T0139917

Lecture Notes in Information Systems and Organisation

Volume 65

Lecture Notes in Information Systems and Organization—LNISO—is a series of scientific books that explore the current scenario of information systems, in particular IS and organization. The focus on the relationship between IT, IS and organization is the common thread of this collection, which aspires to provide scholars across the world with a point of reference and comparison in the study and research of information systems and organization. LNISO is the publication forum for the community of scholars investigating behavioral and design aspects of IS and organization. The series offers an integrated publication platform for high-quality conferences, symposia and workshops in this field. Materials are published upon a strictly controlled double blind peer review evaluation made by selected reviewers.

LNISO is abstracted/indexed in Scopus

Alessandra Lazazzara • Rocco Reina •
Stefano Za
Editors

Towards Digital and Sustainable Organisations

People, Platforms, and Ecosystems

 Springer

Editors
Alessandra Lazazzara
Department of Social and Political Sciences
University of Milan
Milano, Italy

Rocco Reina
Department of Law, Economics and
Sociology
Magna Græcia University of Catanzaro
Catanzaro, Italy

Stefano Za
Department of Management and Business
Administration
University "G. d'Annunzio"
Pescara, Italy

ISSN 2195-4968   ISSN 2195-4976   (electronic)
Lecture Notes in Information Systems and Organisation
ISBN 978-3-031-52879-8   ISBN 978-3-031-52880-4   (eBook)
https://doi.org/10.1007/978-3-031-52880-4

This Springer imprint is published by the registered company Springer Nature Switzerland AG
The registered company address is: Gewerbestrasse 11, 6330 Cham, Switzerland

If disposing of this product, please recycle the paper.

Contents

Digital Transformation and Sustainability Goals: Advancing the "Twin Transition"

Alessandra Lazazzara ⓘ, Rocco Reina ⓘ, and Stefano Za ⓘ

1 Introduction

The digital transformation (DT) journey has long been underway, yielding valuable digital technologies that assist companies in their pursuit of environmentally conscious practices. Moreover, companies are recognizing the inherent synergy between digital innovation and sustainability, as these two forces converge to facilitate mutually reinforcing advancements, greatly enhancing achievable environmental, social, and economic outcomes. In a recent book [1], Za et al. discuss about the surge of two perspectives concerning the intersection of DT and sustainability as discussed within the realm of Information Systems (IS): the perspective of sustainability through DT, centred on how digital artifacts and their adoption can bolster sustainability objectives, and the perspective of sustainability in DT, which focuses on designing the transformation itself to possess sustainability. More recently, the concept of the "twin transition" emerged as a "fancy" term used to describe the utilization of technology and data to propel sustainability objectives, gaining popularity among organizations aiming to enhance their Environmental, Social, and Governance (ESG) performance. Indeed, the emergence of cutting-edge digital technologies has sparked

A. Lazazzara
Department of Social and Political Sciences, University of Milan, Milano, Italy
e-mail: alessandra.lazazzara@unimi.it

R. Reina
Magna Graecia University of Catanzaro, Catanzaro, Italy
e-mail: rreina@unicz.it

S. Za (✉)
Department of Management and Business Administration, University "G. d'Annunzio", Pescara, Italy
e-mail: stefano.za@unich.it

a fresh surge of hope that a diverse spectrum of social, economic, and environmental objectives could finally come to fruition, together with the aspiration for a sustainable, all-encompassing growth. Therefore, although sustainability and digitalization initiatives were previously largely treated as distinct endeavours, they are now viewed as synergistic drivers capable of significantly enhancing intended results.

However, concurrently, apprehensions have emerged concerning the potential adverse consequences linked to the extensive proliferation of these technologies. One specific concern that has garnered significant attention is the possible environmental impact as our world increasingly embraces digitalization [2–4]. These concerns are accompanied by issues such as the escalation of unemployment [5], the deepening of disparities and bias [6], the emergence of malfunctioning democracies [7], and even unregulated advancements in human capabilities [8]. Therefore, a number of questions have arisen within the IS scientific community: Can the concurrent advancement of sustainable and digital transitions coexist harmoniously? Alternatively, could the progress of one potentially offset the benefits of the other? What are the organizational and technological prerequisites for effectively achieving the twin transition?

More generally, DT could accelerate sustainable transitions. However, a number of prerequisites should be ensured to manage potential impacts. Indeed, as it will be fully described into this book, successfully realizing the twin transition poses challenges, encompassing the human and the technological side.

As with any change, humans are the most critical elements in making the change happen. Therefore, engaging and empowering the people within the organization to contribute is imperative. To facilitate effective implementation, it's essential to equip the workforce with appropriate skills, training, infrastructure, processes, and communication. Moreover, to promote involvement and empowerment, cultural factors should be established both within the organization (concerning employees) and externally (in relation to other stakeholders in the ecosystem) [9].

On the technological side, in order to successfully navigate the twin transition, organizations must revamp their utilization of digital technologies and platforms. Leveraging digitization to assess and enhance ESG performance can contribute to increased value and promote productivity and effectiveness. For example, I4.0-based manufacturing systems, which are structured with a cyber-physical system comprising five levels, the 5C architecture: connection, conversion, cyber, cognition, and configuration levels [10], has been adopted to accelerate sustainable manufacturing [11]. Furthermore, Pappas et al. [12] argue that DT, particularly in the domains of Big Data and analytical ecosystems, has the potential to expedite the shift toward sustainability. This acceleration is dependent on a thorough understanding of the interactions among various stakeholders, which subsequently facilitates the creation of value and knowledge. Hence, the analysis of the twin transition should encompass changes in ecosystems and socio-technical systems to comprehend and advance sustainable, comprehensive growth through DT.

The 18 chapters contained in this volume, are the revised version of selected contributions presented at the XIX Conference of the Italian Chapter of AIS (ItAIS 2022), held at the University "Magna Græcia" of Catanzaro on October 14th–15th,

2022, developed through a double-blind review process. They are grouped into two different parts exploring the human and technological prerequisites of the twin transition. The first part provides chapters mainly focused on people and user issues, while the second one discusses several aspects concerning platforms and ecosystems. All the contributions provide a plurality of views that makes this book particularly relevant for scholars but also for practitioners, managers, and policy makers dealing with DT and sustainability decisions.

2   People and Users

The first two chapters of this part are related, albeit in different ways, to the COVID-19 effects. In their chapter, Castelnovo et al. investigate how the COVID-19 pandemic has exacerbated inequalities in the employment context, especially for vulnerable people, such as those with disabilities. Based on a single case study, the authors highlight the role that social cooperatives played in mitigating the negative effects of the pandemic on the work inclusion of people with disabilities during the most acute phase of the COVID-19 crisis in 2020. These results confirm social cooperatives as fundamental actors for social innovation and primary partners for public administration within a plural welfare system. In the following chapter, Spahiu et al. investigate the new working settings introduced on a massive scale in response to the pandemic, such as remote, agile or smart working. These new approaches have removed the constraints of time and place transforming the traditional concept of work into a highly flexible phenomenon that can now be conducted anywhere through digital tools and an array of new technologies. Subsequently, many companies decided to embrace them as a way of improving employees' satisfaction and revolutionizing operations. Despite the benefits often associated with the new ways of work, evidence shows that many companies have struggled to adapt with them. Given the complexity of such adoption, the authors conduct a longitudinal case study of a multinational company that embraced these initiatives before, during and after the pandemic, in order to explore the main challenges and difficulties voiced by both managers and employees. The analysis of the findings reveals that the primary issues relate to excessive supervision, longer working hours, change of team dynamics and inadequate use of technologies. All of these factors call for a change in organizational culture and approach to new ways of working that goes beyond changes in individual tasks and work practices.

Focusing still on individual aspects, Ravarini et al. expand the concept of job-crafting, that is "the physical and cognitive changes individuals make in the task or relational boundaries of their work" [13], by introducing the concept of digital job crafting. An in-depth literature review demonstrated that within the extensive research on job crafting, only limited attention has been dedicated to the effect that digital technology exerts on it. The authors propose using the socio-technical approach to make these impacts explicit and, thus, reframe the concept of job crafting in a new, integrated model. Two case studies are presented to explore the effectiveness of applying the model in different organizational contexts.

Focusing on participatory work activities, Paolini and Raucci investigate the role of doctors heading of Operational Units in Public Healthcare Organizations (PHOs). As budget holders, they have become fundamental actors for the effective functioning of the budgeting planning and control systems. This chapter explores the influence of participative budgeting on doctor-managers' goal clarity and well-being at work. Indeed, the hybrid nature of the doctor-manager's role and the predominant influence of their original clinical culture may lead them to a lack of clarity in setting budgetary goals, which in turn limits the usefulness of the information neutrally provided by such systems for supporting their decision-making. Findings show that participative budgeting positively influence doctor-managers' goal clarity, which, in turn, increases well-being at work, with goal clarity playing a mediating role in this relationship. Conversely, Canonico et al. investigate knowledge transfer and knowledge translation related to digital transformation process in a public domain. Their research examines a digital transformation project triggered by the introduction of the Telematics Civil Process in the Italian final court of appeal. They demonstrate that the project itself may act as a mechanism for knowledge translation. The project is seen as an interactional space where different stakeholders share a framework and develop a common language. This implies that both the project, as a coordination mechanism, and the project's tools have the potential to become a "platform" where participants may effectively enhance knowledge translation, sharing and translating their expertise, adopting a framework, and establishing a common foundation. Berghuis et al. explore and propose an alternative group approach for identifying the more appropriate solution for a process automation. Specifically, their focus is on Robotic process automation (RPA), which is widely adopted in organizations for automating repetitive business processes. Currently, only about half of such projects can be considered successful since organizations struggle to identify simple yet impactful processes for automation. The authors investigate whether and how a group of relevant actors can jointly generate ideas, evaluate them, and select the most salient processes for RPA automation. They ultimately propose a new systematic group approach for identifying and selecting business processes for RPA, which could be applied in a variety of contexts and organizations.

Kautz and Winter focus again on the public sector. Specifically, their interest lies on digitalization initiatives in the public sector, especially those facing pressure to become agile by adopt agile activities, principles, and an agile mindset. Their study investigates challenges and corresponding mitigation measures of scaled agile transformations within such organizations. Utilizing data collected through an Action Research based multiple case studies and drawing on context theory, they identify obstacles related to the political, environmental, and internal context as well as transformation management itself.

Finally, two literature reviews conclude this part. Specifically, one concerns the organizational culture, while the following one is focus on electronic Human Resource Management (e-HRM). Pescatore et al. analyse the bottom-up perspective for the dissemination of organisational culture through the lenses of Socio-technical and Complexity theories. They also compare academic and grey literature to highlight the need for a change in the approach to develop the organizational culture. Sarti at al. develop a bibliometric analysis, mapping the conceptual structure of the body of knowledge regarding e-HRM research field. The bibliometric analysis reveals that there are seven different streams of research in which the e-HRM debate is developed. The chapter provides an examination of the current state of the art of research on e-HRM as well as identify the current areas of analysis in the literature. It may offer some suggestions for future development in the perspective of the new trends in HRM.

3 Platforms and Ecosystems

Bagnoud et al. investigate reputation mechanisms on digital platforms since they are commonly used to reduce information asymmetry, increase trust, and facilitate transactions between users. Despite extensive research on the design challenges of such mechanisms, the specificities of online labor platforms, like the evolution of skills or the heterogenous context in which transactions take place, are not fully addressed in the current literature. Thus, this work aims to determine how to design suitable reputation mechanisms for online labor platforms. Following the Action Design Research approach, the authors provide seven design requirements, which may serve as a guideline for researchers and practitioners in the labor market industry to design adequate reputation mechanisms. Accordino et al. investigate Additive manufacturing (AM) and how firms change the way they create and capture value through AM. For this purpose, the authors perform an explorative qualitative analysis based on a single case study, represented by an innovative Italian start-up operating in the 3D printing industry.

The following three chapters are related to sustainability issues. Ciappa et al. present an analysis of a 3-year time series of pollution data from the European Satellite Sentinel 5p, with a focus on the identification of peaks of pollution in the Arctic region. This research contributes to the literature with a methodology for the automatic identification and geolocation of anomalous peaks of pollution, potentially indicating new or intensifying human activity, either industrial or commercial. While previous research mostly focuses on drawing accurate pollution maps, in this chapter, the authors have designed an algorithm to identify peaks of pollution and, thus, eliminate pollution areas that do not represent an indication of a change in human activity, both on land and at sea, generally considered at risk. Javed and Rapposelli primarily focus on global warming. In this chapter, they examine the relationship between carbon emissions, economic growth, foreign direct investments, oil price, energy consumption and exports in Italy by using yearly data for the period 1970–2019. The findings show that the impact of foreign direct investments on carbon emissions is positive and statistically significant in both the short and long-run, supporting the pollution heaven hypothesis in Italy. In the following chapter, Khan and Rapposelli are interested in how countries can move towards the full adoption of renewable energy resources, as it still represents a challenge for various technological, socio-political, economic and environmental reasons. Specifically, they aim to find a way to select the most optimal mix of energy sources among the existing technologies in the country. For this purpose, the study uses a strategic decision-making tool known as fuzzy SWOT approach to evaluate 7 energy technologies based on a set of 13 sustainability factors. The fuzzy set theory has been employed to address the possibility of uncertainty during the decision-making process. The technologies that exhibit the most strengths and opportunities are considered the most suitable for adoption, whereas those facing weaknesses and threats in the country are to be avoided.

Finally, three literature reviews conclude this part. Mattioli and D'Andreamatteo delve into the academic discourse surrounding digital platforms and digital ecosystems, considering their interconnection with emerging technologies. Their analysis yields research insights and suggestions for exploring the identified knowledge gap, specifically how emerging technologies interact with digital platforms and ecosystems. Trivelli et al. concentrate on the context smart cities, exploring the literature regarding entrepreneurs' behavioural aspects when introducing innovations to the territory. Among the personality traits studied in the literature, they focus on narcissism. They propose a conceptual model that could be further investigated, positing that social capital positively influences innovative acquisitions, where the geographical location of the entrepreneur playing a key role in shaping the performance of the innovative entrepreneurial activity. Scharfe investigates the phenomenon of "smartness" in the digital era, a term widely used and applied in the manufacturing domain. Here, researchers and practitioners discuss concepts such as smart machines, smart manufacturing systems, or smart maintenance services. Despite the common usage of the term "smartness," its precise meaning remains elusive Therefore, the author conducts a systematic review of literature focusing on multiple characteristics associated with the smartness of devices, systems, and services in this domain. The resulting classification framework contributes to the existing body of knowledge by providing a more nuanced understanding of the implementation of smartness in the manufacturing domain and offering manufacturing practitioners a 'guidance tool' for exploring and designing smart devices, systems, and services.

References

1. Za, S., Winter, R., & Lazazzara, A. (Eds.). (2023). *Sustainable digital transformation. Paving the way towards smart organizations and societies.* Springer.
2. Vinuesa, R., Azizpour, H., Leite, I., Balaam, M., Dignum, V., Domisch, S., & Nerini, F. F. (2020). The role of artificial intelligence in achieving the sustainable development goals. *Nature Communications, 11*, 1–10.
3. Coeckelbergh, M. (2021). AI for climate: freedom, justice, and other ethical and political challenges. *AI and Ethics, 1*, 67–72. https://doi.org/10.1007/s43681-020-00007-2
4. Del Río Castro, G., González Fernández, M. C., & Uruburu Colsa, Á. (2021). Unleashing the convergence amid digitalization and sustainability towards pursuing the sustainable

development goals (SDGs): A holistic review. *Journal of Cleaner Production*. https://doi.org/10.1016/j.jclepro.2020.122204

5. Bordot, F. (2022). Artificial intelligence, robots and unemployment: Evidence from OECD countries. *Journal of Innovation Economics & Management, 1*, 117–138. https://doi.org/10.3917/jie.037.0117

6. O'Neil, C. (2016). *Weapons of math destruction: How big data increases inequality and threatens democracy*. Crown.

7. Zuboff, S. (2019). Surveillance capitalism and the challenge of collective action. *New Labor Forum, 28*, 10–29. https://doi.org/10.1177/1095796018819461

8. Bostrom, N. (2017). Strategic implications of openness in AI development. *Global Policy, 8*, 135–148. https://doi.org/10.1111/1758-5899.12403

9. The Conference Board, Inc. (2023). *Digital for green: Leveraging digital technologies to improve sustainability.*

10. Lee, J., Bagheri, B., & Kao, H. A. (2015). A cyber-physical systems architecture for Industry 4.0-based manufacturing systems. *Manufacturing Letters, 3*, 18–23. https://doi.org/10.1016/j.mfglet.2014.12.001

11. Chen, X., Kurdve, M., Johansson, B., & Despeisse, M. (2023). Enabling the twin transitions: Digital technologies support environmental sustainability through lean principles. *Sustainable Production and Consumption, 38*, 13–27. https://doi.org/10.1016/j.spc.2023.03.020

12. Pappas, I. O., Mikalef, P., Giannakos, M. N., Krogstie, J., & Lekakos, G. (2018). Big data and business analytics ecosystems: paving the way towards digital transformation and sustainable societies. *Information Systems and e-Business Management, 16*, 479–491. https://doi.org/10.1007/s10257-018-0377-z

13. Wrzesniewski, A., Berg, J. M., & Dutton, J. E. (2010). Turn the job you have into the job you want. *Harvard Business Review, 88*, 114–117.

Part I
People and Users

The Role of Social Cooperatives in the Work Inclusion of People with Disability During the COVID-19 Crisis: A Case from Italy

Walter Castelnovo ⓘ, Giuseppe Aquino, Paola Consonni, and Federico Rappelli

Abstract One of the more striking effects of the COVID-19 pandemic has been the worsening of inequalities, especially for already vulnerable people. This is the case for people with disability who came into the COVID-19 crisis already facing significant exclusion from employment. Based on a single case study research project concerning an Italian province, the current paper highlights the role social cooperatives played in mitigating the negative effects of the pandemic on the work inclusion of people with disability during the most acute phase of the COVID-19 crisis in 2020. By triangulating multiple sources of evidence (both qualitative and quantitative), the study identifies local embeddedness and organisational hybridity as the most relevant properties that allowed cooperatives to play that role. This result confirms social cooperatives as fundamental actors for social innovation and primary partners for public administration within a plural welfare system.

Keywords Social cooperatives · People with disability · Work inclusion · Local embeddedness · Organisational hybridity · COVID-19

1 Introduction

"In a matter of a few months, the COVID-19 pandemic has turned from a public health crisis with no parallel in living memory into a major economic and jobs crisis whose full extent is still unfolding" ([1], p. 22). This is how a recent OECD report

W. Castelnovo (✉) · G. Aquino · P. Consonni
University of Insubria, Como, Italy
e-mail: walter.castelnovo@uninsubria.it; giuseppe.aquino@unisubria.it;
paola.consonni@uninsubria.it

F. Rappelli
PoliS Lombardia, Milan, Italy
e-mail: federico.rappelli@polis.lombardia.it

© The Author(s), under exclusive license to Springer Nature
Switzerland AG 2024
A. Lazazzara et al. (eds.), *Towards Digital and Sustainable Organisations*,
Lecture Notes in Information Systems and Organisation 65,
https://doi.org/10.1007/978-3-031-52880-4_2

describes the impact of the pandemic on jobs. According to the International Labour Organization, there were unprecedented global employment losses in 2020 of 114 million jobs relative to 2019 [2]. Although with different intensity, the employment crisis hit both developed and developing countries and, within each country, the most developed regions have also been heavily impacted.

In Italy, the National Institute of Statistics [3] reports an unprecedented decrease of employment in 2020 amounting to 456,000 units of personnel, which means a decrease of 2% in the total workforce. In Lombardy, the most populated and economically relevant region in Italy, almost 90,000 jobs were lost by December 2020.

Many international organisations, including the UN, OECD, ILO, the European Foundation for the Improvement of Living and Working Conditions (to mention just a few examples), warned that the COVID-19 crisis would expose the most vulnerable people to additional disadvantages. As pointed out by the OECD, "the impact of COVID-19 is particularly severe for the elderly, low-income earners, women, migrants, children and youth, and those with disabilities and with chronic health conditions" ([1], p. 4).

With public welfare systems already under stress long before its outbreak, the pandemic exacerbated many welfare issues and showed the vulnerabilities of public welfare systems under highly critical conditions. In times of crisis, the need for a plural and community-based welfare model that serves people and communities and finds its strength in people and communities' support emerges. With governments compelled to fight the pandemic on many critical fronts, social dialogue and social partnership can make the difference [4].

Positioned at the crossroads of the market, public policies, and civil society, and with the aim of achieving social goals and responding to collective needs in an entrepreneurial way [5], cooperative enterprises are primary partners for governments' social dialogue and social innovation initiatives. Indeed, in many countries, local and national governments are integrating, with increasing frequency, cooperatives and social enterprises as robust and resilient partners into public relief strategies.

Protecting workers, responding to the needs of society, and acting at the local level are amongst the fundamental principles of the cooperative enterprises. This observation motivates the twofold research question the current qualitative paper intends to address, i.e. (1) *did (social) cooperatives contribute to mitigating the impact of the pandemic on the work inclusion of people with disability?* (in the paper the term is intended as defined by the World Health Organization, i.e. it refers to anyone experiencing disability independent of the duration); and (2) *what properties of the cooperative enterprises allowed them to play that role?*

To answer this research question, the paper performs a qualitative single case study on the work inclusion of people with disability (hereinafter referred to as PWD) within an Italian province during the first year of the pandemic crisis. Based on a survey involving the social cooperatives active in the province, official documents from the Province Administration, and an interview with the manager responsible for the Public Employment Service (PES) of the Province Administration, the paper highlights the positive role played by social cooperatives in mitigating the impacts of the pandemic on the work inclusion of PWD. Local embeddedness and organisational hybridity are identified as the properties of social cooperatives that allowed them to play that role.

The contribution of the paper is twofold. On the one hand, it contributes to bridging a gap in the literature. In fact, although a quite extensive literature has been devoted to how to mitigate the impact of COVID-19 on the employment of PWD [6–10], there is still a scarce number of works that investigate the role of cooperatives and social enterprises. On the other hand, by identifying the positive role played by social cooperatives, the paper highlights their essential role as primary partners for public administration within a plural welfare system based on the principle of horizontal subsidiarity [11].

The paper is structured as follows. In Sect. 2, some properties of the cooperative model, which are relevant when it comes to explaining the role played by social cooperatives in the work inclusion of PWD, are discussed with reference to the relevant literature. Section 3 describes the objectives of the research and the methodological approach. Section 4 introduces the case study, i.e. the work inclusion of PWD in the Italian Northern Province of Lecco. Section 5 presents the results of the survey and the major points emerging from the interview with the PES manager, which are then discussed in Sect. 6. The final section drives the conclusions of the paper, discusses some limitations of the study, and indicates further research directions.

2   The Role of Social Cooperatives in the Work Inclusion of PWD

As actors of the Social and Solidarity Economy, cooperative enterprises are characterised by "collective ownership of institutions which aim to transform labor relations, promote participative democracy, and design new wealth-sharing arrangements" ([12], p. 8). Cooperatives are organisations that "follow social solidarity principles of pursuing social, environmental and redistributive justice through cooperative, associative and solidarity relations" (ibidem). This is what makes cooperatives different from other typical profit-oriented organisations. Nevertheless, cooperatives are enterprises, and, as such, besides pursuing social goals, focusing on democratic values and principles such as solidarity, equality and inclusion [13], cooperatives also pursue business goals [14]. By combining the social orientation of the Social and Solidarity Economy organisations and the business orientation of enterprises, cooperatives are typical hybrid organisations. This property of cooperatives has relevant implications for their role as actors of social innovation and local sustainable development [15].

In organisational studies, hybridity refers to the coexistence, within the same organisation, of different (sometimes even conflicting) institutional logics, typically related to the public, private or third-sector domain [16–18]. Organisational hybridity is one of the main characteristics of cooperatives that pursue multiple goals rather than having a single purpose. In fact, their very raison d'être is to pursue both economic and social goals [19]. For cooperatives, the coexistence of plural logics is a permanent phenomenon [14, 18, 20–22]. It represents a positive aspect [23], since "operating in institutional interstices and combining multiple logics (i.e. considering and adhering to multiple prescriptions) might open up opportunities, as organizations can access broader sets of resources and expand their practices, which allows them to be innovative, to create new products and services and to pioneer new ways of organizing" ([21], p. 715).

Besides hybridity, and strictly related to it, cooperative enterprises are characterised by social embeddedness, i.e., the subordination of economic motivations to values, cultural and social issues, and political ideologies [24, 25]. Cooperatives exhibit high levels of embeddedness, both within the general cooperative movement and within the local community in which they operate [24, 26–29].

Local embeddedness is a defining property of cooperative enterprises, as explicitly stated by principle 7 (*Concern for Community*) of the International Cooperative Alliance Guidance Notes to the Co-operative Principles, according to which cooperatives "emerge from and are rooted in the communities in which they conduct their business operations. Their success is based on their ability to support those communities to develop in a sustainable way" ([30], p. 85). Local embeddedness allows cooperatives to leverage the 'quality of place' as the dimension that contributes to the quality of local economic development based on the social, cultural, and organisational factors that characterise a territory and the population that inhabits it. At the same time, local embeddedness allows cooperative enterprises to exert a beneficial impact on local social and economic development by supporting inclusive and sustainable growth, contributing to the reduction of poverty, and generating new and more stable employment [31].

The local embeddedness and the hybrid nature of cooperatives make this specific type of enterprises particularly fit for understanding local needs and responding, in a quick and dynamic way, to the socio-economic problems of the local communities, which traditional public interventions struggle to solve [15, 29, 32, 33]. Hence, whilst maintaining a strong business orientation that supports their long-term sustainability and also makes them a relevant economic actor, cooperatives can play a fundamental role in local sustainable development and social innovation.

Cooperative enterprises can take a variety of legal structures, also depending on different national legislation, and operate in a variety of domains [28, 34]. Here we are interested in social cooperatives, i.e., cooperatives in which "the prevalence of the external mutuality on the internal interest emerges. This means that they are called to pursue the interests of the overall community, rather than the exclusive interest of their members" ([5], p. 62). Social cooperatives pursue this objective by providing social services to the entire community and generating a general interest effect [35, 36] by leveraging "the surrounding social context to create a mutual benefit within a network of reciprocity enacted by social agents like volunteers, civil society organizations and public and private institutions" ([37], p. 20).

In Italy, the social cooperative model was established by law 381/1991, which distinguishes between social cooperatives providing social, health and educational services (Type-A) and social cooperatives integrating disadvantaged people into jobs (Type-B), the latter representing the only case of Work Integration Social Enterprise in Italy [5, 36]. Type-B social cooperatives are required to employ at least 30% of low employable workers [38, 39], offer stable jobs, and promote entre-preneurial skills for disadvantaged people [5, 36, 40], including: people with physi-cal or mental disabilities, drug addicts, alcoholics, children of working age in difficult family situations, and prisoners. Moreover, Type-B social cooperatives are expected to implement innovative employment schemes for disadvantaged people to grant them jobs within protected work environments (when necessary) or to allow them to express their peculiar capabilities. In fact, workers who fall into the disad-vantaged category often perform certain types of work better than non-disadvantaged workers [41].

Over the years, the social cooperative movement has grown impressively in Italy, and social cooperatives are now central actors of the Italian mixed welfare system [42], especially when it comes to what concerns the work inclusion of PWD. In the Italian Ministry of Labour and Social Affairs' communication to the Parliament concerning the work inclusion of PWD in 2016–2019, it is reported that social cooperatives (mainly Type-B social cooperatives) have been involved in 63% of all the interventions aimed at supporting the work inclusion of PWD [43].

3   Objective of the Research and Methodological Approach

The aim of the paper is to investigate the role of social cooperatives in mitigating the impact of the COVID-19 pandemic on the work inclusion of PWD. To answer our research question, we performed a qualitative single case study [44, 45] on the work inclusion of PWD in the Province of Lecco in the Lombardy Region (Italy).

The study was based on multiple sources of evidence [45]: an online survey involving the social cooperatives (both Type-A and Type-B) active in the Province of Lecco; official reports from the Public Employment Service of the Province Administration, and an interview with the manager responsible for that service.

The survey was based on a questionnaire [46] administered through a Computer Aided Web Interview system to all the social cooperatives active in the Province of Lecco (32 Type-A and 20 Type-B cooperatives), identified by consulting the Minister of Economic Development register of the Italian cooperatives on May 5, 2021. We adopted this methodology as qualitative interviews are particularly useful in contexts in which the phenomenon under study is still unfolding [45], with par-ticular attention paid to avoid possible distortions deriving from the use of this tool [47, 48].

The questionnaire is completely anonymous and includes two parts. The first part was administered to all the social cooperatives active in the Province of Lecco to gather general information on the dimension of the cooperative, the impact of the pandemic on the activities of the cooperative, and the cooperative level of organisa-tional hybridity. The second part of the questionnaire specifically concerns the work inclusion of PWD, and it has been administered to Type-B cooperatives only.

The answers to the questionnaire were collected during May 2021.

Overall, 20 cooperatives out of 52 answered the questionnaire (which means a 38.4% overall response rate). Table 1 summarises the number and the response rate for the two typologies of cooperative involved in the survey.

Since the average response rate for studies that utilise data collected from organ-isations is approximately 35% [49], our response rate is good enough to support some conditional generalisations.

Our second information source comprised the annual reports of the PES of the Province of Lecco, which contain official quantitative data on the work inclusion of PWD. We used those documents to triangulate the results of the survey (data trian-gulation). Finally, the third information source was a semi-structured interview con-ducted on May 20, 2021, with the PES manager. The interview, which lasted approximately 1 h, was transcribed and annotated by two researchers to identify key points to be triangulated with the results of the survey to seek convergent evi-dence [45].

4   The Case Study: Work Inclusion of PWD in the Province of Lecco During the Pandemic

Amongst the Italian provinces, the Province of Lecco represents an interesting case to study, due to the positive results which the local labour market showed for many years before the COVID-19 outbreak—a trend that continued also in 2020. The PES Local Labour Market Observatory reports 150,500 employed people in 2019, and this number remained substantially the same in 2020. Although during the first year of the pandemic the total number of job placements decreased (–15%), the number of job terminations decreased at a higher rate (–21%), which gives a positive bal-ance between placements and terminations (+2800). The local economic system and labour market showed a good capacity of resistance to the pandemic in 2020 [50]. From this point of view, it is interesting to consider whether the same positive results also concerned the work inclusion of PWD.

In Italy, the work inclusion of PWD is regulated by law 68/1999, which promotes the work placement and work integration of PWD based on quotas of compulsory

Table 1 Answers to the questionnaire administered to the social cooperatives

	Number of active cooperatives	Number of cooperatives that answered the questionnaire	Response rate (%)
Type-A	32	11	34.3
Type-B	20	9	45
Total	52	20	38.4

hiring, training courses, internship and business mentoring [51]. However, despite the law provisions, PWD still suffer from low employment rates in Italy. In 2019 (the last year for which official data are available), only 32% of disabled people were employed in Italy, against the 59.8% of non-disabled people employed. Lombardy is the Italian region with the highest number of PWD employed. In 2019, 21.5% of all the PWD employed in Italy were employed in Lombardy [52]. Amongst the 12 provinces of Lombardy, the Lecco province has the highest rate of employed PWD with respect to the total number of inhabitants (0.16% against 0.07% average rate of Lombardy).

In 2020, in the Province of Lecco the PWD job placements were only 400—a significant decrease with respect to the previous year (−28%). Most of them (82%) were placements in firms, followed by social cooperatives (14.5%) and public sector organisations (3.5%). In 2020, the decrease in the PWD placements concerned all the three sectors with the highest decrease in the placements in firms (−29%), followed by social cooperatives (−25%) and public administrations (−17%). The negative impact of the pandemic on job placements was stronger in the case of PWD compared to non-disabled people: 28% against 15% [50].

A further interesting piece of data concerns job-training/internship for PWD, including the so-called 'tirocini di adozione' (adoption internship), which allows firms for which the employment of PWD in mandatory to sign, instead, agreements with the PES to economically support the placement of PWD in protected work environments (most often in social cooperatives). The number of job-trainings/internships for PWD decreased sensibly from 2019 to 2020 at a rate (−28%) aligned with that of the decrease in the PWD job placements, whereas the number of adoption internships decreased less sensibly (−6%). Of particular interest is the sector in which the job-trainings/internships were activated in 2020. The number of job-trainings/internships activated by firms decreased by 81% from 2019 to 2020, whereas it increased by 132% in the case of public administration organisations, and by 151% in the case of cooperatives. These data, together with the data concerning the lower decrease of the number of PWD job placements in social cooperatives with respect to the other firms, suggest that social cooperative played a significant role in mitigating the impact of the COVID-19 on the work inclusion of PWD.

5 The Role of the Social Cooperatives During the COVID-19 Pandemic

The questionnaire administered to the social cooperatives active in the Lecco Province comprised two parts: the first part was administered to both the Type-A and Type-B cooperatives, whereas the second part of the questionnaire only involved Type-B social cooperatives. This allowed us to acquire both general information concerning the scenario within which the social cooperatives operated during the pandemic, and specific information concerning the role of Type-B social cooperatives in the work inclusion of PWD.

5.1   How the Pandemic Affected the Social Cooperatives in the Province of Lecco

The cooperatives that answered the questionnaire were quite homogeneous with respect to their dimensions. Most of them were medium-to-small enterprises: 63.6% in the case of Type-A cooperatives and 55% for Type-B cooperatives. The number of medium-to-large enterprises was higher amongst the Type-B (44.5%) than amongst the Type-A cooperatives (36.4%).

For the cooperatives of both types, the main consequences of the pandemic were the temporary suspension of the activities and the reduction of the work hours. The reorganisation of the activities based on the use of digital technologies was, for most of the cooperatives, the main measure adopted to mitigate the effect of the crisis. Quite interestingly, some cooperatives (two Type-A and three Type-B) reported an increase in their activities during the pandemic, which indicates a greater robustness of the cooperative enterprises with respect to other types of enterprises.

Amongst the elements that most helped them to resist the crisis, the cooperatives (both Type-A and Type-B) indicated the orientation towards the well-being of the members and workers, the local embeddedness, and the capacity to make timely and innovative decisions. As a further relevant element, seven Type-B cooperatives indicated the cooperative financial solidity, which was considered relevant by only two Type-A cooperatives. Type-A and Type-B cooperatives also differed with respect to the importance of the collaboration with local government organisations as an element that helped them to better resist the crisis (this element was indicated by five Type-A and two Type-B cooperatives only).

Within the literature, the cooperative model is often indicated as the one that allows greater resilience after crises. The survey confirmed this result. In total, 10 Type-A cooperatives (91%) and eight Type-B cooperatives (88.9%) reported a recovery of activities in the first semester of 2021. Moreover, seven Type-A cooperatives (out of 11) and four Type-B cooperatives (out of nine) declared that they had restored their activities at a level aligned with that of the years before the pandemic outbreak. Two cooperatives only (one for each type) reported an unvaried level of activity in 2021 compared to 2020.

All the cooperatives defined themselves as hybrid organisations. The pursuing of a public interest (social values and solidarity) was indicated as the most important strategic element by most of the cooperatives (72.8% of the Type-A and 89.9% of the Type-B cooperatives). In total, 54.6% of the Type-A and 100% of the Type-B cooperatives also indicated mutuality as a fundamental value. Finally, 55.5% of the Type-B cooperatives reported that they do not pursue any specific business objective.

5.2 The Role of Type-B Cooperatives in the Work Inclusion of PWD

All the nine Type-B cooperatives that responded to the survey employed people affected by mental or sensory impairments. Seven cooperatives also employed people with physical impairments and five cooperatives employed people with severe disabilities.

Most of the cooperatives implemented measures for the work continuity of their disabled employees during the pandemic. Only two cooperatives did not implement any specific measure. In none of the cooperatives did the COVID-19 crisis favour the introduction of new work accommodation measures for their disabled employees. Seven cooperatives declared that the health crisis did not have any impact on the working conditions of their disabled employees, whereas for two cooperatives the COVID-19 emergency hindered their disabled employees' tasks and working conditions.

Almost all of the cooperatives (eight out of nine) renewed all the fixed-term contracts of their disabled employees in 2020. The remaining one renewed only some of the contracts. Most of the cooperatives (five out of nine) declared that they did not transform their disabled employees fixed-terms contracts into permanent employment contracts in 2020, whereas three cooperatives transformed the contract for at least one of their disabled employees. Only three cooperatives activated at least one adoption internship in 2020.

According to the national legislation, firms subjected to the mandatory employment of PWD can comply with the provision of law 68/1999 by signing agreements with social cooperatives that employ PWD. During the pandemic, Regional Law 3013, issued in March 2020, allowed the temporary suspension of the signed agreements. Only six of the surveyed cooperatives resorted to this measure. However, five of those six cooperatives renewed the agreements at the end of the suspension period.

Finally, only two cooperatives out of nine benefitted from public funding (from the Regional Government of Lombardy) during the pandemic; they declared that this funding had a positive effect on their capacity to mitigate the negative impacts on the work inclusion of PWD during the crisis.

5.3 The Point of View of the Public Employment Service of the Province of Lecco

The survey of the cooperatives was complemented with a semi-structured interview with the manager responsible for the Public Employment Service of the Province of Lecco (the Manager henceforth), with the aim of seeking convergent evidence. The interview allowed a deeper understanding of the measures adopted by the cooperatives to mitigate the impact of the pandemic on the work integration of PWD, as seen from the point of view of the public employment service. Moreover, based on the long-term collaboration between the PES and the social cooperatives, the interview also made it possible to investigate whether, and how, the cooperatives' response to the crisis can be related to the peculiar properties of the cooperative enterprises, such as local embeddedness and organisational hybridity.

The context of the Province of Lecco is characterised by a strong long-term collaboration between the PES and the social cooperatives, most notably Type-B cooperatives. As reported by the Manager, *"the collaboration has been further strengthened during the pandemic, with the aim of elaborating shared strategies and solutions adequate to the seriousness of the situation in order to safeguard the PWD' employment levels and the cooperatives' operational continuity"* (our transcription of the interview).

During the interview, the Manager stressed that social cooperatives *"adopted measures aimed not only at the operational continuity and recovery objective, but also at the reorganisation, in strict collaboration with the PES and the territorial public social services, of the transport of PWD from home to the workplace and the working time hours, with the aim of satisfying the requirements of the COVID-19 security protocols and the specific needs of PWD"* (our transcription).

The social cooperatives behaviour *"has been particularly collaborative both with the workers (employees and interns) and with the public social services of the territory"* (our transcription). More specifically, the cooperatives tried to avoid the suspension of the PWD' employment by implementing *"strategies for the accommodation of the workplace and work hours, so as to assure that all the employees have physical access to the workplace in condition of security, according to the COVID-19 protocols. When, due to the reduction of orders, it has been impossible to maintain the work continuity, the disabled employees (as all the workers) had access to temporary public income replacement programmes. Anyway, when there has been a suspension of the activity, the cooperatives gave priority to the recovery of the jobs of the most vulnerable employees to reduce the negative effects, also from a psychological point of view, that the suspension of work could determine for people with disabilities"* (our transcription).

Some cooperatives resorted to the COVID-19 public income replacement programme in 2020 as a first answer to the crisis. However, only few cooperatives resorted to the measure of temporarily suspending the agreements signed with firms for the work inclusion of PWD stated by Regional Law 3013/2020. In fact, in 2020, 23 new agreements were signed that allowed social cooperatives to employ 39 disabled workers.

The Manager reported positive behaviour of social cooperatives also with respect to the training and internship programmes for PWD. More specifically, *"Type-B social cooperatives showed a resilient attitude strongly orientated towards the well-being of disabled people. As deliberated by the Regional Government, the training and internship programmes had been suspended at the outbreak of the pandemic, but they were successively restored as soon as it was possible to satisfy the COVID-19 security protocols"* (our transcription). Despite the difficulties of the period, many social cooperatives active in the province adhered to the restore programmes promoted by the PES and agreed to host training placements and internships for PWD. The Manager also reported a collaborative attitude of the social cooperatives with respect to the numerous administrative procedures and documents necessary to comply with the requirements of the COVID-19 security protocols to restore the training and internship programmes.

Finally, the Manager pointed out that, in June 2020, Type-B cooperatives signed an agreement with the territorial Unions to facilitate work placement and continuity for people in situations of fragility during social and economic crises. The agreement concerns measures aimed at:

- Automatically renewing all the fixed-term contracts expiring by Decembre 31, 2020
- Keeping active the training programmes for PWD in case of temporary suspension of the cooperative activity
- Supporting, whenever possible, the implementation of remote working solutions (which in Italy is usually referred to as 'smart working') for PWD
- Allowing cooperatives to assign PWD jobs different from those stated in their contracts (even in the case this would amount to a downgrading), but maintaining the same salary level

6   Discussion

Both the survey on the social cooperatives and the interview with the manager responsible for the PES confirmed the robustness and resilience of the cooperative enterprises, as widely discussed within the literature [29, 53–56]. The cooperatives' local embeddedness and their orientation towards pursuing the well-being of the members, the workers and the community, are the elements that most influenced the cooperatives' resistance during the most acute phase of the pandemic and their capacity of restoration when the effects of the pandemic weakened.

Both elements also played a role in the cooperatives' capacity to mitigate the impact of the pandemic on the work inclusion of PWD. As stated by the Manager, the cooperatives' behaviour during the pandemic was characterised by both a *"strong orientation towards pursuing the well-being of their disabled employees within a protected work environment"* and the *"cooperatives capacity of maintaining a continuous and positive dialogue with the Public Employment Service and the territorial public welfare services, also due to the long-term collaborative relationships between the social cooperatives and the PES"* (our transcription).

Local embeddedness and orientation towards people's well-being shaped the social cooperatives' approach to the work inclusion of PWD during the pandemic. This differentiated the cooperatives' approach from that of the more business-oriented enterprises that resorted quite extensively to the suspension of the obligations of law 68/1999 authorised by Regional Law 3013/2020.

Social cooperatives showed "*a strong commitment to maintaining the continuity of the ongoing training and internship programmes for PWD, even in the most acute phase of the pandemic*" (our transcription), in order to "*mitigate the negative consequences, also at the psychological level, that the COVID-19 pandemic and the emergency measures could have for people in situations of fragility*" (our transcription). The firms' answer to the pandemic were quite different: "*they interacted with the PES mainly for information concerning the suspension of the obligations to comply with law 68/1999 and for information concerning the COVID-19 public income restoration programme. They only marginally contacted the PES to report the emerging of critical situations for their disabled employees due to the pandemic, or to ask for advice on the measures for the work continuity of PWD, how to accommodate the work hours and the workplace, and how to implement smart working solutions*" (our transcription).

The triangulation between the data collected through the survey and the content of the interview with the Manager makes it possible to formulate an answer to our twofold research question, i.e. (1) did (social) cooperatives contribute to mitigating the impact of the pandemic on the work inclusion of people with disability? and (2) what properties of the cooperative enterprises allowed them to play that role?

On the one hand, our limited—but nevertheless significant—study highlights a positive role of cooperatives for the work inclusion of PWD during the pandemic. On the other hand, local embeddedness, strict collaboration with public administration, and strong orientation towards pursuing people (especially the most fragile) and community well-being, are the principles that allowed cooperatives to play that role.

Such principles are at the very foundation of the ethics of the cooperative movement and characterise cooperatives as typical hybrid organisations. Hence, to contribute to mitigating the impact of the pandemic on the most vulnerable people, cooperatives just had to behave as such, without being forced to undergo a process of organisational re-orientation, as other firms had to do instead. As confirmed by the data collected through our survey, during the pandemic crisis, the cooperatives did not have to introduce new work accommodations for their disabled employees. The only measures they implemented specifically for PWD concerned the reorganisation of the transport from home to the workplace. All the other measures they adopted were those required by the COVID-19 security protocols for the whole workforce. In fact, implementing conditions that can enable the work inclusion of PWD and help already-employed PWD stay at work in periods of crisis is a direct consequence of the cooperatives' 'normal' way of organising their employees' work. The concern for the sustainable development of communities, which is one of the seven Cooperative Principles, requires cooperatives to be good employers and to be concerned about their employees' well-being and the well-being of their employees' families. The adherence to this fundamental principle makes cooperatives typical hybrid organisations.

Organisational hybridity makes cooperative enterprises relevant actors for sustainable economic development in 'normal' situations. However, as the role played by cooperatives in the work inclusion of PWD during the COVID-19 crisis clearly shows, organisational hybridity also makes cooperatives robust and resilient actors in social and economic systems under stress due to endogenous or exogenous factors.

Two relevant implications can be derived from our study. The first implication concerns enterprises. The focus of their employment policies on the employees' well-being is what allowed cooperatives to operate in a (quasi) 'normal' way during the COVID-19 crisis, thus reducing the pandemic's impact on the employment of PWD. This is a model that could also inspire more business-oriented enterprises to implement their disability management policies as part of their corporate social innovation processes.

The second implication concerns public decision-makers and public managers. The positive role played by cooperatives in mitigating the impact of the pandemic confirms them as fundamental partners of public administration in a system of welfare mix based on the principle of horizontal subsidiarity. In fact, in the case we studied, the strict cooperation between cooperatives and the Public Employment Service has been of paramount importance in shaping the local work system answer during the most acute phase of the crisis. From this point of view, engaging cooperative enterprises in long-term partnerships for the governance of the local work system can represent a strategy for government organisations to increase their response capacity under highly critical conditions impacting the employment of the most vulnerable people.

7   Conclusion, Limitations, and Further Research Directions

The most vulnerable people are the most exposed to the negative consequences of heavy economic and social crises, whose main social effect is the worsening of inequalities. The COVID-19 pandemic had a negative impact on employment worldwide, with particularly critical consequences for the work inclusion of people with disability. In the current paper, we discussed the work inclusion of PWD during the pandemic in the context of the Northern Province of Lecco in the Lombardy Region (Italy). What we find in our study is the positive role played by social cooperatives in mitigating the impact of the pandemic on the work inclusion of PWD. The data we collected show that cooperatives were not only able to reduce the effects of the pandemic during its most acute phase, but also succeeded in restoring their activities at levels aligned with those preceding the crisis outbreak as soon as the pandemic weakened. This had positive effects not only on the work continuity for PWD, but also on the job placement of PWD through training and internship programmes.

From our research it emerges, quite clearly, that the positive role played by social cooperatives depends on two fundamental principles of the cooperative model: the local embeddedness of the cooperative enterprises and their orientation towards pursuing a public interest. Both these elements derive from the organisational hybridity typical of cooperative enterprises, which is what differentiates them from other types of enterprises. This provides an answer to our research question.

Our research included only an Italian province, which is the main limitation of the study, especially when it comes to the possibility of generalising the results of the research. A further limitation is the way we performed the survey on the social cooperatives. On the one hand, we did not select a statistically significant set of cooperatives to be involved in the survey. For this reason, we cannot assure the complete representativeness of the respondents and exclude the possibility of a selection bias in the sample. On the other hand, only 20 cooperatives (out of 52) answered the online questionnaire. Although this gives a response rate higher than the average rate for studies which utilise data collected from organisations, in absolute terms the number of respondents is quite low. Further research is required to overcome these limitations, especially by indagating the role of social cooperatives in other territorial contexts to obtain more evidence with which to support our conclusions.

References

1. OECD. (2020). *OECD Employment Outlook 2020*. OECD.
2. ILO. (2021). *ILO Monitor: COVID-19 and the world of work* (7th ed.). International Labour Organization.
3. ISTAT. (2021). *Audizione dell'Istat presso il Comitato Tecnico Scientifico dell'Osservatorio Nazionale sulla condizione delle persone con disabilità*. Presidenza del Consiglio dei Ministri.
4. CICOPA. (2021). *COVID19: How cooperatives in industry and services are responding to the crisis*. International Organisation of Industrial and Service Cooperatives.
5. Bandini, F., Gigli, S., & Mariani, L. (2021). Social enterprises and public value: A multiple-case study assessment. *VOLUNTAS: International Journal of Voluntary and Nonprofit Organizations, 32*(1), 61–77.
6. Buomprisco, G., Ricci, S., Perri, R., & De Sio, S. (2021). Health and telework: New challenges after COVID-19 pandemic. *European Journal of Environment and Public Health, 5*(2), em0073.
7. Dirks, S., & Kurth, F. (2022) Working from home in the COVID-19 pandemic—Which technological and social factors influence the working conditions and job satisfaction of people with disabilities? In *Computers helping people with special needs*. Springer.
8. Tang, J. (2021). Understanding the telework experience of people with disabilities. *Proceedings of the ACM on Human-Computer Interaction, 5*(CSCW1), 1–27.
9. Matilla-Santander, N., Ahonen, E., Albin, M., Baron, S., Bolíbar, M., Bosmans, K., Burström, B., Cuervo, I., Davis, L., Gunn, V., Håkansta, C., Hemmingsson, T., Hogstedt, C., Jonsson, J., Julià, M., Kjellberg, K., Kreshpaj, B., Lewchuk, W., Muntaner, C., … Bodin, T. (2021). COVID-19 and precarious employment: Consequences of the evolving crisis. *International Journal of Health Services, 51*(2), 226–228.
10. Bouziri, H., Smith, D. R. M., Descatha, A., Dab, W., & Jean, K. (2020). Working from home in the time of COVID-19: how to best preserve occupational health? *Occupational and Environmental Medicine, 77*(7), 509.
11. Savini, V. (2020). How the local welfare system in Italy changes: From planning to co-planning. In J. L. Sarasola Sánchez-Serrano, F. Maturo, & Š. Hošková-Mayerová (Eds.), *Qualitative and quantitative models in socio-economic systems and social work* (pp. 111–121). Springer.

12. ILO. (2019). *Financial mechanisms for innovative social and solidarity economy ecosystems.* International Labour Organization.
13. Kerlin, J. (2010). A comparative analysis of the global emergence of social enterprise. *VOLUNTAS: International Journal of Voluntary and Nonprofit Organizations, 21*(2), 162–179.
14. Camargo Benavides, A. F., & Ehrenhard, M. (2021). Rediscovering the cooperative enterprise: A systematic review of current topics and avenues for future research. *VOLUNTAS (Manchester, England), 32*, 964–978.
15. Ridley-Duff, R. (2019). Cooperative social entrepreneurship: reflections on a decade embedding cooperative studies in social enterprise courses. In T. Woodin & L. Shaw (Eds.), *Learning for a co-operative world: Education, social change and the co-operative college* (pp. 134–153). Trentham Books.
16. Brandsen, T., van de Donk, W., & Putters, K. (2005). Griffins or chameleons? Hybridity as a permanent and inevitable characteristic of the third sector. *International Journal of Public Administration, 28*(9–10), 749–765.
17. Evers, A. (2008). Hybrid organisations—Background, concept, challenge. In S. Osborne (Ed.), *The third sector in Europe* (pp. 279–292). Routledge.
18. Ebrahim, A., Battilana, J., & Mair, J. (2014). The governance of social enterprises: Mission drift and accountability challenges in hybrid organizations. *Research in Organizational Behavior, 34*(C), 81–100.
19. Pestoff, V. (2012). Hybrid tendencies in consumer co-operatives: the case of Sweden. In D. McDonnell & E. Macknight (Eds.), *The co-operative model in practice: International perspectives* (pp. 84–97). CETS—Co-operative Education Trust Scotland.
20. Besharov, M. L., & Smith, W. K. (2014). Multiple institutional logics in organizations: Explaining their varied nature and implications. *Academy of Management Review, 39*(3), 364–381.
21. Mair, J., Mayer, J., & Lutz, E. (2015). Navigating institutional plurality: Organizational governance in hybrid organizations. *Organization Studies, 36*(6), 713–739.
22. Battilana, J. (2018). Cracking the organizational challenge of pursuing joint social and financial goals: Social enterprise as a laboratory to understand hybrid organizing. *M@n@gement, 21*(4), 1278–1305.
23. Kraatz, M., & Block, E. (2008). Organizational implications of institutional pluralism. In R. Greenwood, C. Oliver, & R. Suddaby (Eds.), *The SAGE handbook of organizational institutionalism* (pp. 243–275). Sage.
24. Levi, Y., & Pellegrin-Rescia, M. L. (1997). A new look at the embeddedness/disembeddedness issue: Cooperatives as terms of reference. *The Journal of Socio-Economics, 26*(2), 159–179.
25. Wu, Z., & Pullman, M. E. (2015). Cultural embeddedness in supply networks. *Journal of Operations Management, 37*(1), 45–58.
26. Johanisova, N., Crabtree, T., & Fraňková, E. (2013). Social enterprises and non-market capitals: a path to degrowth? *Journal of Cleaner Production, 38*, 7–16.
27. Becker, S., Kunze, C., & Vancea, M. (2017). Community energy and social entrepreneurship: Addressing purpose, organisation and embeddedness of renewable energy projects. *Journal of Cleaner Production, 147*, 25–36.
28. Defourny, J., & Nyssens, M. (2017). Fundamentals for an international typology of social enterprise models. *VOLUNTAS: International Journal of Voluntary and Nonprofit Organizations, 28*(6), 2469–2497.
29. Billiet, A., Dufays, F., Friedel, S., & Staessens, M. (2021). The resilience of the cooperative model: How do cooperatives deal with the COVID-19 crisis? *Strategic Change, 30*(2), 99–108.
30. ICA. (2015). Guidance notes to the co-operative principles. International Co-operative Alliance: http://www.ica-ap.coop/sites/ica-ap.coop/files/Guidance%20Notes%20EN.pdf.
31. Bodini, R., Cicciarelli, L., Di Meglio, R., Franchini, B., & Salvatori, G. (2017). Putting the "local" in economic development: The role of the social and solidarity economy. In *4th World Forum on Local Economic Development, Praia, Cabo Verde.*

32. Shaw, E., & Carter, S. (2007). Social entrepreneurship: Theoretical antecedents and empirical analysis of entrepreneurial processes and outcomes. *Journal of Small Business and Enterprise Development, 14*(3), 418–434.
33. Dacin, M. T. (2010). *The embeddedness of social entrepreneurship: Understanding variation across local communities*. IESE Business School.
34. Mazzarol, T., Limnios, E. M., & Reboud, S. (2014). An overview of the research. In T. Mazzarol, E. M. Limnios, & S. Reboud (Eds.), *Research handbook on sustainable co-operative enterprise case studies of organizational resilience in the cooperative business model* (pp. 3–21). Edward Elgar.
35. Poledrini, S. (2018). The emergence of new social enterprise models in Italy: First insights from the International ICSEM Project. *Impresa Progetto—Electronic Journal of Management, 2*, 1–19.
36. Thomas, A. (2004). The rise of social cooperatives in Italy. *VOLUNTAS: International Journal of Voluntary and Nonprofit Organizations, 15*(3), 243–263.
37. Pansera, M., & Rizzi, F. (2020). Furbish or perish: Italian social cooperatives at a crossroads. *Organization (London, England), 27*(1), 17–35.
38. Borzaga, C., & Tortia, E. C. (2010). The economics of social enterprises. In L. Becchetti & C. Borzaga (Eds.), *The economics of social responsibility. The world of social enterprises*. Routledge.
39. Borzaga, C., Depedri, S., & Bodini, R. (2010). *Cooperatives: The Italian experience*. Euricse.
40. Borzaga, C., Bodini, R., Carini, C., Depedri, S., Galera, G., & Salvatori, G. (2014). *Europe in Transition: The role of social cooperatives and social enterprises* (Euricse Working Papers, pp. 1–17).
41. Poledrini, S. (2015). Unconditional reciprocity and the case of Italian Social Cooperatives. *Nonprofit and Voluntary Sector Quarterly, 44*(3), 457–473.
42. Borzaga, C. (2020). *Social enterprises and their ecosystems in Europe—Country report Italy*. Publications Office of the European Union.
43. MLPS. (2021). *Nona relazione sullo stato di attuazione della legge recante norme per il diritto al lavoro dei disabili (Anni 2016, 2017 e 2018)*. Camera dei Deputati.
44. Baxter, P., & Jack, S. (2008). Qualitative case study methodology: Study design and implementation for novice researchers. *The Qualitative Report, 13*(4), 544–559.
45. Yin, R. K. (2017). *Case study research and applications. Design and methods* (6th ed.). Sage.
46. Groves, R. M., Fowler, F. J., Jr., Couper, M. P., Lepkowski, J. M., Singer, E., & Tourangeau, R. (2004). *Survey methodology*. Wiley.
47. Belson, W. A. (1983). *Design and understanding of survey questions*. Lexington Books.
48. Gillham, B. (2008). *Developing a questionnaire*. Continuum International Publishing Group.
49. Baruch, Y., & Holtom, B. C. (2008). Survey response rate levels and trends in organizational research. *Human relations (New York), 61*(8), 1139–1160.
50. PTSCLAS, Osservatorio Provinciale del Mercato del Lavoro. (2021). Report 29.
51. Agovino, M., & Rapposelli, A. (2014). Employment of disabled people in the private sector. An analysis at the level of Italian Provinces according to article 13 of law 68/1999. *Quality & Quantity, 48*(3), 1537–1552.
52. FSCL. (2019). *L'inclusione lavorativa delle persone con disabilità in Italia*. Fondazione Studi Consulenti del Lavoro.
53. Ammirato, P. (2018). *The growth of Italian Cooperatives: Innovation, resilience and social responsibility*. Routledge.
54. Birchall, J., & Ketilson, L. H. (2009). *The resilience of the cooperative business model in time of crisis*. International Labour Organization.
55. OECD. (2021). *La dimensione territoriale della produttività nelle cooperative italiane*. OECD.
56. Roelants, B., Dovgan, D., Eum, H., & Terrasi, E. (2012). *The resilience of the cooperative model*. CECOP-CICOPA Europe.

Moving to New Ways of Working Across the Pandemic Crisis: Managerial Challenges and Human-Technology Configurations

Esli Spahiu ⓘ, Niloofar Kazemargi ⓘ, Eugenio Nunziata, and Paolo Spagnoletti ⓘ

Abstract New working modalities such as smart working have removed the constraints of time and place and turned the traditional concept of work into a highly flexible phenomenon that can now be conducted anywhere through digital tools and an array of new technologies. After having experienced it in an unprecedented rate worldwide, following the Covid-19 pandemic, many companies have vowed that these new work configurations are here to stay and will become increasingly common. Organizations will continue to embrace them as a way of improving employees' satisfaction and revolutionizing operations. Despite the benefits often associated with the new ways of work, evidence shows that many companies have struggled to cope with it. In light of the complexity of such adoption, we investigate through a longitudinal case study of a multinational company that embraced such initiatives before, during and after the pandemic, the main challenges and difficulties voiced by both managers and employees. The analysis of the findings shows that the main issues relate to excessive supervision, longer working hours, change of team dynamics and insufficient use of technologies—all of which call for a change in organizational culture and approach towards new ways of working that goes beyond changes in individual tasks and work practices.

Keywords Smart working · Remote work · Work behavior · Employee experience

E. Spahiu · E. Nunziata
Luiss University, Rome, Italy

N. Kazemargi
University of Chieti-Pescara, Pescara, Italy

P. Spagnoletti (✉)
Luiss University, Rome, Italy

University of Agder, Kristiansand, Norway
e-mail: pspagnoletti@luiss.it

© The Author(s), under exclusive license to Springer Nature
Switzerland AG 2024
A. Lazazzara et al. (eds.), *Towards Digital and Sustainable Organisations*,
Lecture Notes in Information Systems and Organisation 65,
https://doi.org/10.1007/978-3-031-52880-4_3

1   Introduction

Many organizations have adopted new ways of working, where work is fully or partially performed outside of the workplace. Although many scholars have recently focused on the Covid-19 restrictions, new ways of working were also studied in the pre-pandemic. The development and adoption of digital workplace technologies has been a driver of change in many work practices and in some cases has altered the nature of work. For instance, mobile technologies enable mobile working where employees can work outside of the workplace for a limited period of time or in case of any displacement required by the nature of work [1]. Today we are also witnessing how the role of these workplace technologies has shifted from being mere supportive tools of the work in the office, to playing an important role in shaping different forms of community building within the organization [2]. This goes to also support a recent shift from the old human-tech dichotomy towards a reconceptualized rhetoric that a new way of interaction between human and machines is taking place and should be acknowledged as such [3, 4]. Dery et al. [5] go further by suggesting redesigning the "physical, cultural and digital arrangements that simplify working life" to become customer-centered organizations that monitor and respond in a timely manner to customers' demands [6]. They highlight that the traditional command-and-control based on hierarchy and direct supervision is no longer appropriate to address changes in the business environments. Thus, organizations need to redesign work and workplace focusing on agility, team working, collaboration with internal and external actors and a non-hierarchical control. In this regard managers should also focus on communication, improvisation and learning new competences as a way of aligning with the development of different agile capabilities [7]. Such transformation has been reinforced by the needs and working styles of the new workforce [8]: new workforce is expected to perform "knowledge based, flexible, and adaptive tasks" rather than repeated structured work [9].

The adoption of new ways of working, however, seems to be difficult for some organizations—especially during the health emergency, organizations needed to transform how their employees work overnight. Organizations needed to cope with tensions and paradoxes both at individual and intra-organizational levels. Previous studies illustrate the antecedents and consequences of new ways of working. However, as will also be highlighted in the next section, most of the existing knowledge so far was either conducted when remote working was implemented partially or infrequently and not at such a unique rate as in the last 2 years, or it was only considered by some organizations and not to such extend as today where almost every employee expects some flexible working arrangement from companies. In view of the lack of studies in this regard, this paper aims at addressing the following research question: *What are the challenges faced and lessons learned by organizations when adopting new forms of work?* In answering this question, the research conducted is based on a longitudinal case study of a big organization operating worldwide that decided to embark on a transformative journey with regard to the new ways of working. The results from this study aim at paving the way for future research on digital/human work configurations and bridging existing challenges with effective ways to address them, in an attempt to establish even better organization-employer relationships in the future.

2 Literature Review

2.1 Definition of New Forms of Work

New way of working as a terminology is often confusing and not always used consistently. Terms such as remote working, flexible working and smart working are often used interchangeably, when in fact in literature they refer to different types of work practices. During the health emergency, remote work mainly referred to working from home [10]. New ways of working are facilitated by workplace technologies such as mobile and e-collaboration tools. In mobile working, the focus remains still on efficiency and productivity relying on traditional organizational and management structures: still workers need to perform structured tasks, where supervisors monitor and control the performance of workers [11]. "Smart working" has recently received attention from both academics and practitioners as a new way of working, which refers to "a flexible working system" [12]. Smart working exploits and combines new technologies to make human activities less related to office spaces or to the physical presence at one's desk. Dery et al. [5] coin the term "digital workplaces" where a new workplace system supports employees in addressing business uncertainty. They highlight that the new workplace should focus on employees' experience, which demands a rearrangement of the organizational structure, culture, workspace and IT infrastructure. Such evolution of new workplaces has also led to the emergence of new notions in literature such as digital/human configurations, that apart from recognizing the relation between human and technology, also emphasize the importance of "work" or the extra effort needed to manage such relations due to the addition of digitalization [2].

The literature also provides insights on the outcomes of the new ways of working. Mainly prior studies regard new ways of working with autonomy: new work practices give opportunity to knowledge workers to perform their tasks wherever and whenever they opt and hence, remove temporal and spatial organizational boundaries and increase flexibility of employees [6]. In addition, the empirical studies show relationships between remote working and job performance [13], job satisfaction [14]; and well-being [15]. Nevertheless, considering how the new working modalities require new adjustments, it would be expected for organizations to face some challenging aspects. Such studies though, focus only on the end results and the effect of the new ways of working on different aspects of work/job. There is a lack of references with regard to the process itself and what were the lessons learned, which would provide an important roadmap for future adoptions.

2.2   Antecedents of New Ways of Working

The nature of work has shifted away from structured tasks, uncertainty has increased and thus, the traditional approach is not effective anymore for monitoring and controlling [16]. New organizational structures should focus less on efficiency and more on innovation: they should enable workers to generate and exchange ideas, collaborate, experiment, and prototype. Adoption of new way of working goes beyond the traditional organizational and management structures. This has implications on organizational structure, monitoring, control, and reward systems [2]. In the new ways of working, the focus is on enhancing autonomy of workers and collaboration internally and externally. Providing workers with autonomy gives them the freedom to choose where, when and how to perform the work assigned. This enables workers to respond to changing business environments and enhances flexibility. In such workplace, the employer-employee relationship has shifted from hierarchical, command-and-control and well-structured tasks to a new paradigm in organizing based on mutual trust, autonomy and flexibility [17]. This has brought some recent studies to see the need for proper leadership style in coordination and well-being of remote workers that would fit the new changes [18]. Whereas traditional office layouts constrain flexibility and cross team collaboration, the redesigning of workplaces aims at enhancing not only the well-being of workers but also the intra-organizational collaboration and communication. Many organizations now have redesigned their spaces to small group meetings (using applications to book meeting rooms in efficient ways), brainstorming sessions, shared social areas to enhance collaboration and generation of new ideas. Some even go further, by designing customer centers within workplace where workers closely interact with customers during innovation processes [7].

Digital technologies play a key role in enabling the new ways of working. Mobile devices (such as smartphones, laptops, and tablets) enable workers to access and share data with peers, managers, or even with external actors such as customers or suppliers. Using mobile devices removes temporal and spatial constraints: workers can be connected to the workplace wherever and whenever they opt to [19]. To support connectivity, some workers use their own devices at workplace and the "Bring Your Own Device" (BYOD) idea provides innovative opportunities for organizations [20]. As technology evolves, Attaran et al. [9] explain that organizations are redesigning the workplace by embedding new digital technologies to support individuals in performing their work (e.g. self-services, data gathering and analytics systems), to facilitate virtual collaboration and communication at team level (e.g. collaborative tools, project management and video conferences), to support knowledge sharing and decision making process (e.g. enterprise social media, platforms, decision making support systems). Moreover, digital technologies are significantly changing the way organizations coordinate and control. For instance, digital platforms and algorithms enable organizations to coordinate human resources even beyond the organizational boundaries [21]. While other new workplace technologies in what is considered an intelligent augmentation layer, make use of as AI capabilities or robotic process automations to offer advanced integrated office plat-forms to leverage people [2].

2.3   Challenges of New Ways of Working

The literature reveals multiple challenges with regard to the new ways of working mainly at individual level. For remote workers the boundaries between work and life are blurred [22]. In the new ways of working, while remote workers are autono-mous in managing their work (e.g. time, location and how to perform work), in practice remote workers are faced with the paradox of autonomy where they feel a tension "between their personal autonomy and their professional commitment to others" and thus feeling the need to be always online [23].While new policies and practices remove the emphasis on work context, some studies show the "dual role of the location" for remote workers where location "does and don'ts" are not important [24]. Dery and Hafermalz [25] argue that remote workers may feel ignored or iso-lated at workplace and they see the need for new capabilities in creating and main-taining an identity virtually. Wang et al. [26] identified four challenges that employees in China faced during the pandemic: the inability to balance their work and personal life, distractions, loneliness and lack of communication. Fan and Moen [27] study the amount of working time for remote workers by gender during the COVID-19 pandemic. They find that some challenges are more evident for women remote workers who were shown to have had more issues in managing their life-work balance due to the longer working hours [28]. Other studies show that the new way of working was more difficult for managers than employees [29]. In other stud-ies the new way of working had an additional dark side as for many it means less opportunities in career development [30].

Other studies point out that organizations face paradoxes while the nature of the work becomes more digital or performed by mobile devices. In particular, the devel-opment of technologies makes the behaviors of people (e.g. employees) to be more visible [31]. Such visibility of employees' behaviors could create tensions that make it difficult for organizations to manage and coordinate work. For instance, Leonardi and Treem [31] show that employees seek to respond to expected connec-tivity by organizations or to make their performance visible. Despite such a new wave of studies though, to our knowledge, however, little attention has been paid to challenges at the top level on how new ways of working can be integrated in the organization, which is why this study wishes to offer a holistic view in terms of challenges as observed from both the higher levels (supervisors/managers) and all the other employees.

3   Methodology

For the purpose of this research and in order to understand the organization's approach to new ways of working, it was imperative to first consider as many organizational components as possible, such as organizational structure, professional population and supporting technologies in addition to the methods, attitudes, and levels of adoption with regard to different types of remote working. In this regard, qualitative field surveys and semi structured interviews were conducted with different clusters representing different profiles of interest in agile working such as different employees and individual contributors on the one hand, and managers/supervisors/coordinators on the other hand, in order to see the different perspectives as intended by the objective of this research. The focus of both the survey and the interviews was based on the organizational dimensions which were impacted the most by "agile work", therefore, evaluating the contribution of the people involved, what is the role they play, the organization itself and its contribution to a successful agile work, and lastly, the technologies used or adopted as a crucial part of this new form of executing work. A detailed summary with regard to the interviews and survey conducted can be found in Fig. 1.

The survey provided an efficient way of gathering information due to its unique capability of being easy to administer. Considering that this research was undertaken during the first wave of the pandemic where close contact was impossible, surveys provided a good source of data from the company managers. The surveys were anonymous, which would allow for respondents to be more candid and honest when answering, and that in turn would also provide more unambiguous responses. The survey was distributed through an online service provider to seven of the senior level managers in the organization, who had been in the first line of engaging and

Primary Data		
Type of Data	**Description**	**Quantity**
Interviews	Semi-structured interviews with managers, supervisors, and employees	20 interviews to managers and employees
Survey	14 open ended and close ended questions	7 surveys to top level managers
Secondary Data		
Type of Data	**Description**	**Quantity**
Site visits	On site observations of working modalities, spaces, and technology	2 full days on site
Archival documents	Reports, presentations, press releases	7 reports

Fig. 1 Dataset overview

facing the new ways of working, in order to understand better the main themes on which to base the interviews later. The findings were subsequently used to structure a set of 20 semi-structured interviews which would follow the survey. The aim of the interviews was to have the chance to observe whether corporate e-business strategies and policies aimed at stimulating smart working would be in synergy with one another inside the organization, from the point of view of both managers and other employees. Interviews conducted were divided into two sets: in the first set interviews were conducted with managers and employees who had adopted the new forms of working for a significant period of time, whilst the second set of interviews were conducted with a "control" group with similar job characteristics as the individuals in the first set, but who had not adopted any agile or smart working practices. All hierarchical levels were represented by the interview sample—including individuals pertaining to roles that involve both a certain level of mobility and roles that involve only "desk activities". The interviews were conducted through a digital tool, due to the lockdown constraints in place at the time. Whilst the questions of the survey were the same for everyone taking it, in the case of the interviews the themes remained the same, but since they were semi-structured in nature, it allowed for diversion from the predefined questions when important points would be raised. More details on the themes and subtopics have been summarized in Fig. 2.

NVivo was used for the data analysis and coding, which was performed following Corbin and Strauss [32] approach through which open coding was conducted as a first step into pointing out similar patterns in the data. Axial coding and selective coding subsequently followed the data analysis which allowed for an eventual regrouping of the main emerging categories. Both the survey and the interviews were conducted in Italian. Apart from primary data, secondary data was also acquired from the organization, which was particularly important in understanding the context and the level of implementation of such practice.

In order to ensure the validity of the study and also limit any potential biases, the authors implemented key measures in order to overcome any issues with regard to validity and biases. Following Yin's [33] methodology, primary and secondary data were acquired for triangulation between them in order to enforce the construct validity of the study. In addition, the different seniority levels of the interviewees, which included not only employees but also managers from different sectors within the organization would help establish the internal validity of the study, whilst also limit any design and selection bias. With regard to any interview biases, authors followed Saunders et al. [34] proposals in establishing trust by sending an interview guide and the necessary contact details before each interview in case of any question concerning the procedure. In addition, to establish a sound reliability of the data collected during the interviews, results were compiled into full records shortly after the interviews [35].

Interview Guide		
Themes	**Main Question**	**Probes**
Opening remarks & Personal experience	What is your personal experience with remote/agile/smart work?	• How prone are new ways of work to be adopted in your line of work? • What are the main differences in the way work is conducted?
Productivity	How is productivity being measured?	• What are the criteria on which judgments about productivity are made? • What is the effect of new ways of work on productivity?
Coordination	How is coordination exercised?	• What are the ways used to coordinate, integrate and supervise work? • How has coordination between teams changed after the new ways of work?
Cooperation	How do you cooperate with internal/external offices/teams/projects?	• What are the main tools adopted after the introduction of new ways of work? • What is the frequency of using certain tools (before/after new ways of work)
Perceived Risks, & Closing remarks	What are the perceived risks associated with new ways of work?	• What are the fears expressed by who has adopted new ways of work? • What should change for a more successful adoption of new ways of work?

Fig. 2 Interview guide

4 Background of the Organization

Avios is the anonymized name of an international fleet managing and lease company operating worldwide, which decided to embark on transforming the workplace and adopting new ways of working following the redesign of their headquarter structure in Italy. This was a strategic choice in reconfiguring what were known to be as the classical operating practices at the time. Such a step was in many ways dictated by a similar wave of change adopted by other companies due to the reduction of logistical costs associated with a more mobile workforce and a decreasing need to have dedicated workstations. The HR unit of the Avios became the promoter of the policy designed to legitimate the so-called "smart working" through different protocols that had allowed for more employees to choose, in agreement with managers and for 1 day a week, to work outside their place of work. Nevertheless, the HR initiative initially was not accompanied by an explicit strategic vision and a clear awareness strategy on behalf of the company management with regard to the

Phases	Modes of work	Period of Implementation	Description
Phase 1	Agile work	May 2017 - March 2020	Progressive adoption of agile work with individual protocols
Phase 2	Total remote work	March/November 2020	Total remoteness of work due to the pandemic crisis
Phase 3	Partial remote work	November 2020/to date	Partial job remoteness due to health concerns
Phase 4	Policy reformulation for agile work	Post-pandemic	Internal strategic reformulations of the current policies regarding agile work
Phase 5	Wider adoptions of remote work	Post-pandemic	Normalizing smart working

Fig. 3 Phases and modes of work at Avios

advantages of such opportunities. Considering the extent to which the smart working was embraced due to the Covid-19, total remoteness of work due to the pandemic crisis was then implemented abruptly in the organization due to the sudden change of circumstances that modified the motivations behind the adoption of remote working. The main phases through which the organization embraced new modes of work are summarized in Fig. 3. Whilst the first three phases describe what has already been implemented, phases 4 and 5 relate to the upcoming objectives and long-term reforms expected to be undertaken by the organization after the pandemic crisis aimed at a wider application of smart working.

Considering that Avios would be relatively new to all the new ways of working remotely compared to other organizations that have embraced working remotely for a longer period of time, which in turn has given them time to adjust, Avios provided the perfect conditions for analyzing the take on such modalities. The interviews and surveys, which were conducted after the organization had embraced smart working and total remoteness due to Covid, compared to other counterparts in the industry would provide meaningful evidence of how the process went, its strengths and weaknesses. Providing such evidence would allow us to showcase a list of the lessons learned and important considerations that companies in similar conditions can make prior to embarking on a similar journey. This would be important considering the shift in work modalities in the recent 2 years and the expectations that employees have from companies to provide for them.

5   Findings

There are many organizational dimensions involved in the new work practices such as enabling technologies, restructuring of processes, reconfiguration of roles and responsibilities and alternating between different managerial and coordination approaches. Each of these dimensions would require particular policies in order to ensure the highest levels of consistency with regard to the changes happening due to the new work practices. When new policies such as the ones mentioned above are lacking or limited in scope, the following list of challenges can emerge:

5.1   Remote Working for Everyone?

First and foremost, the analysis of the findings showed that there was an imbalance between employees that were given greater autonomy with regard to their use of time and space based on the professional roles played within the organization. This meant that one of the main challenges observed was based on the fact that not everyone working in the organization was given the same level of flexibility as others. In this regard, the roles who were more mobile and who could work more easily from remote tended to be the ones oriented towards achieving non quantitative results. Their results and work performance were instead measured in level of effective implementation of provisions or service offerings. The opposite was evidenced for roles whose work requires more tangible results as part of their day-to-day job engagements. Based on the responses collected by supervisors and managers, such a lack of uniformity in terms of remote working was argued to be mainly due to a lack of trust in offering the same rights to be more flexible to everyone indistinctively of the role, responsibilities and seniority within the organization. Such lack of trust had also led managers to be less propense to allow working remotely in general. Nevertheless, further inquiry into the matter revealed that the main cause for such a disparity was due to the inconvenience of supervisors stemming from having to coordinate teams remotely. Because of the latter, the organization had made a selective choice in assigning more flexible attributes to some individuals and not others, based on the leadership style of supervisors/managers, despite the fact that well-being at work is the result of work flexibility that should be enjoyed by everyone. Not extending the same opportunities to all the workforces can be damaging both to the employees' wellbeing and in extreme cases to the reputation of the organization. It is imminent in this context, to teach managers the tools and give them the know-hows of coordinating through the use of technology, which would give them the opportunity to supervise the employees easily despite the new working modalities. On the other hand, through the use of similar technological means employees should be taught how to showcase their work and make it more transparent, which in turn would help managers evaluate their work better.

5.2   Managing Without Seeing

When looking at the emerging issues evidenced from the resources operating in agile work, a change in direct supervision was perceived as yet another of the main issues of concern. For some of the employees there was a lack of direct supervision exercised over them compared to the time when physically present at the office. This had then led to employees feeling a greater need to self-engage and self-regulate in the team. Despite this aspect being different from what the employees were used to, the findings showed that eventually, the lack of direct supervision, which led employees to learn to work more independently, was integral in learning to have more responsibility, and in doing so learn new skills. Whilst this was evident for some teams, the opposite was evidenced from others who said that control at times could be excessive due to what they perceived to be a lack of trust. It was evident that old stereotypes regarding the need to be nonstop present at work was very persistent. With regard to these issues, managers said that at times they felt the need to be more controlling which, was translated into more phone calls, meetings, or number of e-mails since they felt such measures were the only way they felt they could make sure to supervise their employees, despite understanding the concern coming from their teams about over control. In this regard, the research showed how the managers should understand what is described as a shift from "at desk" culture where supervision can be visually accessible, to the need to develop a new way of "managing without seeing". Such an approach can be achieved through a series of shifts including the need to prioritize tasks and enabling data to showcase the result of the work done by the employees. Because of the emergence of new working modalities, where working remotely outside the office space has become predominant in such modalities, remote management has also been introduced as a new way of supervising along its own specific traits. This includes being able to assign tasks for remote team members, track a remote team's progress and addressing any possible challenges that come with working remotely. Such a managerial style should be understood to be different from the classical managerial role since it is envisioned to fit the needs of team members working in isolation from one another. In the organization under review, such a managerial style was lacking and a disparity between old ways of working and adapting to the new ways, was not an easy transition to make.

5.3   Performance Without Pressure

In line with the previous concern regarding excessive supervision, another emerging issue regarding the new modality of work was the fact that employees felt that their working hours instead of being flexible, were longer than usual due the fact that they perceived the unspoken pressure to work longer in order to show that they were indeed doing their job. The interviewees expressed concern that this would be counterproductive and in fact play a negative role with regard to the approach they would have to smart working in the future. When asked for the reasons that lead to such a behavior, respondents said that this was at part due to the abrupt need to go fully remote because of the pandemic, but also due to the organizational culture which had not gone through any prior transformation/adjustment in line with the changes happening in the business world with regard to the new ways of working. By not being fully ready to engage with smart working, the findings showed how the line between the office and home were blurred and despite employees having the right to sign off of their work in the designated hours, that was not the case.

Most employees said that apart from working long hours, without making use of the flexibility that should come with such working modalities, they would also find themselves stuck at work at all times. In this context, there was a lack of a proper example set by the supervisors and managers who were also doing the same, and in doing so leading their teams to exhaustive work shifts. Despite, smart working showing an increase in productivity, it should be noted that it can do so only under the right circumstances and failing to set the record straight with regard to what smart working consists of, could lead to undesirable effects such as in this case. Sometimes this was caused due to the larger number of meetings that would take place remotely when compared to when physically present in the office, which would take away valuable time that would otherwise be dedicated on the required tasks. Overall, it was evident from the analysis that a lack of the right balance of all such issues as absence of flexibility, longer working hours and impossibility to "shut down" was a leading cause of many of the challenges observed throughout the period on question. In this regard, there was a lack of directives and clear information coming from the organization itself on what are the correct work modalities under these new circumstances which eventually lead to undesirable effects such as in this case.

5.4   Communication as a Workflow

Another grey area where employees felt the need for the organization to be paying more attention regarded teamwork. The resources that operate in agile work mode appeared to have been significantly affected by the discomfort deriving from the loss of teamwork once the ability to share a physical space was not possible. This was evident given that the interactions between employees appeared to be suffering from a distress stemming from the physical distance. By losing informal relationships resulting from sharing the same physical space, there appeared an increased sense of being isolated that diminished the opportunity to exchange work experiences. This had led to more meetings being planned ad hoc via shared communication channels in order to satisfy the need to feel aligned on tasks and objectives and to make one's contribution evident to colleagues and supervisors.

What can help in this regard more, and which was agreed by everyone, was the fact that communication should be considered as a workflow and the number of meetings should be in accordance with the need to align, the need to set objectives and show how these objectives are assumed to be measured. This in turn would be expected to be more beneficial with regard to knowing one's responsibilities despite not being at constant contact with other team members. This would prove beneficial in cases where some members of the team work remotely and others not, which in some situations could also lead the ones working remotely to feel more alienated compared to the others working from the office. Apart from this, by investing more into looking at communication as a workflow should be seen as beneficial in the long term as well, since it would help in the diffusion of smart working and would also aid in making every employee, despite their working modalities, feel that they are involved equally.

5.5 Encouraging Technology Embracement

During the interviews, all employees were asked to name which were the tools that they used the most to collaborate before engaging in new working modalities and those that they use the most after doing so. What emerged was that despite the organization investing in technology and technological infrastructures that would aid smart working, most of the remote collaboration was achieved through the same channels as when present physically in the same space at work (e.g., video/voice calls, via email), with little exploitation of other options. This fact was observed in all of professional roles under review by this study. Technology should be understood as the main vehicle of communication, engagement and attaining desirable results, and as such plays a huge role in providing the necessary tools to not only reach the work objectives but doing so through the most effective and efficient way. The same way managers should learn to exercise new ways of supervising the employees, teams are also expected to step outside their comfort zone and learn new ways of collaborating through means of new digital tools. Albeit challenging at first, this is an important step in making the most out of the new ways of work that require a reconfiguration of certain aspects of how the job is carried out.

In most cases the reason for not making use of new technology was due to hesitation in making things differently. Nevertheless, in some instances, the findings from the data collected suggested that some of the limitations when it comes to the usage of technology stems from privacy concerns with regard to the data. Employees showed concern that sharing and receiving data when working remotely can be hazardous. This is why it is important for organizations to always be on the hunt for reliable tools that address such concerns and in turn offer a seamless user experience for the employees making use of them. Managers and supervisors on the other hand should be reassured on the reliability of the new tools made available to them. Additionally, employees should be persuaded more into making use of and exploiting digital tools and alternative working spaces that would allow them to make use of the full experience of smart working and aid in putting them in the right mindset of such new work modalities.

6 Discussion

The main findings from the analysis of surveys and interviews suggest that in order for organizations to fully embrace the potential that comes with smart working, there is a series of considerations that should be made prior. Actions should be subsequently taken aligned with such considerations that mostly relate to a shift in organizational behavior, that would in turn modify the paradigms that have governed the way work is conducted prior to smart working. The findings of our analysis are supported by similar emerging outcomes of studies in the business world with regard to what employees agree is important today for their work to be made visible, despite the different working modalities, and what are the management shifts that need to take place to support the new ways of working [36, 37].

These findings enforce previous studies reflecting on the importance of the right balance between working shifts and flexibility as a key ingredient to employees' wellbeing [38]. Working outside a fixed station is becoming a new way of engaging with our working responsibilities and accountabilities. The liberty to choose the physical space has shown to increase productivity and well-being and not the other way around [39]. For employees today, it is important to shape the working shifts around other important activities that they deem necessary. This is far beyond the dull picture painted by managers decades ago that such approach would damage productivity. In the contrary, allowing a certain degree of flexibility in terms of choosing the time and space can prove quite beneficial [40].

In order to make the most out of the new working modalities, apart from the good intentions of simply offering the possibility to employees, it is important to also aid the process of transitioning towards smart working. This would require enabling the digital capabilities of employees, which would mean providing the right mix of digital maturity and digital tools that would allow them to connect quickly and be at ease at working remotely [41]. By making sure that the employees have the right tools and knowledge on how to make use of them, would ensure that they develop collaborations and produce value, whether they are working individually or in teams. Technology is the glue that pulls everything together in such working modalities, so organizations should be investing in making sure that they have all the necessary tools in this regard, but also ensure that the employees and teams working remotely can make the most out of them [42].

One of the main concerns that emerged also regarded the issue that working remotely was considered to make the work harder to be noticed. In this context it is important to make the invisible visible by making the work done outside the physical office transparent. This can be done only by adopting workflow tools that aid in managing a fluid communication internally. This goes back to the previous point about the importance of technology that can help keep track of communication. It should be noted though that under the new working circumstances real-time collaboration is useful but not always essential in the virtual environment, which means that organizations should find new ways of showcasing each other's work.

Another important consideration is the fact that managers play a crucial role in the well-functioning of the new working system. The analysis showed how managers feel the need to have more control on their teams when working remotely, which makes the employees be more tense with regard to their day-to-day activities. It is therefore important to develop a new set of management behaviors to guide people and teams to work remotely as the only way of addressing this issue [43]. There is the need to focus on results (objectives) with respect to the effort (activities). It is important to give people the flexibility they need, provide and promote delegation and empowerment, which in turn would create a new management style without being too overcontrolling, but rather exhibit confidence towards the employees [44]. From the employees' side this would be transmitted as having the adequate space to perform without pressure and feel they are trusted. By changing the ways team operate and behave is expected to increase productivity and the value of the contributions made by our remote workers. By empowering the people while equipping them with the skills and tools needed to meet the challenges of the virtual world, there is a better chance of making the most out of the flexibility provided by new forms of work, whilst also creating more productive and efficient ways of sharing and communicating within teams.

7   Implications

7.1   Theoretical Implications

Although previous studies have focused on the antecedents and consequences of new way of working at individual or organizational level, such studies do not yet provide insights into the challenges and practices of human-technology reconfigurations experienced by organizations identified in literature [3, 4]. By exploring the challenges that organizations face, this study makes important contribution to the existing literatures in terms of job performance, leadership and how the new nature of work is depicted by both managers and employees. The latest studies suggest how leaders and coordination plays an important role of remote workers [18], which in our research was evidenced through the issues arising from the lack of supervision or when the latter was more exhaustive when working in smart working. Job performance and job satisfaction have been proven to go hand in hand and to have an important effect on one other [14]. Our study extends this notion by showing through concrete examples how productivity is not related to work modalities, but rather on whether the employees are given the right tools, space and flexibility that the new working modalities command. Otherwise, the new working modalities can be counter productive and increase tensions. Our findings on the other hand, also complement other similar analyses with regard to the fact that longer hours can have a negative effect of working remotely that blures the lines of work and private life [22]. To conclude this study also extends our understanding of the new governance process dynamics of digital/human configurations as an emerging phenomena during the organisational transformation resulting from digital work [2].

7.2 *Practical Implications*

A successful implementation of any form of remote work depends predominantly on the course of action taken by the organization and as such this study is important for managers to understand the key issues to consider before implementation, or even if they have already started managing employees and teams working in remote modalities. The findings in this research showed that customizing policies for such working modalities is important to make the work environment appropriate for smart working with regard to the flexible use of workspaces, flexible management of work and working hours and the enabling technologies for the creation and maintenance of virtual workspaces. Policies in this regard should address, but not be limited to, policies designed to legitimize the process of organizational change as a result of the spread of smart working, definition, and legitimization of the directive regarding the path to follow in these instances, new organizational and individual performance evaluation systems that match the new modalities. In addition, to such policies, the analysis also showed the importance of actions for the development of a digital culture and how digitalization and technology are among the most important pillars from where to start building on the smart working. While the implementation of different policies that would aid the development of smart working are the first step into embracing the later, it should be noted that such implementation is important to be subsequently followed with new monitoring mechanisms in terms of business KPIs, perceived tangible and intangible benefits, and frequent evaluation of the customer and employee satisfaction.

8 Limitations and Future Research

There are two main limitations with regard to this study. The first limitation regards the fact that this research is based on a single case study and the analysis, and the results pertain to the selected case study alone. This can result in limitations with regard to generalization based on this case study alone. With regard to generalization, it should be noted that the organization culture of this particular company could have also played a role in the process of adoption of the new ways of work, which can also restrict the possibility of generalized conclusions. In order to enhance generalizability, future studies could be replicated across different organizations, sectors and industries. The second limitation regards the fact that the organization under review is based in Italy and as such the regulatory context can lead to differences with regard to other companies operating in other countries. Nevertheless, this research gives the opportunity for subsequent research to analyze other companies, which are also newcomers to the idea of smart working and see how the main considerations in this paper compare. Other limitations that can result from the use of a case study approach such as construct, and internal validity should also be noted. In order to mitigate such limitations, as noted in Sect. 3, for the purpose of this research, the interviewees were chosen from all levels, roles and seniorities which had at least in some point during their career with the organization make use of the remote working opportunities. With regard to the data gathering and analysis, secondary data was also analyzed for triangulation purposes in order to address the aforementioned limitations.

With regard to future research, having identified some key challenges faced by the new ways of working, upcoming work should focus in addressing the issues from both perspectives: managers and employees. In accordance with this point, studying the possibility of compiling appropriate guidelines based on best practices for achieving a smooth transition could also be another avenue of research. This could be preceded first by employee readiness analysis that would evaluate the organizational needs in terms of managerial and technological skills. With more organizations adopting new working modes, more research will have to eventually focus on the changes in terms of organizational dynamics, new business models and operating structure designs. Lastly, since it is already hard to ignore the fact that employees are more and more demanding flexible working options, sustainability of remote working would also need to be evaluated as a sustainable workplace framework.

9   Conclusion

The new ways of working have been proven to drive productivity, efficiency, whilst also providing a new definition of freedom for employees to leave their desks and profit from the greater benefits that come along such new modalities. Through the development of existing technologies and the adoption of new ones, new models of work have emerged extensively. Such models proved to be extremely useful in carrying out work in the last few years in spite of the challenging situation being faced due to the pandemic. Having proven its worth, smart working is here to stay and requires a new paradigm on how work is being executed. By focusing on a recent case of a company jumping on the bandwagon of smart working, this paper focused on the emerging concern and issues faced in the process. It showcased how apart from good intentions, a successful implementation required a cultural revolution that guides managers and employees on how to understand and evaluate work. It requires an ideological change that would revise teamwork, collaboration, use of technology and work evaluation. The emerging issues that were evidenced throughout this paper aim at offering insights on the adoption journey of an organization and contribute to both theory and practice regarding new ways of work. Future studies should focus on addressing the main challenges as evidenced by this paper, whilst also exploring new avenues of research with regard to the new ways of working in terms of best practices, organizational changes and sustainability.

References

1. Yuan, Y., Archer, N., Connelly, C. E., & Zheng, W. (2010). Identifying the ideal fit between mobile work and mobile work support. *Information & Management, 47*(3), 125–137.
2. Baptista, J., Stein, M. K., Klein, S., Watson-Manheim, M. B., & Lee, J. (2020). Digital work and organisational transformation: Emergent digital/human work configurations in modern organisations. *The Journal of Strategic Information Systems, 29*(2).
3. Suchman, L. (2012). Configuration. In C. Lury & N. Wakeford (Eds.), *Inventive methods: The happening of the social* (pp. 48–60). Taylor and Francis.
4. Suchman, L. (2007). *Human-machine reconfigurations: Plans and situated actions.* Cambridge University Press.
5. Dery, K., Sebastian, I. M., & van der Meulen, N. (2017). The digital workplace is key to digital innovation. *MIS Quarterly Executive, 16*(2), 135–152.
6. Chatterjee, S., Sarker, S., & Siponen, M. (2017). How do mobile ICTs enable organizational fluidity: toward a theoretical framework. *Information & Management, 54*(1), 1–13.
7. Spagnoletti, P., Kazemargi, N., & Prencipe, A. (2021). Agile practices and organizational agility in software ecosystems. *IEEE Transactions on Engineering Management, 69*(6), 3604–3617.
8. Colbert, A., Yee, N., & George, G. (2016). The digital workforce and the workplace of the future. *Academy of Management Journal, 59*(3), 731–739.
9. Attaran, M., Attaran, S., & Kirkland, D. (2019). The need for digital workplace: Increasing workforce productivity in the information age. *International Journal of Enterprise Information Systems, 15*(1), 1–23.
10. Ghislieri, C., Molino, M., Dolce, V., Sanseverino, D., & Presutti, M. (2021). Work-family conflict during the Covid-19 pandemic: teleworking of administrative and technical staff in healthcare. An Italian study. *La Medicina Del Lavoro, 112*(3).
11. Porter, A. J., & Van Den Hooff, B. (2020). The complementarity of autonomy and control in mobile work The complementarity of autonomy and control in mobile work. *European Journal of Information Systems, 00*(00), 1–18.
12. Lee, J. (2016). Drivers and consequences in transforming work practices. In J. Lee (Ed.), *The impact of ICT on work* (pp. 71–92). Springer.
13. Golden, T. D., & Gajendran, R. S. (2019). Unpacking the role of a telecommuter's job in their performance: Examining job complexity, problem solving, interdependence, and social support. *Journal of Business and Psychology, 34*(1), 55–69.
14. Gajendran, R. S., & Harrison, D. A. (2007). The good, the bad, and the unknown about telecommuting: meta-analysis of psychological mediators and individual consequences. *Journal of Applied Psychology, 92*(6).
15. Dettmers, J. (2017). How extended work availability affects well-being: The mediating roles of psychological detachment and work-family-conflict. *Work & Stress, 31*(1), 24–41.
16. Frost, J., Osterloh, M., & Weibel, A. (2010). Governing knowledge work: Transactional and transformational solutions. *Organizational Dynamics, 39*(2), 126–136.
17. De Kok, A. (2016). The new way of working: bricks, bytes, and behavior. In J. Lee (Ed.), *The impact of ICT on work* (pp. 9–40). Springer.
18. Dolce, V., Vayre, E., Molino, M., & Ghislieri, C. (2020). Far away, so close? The role of destructive leadership in the job demands–resources and recovery model in emergency telework. *Social Sciences, 9*(11), 1–22.
19. Dery, K., & MacCormick, J. (2012). Managing mobile technology: The shift from mobility to connectivity smartphone. *MIS Quarterly Executive, 159, 10*(2), 115–117.
20. Scheepers, R., & Middleton, C. (2013). Personal ICT ensembles and ubiquitous information systems environments: Key issues and research implications. *Communications of the Association for Information Systems, 33*(1), 22.

21. Möhlmann, M., Zalmanson, L., Henfridsson, O., & Gregory, R. W. (2021). Algorithmic management of work on online labor platforms: When matching meets control. *MIS Quarterly, 45*(4), 1999–2022.
22. Song, Y., & Gao, J. (2020). Does telework stress employees out? A study on working at home and subjective well-being for wage/salary workers. *Journal of Happiness Studies, 21*(7), 2649–2668.
23. Mazmanian, M., Orlikowski, W. J., & Yates, J. A. (2013). The autonomy paradox: The implications of mobile email devices for knowledge professionals. *Organization Science, 24*(5), 1337–1357.
24. Kietzmann, J., Plangger, K., Eaton, B., Heilgenberg, K., Pitt, L., & Berthon, P. (2013). Mobility at work: A typology of mobile communities of practice and contextual ambidexterity. *Journal of Strategic Information Systems, 22*(4), 282–297.
25. Dery, K., & Hafermalz, E. (2016). Seeing is belonging: Remote working, identity and staying connected. In J. Lee (Ed.), *The Impact of ICT on work*. Springer.
26. Wang, B., Liu, Y., Qian, J., & Parker, S. K. (2021). Achieving effective remote working during the COVID-19 pandemic: A work design perspective. *Applied Psychology, 70*(1), 16–59.
27. Fan, W., & Moen, P. (2022). Working more less or the same during COVID-19? *A Mixed Method Intersectional Analysis of Remote Workers Work and Occupations, 49*(2), 143–186. https://doi.org/10.1177/07308884211047208
28. Fan, W., & Moen, P. (2021). Working more, less or the same during COVID-19? A mixed method, intersectional analysis of remote workers. *Work and Occupations, 49*(2), 143–186.
29. Baert, S., Lippens, L., Moens, E., Weytjens, J., & Sterkens, P. (2022). The COVID-19 crisis and telework: A research survey on experiences, expectations and hopes. *The European Journal of Health Economics, 23*, 729–753.
30. Bolisani, E., Scarso, E., Ipsen, C., Kirchner, K., & Hansen, J. P. (2020). Working from home during COVID-19 pandemic: Lessons learned and issues. *Management & Marketing. Challenges for the Knowledge Society, 15*(1), 458–476.
31. Leonardi, P. M., & Treem, J. W. (2020). Behavioral visibility: A new paradigm for organization studies in the age of digitization, digitalization, and datafication. *Organization Studies, 41*(12), 1601–1625.
32. Corbin, J. M., & Strauss, A. (1990). Grounded theory research: Procedures, canons, and evaluative criteria. *Qualitative Sociology, 13*(1), 3–21.
33. Yin, R. (2018). *Case study research and applications*. Sage.
34. Saunders, M., Lewis, P., & Thornhill, A. (2003). *Research methods for business students*. Prentice Hall: Financial Times.
35. Robson, C. (2002). *Real world research: A resource for social scientists and practitioner-researchers*. Wiley-Blackwell.
36. Gastaldi, L., Corso, M., Raguseo, E., Neirotti, P., Paolucci, E., & Martini, A. (2014). Smart working: Rethinking work practices to leverage employees' innovation potential. In *Proceedings of the 15th international CINet conference* (Vol. 100). CINet.
37. Tagliaro, C., & Ciaramella, A. (2016). Experiencing smart working: a case study on workplace change management in Italy. *Journal of Corporate Real Estate, 18*(3), 194–208.
38. Kossek, E. E., Valcour, M., & Lirio, P. (2014). Organizational strategies for promoting work–life balance and wellbeing. *Work and Wellbeing, 3*, 295–318.
39. Angelici, M., & Profeta, P. (2020). *Smart working: Work flexibility without constraints* (CESifo Working paper no 8165).
40. Choudhury, P., Foroughi, C., & Larson, B. (2021). Work-from-anywhere: The productivity effects of geographic flexibility. *Strategic Management Journal, 42*(4), 655–683.
41. Iapichino, A., Rosa, A. D., & Liberace, P. (2018). Smart organizations, new skills, and smart working to manage companies' digital transformation. In L. Pupillo, E. Noam, & L. Waverman (Eds.), *Digitized labor* (pp. 215–227). Palgrave Macmillan.
42. Hirsch, A. S. (2019). *Building and leading high-performing remote teams*. SHRM.

43. Parker, S. K., Knight, C., & Keller, A. (2020). Remote managers are having trust issues. *Harvard Business Review, 30.*
44. Janene-Nelson, K., & Sutherland, L. (2020). *Work together anywhere: A handbook on working remotely-successfully-for individuals, teams, and managers.* Wiley.

Digital Job Crafting: Toward an Integrated Socio-technical Model

Aurelio Ravarini ⓘ, Luisa Varriale ⓘ, and Roberta Cuel ⓘ

Abstract In this paper, we introduce digital job crafting as an evolution of the concept of job crafting. An in-depth literature review demonstrated that in the broad research dedicated to job crafting, only limited attention has been dedicated to the effect that digital technology exerts on job crafting practices. We propose using the socio-technical approach to make these impacts explicit and, thus, reframe the concept of job crafting in a new, integrated model. Two case studies are presented to explore the effectiveness of applying the model in different organizational contexts.

Keywords Digital job crafting · Socio-technical approach · Do-it-yourself · Job design · Future of work

1 Introduction

Over the last two decades, "job crafting" has received increasing attention from the scholars and practitioners who broadly investigate this phenomenon, especially those in the job design field, who have proposed numerous definitions and theoretical models.

Most research on job crafting conceptualizes and operationalizes the phenomenon by outlining positive outcomes for individuals and organizations [1, 2]. Other studies argue that work design matters more than ever in a digital world and vice versa; digital transformation affects work design [3]. However, few studies

A. Ravarini
Università C. Cattaneo LIUC, Castellanza (VA), Italy

L. Varriale
Università degli Studi di Napoli "Parthenope", Napoli, Italy

R. Cuel (✉)
Università di Trento, Trento, Italy
e-mail: roberta.cuel@unitn.it

A. Lazazzara et al. (eds.), *Towards Digital and Sustainable Organisations*,
Lecture Notes in Information Systems and Organisation 65,
https://doi.org/10.1007/978-3-031-52880-4_4

47

investigate the phenomenon of "digital job crafting," which is how workers craft their jobs while accounting for technology and digital solutions, combining job design and digital design [4].

After a brief review of job crafting and digital job crafting, this qualitative study presents the results of a multiple-case study that compares two specific experiences of exploring the concept of digital job crafting through the socio-technical systems (STS) model.

Our primary research goal was to identify fruitful future research directions through the lens of the STS model of digital job crafting. This study highlights key areas that researchers and practitioners should prioritize: investigating work design that accommodates the continuous changes that are occurring in the workplace and workforce, primarily due to technology; identifying the value of work design from long-term and more strategic perspectives; analyzing the effects and role of technology in job crafting; and outlining the relevance of social and technical aspects in crafting jobs.

In the following sections, the literature review and the research gap are presented, the STS framework is proposed, and the research question and methodology are defined. The case studies are presented and thoroughly analyzed. Finally, a discussion of the theoretical and practical contributions of this study is provided.

2   Literature Review and Research Gap

Job crafting concerns "the physical and cognitive changes individuals make in the task or relational boundaries of their work" ([5]: 179). Workers who craft their jobs proactively make their work more satisfying and better aligned with their needs and skills [5]. Thus, in the job design field, job crafting is revolutionary compared to traditional job organizational models, in which workers could not design their jobs directly and independently to meet their expectations, needs, and skills [6]. Most scholars agree that designing jobs to incorporate workers' characteristics and the job's effects on workers' satisfaction and, thus, performance at the individual, team, and organizational levels is crucial [7, 8].

Wrzesniewski and Dutton [5, 9] introduced the concept of job crafting, and many others have recently investigated the phenomenon, generating interesting studies on the topic [7, 10]. In addition, many decades before the terminology developed, scholars had some original ideas about job crafting. For instance, Williamson et al. [11] discuss "non-standardized (idiosyncratic) exchange" (job idiosyncrasy), where, to better understand the employment relationship, it is possible to design jobs to respond better to workers' interests, expectations, and skills. Yet other authors suggested that workers tend to exhibit several levels of job commitment by behaving differently, acting, for instance, as custodians or guardians, or innovators of job content or roles [12]. For example, workers tend to behave differently at work overtime, becoming much more involved, committed, and tied to the organizational dynamics of their workplaces [13]. In the 1980s, some scholars suggested that workers could be considered "sculptors" of their organizational roles when they acted to make their jobs more satisfying and stimulating [14, 15]. Similarly, Deci and Ryan [16, 17], introducing self-determination theory, argue that individuals are active and always seek to improve their status; therefore, from a motivation perspective, workers tend to perform better on stimulating activities that satisfy their goals and their need for achievement [16], which occurs more often where the work environment is more flexible and positive [18].

Fascinating contributions to the conceptualization of job crafting come from the psychological and sociological perspectives [5, 7, 19, 20]. We can distinguish two main theoretical models of job crafting: the job identity model [5] and the Job Demands-Resources (JD-R) model [7, 21]. According to the job identity model, job crafting results from three proactive behaviors that workers adopt to do their jobs according to their personal characteristics: task crafting, relational crafting, and cognitive crafting. According to the JD-R model, job crafting intends to fill any gaps between the available resources and the needs that arise from job tasks (commonly referred to as "job demand").

In their recent review, Zhang and Parker [22] agree that these theories represent the two dominant perspectives of job crafting. On one hand, Wrzesniewski and Dutton [5] argue that employees can revise their work identities and enhance the meaning of their work in three ways: task crafting (changing the number, scope, or type of job tasks), relational crafting (changing the relational aspects of the job, such as the quality or quantity of interactions with others at work), and cognitive crafting (changing how the job is framed or viewed). On the other hand, Tims et al. [7], inspired by work design theory and job demands-resources theory [21], define job crafting as "the changes that employees may make to balance their job demands and job resources with their personal abilities and needs" ([7]: 174). From this perspective, job demands include job aspects related to the physical, emotional, or mental effort required for the job, and job resources include job aspects that support personal growth and development by reducing job demands or achieving work goals [21]. Tims et al. [7, 8] identified four dimensions of job crafting: enhancing structural job resources, increasing social job resources, increasing challenging job demands, and reducing hindering job demands. From both theoretical perspectives, workers' jobs and roles can be expanded (e.g., by adding tasks or relationships) or contracted (e.g., by reducing the workload).

Zhang and Parker [22] outline two main differences between these theoretical models (127–128): "The definition of the content of crafting where the job identity model focuses on changes in task/relational/cognitive boundaries, whereas the JD-R emphasizes changes in job characteristics; the purpose/aims to justify crafting, the first model conceives crafting as a way to improve meaning and work identity, whereas the second one considers crafting as a way to balance job resources and demands for achieving person–job fit". In addition, other scholars, confirming these two perspectives in the job crafting literature, outline that the task, cognitive, and relational job crafting that Wrzesniewski and Dutton [5, 9] describe is mainly assessed via qualitative research designs, while crafting job demands and job resources [7] are generally considered through quantitative research designs investigating the antecedents of job crafting and their links to work-related well-being and performance [2].

Starting from the incongruity that these perspectives reveal, Zhang and Parker [22, 23] describe the main challenges of defining job crafting: identifying behaviors that qualify as job crafting or not, including criticisms about mapping the construct according to certain perspectives; the debate about whether cognitive job crafting is a type of job crafting; difficulties in identifying the similarities of job crafting to other concepts, especially other proactive behaviors; and disagreement about how to measure job crafting, i.e., identifying the antecedents, outcomes, and mechanisms of job crafting.

Further studies tend to follow the two theoretical perspectives separately, mostly adopting the JD-R perspective [24, 25]. Studies that attempt to integrate these two theoretical frameworks are rare in the literature, except Bruning and Campion [26]. who summarize six specific characteristics of job crafting, integrating the two perspectives and conceiving of job crafting as changes workers make to the job to improve themselves (job crafting is self-targeted and tends to benefit individuals; involves volitional, conscious, and intentional change; requires a noticeable deviation between the crafted and pre-crafted job; should result in permanent or semi-permanent changes; aims to change the job role rather than leisure time; applies to a job with a clear description and specified tasks rather than self-created jobs, such as being a self-employed consultant).

Few studies unify the two main perspectives on job crafting, and Vanbelle et al. [27] assume that in both models, job crafting describes self-initiated alterations workers make to improve their jobs. Vanbelle et al. ([27]: 26) define job crafting as "the changes employees make in their job to optimize their functioning in terms of wellbeing, work-related attitudes or behavior".

Zhang and Parker [22] synthesize these two main theoretical perspectives with a three-level hierarchical structure of job crafting, identifying the aggregate/superordinate nature of each significant job crafting construct. Zhang and Parker's integrated perspective [22] conceives of job crafting as a proactive behavior, that is, a self-directed and future-oriented activity in which people achieve the goal of improving the context or themselves [28]. In this approach, job crafting consists of proactive activity, or proactive person–environment fit behavior. Zhang and Parker [22] propose that the first level of the structure, the job crafting orientation, is approach-oriented rather than avoidance-oriented crafting. The second hierarchical level concerns the form of job crafting, which may be behavioral or cognitive. The third and final level of the construct addresses job crafting content, i.e., the target that crafting seeks to change: job resources and job demands, or different ways that individuals craft their jobs. With this integrated hierarchical structure, the authors can review job crafting antecedents and outcomes from both perspectives.

In the scenario briefly described above, most jobs can be done automatically thanks to the rapid global spread of technology. However, job crafting research has not yet investigated the link between technology and work tasks. Studies do not prioritize or analyze the effects and role of technology on crafting jobs, specifically, whether technology can support workers in crafting job content, tasks, and characteristics to better respond to their needs, expectations, and interests, as well as the jobs' demands and resources. We can observe that the numerous existing contributions in the literature are mainly focused on addressing issues related to the conceptualization, functioning, and construction of job crafting via several theoretical frameworks, while few studies define and operationalize job crafting that is explicitly associated with technology, going on to produce the term "digital job crafting".

Many scholars show and investigate how technology supports workers in making jobs easier and more satisfying. For instance, innovative work methods, e.g., smart working or the technological rethinking of classic activities, have been changing the nature of work worldwide, mainly because of the Covid-19 pandemic, which has accelerated the digitalization of the workplace. As they increasingly adopt technology, firms must create innovative work solutions that use time more effectively and make workers feel better in the workplace [1]. Technology must support workers, but the human factor remains crucial [29]. Thus, the technological and digital revolution has fundamentally changed organizational, work, and management practices, as well as workers' involvement and job interactions [30–33]. Digital work platforms and subsequent changes within organizations, work structures, and employment practices will promote an increase in digital employees, as well as the emergence of the gig economy and gig employees in many sectors [34–36].

Therefore, considering technology's role and contributions to the workplace, especially in terms of the need to redesign jobs, some authors propose a conceptual model for investigating the dynamics of digital competencies and worker behavior in the public sector. They hypothesize that public workers with digital competencies behave like job crafters, and, consequently, they can work better and more productively; thus, digital competencies are positioned as antecedents of job crafting [1]. Other authors analyze whether and how technology can change work processes, increase flexibility, or permit innovative task completion. Yet other scholars consider the role that technology plays in the world economy and workplace and conduct quantitative studies focused on digital employees to investigate how individual and collaborative job crafting can be positively related to the senses of organizational inclusion and career satisfaction that digital employees might develop [37]. Some scholars also show that task crafting can enable digital employees in the gig economy to identify and select appropriate tasks and job schedules by responding to their job assessment and time requirements [2, 5, 8]. Furthermore, Claes and Moens [38] of Odisse University proposed JOS, a job crafting app developed for and with people with disabilities, that can support workers in crafting their jobs through questions focused on helping them know themselves and their jobs, how well the job fits them, and how to craft the job to accommodate their specific needs and characteristics. In addition, according to JD-R theory, Jenny, Kerksieck, and Bauer [39] developed a "Crafting Playbook" for workers and "a website for self-experimentation to make work more motivating and meaningful". In these digital solutions, IT components from the "wecoach" platform (such as surveys and whiteboards) have been combined with the job crafting construct.

Likewise, other scholars use the expression "digital job crafting" to conceptualize the phenomenon of job crafting alongside technology. Specifically, "digital job crafting" has been conceptualized as "job crafting where crafting interaction designs is an important part" with technological support ([4]: 123).

According to previous studies of the phenomenon, digital job crafting incorporates two main features: using IT to support leaders and facilitators in encouraging employees to perform more job crafting [39, 40] and performing job crafting that prioritizes the digitalized parts of the job [41]. Specifically, Kehr et al. [40] investigated how IT can support job crafting, presenting some early research into the design model for "job crafting information systems" (JCISs). In this case, the authors follow the information systems design tradition, using specific knowledge to derive design principles and methods for implementing and evaluating these systems. Thus, their idea consists of using the model to design artifacts with good user experiences that become complete, defined guides for employees' individual and organizational job crafting, helping employees acquire awareness about how working processes support them, especially in understanding and managing the opportunities of change, shaping both individuals and organizations (and vice versa), and providing a kind of guide to positive and negative job crafting behaviors. Other scholars found that the quality of information technology improved the work–life balance of knowledge workers [41]. Their survey of 11,140 physicians found that the quality of IT services was positively associated with work–life balance, with fewer effects due to long and unpredictable work hours, colleague support, complex patients, or part-time employment.

As defined by Clemmensen [4], digital job crafting has been chiefly conceptualized as a form of job crafting in which the digitalization of the work design is crucial; that is, workers who craft their jobs by prioritizing digital technology and IT solutions in general, including virtual settings such as remote work, virtual teams, and smart working. The main point of this conception concerns crafting jobs by adopting digital solutions and creating a unique environment where job design and digital design are associated and operate together. This combination of job and digital design for job crafting has been considered by Laenen [42], who created a process to facilitate continuous and autonomous job crafting in the home environment. Laenen [42] tested an application called The Job Crafting Journey, showing that several factors contribute to independent, continuous job crafting support. Then, the new, ongoing action–reflection job crafting process proposed can be implemented in digital job crafting applications. Thus, the job crafting process is supported, providing users with "more control over their demands & resources, documenting their job crafting process (e.g., creating an overview of past challenges using videos and images too), and providing additional support and feedback (e.g., with an interactive timeline)" ([42]: 9–10).

Another stream of research builds on studies of Do-It-Yourself (DIY) behavior to investigate the DIY practices that digital technology enables. Digital DIY (DiDIY) has been defined as a phenomenon emerging from the convergence of the widespread availability of easy-to-use digital artifacts and the growing accessibility, often through open online communities, of relevant knowledge, designs, and other data [43].

Salvia [44] showed the impact of such practices on design activities, while Ravarini et al. [45, 46] proposed considering them as alternative elements of a taxonomy of the applications of digital technologies in work environments, alongside automation, virtualization, and self-service. Cremona et al. [47] identified a set of properties that characterize DiDIY workers and workplaces where DiDIY practices occur.

Otherwise, scholars have not defined any "specific technology-related crafting forms;" therefore, this subject remains under investigation [1, 2]. In summary, only a few studies analyze job crafting in virtual work environments and among digital employees [26, 37, 48–50]. Mousa et al. [37] investigated job crafting for digital employees of three gig economy crowdsourcing platforms and outline that individual and collaborative job crafting can significantly promote digital employees' sense of organizational inclusion and feeling of career satisfaction [37].

Furthermore, Bruning and Campion [26], in a qualitative and quantitative study, outline how the use of technology or other information systems can improve the work process. Specifically, the active and goal-directed use of technology and other sources of knowledge can alter a job and enhance the work process. Sturges' [49] qualitative study recognizes the proactive use of technology for maintaining work processes' and jobs' flexibility, showing that individuals use these to shape their work–life balance, and these behaviors have been conceptualized as physical, relational, and cognitive work–life balance crafting.

In the educational field, Grant-Vallone and Ensher [48] report that mid-career faculty have high levels of autonomy and flexibility in crafting tasks to achieve their long-term teaching and research goals via technology and online teaching solutions.

In summary, considering the evolution of the workplace and the growth of alternative work arrangements—e.g., remote work, gig work, freelancing, etc. [51]—research on job crafting should be amplified and enriched by updating and reframing the characteristics of job crafting as they have been described so far. Therefore, studying boundaryless, ubiquitous digital workplaces is recommended [2, 52]. Although the adoption of new technologies and digital design, in general, have been investigated in research on job crafting, the phenomenon of digital job crafting remains an emerging category that is not yet fully explored and requires further investigation. To meet this need, this paper explores STS for job crafting.

3 Socio-technical Systems and Job Crafting

The introduction of advanced automation, the IoT, big data, and AI to the twentieth-century workplace are transforming the fundamental nature of work, employment relationships, and organizations' coordination processes [53, 54].

This trend recalls the adoption of a phenomenological approach to the study of technology in organizations, considering organizational choices and socio-economic contexts as fundamental features of technology adoption. In other words, human-centered design and natural systems are essential to the analysis of digital transformation.

More specifically, as Bednar and Welch [55] stated, a contemporary socio-technical perspective should be the "cornerstone in discussions about smart working in Industry 4.0 and 5.0," and organizational change that maximizes technological capacity must be based on "human-centered design" (291–292). Cuel et al. [56, 57] noted that the STS model provides a perfect framework for analyzing the evolution phases of technology adoption in organizations. This return to STS is underpinned by the broader recognition that organizational choices about how digital technology is introduced, understood, adopted, and used affect job quality [58].

Pasmore et al. [59] stated that the principles of STS model represent a compass to interpret organizational transformation. Similar considerations arise in adopting the lens of the fourth industrial revolution [43]: The changes synthesized in the concept of Industry 4.0 find an appropriate representation "considering the impact of the socio-technical system on people, infrastructure, technology, processes, culture, and goals" ([60]: 1).

Figure 1 presents a typical representation of an STS approach [61–65]:

- The technical subsystem includes organizational variables that interact in business processes (subdivided into activities and tasks) and convert inputs to outputs and technological variables, i.e., technologies, means, and tools that are recognized as the main engines for implementing processes
- The social subsystem includes human variables related to the characteristics of the people who operate in the organizational system (qualifications, attitudes,

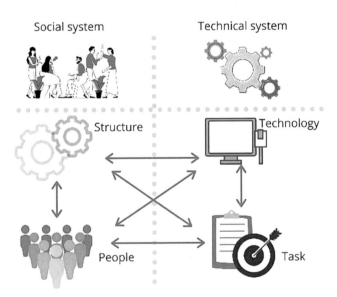

Fig. 1 Socio-technical systems (source: [56])

motivation, personality); and social variables, i.e., the set of interpersonal relationships that people create within the organizational system and formalize through the organizational structure

Technology should be considered a socially constructed artifact as it is the product of human action in a given social context and actors socially construct it through the different meanings, they attach to it and the various features they emphasize and use. According to Orlikowski ([66]: 409), "The structurational model of technology comprises the following components: (1) human agents-technology designers, users, and decision-makers, (2) technology-material artifacts mediating task execution in the workplace; and (3) institutional properties of organizations, including organizational dimensions such as structural arrangements, business strategies, ideology, culture, control mechanisms, standard operating procedures, division of labor, expertise, communication patterns, as well as environmental pressures such as government regulation, competitive forces, vendor strategies, professional norms, state of knowledge about technology, and socio-economic conditions." See Fig. 2 for definitions of the types of influence and how they manifest according to this model.

More recently, within the information system (IS) discipline, other studies have been introduced to analyze the acceptance of technology in organizations. One of the most common theories adopted in the last 20 years is the technology acceptance model (TAM), which measures the intention to use a system and the antecedent factors of its perceived usefulness and perceived ease of use [67–69]. The TAM derives

TYPE OF INFLUENCE	NATURE OF INFLUENCE
Technology as a Product of Human Action	Technology is an outcome of such human action as design, development, appropriation, and modification
Technology as a Medium of Human Action	Technology facilitates and constrains human action through the provision of interpretive schemes, facilities, and norms
Institutional Conditions of Interaction with Technology	Institutional Properties influence humans in their interaction with technology, for example, intentions, professional norms, state of the art in materials and knowledge, design standards, and available resources (time, money, skills)
Institutional Consequences of Interaction with Technology	Interaction with technology influences the institutional properties of an organization, through reinforcing or transforming structures of signification, domination, and legitimation

Fig. 2 Structurational model of technology (source: [66])

from the theory of reasoned action (TRA) model, which is based on individual attitudes and social influences on behaviors.

Another standard model in the IS discipline is the unified theory of acceptance and use of technology (UTAUT) model [70]. Its antecedent factors are performance expectancy, effort expectancy, social influence, and enabling conditions.

Analyzing digital job crafting from the STS perspective results in the model represented in Fig. 3. In this case, two common theories on job crafting are incorporated: the model proposed by Wrzesniewski and Dutton [5, 9] and developed by Kim and Beehr [71] and Kooji et al. [72] and the hierarchical model introduced by Zhang and Parker [22] and Zang et al. [23].

As depicted in Fig. 3, the relationship between STS and the two models shows technology's role in an organization. While Zhang and Parker [22, 23] mainly model human and behavioral dimensions, Wrzesniewski and Dutton [5] focus on various aspects of job design that derive from people, structures, tasks, and technology.

We can also deduce that job design models consider technology mainly a transparent means in organizations; namely, there are no discussions of how technology and digitization are introduced (relational and environmental crafting), understood by workers (cognitive crafting), adopted and used to perform tasks and activities (task crafting), coordinated (relational crafting), or exploited to develop workers' careers (developmental crafting—a subset of relational crafting).

Previous studies state that "job crafting may support organizational alignment in cases where the organizational strategy is an employee (worker)-centric" ([4]: 122). Adopting a socio-technical HCI (human computer interaction) design can significantly help in aligning organizational strategy in terms of IT and business strategy and facilitate digital job crafting [4]. Most studies focus on leadership style as an enabler of employees' and managers' job crafting [73, 74]. This issue, that is, the leadership involved in digital job crafting, has been primarily investigated via socio-technical design projects. However, just as leadership must concern itself with both social and technical aspects, digital job crafting requires these aspects to be considered in an integrated fashion that accommodates multiple and different outcomes over time.

From this perspective, relevant insights come from Wang et al.'s [75] study, which adopted the theoretical perspective of work design that encompasses the notion of remote work and is crucial for other contemporary work changes, such as the digital era [3, 75, 76]. Specifically, this mixed-methods study explores the challenges that remote workers experienced during the Covid-19 pandemic, as well as how virtual work characteristics and individual differences affected work design in terms of defining job characteristics and work processes. The authors observe that virtual work characteristics (i.e., the characteristics of remote work) were decisive in shaping work experiences.

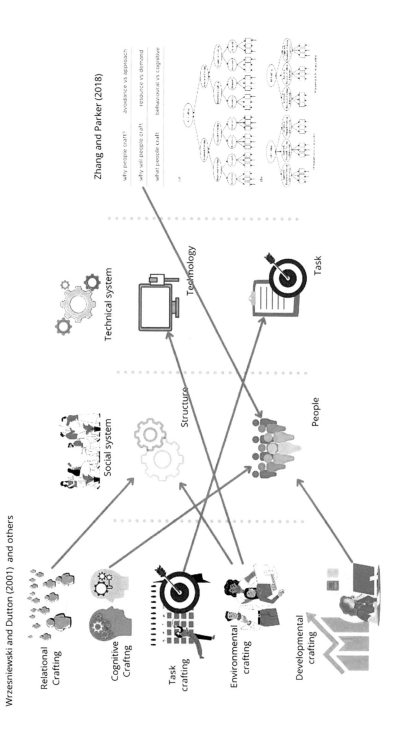

Fig. 3 Job crafting and socio-technical systems

3.1 Technical System

From the perspective of technical systems (tasks and technology), job crafting is affected by technological solutions, such as digital platforms and software applications, workplace collaboration and video-conferencing tools, and help-desk services that affect how people design their jobs [68].

At the individual level, the choice of technological equipment is opaque and depends on how the tools are understood, adopted, and interpreted to craft a job. In this regard, different levels of technical skill in the use of software radically affect workers' propensity to craft jobs and tasks. Therefore, a one-size-fits-all model could prove dramatically inadequate [77], and recommendations should be given to support job crafting.

3.2 Social System

From the perspective of the social system, both Zhang and Parker's and Wrzesniewski and Dutton's models address structure and people [5, 9, 22]. In this sense, technology radically affects how work and jobs are designed and how roles and coordination processes are determined.

The replacement of physical interaction with digital interaction, combined with a culture of constant connection, is compounding digital overload and powerfully affects job design [78]. Therefore, the constraints on interpersonal communication that arise from the physical distance between individuals, the allocation of tasks, the increased autonomy in task management, the temporal distribution of each worker's tasks to ensure a proper work–life balance, and the management of diversity and disabilities must be considered. Managing communication processes and workers' sense of belonging is also essential.

Companies should support the development of workers' abilities to design, plan, and control objectives [79, 80]. In a context of massive virtualization and the relocation of work, employees must learn how to define and plan tasks and activities, schedule them, optimize their time and process management, and cope with the information overload associated with the high quantity and rate of information received in "push" mode from multiple sources, such as workplace collaboration applications, corporate messaging tools, video-conferencing systems, and work and personal devices.

Employees also need to develop the proper skills to master new digital collaboration tools, run digital meetings, and provide management feedback as required.

Moreover, managers should be trained for new roles, learn to work according to objectives, strengthen their employees' skills for effective virtual interaction with their colleagues, and adopt more effective communication techniques.

4 Research Methodology: Multiple Case Study Approach

A qualitative research approach was deemed the most appropriate for this study as it permits researchers to "understand those being studied from their perspective" [51]. Qualitative studies are "designed to help researchers understand people and the social and cultural contexts within which they live" ([81]: 278).

The case study approach is intended to explore a specific phenomenon in a bounded system or multiple bounded systems over time "within its real-life context" ([82]: 13) and seek an in-depth understanding of the phenomenon.

According to Stake [83], it is important to concentrate "on each single case almost as if it is the only one;" multiple case studies should be investigated "one case at a time". Therefore, our analysis involved developing a report for each case study, followed by a cross-case analysis.

In the following section, we present the cases of two organizations in very different industries: an industrial gas producer and a consulting company. In both organizations, we conducted interviews following the same protocol. A preliminary semi-structured interview enabled the researchers to identify digital job crafting practices and the involved actors. Researchers interviewed actors working in three organizational roles: job crafters, their direct managers, and the company's IT managers.

This study used semi-structured interviews, in which questions are prepared in advance but not strictly followed during the interview [84]. Although semi-structured interviews follow a series of pre-determined questions, they normally unfold in a way that allows interviewers to investigate or discuss themes that arise and seem essential or worthy of attention [85, 86].

Each interview lasted for about 1 h and consisted of two sections. The first section sought to collect information about the effects of the adoption of digital technology on the organization in general through tasks, roles, and organizational culture. The second section explored the characteristics of the workers involved in job crafting and the properties of the workplace where job crafting occurred in greater detail. The structure of this second section was based on the worker and workplace elements characterized by the digital DIY practices mentioned in the literature review [47]. All the interviews were recorded, transcribed, and deeply analyzed to identify the most relevant categories that emerged.

5 Case Studies

Company ABC
Company ABC is an Italian company with more than 2000 employees that was founded in Italy in 1922 and is managed by a board of managers, although it is owned by two families, following a typical tradition of Italian industry. Its core business concerns the supply of various types of gas for different uses: food,

environmental, and energy; biotechnological, chemical, and pharmaceutical; electronic, mechanical, and metallurgical; and health, glass, and cement.

In 2018, the company introduced the corporate hackathon. During this event, employees were asked to voluntarily submit project ideas to facilitate their work or optimize a business process. A committee selected 50 projects (from 170 employees' ideas) that were developed during the 48-h event. At the end of the hackathon, the company selected ten projects that were launched through cross-functional teams in the subsequent months.

More than achieving concrete development from the projects, the hackathon was meant to involve employees by "making them part of the ABC family," highlighting and rewarding the contributions they can make and, thus, creating a virtuous cycle of innovation. One project, called "ABC Push," proved successful. The "ABC Push" is a device inspired by and similar to the more famous "Amazon Dash Button": It is a button connected to the internet. Company ABC loans the ABC Push to customers; they install it in an area of the client plant close to a daily operation that requires gas. Whenever a new supply of gas is needed, any operator can push the button. This instantly generates an order of a standard quantity of gas in Company ABC's information system.

The proposer of the project idea was a sales agent who noticed that many customers, especially artisans and freelancers, worked on days when ABC was closed (preventing them from accepting orders). With the ABC Push, customers can send orders directly to the Company ABC information system via a specific IoT protocol. However, while the sales agent could identify a possible solution to a work-related problem by imitating the features of the Amazon Dash Button, he lacked the technical skills to enact the project alone.

By analyzing the interviews, various components of digital job crafting can be framed through the socio-technical model, as the previous section outlined.

Technology: The set of digital technologies contained in the ABC Push are relevant not because they are innovative (they were quite mature at the time of the invention) but because they were necessary elements to allow the crafting of the job.

People: A crucial aspect of this case study is the employees' proactivity and willingness to revisit their jobs by transforming the organization–client relationship. By proposing the ABC Push, multiple goals were achieved: (1) a new way to perform and (2) a radical improvement of the order task, streamlining the activity and permitting 24/7 ordering, which reduced the time to delivery and increased customers' satisfaction and loyalty.

Structure: Company ABC was able to create a fertile ground for its workers to craft their jobs using digital technologies. The organization made the project successful by introducing a knowledge-sharing practice, encouraging idea generation (rather than raising barriers against it), and providing resources and support teams. People in several organizational roles were involved in the success of the project: the sales agent, the sales director, the IT department director and IT experts, the operations department, and even the CEO. As a result, Company ABC has activated a virtuous cycle, stimulating other employees to participate in similar initiatives in the future.

Company XYZ

Company XYZ was the second case study. It is a small consultancy firm focused on digitalization projects for small-to-medium companies. In 2018, Company XYZ launched a series of initiatives to favor proactivity and innovation at any level, represented by its iconic "Youniversity" (a corporate academy) and the promotion of the newly coined term "employeneur" to incentivize employees to develop an entrepreneurial attitude.

In this context, several instances of job crafting enabled by digital technology can be found. As a representative example, in 2019, a software developer was working to implement firmware for a customer. During the project, he encountered the activity of debugging the software code by searching for errors, correcting, and translating them into another programming language. Conventionally, this activity would have been done manually and required about 2 weeks of work. The employee, an expert and passionate user of coding, decided to write code that could automatically perform the same task in a few minutes. The coding required a few hours of work, but halved the overall time needed for the project: This also had the advantage of strengthening the relationship with the customer. The crafted solution was then shared with all of Company XYZ's employees and added to the organization's knowledge base of suggested good work practices.

Following the STS approach, the experience can be reframed as follows:

Technology: The role that technology played is different from that in the previous case study: here, digital technology is the means through which the job is crafted, rather than a result of crafting a new component of a product/service, as for the ABC Push.

People: The term "employeneur" itself is evidence of the organization's effort to promote competencies and attitudes that enable the improvement of job practices by leveraging individuals' will and initiative. The effect on the task mentioned in the case study is exemplary not only for the extent of the improvement but also for its ease of transferability to the organization's other activities.

Structure: the organization created a fertile ground for the worker to carry out digital job crafting. Company XYZ set up several mechanisms of informal and transversal communication and knowledge-sharing, such as the "Youniversity" and the "Pizza Sessions."

6 Discussion and Contributions

The two case studies show that STS effectively describes the properties of the transformation that job crafting practices enabled by digital technology can enact.

Zhang and Parker's [22] taxonomy can be used to classify the outcomes of the empirical investigation: the cases appear to be examples of approach crafting as both involve workers seeking to improve and enrich existing work practices. Specifically, the job crafting at Company ABC is behavioral crafting applied to the job resources, while the example at Company XYZ is a kind of cognitive crafting applied to both the job resources and demands. Through the lens of this taxonomy, the job crafting practices enabled by digital technology do not appear to possess properties that justify extending or modifying Zhang and Parker's [22] model.

The model we propose aims to describe not merely the motivation (approach or avoidance) and the location in terms of the organizational domains (behavioral or cognitive, acting on job resources or demands) in which the crafting occurs. Instead, it focuses on the organizational variables that are affected by digital job crafting: The lens of STS theory allows us to represent the job crafting enabled by digital technology in terms of the transformation of work practices, which is characterized by systemic effects amongst an organization's components (tasks, people, structures).

Therefore, the academic contribution of our study consists of reframing the representation of the phenomenon of job crafting. In this sense, the STS perspective can be used for descriptive purposes. At the practitioner level, we argue that the results of these case studies suggest that our model could also be used for prescriptive goals, to draw guidelines for organizational design. An organization that is willing to facilitate the diffusion of digital job crafting practices should leverage workers' characteristics, starting with the recruitment process and continuing through training activities, as well as via the features of the workplace.

Finally, the STS perspective also allows us to identify different "stereotypes" of digital job crafting. Although job crafting happens in both case studies, two distinct profiles of digital job crafting were discovered. In both cases, it was enabled by digital technology, but in two different manners: in Company ABC, digital technology is included in the result of the job, and in Company XYZ, it is used to craft the tasks that comprise the job. Further research might search for other digital job crafting types and create a structured taxonomy of digital job crafting.

7 Conclusions

In this paper, we propose the concept of digital job crafting as an evolution, possibly an update, of the concept of job crafting. An in-depth literature review allowed us to recognize that, among the studies dedicated to job crafting, only limited attention has been dedicated to the effect digital technology can have on job crafting practices. We proposed adopting a socio-technical approach to make these effects explicit and reframe the concept of job crafting.

After the in-depth literature review of the phenomenon investigated, we conducted a multiple-case study comparing two experiences where job design solutions that represent digital job crafting were analyzed through the lens of the STS model.

However, this study encompasses some limitations, mostly related to its qualitative exploratory nature: It considers only two case studies in one country; therefore, the findings cannot be generalized. Despite these limitations, we consider this exploratory study a starting point for further investigation into the phenomenon of digital job crafting through the lens of the STS model. Therefore, these limitations can be used as a foundation from which to suggest interesting future research directions. For example, replicating this study in other industries and countries might prove valuable, as might focusing greater research attention on further features of digital job crafting and drawing on a larger sample of cases.

References

1. Buonocore, F., de Gennaro, D., Russo, M., & Salvatore, D. (2020). Cognitive job crafting: A possible response to increasing job insecurity and declining professional prestige. *Human Resource Management Journal, 30*(2), 244–259.
2. Lazazzara, A., Tims, M., & De Gennaro, D. (2020). The process of reinventing a job: A meta-synthesis of qualitative job crafting research. *Journal of Vocational Behavior, 116*, 103267.
3. Parker, S. K., & Grote, G. (2020). Automation, algorithms, and beyond: Why work design matters more than ever in a digital world. *Applied Psychology.* https://doi.org/10.1111/apps.12241
4. Clemmensen, T. (2021). *Human work interaction design: A platform for theory and action.* Springer.
5. Wrzesniewski, A., Berg, J. M., & Dutton, J. E. (2010). Turn the job you have into the job you want. *Harvard Business Review, 88*(6), 114–117.
6. de Gennaro, D., Buonocore, F., & Ferrara, M. (2017). Il significato del job crafting nell'organizzazione del lavoro: Inquadramento teorico, tendenze evolutive e prospettive manageriali. *Electronic Journal of Management, 2*, 1–20.
7. Tims, M., Bakker, A. B., & Derks, D. (2012). Development and validation of the job crafting scale. *Journal of Vocational Behavior, 80*(1), 173–186.
8. Tims, M., Bakker, A. B., Derks, D., & Van Rhenen, W. (2013). Job crafting at the team and individual level: Implications for work engagement and performance. *Group & Organization Management, 38*(4), 427–454.
9. Wrzesniewski, A., & Dutton, J. E. (2001). Crafting a job: Revisioning employees as active crafters of their work. *Academy of Management Review, 26*(2), 179–201.
10. Bakker, A. B., Tims, M., & Derks, D. (2012). Proactive personality and job performance: The role of job crafting and work engagement. *Human Relations, 65*(10), 1359–1378.
11. Williamson, O. E., Wachter, M. L., & Harris, J. E. (1975). Understanding the employment relation: The analysis of idiosyncratic exchange. *The Bell Journal of Economics, 6*, 250–278.
12. Schein, E. H. (1971). The individual, the organization, and the career: A conceptual scheme. *The Journal of Applied Behavioral Science, 7*(4), 401–426.
13. Van Maanen, J., & Schein, E. H. (1979). Toward a theory of organizational socialization. In B. M. Staw (Ed.), *Research in organizational behavior* (pp. 209–264). JAI.
14. Bateman, T. S., & Crant, J. M. (1993). The proactive component of organizational behavior: A measure and correlates. *Journal of Organizational Behavior, 14*, 103–118.
15. Bell, N. E., & Staw, B. M. (1989). People as sculptors versus sculpture: the roles of personality and personal control. *Handbook of Career Theory, 11*, 232.
16. Deci, E. L., & Ryan, R. M. (2000). The "what" and "why" of goal pursuits: Human needs and the self-determination of behavior. *Psychological Inquiry, 11*(4), 227–268.
17. Deci, E. L., & Ryan, R. M. (2002). Self-determination research: Reflections and future directions. In E. L. Deci & R. M. Ryan (Eds.), *Handbook of self-determination research* (pp. 431–441). University of Rochester Press.
18. Gagné, M., & Deci, E. L. (2005). Self-determination theory and work motivation. *Journal of Organizational Behavior, 26*(4), 331–362.
19. Bakker, A. B., & Demerouti, E. (2014). Job demands—Resources theory. In P. Y. Chen & C. L. Cooper (Eds.), *Work and wellbeing: Wellbeing: A complete reference guide* (Vol. III, pp. 37–64). Wiley-Blackwell.

20. Leana, C., Appelbaum, E., & Shevchuk, I. (2009). Work process and quality of care in early childhood education: The role of job crafting. *Academy of Management Journal, 52*(6), 1169–1192.
21. Bakker, A. B., & Demerouti, E. (2007). The job demands-resources model: State of the art. *Journal of Managerial Psychology, 22*(3), 309–328.
22. Zhang, F., & Parker, S. K. (2019). Reorienting job crafting research: A hierarchical structure of job crafting concepts and integrative review. *Journal of Organizational Behavior, 40*(2), 126–146.
23. Zhang, F., Wang, B., Qian, J., & Parker, S. K. (2021). Job crafting towards strengths and job crafting towards interests in overqualified employees: Different outcomes and boundary effects. *Journal of Organizational Behavior, 42*(5), 587–603.
24. Lichtenthaler, P. W., & Fischbach, A. (2016a). Job crafting and motivation to continue working beyond retirement age. *Career Development International, 21*, 477–497.
25. Rudolph, C. W., Katz, I. M., Lavigne, K. N., & Zacher, H. (2017). Job crafting: A meta-analysis of relationships with individual differences, job characteristics, and work outcomes. *Journal of Vocational Behavior, 102*, 112–138.
26. Bruning, P. F., & Campion, M. A. (2018). A role–resource approach–avoidance model of job crafting: A multimethod integration and extension of job crafting theory. *Academy of Management Journal, 61*(2), 499–522.
27. Vanbelle, E., Van Den Broeck, A., & De Witte, H. (2017). Job crafting: Autonomy and workload as antecedents and the willingness to continue working until retirement age as a positive outcome. *Psihologia Resurselor Umane, 15*(1), 25–41.
28. Parker, S. K., Bindl, U. K., & Strauss, K. (2010). Making things happen: A model of proactive motivation. *Journal of Management, 36*, 827–856.
29. Deloitte. (2018). *The rise of the social enterprise: 2018 global human capital trends*. Deloitte Development LLC.
30. Geissinger, A., Laurell, C., Öberg, C., Sandström, C., & Suseno, Y. (2021). The sharing economy and the transformation of work: Evidence from Foodora. *Personnel Review, 51*(2), 584–602.
31. Howcroft, D., & Bergvall-Kåreborn, B. (2019). A typology of crowdwork platforms. *Work, Employment and Society, 33*(1), 21–38.
32. Mahato, M., Kumar, N., & Jena, L. K. (2021). Re-thinking gig economy in conventional workforce post-COVID-19: A blended approach for upholding fair balance. *Journal of Work-Applied Management, 13*(2), 261–276.
33. Rahman, K. S., & Thelen, K. (2019). The rise of the platform business model and the transformation of twenty-first-century capitalism. *Politics & Society, 47*(2), 177–204.
34. Kuhn, K. M., & Galloway, T. L. (2019). Expanding perspectives on gig work and gig workers. *Journal of Managerial Psychology, 34*(4), 186–191.
35. Peticca-Harris, A., DeGama, N., & Ravishankar, M. N. (2020). Postcapitalist precarious work and those in the 'drivers' seat: Exploring the motivations and lived experiences of Uber drivers in Canada. *Organization, 27*(1), 36–59.
36. Stewart, A., & Stanford, J. (2017). Regulating work in the gig economy: What are the options? *The Economic and Labour Relations Review, 28*(3), 420–437.
37. Mousa, M., Chaouali, W., & Mahmood, M. (2022). The inclusion of gig employees and their career satisfaction: do individual and collaborative job crafting play a role? *Public Organization Review, 23*(3), 1055–1068.
38. Claes, C., & Moens, B. (2022). The JOS-app, a digital job crafting tool: a way to reduce challenges and barriers in the workplace. In *EUSE2022, 2022/06/20–2022/06/22, European Union of Supported Employment (EUSE), Oslo*.
39. Jenny G. J., Kerksieck, P., & Bauer, G. (2022). Digital job crafting for teams and individuals—Apps, roadmaps and field experiences. Paper proceedings in van den Brand, W., Nikolova, I., & Caniëls, M. C. (2022, July). Empowering leadership, professional isolation, and emotional exhaustion: a daily diary investigation. In *15th European Academy of Occupational*

Health Psychology Conference: Supporting knowledge comparison to promote good practice in occupational health psychology (pp. 602–603). European Academy of Occupational Health Psychology.

40. Kehr, F., Bauer, G., Jenny, G. F., Güntert, S. T., & Kowatsch, T. (2013). Towards a design model for job crafting information systems promoting individual health, productivity and organizational performance.

41. Bardoel, E. A., & Drago, R. (2016). Does the quality of information technology support affect work–life balance? A study of Australian physicians. *The International Journal of Human Resource Management, 27*(21), 2604–2620.

42. Laenen, J. J. (2020). *Continuous and autonomous Job Crafting support in the home-work environment.* Extended abstracts, April 25–30, 2020, Honolulu, HI, USA. ACM ISBN 978-1-4503-6819-3/20/04. https://doi.org/10.1145/3334480.

43. Margherita, E. G., & Braccini, A. M. (2021). Exploring the socio-technical interplay of Industry 4.0: a single case study of an Italian manufacturing organisation. arXiv preprint. https://doi.org/10.48550/arXiv.2101.05665.

44. Salvia, G. (2016). The satisfactory and (possibly) sustainable practice of do-it-yourself: the catalyst role of design. *Journal of Design Research, 14*(1), 22–41.

45. Locoro, A., Ravarini, A., Cabitza, F., & Mari, L. (2017). Is making the new knowing? Tangible and intangible knowledge artifacts in DiDIY. In *Proceedings of the 25th European Conference on Information Systems (ECIS), Guimarães, Portugal, June 5–10, 2017.* ISBN 978-989-20-7655-3

46. Ravarini, A., & Strada, G. (2018). From smart work to Digital Do-It-Yourself: a research framework for digital-enabled jobs. In *Network, smart and open* (pp. 97–107). Springer.

47. Cremona, L., & Ravarini, A. (2017). Digital do-it yourself in work and organizations: Personal and environmental characteristics. In *ICT and innovation* (p. 97).

48. Grant-Vallone, E. J., & Ensher, E. A. (2017). Re-crafting careers for mid-career faculty: A qualitative study. *Journal of Higher Education Theory and Practice, 17*(5), 10–24.

49. Sturges, J. (2012). Crafting a balance between work and home. *Human Relations, 65*(12), 1539–1559. https://doi.org/10.1177/0018726712457435

50. Wong, S. I., Kost, D., & Fieseler, C. (2021). From crafting what you do to building resilience for career commitment in the gig economy. *Human Resource Management Journal, 31*(4), 918–935.

51. Gorman, G. E., & Clayton, P. (1997). *Qualitative research for the information professional: A practical handbook.* Facet.

52. Prus, I., Nacamulli, R. C., & Lazazzara, A. (2017). Disentangling workplace innovation: A systematic literature review. *Personnel Review, 46*(7), 1254–1279. https://doi.org/10.1108/PR-10-2016-0267

53. Vallas, S. P., & Kovalainen, A. (Eds.). (2019). *Work and labor in the digital age.* Emerald.

54. Warhurst, C., & Dhondt, S. (2020). The challenges and opportunities in the digitalisation of production. In *47th OeNB Economics Conference, The EU's "northern" enlargement 25 years on: A comparative stocktaking and outlook in cooperation with SUERF, Bank of Finland, Sveriges Riksbank and Norges Bank* (p. 51).

55. Bednar, P. M., & Welch, C. (2019). Socio-technical perspectives on smart working: Creating meaningful and sustainable systems. *Information Systems Frontiers, 21*, 1–18.

56. Cuel, R., Ravarini, A., & Varriale, L. (2020). *Technology in organisation: Digital transformation and people.* Maggioli. ISBN: 9788891646088.

57. Cuel, R., Ravarini, A., Ruffini, R., & Varriale, L. (2021, September 10–11). Smart working in the Italian Public Administration: A socio-technical analysis. In *Workshop dei Docenti e dei Ricercatori di Organizzazione Aziendale 2021: "Organizing for what? Meaning and purpose in human action", Genova: Ithum srl, 2021. Atti di: WOA 2021, Genova.*

58. Dhondt, S., Kraan, K. O., & Bal, M. (2021). Organisation, technological change and skills use over time: A longitudinal study on linked employee surveys. *New Technology, Work and Employment*, 1–20.

59. Pasmore, W., Winby, S., Mohrman, S. A., & Vanasse, R. (2019). Reflections: sociotechnical systems design and organization change. *Journal of Change Management, 19*(2), 67–85.
60. Sony, M., & Naik, S. (2020). Industry 4.0 integration with socio-technical systems theory: A systematic review and proposed theoretical model. *Technology in Society, 61*, 101248.
61. Bostrom, R. P., & Heinen, J. S. (1977). MIS problems and failures: A socio-technical perspective. *MIS Quarterly, 1*(3), 17–32.
62. Cherns, A. (1976). The principles of sociotechnical design. *Human Relations, 29*(8), 783–792.
63. Cooper, R., & Foster, M. (1971). Sociotechnical systems. *American Psychologist, 26*(5), 467.
64. Sutcliffe, A. G. (2000). Requirements analysis for socio-technical system design. *Information Systems, 25*(3), 213–233.
65. Yurtseven, M. K., & Buchanan, W. W. (2013, March). Socio-technical system design: A general systems theory perspective. In *Proceedings of the international conference on engineering and computer education-ICECE'2013.*
66. Orlikowski, W. (1992). The duality of technology: rethinking the concept of technology in organizations. *Organization Science, 3*(3), 398–427.
67. Davis, F. D. (1989). Perceived usefulness, perceived ease of use, and user acceptance of information technology. *MIS Quarterly, 13*(3), 319–340.
68. Davis, F. D. (1993). User acceptance of information technology: system characteristics, user perceptions and behavioral impacts. *International Journal of Man-Machine Studies, 38*(3), 475–487.
69. Davis, F. D., Bagozzi, R. P., & Warshaw, P. R. (1989). User acceptance of computer technology: a comparison of two theoretical models. *Management Science, 35*, 982–1003.
70. Venkatesh, V., Thong, J. Y., & Xu, X. (2012). Consumer acceptance and use of information technology: extending the unified theory of acceptance and use of technology. *MIS Quarterly, 36*, 157–178.
71. Kim, M., & Beehr, T. A. (2021). The role of organization-based self-esteem and job resources in promoting employees' job crafting behaviors. *The International Journal of Human Resource Management*, 1–28.
72. Kooij, D. T., De Lange, A. H., & Van De Voorde, K. (2022). Stimulating job crafting behaviors of older workers: The influence of opportunity-enhancing human resource practices and psychological empowerment. *European Journal of Work and Organizational Psychology, 31*(1), 22–34.
73. Shin, Y., Hur, W. M., Kim, H. G., & Cheol Gang, M. (2020). Managers as a missing entity in job crafting research: Relationships between store manager job crafting, job resources, and store performance. *Applied Psychology, 69*(2), 479–507.
74. Xin, X., Cai, W., Zhou, W., Baroudi, S. E., & Khapova, S. N. (2020). How can job crafting be reproduced? Examining the trickle-down effect of job crafting from leaders to employees. *International Journal of Environmental Research and Public Health, 17*(3), 894.
75. Wang, B., Schlagwein, D., Cecez-Kecmanovic, D., & Cahalane, M. C. (2020). Beyond the factory paradigm: Digital nomadism and the digital future (s) of knowledge work post-COVID-19. *Journal of the Association for Information Systems, 21*(6), 10.
76. Bélanger, J. J., Lafrenière, M. A. K., Vallerand, R. J., & Kruglanski, A. W. (2013). Driven by fear: The effect of success and failure information on passionate individuals' performance. *Journal of Personality and Social Psychology, 104*(1), 180–195.
77. Hitchcock, A., Laycock, K., & Sundorph, E. (2017). *Work in progress. Towards a leaner, smarter public-sector workforce.* Available at https://reform.uk/sites/default/files/2018-10/Work%20in%20Progress%20Reform.pdf.
78. Rosen, L., & Samuel, A. (2015). Conquering digital distraction. *Harvard Business Review, 93*(June), 110–113.
79. Marović, I., & Bulatović, G. (2020). Development of a hybrid agile management model in local self-government units. *Tehnički vjesnik, 27*(5), 1418–1426.
80. Mergel, I., Ganapati, S., & Whitford, A. B. (2020). Agile: A new way of governing. *Public Administration Review, 81*(1), 161–165.

81. Myers, M. D. (1997). Qualitative research in information systems. *Management Information Systems Quarterly, 21*(2), 241–242.
82. Yin, R. K. (2013). *Case study research: Design and methods.* Sage.
83. Stake, R. E. (2006). *Multiple case study analysis.* Guilford.
84. Patton, M. Q. (1990). *Qualitative evaluation and research methods.* Sage.
85. Cassell, C., & Symon, G. (Eds.). (2004). *Essential guide to qualitative methods in organizational research.* Sage.
86. Saunders, M., Lewis, P., & Thornhill, A. (2015). *Research methods for business students* (7th ed.). Pearson.

Participative Budgeting Effects on Doctor-Managers' Well-Being

Manuela Paolini and Domenico Raucci

Abstract Doctors heading Operational Units in Public Health care Organizations (PHOs), as budget holders, have become fundamental actors for the effective functioning of the budgeting planning and control systems. However, the hybridization of doctor-manager's role and the predominant influence of their original clinical culture may cause them a lack of budgetary goal clarity, setting limits to the usefulness of the information neutrally provided by such systems for supporting their decision-making. This perceived ambiguity of budgetary goals may cause doctor-managers' adverse reactions, which negatively influence their well-being at work, re-proposing the advantages of a greater integration of "behavioural" perspectives into the "structuralist" ones within the approaches to management control, also in PHOs' context. Searching for such integrated approaches to budgeting systems, health care literature developing the behavioural perspective in some lines of interpretative research suggest to enhancing the patterns of doctor-managers' cooperation with PHOs' controllers and top management.

Within the lines of Behavioural Management Accounting (BMA) research, based on the assumptions of Person-Organization Fit Theory, this paper explores the influence of participative budgeting on doctor-managers' goal clarity and well-being at work. This model was tested through questionnaires from 332 doctor-managers of Italian PHOs. Findings show that participative budgeting positively influence doctor-managers' goal clarity, which, in turn, increases well-being at work, and the mediating role of goal clarity in such relation. Our study contributes to the BMA research on the budgeting practices in PHOs context, shedding a light on doctor-managers' well-being effects of participative budgeting.

Keywords Participative budgeting in PHOs · Goal clarity · Well-being at work

---

M. Paolini (✉) · D. Raucci
Department of Economics, University of Studies "G. d'Annunzio", Chieti-Pescara, Italy
e-mail: manuela.paolini@unich.it; domenico.raucci@unich.it

© The Author(s), under exclusive license to Springer Nature
Switzerland AG 2024
A. Lazazzara et al. (eds.), *Towards Digital and Sustainable Organisations*,
Lecture Notes in Information Systems and Organisation 65,
https://doi.org/10.1007/978-3-031-52880-4_5

1   Introduction

The reform processes affecting Public Health care Organizations (PHOs) in recent decades [1–3] have caused the progressive involvement of doctors heading Operational Units (OUs) in PHOs' management, making them fundamental actors of the performance measurement systems and, specifically, of the effective functioning of the budgeting planning and control ones [4–7]. These reforms, in fact, have devolved them a new financial accountability, as budget holders, which has been added to their traditional professional responsibilities, as clinicians [8–10].

With respect to this role of doctor-managers [11, 12], formal budgeting systems within PHOs are aimed both at supporting their decisions on the efficient resource consumption for OUs health care activities and clarifying the budgetary objectives to achieve, which means mitigate the potential ambiguities deriving from this overlapping of responsibilities [13, 14]. Doctor-managers' responses to these functions of budgeting control decide to what extent this latter will bring managerial performance improvement [15–17].

In fact, phenomena as the hybridization of their role of middle managers [18, 19] the traditional hierarchical implementation of these management control systems, generally made for complying with normative requirements, rather than for satisfying the management needs of these budget holders [20], the divergences between their clinical professional culture and the economic one inspiring PHOs' controllers and top management can put at risk doctor-managers' budgetary goal clarity [21, 22].

As underlined by the performance measurement literature focusing on the various dimensions of ambiguity [10, 23, 24], goal clarity refers to the individuals' cognitive mental representation of their clear understanding of the organizational expectations associated with the goals and the objectives of their work role [17, 25, 26]. So, the formal assignment of objectives, alone, may be not sufficient to clarify these latter and empower doctor-managers' behaviours for their pursuit. Further, a lack of goal clarity, by favoring the interpretative ambiguities, can limit the perception of usefulness of these performance measurement systems in supporting the managerial role of the recipients, like doctor-managers in PHOs [27–29]. In detail, it can cause adverse reactions in terms of cognitions and mental states, negatively influencing, among the others, their well-being at work [30]. Similar risks of dysfunctional effects must be taken seriously, considering that managers' well-being at work expresses the overall quality of their subjective experiences and functioning in operational activities related to their role [31, 32]. Besides being an end in itself, it is an important factor for effective decision-making [33] and better managerial performance [34], mostly in complex organizations like PHOs [35].

In these organizations, some lines of research on the topic suggest valuing the function of performance information, including the budgetary one, to increase doctor-managers' knowledge and clear sense of the assigned objectives [19, 24, 28, 36], avoiding the adverse psychological reactions which may derive from their interpretations of the budgetary responsibilities compared to the clinical one [3, 13, 15, 37].

To this end, such health care research has its roots in the historical debate of the generalist literature between the "structuralist" and "behavioural" perspectives on the design of management accounting systems [38–40].

The theoretical studies from a structuralist perspective identify in the sophistication of technical-accounting approaches, standards, and performance indicators the informational function of management accounting, defined by Burchell et al. ([41], p. 14) of "answer machine", able to provide clarity, knowledge, and rational orientation of managerial decision-making for the achievement of objectives. In this approach, the integrations with the ICT tools [7, 42–45] and the applications of the various Digital Technologies [46–49] allow to expand similar cognitive-informational functions and, thus, increase goal clarity, also for PHOs' doctor-managers [8, 36, 50].

The empirical results, however, show that such technical dimensions in the management accounting systems design, even if sophisticated and formalized, do not assure, alone, the understanding and the pursuit of organizational objectives by the recipients [39, 51, 52]. In PHOs, the inadequacies of information "neutrally" provided by the budgeting system are emphasized by its limited contribution in mitigating doctor-managers' goal ambiguity, their widespread perceptions of its scarce usefulness for management purposes [14, 15, 20] and their cultural resistance towards its use for decision-making [6, 16, 28, 29].

Thus, the rational and mechanistic nature underlying this approach of management accounting systems opens to the perspectives of "behavioural" analysis, proposing more fruitful model of systemic integration, widely accepted by the subsequent developments in the national and international literature [53–56].

In particular, the approaches to the definition of the budgeting system, also in the context of PHOs [21, 57–59], aim at developing more effective integrations of its functions of programming, control, and performance evaluation, with those of coordination, motivation, and behavioural influence of budget holders [3, 37, 60].

More broadly, similar convergences of the "structuralist" perspectives with the "behavioural" ones are sought, both in the generalist and the health care literature, starting from different areas of investigation of management accounting systems.

The studies originated from formalized approaches to the accounting information systems and interested in the application developments of ICT and Digital Technologies seek similar integrations with the "human" factors by elaborating implementation logics referable to the dimensions of Technology Acceptance Model by Davis [61], its evolutions [62] and the subsequent integrations in the Unified Theory of Acceptance and Use of Technology [63]. In such models, the design and the adoption of these systems are not confined only to the evaluations of the *designers* and the *implementers* within the organization, but also incorporate the influences exerted by the psychological, behavioural, and social dimensions of their *users*, including managers at the various hierarchical levels. This is to improve the instrumental cognitions of these latter, their perceptions of information usefulness for decision-making, and their levels of understanding and clarification of the assigned organizational objectives [64]. However, there are also observations on the limitations of such models, especially in knowledge-intensive contexts, such as those of PHOs [65, 66]. In fact, it has been underlined the excessive simplification of the complexity of the health care decision-making processes and, above all, the limited attention to how goal perceptions and positive behaviours evolve because of interactions among different organizational actors [67, 68].

These dimensions, instead, are deepened by the health care literature interested in searching for integrated approaches to management accounting systems, by developing the "behavioural" perspective in some lines of interpretative research [19, 51, 69]. By focusing on the *soft* factors affecting the design and use of such systems, including the budgetary ones, these studies suggest to enhancing the mechanisms of doctor-managers cooperation with PHOs' controllers and top management [6, 37], through the improvements in the quality of internal communication offered by ICT [20, 42].

In these perspectives, we believe that this driver of doctor-managers' involvement can be fruitfully explored in the fields of participative budgeting practices [70, 71] within the Behavioural Management Accounting (BMA) studies [72–74]. In fact, according to Shields and Shields [75], participative budgeting exists to allow processes of communication and vertical information sharing for reducing the risks of environmental and task uncertainties and information asymmetry. So, in these processes, configurated according to contingency-based approaches [55, 73], greater collaboration with top management and controllers can improve doctor-managers' interpretations and understanding of budgetary information provided. These improvements allow to increase the levels of knowledge and clarity of economic objectives and, consequently, to mitigate the possible tensions with the clinical ones [14, 15, 19, 21]. In this framework, adopting the interpretative lenses of Person-Organization (P-O) Fit Theory [76, 77], participative budgeting allows doctor-managers to reach a perceived fit with PHOs, as impersonated by their interlocutors, in terms of beliefs, goals and related expectations. Such a fit might boast positive cognitions of budgetary objectives, improving doctor-managers' goal clarity, which, in turn, by simplifying OUs' managerial tasks, positively affects their well-being at work.

The few studies on PHOs' participative budgeting practices from BMA research perspectives have mainly investigated the links to doctor-managers' performance, exploring the role of motivation, behaviours, and other psychological factors [22, 78, 79], also following the intensification of their involvement through greater levels of organizational openness in communication [80]. However, there's a scarcity of studies empirically testing how the intensification of this organizational driver of doctor-managers' involvement, in PHOs' participative budgeting practices, can reduce their ambiguities linked to the budgetary objectives, and, thus, enhance their psychological states in carrying out the managerial role in the OUs' work context.

Therefore, based on the core assumptions of P-O Fit Theory, this study explores how participative budgeting influences doctor-managers' goal clarity and how this, in turn, affects their well-being at work. We also analyse the mediating role of goal clarity in this relation between participative budgeting and well-being at work.

The paper contributes to the BMA research in the health care sector interested in promoting the involvement of doctors-managers in the budgeting practices of PHOs. To this end, more specifically, we aim to respond to the call for research of Siverbo [17] on how different management control tools affect managerial role clarity, of which goal clarity is a core dimension, and well-being at work.

Our model was tested through survey questionnaires from 332 doctor-managers of Italian PHOs.

The work is structured as follows: Sect. 2 provides the theoretical framework on participative budgeting and P-O Fit Theory and the research hypotheses; Sect. 3 illustrates the sample and the methodology; Sect. 4 shows the results, Sect. 5 presents their discussions and drives conclusions.

2 Theoretical Framework: Participative Budgeting Within PHOs

In the various interpretative perspectives of participative budgeting proposed by the literature, Shields and Shields [75] conceptualize this practice as an important factor for strengthening the process of communication and information sharing among different organizational levels.

In this sense, theoretical studies have highlighted how the opportunity to communicate in the budgeting process allows budget holders to develop a more precise knowledge and clear sense about the expectations and behaviours associated with the managerial role, making them less exposed to environmental and job uncertainties and to the related stressors [75, 81]. Participative budgeting can favour a reduction of the tensions connected to the goal ambiguity, since it can be perceived by middle managers as a means through which the organization take care of their psychological tensions and well-being at work [70, 82]. In PHOs context, this care devoted from organization to their role of doctor-managers allows also to increase their acceptance of managerial responsibilities [8, 13, 28], reducing the correlated risks of dysfunctional behaviours for the achievement of budgetary objectives [11, 15, 83].

In these perspectives, the few empirical contributions on PHOs' adoption of participative budgeting practices, within the lines of BMA [21], have deepened the role of participation in the budgeting process in enhancing doctor-managers' managerial performance, mainly showing the interactions of motivation, attitudes, and behaviours in this link [26, 84]. Only some of these empirical studies have focused on the influences of participative budgeting on doctor-managers' perceptions, cognitions, and mental states. Most of them explored these influences on the interpretations of budgetary information, in terms of accuracy, usefulness [80, 85], and on the related levels of satisfaction [86, 87], while few studies have investigated the direct effects of participative budgeting on the overall job satisfaction and similar mental states of doctor-managers [79, 88]. Further, some scholars addressed the relationship between role clarity, deriving from the participation in the budgeting process, and some affective and behavioural responses, highlighting how it increases the alignment of individual objectives with the organizational ones [89], and the identification levels with PHOs' overall values and objectives [22, 78]. Nevertheless, despite the interest of the literature on the psychological effects of participation in the budgeting process, there are still no substantial empirical evidence in PHOs context on the causal role of participative budgeting in increasing doctor-managers' goal clarity and its influences on their well-being at work. However, well-being at work is an important outcome [30], since, as we previously underlined, doctor-managers experiencing it are more likely to make decisions and behave consistently with assigned organizational objectives [90, 91]. In these perspectives, we try to fill this gap within participative budgeting literature by responding to the call for research of Siverbo [17] on the influences of the design and use of different management control tools on public managers' role clarity, especially in its core dimension of goal clarity, and how this impacts, in turn, on their well-being at work. To this end, we build on the conceptual assumptions of P-O Fit Theory.

The P-O Fit Theory [76, 77] has its roots in the P-E Fit Theory, which relies on the concept of fit between the individuals and their environment through process of continuous interactions [92–94]. More in depth, P-E Fit is interpreted as the perceived congruence, compatibility, match, similarity or correspondence between the single person and the environment [95]. Within this general definition, P-O Fit refers to the perceived level of congruence existing between individuals' values, norms, beliefs or goals [96] and those of organization, as impersonated by top management [60, 76, 97], attributable to the exchange dynamics at the various organizational levels. Such perceived fit might induce individuals to mature an overall perception of goal clarity [23, 98] and boast several positive outcomes for both them and the organization. In fact, when individuals perceive to fit with their work environment, they tend to develop a more positive well-being [99] and a greater job satisfaction [100]. Therefore, they are more likely to improve their motivation and commitment [96] and perform better within the organizational context [95].

In these studies, on the psychological dynamics powered by the fit, it is possible to include the analysis of the individual influences activated by participative budgeting from doctor-managers point of view. We believe that doctor-managers' interactions with PHOs' top management and controllers, within participative budgeting practices, by stimulating positive effects on the personal learning, the interpretation of the meaning, the value and the usefulness of budgetary information for decision-making process, might develop a perception of fit between doctor-managers' goals, beliefs and expectations and those of top management of PHOs; this latter will likely address greater goal clarity, developing a deeper understanding and more precise idea of budgetary goals, and how to achieve them, which, in turn, increases their well-being at work.

2.1 Research Hypotheses

Based on the central concepts of literature on participative budgeting and P-O Fit Theory, our work develops a research design predicting that participative budgeting influences doctor-managers' goal clarity, which, in turn, increases their well-being at work. Further, we add the mediating role of goal clarity in the relation between participative budgeting and well-being at work (see Fig. 1).

Participation in the budgeting process contributes to increase doctor-managers' goal clarity, since it provides them with valuable information that allows to understand the expectations associated with their managerial responsibilities. In line with this assumption, Chong and Chong [101] demonstrated that participative budgeting provides an opportunity for the involved actors to gather, exchange and disseminate job-relevant information enhancing their decision-making. Consistently, within the general literature on participative budgeting [102], the findings of Chenhall and Brownell [70] supported the positive influence of participative budgeting on the overall role ambiguity. In PHOs context there are less research examining these links but, while Cattaneo and Bassani [89] highlighted how the mechanisms of involvement and integration in PHOs' budgeting process are vectors for internalizing organizational values and objectives and aligning them with the individual ones, Macinati et al. [26] showed that participation in the budgeting process by doctor-managers increases their role clarity. According to such evidence, we expect participative budgeting to be a variable through which doctor-managers' experience that outcome goals and objectives are clear. Consequently, we test the following hypothesis:

H1: Participative budgeting is positively associated with doctor-managers' goal clarity.

Goal clarity increases doctor-managers' well-being at work because it makes them knowledgeable of their responsibilities, and the economic consequences of their decision-making, thus reducing the associated stressors. Previous empirical studies demonstrated that the overall role clarity has positive effect on job satisfaction [103], psychological empowerment [25], job-based psychological ownership [104], and job performance [44, 105]. Instead, the lack of role clarity leads to greater job uncertainties and unproductive, misguided, and unsatisfactory managerial efforts [70, 106].

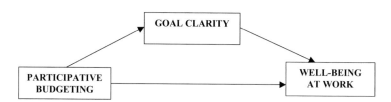

Fig. 1 Theoretical framework

In line with these general findings, empirical research on participative budgeting in the health care context, highlighted that the overall role clarity has an evident effect on cognitive, attitudinal, and behavioural variables, such as doctor-managers' job-based psychological ownership, affective commitment towards managerial role [22], managerial self-efficacy and managerial performance [78]. However, there are no studies examining, within PHOs' participative budgeting dynamics, the effect of goal clarity on well-being at work. Thus, we expect that increased goal clarity from participative budgeting is likely to improve doctor-managers' well-being at work. Accordingly, we test the following hypothesis:

H2: Goal clarity is positively associated with doctor-managers' well-being at work.

Siverbo [17] highlighted the influences of design and use of management control tools on goal clarity of public managers and how this clarity positively affects their well-being at work. In this sense, some research in PHOs, context, similarly to the generalist one on participative budgeting [70, 82, 102, 107], showed that doctor-managers' participation in the budgeting process lead them to experience positive effects on their well-being at work, which translate in increased level of job satisfaction [79, 88], as they perceive to be an active part in this process and to be able to achieve clearer levels of understanding and awareness of organizational expectations on their managerial responsibilities [26, 80]. Nevertheless, there's still a lack of evidence on the effects of goal clarity in the link participative budgeting—doctor-managers' well-being at work. Thus, we also test the following hypothesis:

H3: Goal clarity mediates the relation between participative budgeting and doctor-managers' well-being at work.

3   Methods

3.1   Sampling, Data Collection and Analysis

In the Italian National Health Service (NHS), the central government is responsible for defining and overseeing the basic free-of-charge universal coverage provided to the population, while the Regions are responsible for the local organization and administration of the health care services through a network of PHOs, namely Local Health care Authorities (LHAs), which, in turn, are responsible for yearly defining their organizational strategies, priorities, and goals. Doctors heading of OUs in Italian PHOs, as budget holders, represent the unit of analysis of our study. Their significant hybridization in the role of doctor-managers makes them particularly exposed to goal ambiguity issues and, thus, a useful sample of analysis, also applied in other similar research [12, 108].

The study used data from a survey. A first version of the questionnaire we chose to adopt for our purposes [109] was pilot tested to consider the opportunity of changes in wording and in the order of questions, for needs of better clarity and comprehension of its content, as well as to check if the length of the questionnaire was acceptable.

The final version of the questionnaire was administered to doctor-managers operating in the four Italian LHAs situated in the Region Abruzzo. More in depth, there were 99 doctor-managers working in the LHA Lanciano-Vasto-Chieti, 89 operating in the LHA Avezzano-Sulmona-L'Aquila, 80 belonging to the LHA of Pescara and 64 belonging to the LHA of Teramo. The survey was conducted in person on site. Participants received a description of the purpose of the survey and were asked them to sign an informed consent, in accordance with the Italian data protection laws. The privacy and confidentiality of the answers have always been guaranteed. It was not allowed them to use smartphones or other IT and non-IT tools. Out of a total of 332 headings of OUs operating within the public hospitals of the Region Abruzzo, as resulting from the organizational documents consulted on LHAs' websites, 146 doctor-managers agreed to answer the questionnaire. After excluding the questionnaires with missing information, the final sample for the statistical analysis consisted of 131 doctor-managers.

A quality check procedure ascertained that the measurement scales had satisfactory psychometric properties, in terms of reliability, convergent and discriminant validity, as well as of appropriateness.

Data obtained from the survey were firstly analysed through descriptive and correlation statistics.

Thus, OLS linear regression analysis was used to test the hypotheses.

3.2 Measures

We selected seven-point Likert scales for all survey items. Respondents reported their degree of agreement with the different statements.

Participative budgeting was measured through the scale developed by Milani [110], which contains three items exploring the extent to which doctor-managers perceive to be involved in the budgeting process (e. g. "I'm involved in the definition process of budget"; "I'm involved in the revision process of budget"). Cronbach's alpha of 0.94 (above the threshold of 0.70) confirmed the reliability of the scale [111]. The Kaiser-Meyer-Olkin (KMO) test showed a value above the cut-off of .60 (equal to 0.70), confirming the appropriateness of data.

Goal clarity was measured by five survey items, according to the scale used by Siverbo [17], as developed by Sawyer [112] and applied to management control research by Hall [25] (e. g. "The expected results of my work are clear"; "I know which are my responsibilities"). Cronbach's alpha is 0.87. The KMO test is 0.70.

According to Grant et al. [31], well-being at work can be interpreted in relation to the happiness and the fulfilling of subjective experiences by managers in their workplace. In these perspectives, we measured well-being at work, based on the main conceptual models and empirical studies, which captured these positive experiences, also in the health context, with job satisfaction [32, 113] and measured it through a single item scale ("Overall, I am very satisfied with my job and I couldn't be more satisfied") [114].

Further, in the regression model we included the managerial experience, in terms of years as heading of OUs, as control variable.

After psychometrically testing these measures with KMO test and Cronbach's alpha, we verified the validity of the scales through an Exploratory Factor Analysis (EFA) [115]. Factor loadings above 0.50 for all the items allowed to verify the convergent validity of all the scales. The absence of major cross-loadings between factors confirmed the discriminant validity of the same.

4 Results

4.1 Descriptive Statistics

Before testing research hypotheses, descriptive and correlation analyses were performed. They are presented in Table 1.

Considering the extension of the measurement scale, the mean of participative budgeting, equal to 3.32, showed a moderate perception of involvement in the budgeting process from doctor-managers' perspective. Higher averages values occurred for the dependent variables of our model. In fact, the average value of goal clarity, slightly lower than 4 (3.95), located such perception in a median position. Further, the average value of well-being at work, much higher than the neutrality threshold (4.73), suggested a great satisfaction and pleasure for the managerial job.

Results of Spearman correlation analysis offer some preliminary evidence on the association between variables, highlighting how participative budgeting correlated positively with goal clarity ($r = 0.71$, $p \leq 0.001$), which, in turn, correlated positively with well-being at work ($r = 0.49$, $p \leq 0.001$).

4.2 Hypotheses Testing

We conducted the OLS regression analysis to test the research hypotheses.
In Table 2, regression results are reported.

Table 1 Descriptive and correlation analyses

Variable	Mean	SD	Min	Max	1st quart.	Median	3rd quart.	1.	2.	3.
1. Participative budgeting	3.32	1.77	1	7	1.67	3.35	4.90	1		
2. Goal clarity	3.95	1.20	1	7	3.20	3.97	4.73	0.71***	1	
3. Well-being at work	4.73	1.13	1	7	3.80	5	5.40	0.44***	0.49***	1

***p-value ≤ 0.001

Table 2 Regression results

Dependent variable	Independent variable		Control variable	R^2	Hypotheses tested
	Participative budgeting	Goal clarity	Managerial experience		
Goal clarity	0.49*** (0.04)	–	0.00 (0.01)	0.51	H1
Well-being at work	–	0.46*** (0.07)	–0.00 (0.01)	0.25	H2
	0.12 (0.07)	0.34** (0.10)	0.00 (0.01)	0.26	H3

Standard error in brackets
**p-value ≤ 0.01; ***p-value ≤ 0.001

Table 3 Mediation effect

Dependent variable	Independent variable	Mediation variable	Direct effect	Indirect effect	Total effect	Type of mediation
Well-being at work	Participative budgeting	Goal clarity	0.120	0.168***	0.288***	Total

***p-value ≤0.001

Our evidence found that participative budgeting has the expected significant association to goal clarity (β = 0.49, p ≤ 0.001), which means that H1 about a positive relationship between participative budgeting and goal clarity is confirmed. Also, as expected, goal clarity is positively associated with well-being at work (β = 0.46, p ≤ 0.001), providing support for H2. Then, by applying the Baron and Kenny [116] stepwise procedure to test the mediating effect, we documented: a positive significant relation between participative budgeting and well-being at work (β = 0.288, p ≤ 0.001) (Table 3); a positive significant relation of participative budgeting with goal clarity (β = 0.49, p ≤ 0.001); however, following the inclusion of the mediation variable namely goal clarity, there's still a positive significant relation between goal clarity and well-being at work (β = 0.34, p ≤ 0.01), but the direct link between participative budgeting and well-being at work decreases and becomes not significant (β = 0.12). The table shows the decomposition of the total effect into direct and indirect effect.

The mediating effect of goal clarity (0.168) was calculated with the method of the product of the coefficients [116]. On the basis of our results, we can affirm that goal clarity totally mediates the relation between participative budgeting and well-being at work, confirming H3.

All in all, the associations between the variables supported the theoretical model. More in depth, such results contributed to confirm the theoretical assumptions on the potential of participative budgeting, as well as to fill the underlined empirical gap on the psychological outcomes of such practice, mostly in the health care sector, which suggest the adoption of approaches strengthening the collaboration patterns of doctor-managers, to better support their decision-making and, in turn, favour better managerial performance. These results are better discussed in the following section.

5 Discussion and Conclusions

The "hybrid" nature of doctor-managers and the influences of their traditional clinical-professional culture may cause a lack of budgetary goal clarity in their perceptions, setting limits to the functioning of PHOs' budgetary systems and to the usefulness of the information neutrally provided to these budget holders for supporting their decision-making. These adverse reactions, which are able to negatively influence their well-being at work and, thus, the related performance, lead to seek, even in the budgetary systems of PHOs, greater convergences of the "behavioural" perspective with the "structuralist" one, as underlined by the generalist literature.

In particular, theoretical health care studies on participative budgeting have highlighted its key role in mitigating the risks deriving from doctor-managers' goal ambiguity, as to address their cognitions, mental states and, thus, behaviours towards better performance. Previous empirical research shows positive effects from participative budgeting on several psychological variables related to doctor-managers, but little is known about well-being at work effects and which causal mechanism is involved when such well-being is strengthened, even if this condition allows better decision-making processes. Therefore, this study, building on participative budgeting literature, P-O Fit Theory, and survey responses from 332 doctors heading of OUs in Italian PHOs sheds light on how participative budgeting increases doctor-managers' well-being at work by the indirect and mediating effect of goal clarity.

First, we found that participative budgeting directly improves doctor-managers' goal clarity. This positive effect is consistent with the perspective of P-O Fit Theory on the role of interactions to reach a fit inducing individuals to mature perceptions of goal clarity [23, 92, 98]. Further, it is in accordance with previous general studies on the potential of participative budgeting to reduce goal ambiguity [101], as well as with those conducted in the context of PHOs [26, 89], highlighting how the involvement in the budgeting process allows to internalize the budgetary organizational objectives, thanks to the improvements in the personal learning and the interpretation of budgetary information. This finding is also in line with the previous BMA empirical evidence on the cognitive role of openness in internal communication processes, within PHOs' participative budgeting practices, which reduces information asymmetry, thus favouring the mitigation of the ambiguities related to the managerial role of doctor-managers and enhancing their perceptions of utility of budgetary information for decision-making [80].

Second, our study showed that goal clarity, within participative budgeting practices, is able to increase doctor-managers' well-being at work, revealing how being knowledgeable of their objectives mitigate the possible latent stressors. These positive effects are in line with the generalist studies on participative budgeting [83] and the health care ones [21, 79, 87], according to which the positive psychological states are explained by the job uncertainty-reduction dynamics associated with participative budgeting.

Third, we found that goal clarity totally mediates the link between participative budgeting and well-being at work. This finding allows to unleash the potential of participative budgeting in addressing positive feelings at work, thanks to the empowerment of the perceived clearly stated goals and objectives related to their managerial role. Thus, our results are consistent with both the generalist literature on the role of participative budgeting [70, 102] and on the specific one set in PHOs' context [26, 79].

Thus, on this basis, our findings explain how it is possible to overcome the issues concerning the scarce usefulness of budgeting approaches in the only mechanistic structuralist perspective, by using models, like that we have analysed, which favour the integration with the psychological-behavioural factors. For these purposes, the study highlights the effectiveness of participative budgeting practices in promoting a more clear understanding of budgetary objectives and, consequently, better psychological conditions at work for good doctor-managers' decision-making in the health care activities of OUs.

The paper aimed at contributing to the BMA research in the health care sector promoting the involvement of doctors-managers in the budgeting practices of PHOs. In this perspective, assuming participative budgeting as a practice enhancing the internal communication process and vertical information sharing, our study expands the literature on this budgeting practice, offering further evidence about the still unexplored psychological outcomes of doctor-managers' participation in the budgeting process within PHOs' context. To this end, on the one hand, we add relevant insights on the role of participative budgeting practices in affecting doctor-managers' goal clarity, on the other hand, we shed a light on how their goal clarity influences their well-being at work within these budgeting practices, validating the causal model described by P-O Fit Theory. In doing so, all in all, we respond to the call for research of Siverbo [17] on how different management control designs and uses affect the overall managerial role clarity, of which goal clarity is a core dimension, and well-being at work of public managers. We offer our contribution to such response by focusing on doctor-managers and expanding such dynamics by exploring the participative budgeting practices from the point of view of these budget holders of PHOs' context.

Further, the study suggests to PHOs' governance and health care policy makers the adoption of managerial approaches and policies aimed at creating a fit of doctor-managers' goals, beliefs and expectations with those of top management and controllers. To this end, it proposes the use of practices that value the human potential by strengthening the collaboration patterns among these organizational actors rather than the only neutral hierarchical implementation of budgeting system. Similar involvement, in fact, would allow a process of managerial learning able to change doctor-managers' cognitive and behavioural orientation towards the budgeting process and purposes. The enhancement of these soft variables of PHOs' budgeting systems, allowing to fruitfully integrate them in the "structuralist" perspective, would allow to increase the usefulness of these systems, mostly of the information provided to support decision-making and, thus, the performance of these health care budget holders.

Nevertheless, the limitations of the study require to interpret with some caution our results. First, since these latter rely on doctor-managers' self-reported perceptual data, they are influenced by the contextual factors and the subjectivity with which they are interpreted, hindering generalizations. Enlarge the research sample, also at an international level, could allow to better interpretate our results. At the same time, the integration with other source of data could allow to mitigate the risks of common method variance. Second, our results are based on the core assumptions of P-O Fit Theory, which address the causal relations between the variables. Thus, using different theoretical frameworks could serve to draw different conclusions. Third, we stated that participative budgeting activates a fit which increases goal clarity; however, P-O Fit was not directly measured. Therefore, future studies should adopt more explicit measure of doctor-managers' fit with top management and controllers. Fourth, it could be deepened the role of other interacting variables in the relationships among participative budgeting, goal clarity and well-being at work. Mostly, it could be deepen how the participation in the budgeting process empowers the characteristics or the role of ICT tools and of the new Digital Technologies and how they interact with goal clarity and well-being at work. Moving on this way, future research could explore if the budgeting process can be perceived as less threatening to well-being at work when doctor-managers are involved both in its design and implementation, showing potential insights for the enabling design of participative budgeting. Further, since our analysis is based on data prior to the pandemic period, future works could investigate the impact of Covid-19 on the tested relations. Lastly, consistently with BMA focus, the study does not consider the influences exerted by incentive systems linked to participative budgeting practices. This offers a subsequent integration of the study useful for evaluating the effects generated by these variables as well.

References

1. Anselmi, L. (a cura di). (1996). *L'equilibrio economico nelle aziende sanitarie, Il Sole 240re*.
2. Gebreiter, F. (2021). Accountingization, colonization and hybridization in historical perspective: the relationship between hospital accounting and clinical medicine in late 20th century Britain. *Accounting, Auditing & Accountability Journal, 35*(5), 1189–1211.
3. Macinati, M. S., & Anessi-Pessina, E. (2014). Management accounting use and financial performance in public healthcare organisations: Evidence from the Italian National Health Service. *Health Policy, 117*(1), 98–111. https://doi.org/10.1016/j.healthpol.2014.03.011
4. Abernethy, M. A. (1996). Physicians and resource management: the role of accounting and non-accounting controls. *Financial Accountability & Management, 12*(2), 141–156.
5. Nuti, S., Noto, G., Grillo Ruggieri, T., & Vainieri, M. (2021). The challenges of hospitals' planning & control systems: the path toward public value management. *International Journal of Environmental Research and Public Health, 18*(5), 27–32.
6. Padovani, E., Orelli, R. L., & Young, D. W. (2014). Implementing change in a hospital management accounting system. *Public Management Review, 16*(8), 1184–1204.
7. Quagli, A., Dameri, R. P., & Inghirami, I. E. (2005). *I sistemi informativi gestionali*. FrancoAngeli.
8. Abernethy, M. A., Chua, W. F., Grafton, J., & Mahama, H. (2006). Accounting and control in health care: Behavioural, organisational, sociological and critical perspectives. In

C. S. Chapman, A. G. Hopwood, & M. D. Shields (Eds.), *Handbooks of management accounting research* (Vol. 2, pp. 805–829). Elsevier. https://doi.org/10.1016/S1751-3243(06)02014-1

9. Corsi, K., Ezza, A., Fadda, N., Giovanelli, L., Pinna, M., & Rotondo, F. (2016). *Modelli di management nel settore sanitario. Criticità e prospettive.* Giappichelli Editore.

10. Grossi, G., Kallio, K. M., Sargiacomo, M., & Skoog, M. (2020). Accounting, performance management systems and accountability changes in knowledge-intensive public organizations: A literature review and research agenda. *Accounting, Auditing & Accountability Journal, 33*(1), 256–280.

11. Hardy, M. E., & Hardy, W. L. (1988). Role stress and role strain. *Role Theory: Perspectives for Health Professionals, 2,* 159–240.

12. Sartirana, M., Prenestini, A., & Lega, F. (2014). Medical management: hostage to its own history? The case of Italian clinical directors. *International Journal of Public Sector Management, 27*(5), 417–429.

13. Lega, F., & Vendramini, E. (2008). Budgeting and performance management in the Italian national health system (INHS): assessment and constructive criticism. *Journal of Health, Organisation and Management, 22*(1), 11–22. https://doi.org/10.1108/14777260810862371

14. Macinati, M. S. (2010). NPM reforms and the perception of budget by hospital clinicians: Lessons from two case-studies. *Financial Accountability & Management, 26*(4), 422–442. https://doi.org/10.1111/j.1468-0408.2010.00509.x

15. Abernethy, M. A., & Vagnoni, E. (2004). Power, organization design and managerial behaviour. *Accounting, Organizations and Society, 29*(3–4), 207–225. https://doi.org/10.1016/s0361-3682(03)00049-7

16. Pollitt, C., Harrison, S., Hunter, D., & Marnoch, G. (1988). The reluctant managers: Clinicians and budgets in the NHS. *Financial Accountability & Management, 4*(3), 213–233.

17. Siverbo, S. (2021). The impact of management controls on public managers' well-being. *Financial Accountability & Management, 39*(1), 60–80.

18. Hoff, T. J. (2001). The physician as worker: What it means and why now? *Health Care Management Review, 26*(4), 53–70.

19. Pettersen, I. J., & Solstad, E. (2014). Managerialism and profession-based logic: The use of accounting information in changing hospitals. *Financial, Accountability & Management, 30*(4), 363–382.

20. Oppi, C., Campanale, C., Cinquini, L., & Vagnoni, E. (2019). Clinicians and accounting: A systematic review and research directions. *Financial Accountability & Management, 35*(3), 290–312. https://doi.org/10.1111/faam.12195

21. Abernethy, M. A., & Stoelwinder, J. U. (1991). Budget use, task uncertainty, system goal orientation and subunit performance: A test of the 'fit' hypothesis in not-for-profit hospitals. *Accounting, Organizations and Society, 16*(2), 105–120.

22. Macinati, M. S., & Rizzo, M. G. (2016). Exploring the link between clinical managers involvement in budgeting and performance: Insights from the Italian public health care sector. *Health care Management Review, 41*(3), 213–223. https://www.jstor.org/stable/48516220

23. Oppi, C., Campanale, C., & Cinquini, L. (2021). Il problema dell'ambiguità nei sistemi di misurazione della performance nel settore pubblico: un'analisi della letteratura internazionale. *Management Control, 2,* 11–38.

24. Jung, C. S. (2011). Organizational goal ambiguity and performance: Conceptualization, measurement, and relationships. *International Public Management Journal, 14*(2), 193–217.

25. Hall, M. (2008). The effect of comprehensive performance measurement systems on role clarity, psychological empowerment and managerial performance. *Accounting, Organizations and Society, 33*(2–3), 141–163.

26. Macinati, M. S., Bozzi, S., & Rizzo, M. G. (2016). Budgetary participation and performance: The mediating effects of medical managers' job engagement and self-efficacy. *Health Policy, 120*(9), 1017–1028. https://doi.org/10.1016/j.healthpol.2016.08.005

27. Cifalinò, A., Mascia, D., Morandin, G., & Vendramini, E. (2021). Perceived goal importance, knowledge and accessibility of performance information: Testing mediation and

moderation effects on medical professionals' achievement of performance targets. *Financial Accountability & Management,* 1–22.

28. Demartini, C., & Trucco, S. (2017). Are performance measurement systems useful? Perceptions from health care. *BMC Health Services Research, 17*(1), 96. https://doi.org/10.1186/s12913-017-2022-9
29. Michel Sørup, C., & Jacobsen, P. (2013). Healthcare performance turned into decision support. *Journal of Health Organization and Management, 27*(1), 64–84. https://doi.org/10.1108/14777261311311807
30. Cäker, M., & Siverbo, S. (2018). Effects of performance measurement system inconsistency on managers' role clarity and well-being. *Scandinavian Journal of Management, 34*(3), 256–266.
31. Grant, A. M., Christianson, M. K., & Price, R. H. (2007). Happiness, health, or relationships? Managerial practices and employee wellbeing tradeoffs. *Academy of Management Perspectives, 21,* 51–63.
32. Van De Voorde, K., Paauwe, J., & Van Veldhoven, M. (2012). Employee well-being and the HRM–organizational performance relationship: a review of quantitative studies. *International Journal of Management Reviews, 14*(4), 391–407.
33. Danna, K., & Griffin, R. W. (1999). Health and well-being in the workplace: A review and synthesis of the literature. *Journal of Management, 25*(3), 357–384.
34. Harter, J. K., Schmidt, F. L., & Hayes, T. L. (2002). Business-unit-level relationship between employee satisfaction, employee engagement, and business outcomes: a meta-analysis. *Journal of Applied Psychology, 87*(2), 268.
35. Abernethy, M. A., & Stoelwinder, J. U. (1995). The role of professional control in the management of complex organizations. *Accounting, Organizations and Society, 20*(1), 1–17.
36. Calciolari, S., Cantù, E., & Fattore, G. (2011). Performance management and goal ambiguity: Managerial implications in a single payer system. *Health Care Management Review, 36*(2), 164–174.
37. Eldenburg, L., Krishnan, H. A., & Krishnan, R. (2017). Management accounting and control in the hospital industry: A review. *Journal of Governmental & Nonprofit Accounting, 6*(1), 52–91.
38. Ansari, S. L. (1977). An integrated approach to control system design. *Accounting, Organizations and Society, 2*(2), 101–112.
39. Flamholtz, E. G., Das, T. K., & Tsui, A. S. (1985). Toward an integrative framework of organizational control. *Accounting, Organizations and Society, 10*(1), 35–50.
40. Ouchi, W. G. (1979). A conceptual framework for the design of organizational control mechanisms. *Management Science, 25*(9), 833–848.
41. Burchell, S., Clubb, C., Hopwood, A., Hughes, J., & Nahapiet, J. (1980). The roles of accounting in organizations and society. *Accounting, Organizations and Society, 5*(1), 5–27.
42. Chiarini, A., Vagnoni, E., & Chiarini, L. (2018). ERP implementation in public healthcare, achievable benefits and encountered criticalities-an investigation from Italy. *International Journal of Services and Operations Management, 29*(1), 1–17.
43. Mancini, D., Lombardi, R., & Tavana, M. (2021). Four research pathways for understanding the role of smart technologies in accounting. *Meditari Accountancy Research, 29.*
44. Marginson, D., Mcaulay, L., Roush, M., & Van Zijl, T. (2014). Examining a positive psychological role for performance measures. *Management Accounting Research, 25*(1), 63–75.
45. Raucci, D., Santone, A., Mercaldo, F., & Dyczkowski, T. (2020). BPM perspectives to support ICSs: Exploiting the integration of formal verifications into investment service provision processes. *Industrial Management & Data Systems, 120*(7), 1383–1400.
46. Bonsòn, E., Lavorato, D., Lamboglia, R., & Mancini, D. (2021). Artificial intelligence activities and ethical approaches in leading listed companies in the European Union. *International Journal of Accounting Information Systems, 43.*

47. Kraus, S., Schiavone, F., Pluzhnikova, A., & Invernizzi, A. C. (2021). Digital transformation in healthcare: Analyzing the current state-of-research. *Journal of Business Research, 123,* 557–567.

48. Lombardi, R., Trequattrini, R., Schimperna, F., & Cano-Rubio, M. (2021). The Impact of Smart Technologies on the Management and Strategic Control: A Structured Literature Review. *Management Control, 1,* 11–30.

49. Palozzi, G., Falivena, C., & Chirico, A. (2019). Designing the function of health technology assessment as a support for hospital management. In *Service design and service thinking in healthcare and hospital management* (pp. 233–257). Springer.

50. Preston, A. M., Cooper, D. J., & Coombs, R. W. (1992). Fabricating budgets: A study of the production of management budgeting in the national health service. *Accounting, Organizations and Society, 17*(6), 561–593.

51. Eldenburg, L., Soderstrom, N., Willis, V., & Wu, A. (2010). Behavioral changes following the collaborative development of an accounting information system. *Accounting, Organizations and Society, 35*(2), 222–237. https://doi.org/10.1016/j.aos.2009.07.005

52. Malmi, T., & Brown, D. A. (2008). Management control systems as a package—Opportunities, challenges and research directions. *Management Accounting Research, 19*(4), 287–300.

53. Chiucchi, S., Iacoviello, G., & Paolini, A. (a cura di). (2021). *Controllo di gestione. Strutture, processi, misurazioni.* Giappichelli.

54. Marchi, L. (2003). *I sistemi informativi aziendali.* Giuffrè.

55. Otley, D. (2016). The contingency theory of management accounting and control: 1980–2014. *Management Accounting Research, 31,* 45–62.

56. Rea, M. A. (2003). *Il modello aziendale in sanità.* Aracne.

57. Del Bene, L. (2000). *Criteri e strumenti per il controllo gestionale nelle aziende sanitarie.* Giuffrè.

58. Sargiacomo, M. (2002). Benchmarking in Italy: The first case study on personnel motivation and satisfaction in a Health Business. *Total Quality Management, 13*(4), 489–505.

59. Vagnoni, E., & Maran, L. (2013). *Il controllo di gestione nelle aziende sanitarie pubbliche, 103.* Maggioli Editore.

60. Merchant, K. A., & Riccaboni, A. (2001). *Il controllo di gestione.* McGraw-Hill.

61. Davis, F. D. (1989). Perceived usefulness perceived ease of use, and user acceptance of information technology. *MIS Quarterly, 13*(3), 319–339.

62. Venkatesh, V., & Davis, F. D. (2000). A theoretical extension of the technology acceptance model: Four longitudinal field studies. *Management Science, 46*(2), 186–204.

63. Venkatesh, V., Morris, M. G., Davis, G. B., & Davis, F. D. (2003). User acceptance of information technology: toward a unified view. *MIS Quarterly, 27*(3), 425–478.

64. Venkatesh, V. (2006). Where to go from here? Thoughts on future directions for research on individual-level technology adoption with a focus on decision making. *Decision Sciences, 37*(4), 497–518.

65. Shibl, R., Lawley, M., & Debuse, J. (2013). Factors influencing decision support system acceptance. *Decision Support Systems, 54*(2), 953–961.

66. Venkatesh, V., Thong, J. Y., & Xu, X. (2016). Unified theory of acceptance and use of technology: A synthesis and the road ahead. *Journal of the association for Information Systems, 17*(5), 328–376.

67. Catrini, E., Ferrario, L., Mazzone, A., Varalli, L., Gatti, F., Cannavacciuolo, L., Ponsiglione, C., & Foglia, E. (2022). Tools supporting polypharmacy management in Italy: Factors determining digital technologies' intention to use in clinical practice. *Health Science Reports, 5*(3), e647.

68. Holden, R. J., & Karsh, B. T. (2010). The technology acceptance model: its past and its future in health care. *Journal of Biomedical Informatics, 43*(1), 159–172.

69. Campanale, C., & Cinquini, L. (2016). Emerging pathways of colonization in healthcare from participative approaches to management accounting. *Critical Perspectives on Accounting, 39,* 59–74. https://doi.org/10.1016/j.cpa.2015.12.001

70. Chenhall, R. H., & Brownell, P. (1988). The effect of participative budgeting on job satisfaction and performance: Role ambiguity as an intervening variable. *Accounting, Organizations and Society, 13*(3), 225–233. https://doi.org/10.1016/0361-3682(88)90001-3
71. Shields, M. D., & Young, S. M. (1993). Antecedents and consequences of participative budgeting: evidence on the effects of asymmetrical information. *Journal of Management Accounting Research, 5*(1), 265–280.
72. Covaleski, M. A., Evans, J. H., III, Luft, J. L., & Shields, M. D. (2003). Budgeting research: three theoretical perspectives and criteria for selective integration. *Journal of Management Accounting Research, 15*(1), 3–49. https://doi.org/10.2308/jmar.2003.15.1.3
73. Hall, M. (2016). Realising the richness of psychology theory in contingency-based management accounting research. *Management Accounting Research, 31*, 63–74. https://doi.org/10.1016/j.mar.2015.11.002
74. Macinati, M. S. (2012). *Behavioural management accounting.* Franco Angeli.
75. Shields, J. F., & Shields, M. D. (1998). Antecedents of participative budgeting. *Accounting, Organizations and Society, 23*(1), 49–76.
76. Chatman, J. A. (1989). Improving interactional organizational research: A model of person-organization fit. *Academy of Management Review, 14*(3), 333–349.
77. Kristof, A. L. (1996). Person-organization fit: An integrative review of its conceptualizations, measurement, and implications. *Personnel Psychology, 49*(1), 1–49.
78. Macinati, M. S., Cantaluppi, G., & Rizzo, M. G. (2017). Medical managers' managerial self-efficacy and role clarity: How do they bridge the budgetary participation–performance link? *Health Services Management Research, 30*(1), 47–60. https://doi.org/10.1177/0951484816682398
79. Raucci, D., & Paolini, M. (2021). Soddisfazione lavorativa e work engagement nelle budgeting practices delle aziende sanitarie pubbliche. *Una verifica empirica. Management Control, 1*, 13–32. https://doi.org/10.3280/MACO2021-001002
80. Raucci, D., & Paolini, M. (2022). Openness in communication and budgetary information in the participative budgeting research. The case of Italian public healthcare organizations. In *Sustainable Digital Transformation: Paving the Way Towards Smart Organizations and Societies* (pp. 95–115). Springer International Publishing.
81. Brownell, P. (1982). The role of accounting data in performance evaluation, budgetary participation, and organizational effectiveness. *Journal of Accounting Research, 20*, 12–27.
82. Maiga, A. S. (2005). Antecedents and consequences of budget participation. *Advances in Management Accounting, 14*(1), 211–231. https://doi.org/10.1016/S1474-7871(05)14010-6
83. Macinati, M. S., Rizzo, M., & Ippolito, B. (2012). Partecipazione, commitment e informazioni di budget. I risultati di una ricerca empirica. *Mecosan, 82*, 25.
84. Longo, F., Mele, S., Salvatore, D., Tasselli, S., Monchiero, G., & Pinelli, N. (2013). *Il governo dei servizi territoriali: budget e valutazione dell'integrazione: Modelli teorici ed evidenze empiriche.* Egea.
85. Macinati, M. S., Rizzo, M. G., & D'Agostino, G. (2014). Partecipazione al processo di budget, accuratezza e utilità delle informazioni di budget e performance. I risultati di un caso studi. *Mecosan, 92.*
86. Macinati, M. S., & Rizzo, M. G. (2012). Partecipazione, commitment e informazioni di budget. I risultati di una ricerca empirica. *Mecosan, 82*, 25–41. https://doi.org/10.3280/MESA2014-092004
87. Macinati, M. S., & Rizzo, M. G. (2014). Budget goal commitment, clinical managers' use of budget information and performance. *Health Policy, 117*(2), 228–238. https://doi.org/10.1016/j.healthpol.2014.05.003
88. Rizzo, M. G. (2014). La relazione tra il livello di coinvolgimento nel processo di budget, il commitment verso gli obiettivi, la soddisfazione lavorativa ei relativi risvolti sulla performance manageriale. I risultati di un caso studio. *Management Control, 1*, 9–34. https://doi.org/10.3280/MACO2014-001002

89. Cattaneo, C., & Bassani, G. V. (2016). Il processo di budget e l'interiorizzazione dei valori: il caso di un ospedale italiano. In L. Marchi, R. Lombardi, & L. Anselmi (Eds.), *Il governo aziendale tra tradizione e innovazione*. FrancoAngeli.

90. Conrad, L., & Uslu, P. G. (2011). Investigation of the impact of 'payment by results' on performance measurement and management in NHS trusts. *Management Accounting Research, 22*(1), 46–55.

91. Favero, N., Meier, K. J., & O'Toole, L. J., Jr. (2016). Goals, trust, participation, and feedback: Linking internal management with performance outcomes. *Journal of Public Administration Research and Theory, 26*(2), 327–343.

92. Bandura, A. (1977). *Social learning theory*. Prentice-Hall.

93. Caplan, R. D. (1987). Person-environment fit theory and organizations: Commensurate dimensions, time perspectives, and mechanisms. *Journal of Vocational behavior, 31*(3), 248–267.

94. Edwards, J. R. (1996). An examination of competing versions of the person-environment fit approach to stress. *Academy of Management Journal, 39*(2), 292–339.

95. Greguras, G. J., & Diefendorff, J. M. (2009). Different fits satisfy different needs: linking person-environment fit to employee commitment and performance using self-determination theory. *Journal of Applied Psychology, 94*(2), 465.

96. Kristof-Brown, A. L., Zimmerman, R. D., & Johnson, E. C. (2005). Consequences of individuals' fit at work: A meta-analysis of person–job, person–organization, person–group, and person–supervisor fit. *Personnel Psychology, 58*(2), 281–342.

97. Cable, D. M., & De Rue, D. S. (2002). The convergent and discriminant validity of subjective fit perceptions. *Journal of Applied Psychology, 87*(5), 875.

98. Sun, R., Peng, S., & Pandey, S. K. (2014). Testing the effect of person-environment fit on employee perceptions of organizational goal ambiguity. *Public Performance & Management Review, 37*(3), 465–495.

99. Vilela, B. B., González, J. A. V., & Ferrín, P. F. (2008). Person–organization fit, OCB and performance appraisal: Evidence from matched supervisor–salesperson data set in a Spanish context. *Industrial Marketing Management, 37*(8), 1005–1019.

100. Bretz, R. D., Jr., & Judge, T. A. (1994). The role of human resource systems in job applicant decision processes. *Journal of Management, 20*(3), 531–551.

101. Chong, V. K., & Chong, K. M. (2002). Budget goal commitment and informational effects of budget participation on performance: A structural equation modeling approach. *Behavioral Research in Accounting, 14*(1), 65–86. https://doi.org/10.2308/bria.2002.14.1.65

102. Sholihin, M., Pike, R., Mangena, M., & Li, J. (2011). Goal-setting participation and goal commitment: Examining the mediating roles of procedural fairness and interpersonal trust in a UK financial services organisation. *The British Accounting Review, 43*(2), 135–146. https://doi.org/10.1016/j.bar.2011.02.003

103. Moynihan, D. P., & Pandey, S. K. (2007). Finding workable levers over work motivation: Comparing job satisfaction, job involvement, and organizational commitment. *Administration & Society, 39*(7), 803–832.

104. Pierce, J. L., Kostova, T., & Dirks, K. T. (2003). The state of psychological ownership: Integrating and extending a century of research. *Review of General Psychology, 7*(1), 84–107.

105. Burney, L., & Widener, S. K. (2007). Strategic performance measurement systems, job-relevant information, and managerial behavioral responses—Role stress and performance. *Behavioral Research in Accounting, 19*(1), 43–69.

106. Merchant, K. A., & Van der Stede, W. A. (2007). *Management control systems: performance measurement, evaluation and incentives*. Pearson Education.

107. Vandenberg, R. J., & Lance, C. E. (1992). Examining the causal order of job satisfaction and organizational commitment. *Journal of Management, 18*(1), 153–167.

108. Di Vincenzo, F., Angelozzi, D., & Morandi, F. (2021). The microfoundations of physicians' managerial attitude. *BMC Health Services Research, 21*(1), 1–8.

109. Fowler, F. J., Jr. (2013). *Survey research methods*. Sage.

110. Milani, K. (1975). The relationship of participation in budget setting to industrial supervisor performance and attitudes: a field study. *The Accounting Review, 50*, 274–284.
111. Stock, J. H., & Watson, M. W. (2005). *Introduzione all'econometria*. Pearson Italia Spa.
112. Sawyer, J. E. (1992). Goal and process clarity: Specification of multiple constructs of role ambiguity and a structural equation model of their antecedents and consequences. *Journal of Applied Psychology, 77*, 130–142.
113. Akdere, M. (2009). A multi-level examination of quality focused human resource practices and firm performance: evidence from the US healthcare industry. *International Journal of Human Resource Management, 20*, 1945–1964.
114. Gould-Williams, J. (2003). The importance of HR practices and workplace trust in achieving superior performance: a study of public-sector organizations. *International Journal of Human Resource Management, 14*, 28–54.
115. Kaiser, H. F. (1958). The varimax criterion for analytic rotation in factor analysis. *Psychometrika, 23*(3), 187–200. https://doi.org/10.1007/BF02289233
116. Baron, R. M., & Kenny, D. A. (1986). The moderator–mediator variable distinction in social psychological research: Conceptual, strategic, and statistical considerations. *Journal of Personality and Social Psychology, 51*(6), 1173.

Investigating Digital Public Administration and Organizational Change in a Knowledge Translation Perspective

Paolo Canonico, Ernesto De Nito, Vincenza Esposito, Marcello Martinez, and Mario Pezzillo Iacono

Abstract The paper responds to the call to shed more light on the knowledge transfer and knowledge translation related to digital transformation process in a public domain. Our research has considered a digital transformation project triggered by the introduction of the Telematics Civil Process in the Italian final court of appeal. We show that the project of change itself may act as a knowledge translation mechanism. The project is interpreted as the interactional space where different players share the framework and develop a common language. This means that both project, as coordination mechanism, and project tools themselves have the potential to become a "place" where participants may effectively enhance knowledge translation, sharing and translating their expertise, adopting a framework and developing a common ground.

Keywords Digital transformation · Organizational change · Knowledge transfer · Knowledge translation · Civil court

P. Canonico
University of Naples Federico II, Naples, Italy

E. De Nito
University of Salerno, Salerno, Italy

V. Esposito
University of Sannio, Benevento, Italy

M. Martinez · M. Pezzillo Iacono (✉)
University of Campania Luigi Vanvitelli, Capua, Italy
e-mail: mario.pezzilloiacono@unicampania.it

© The Author(s), under exclusive license to Springer Nature
Switzerland AG 2024
A. Lazazzara et al. (eds.), *Towards Digital and Sustainable Organisations*,
Lecture Notes in Information Systems and Organisation 65,
https://doi.org/10.1007/978-3-031-52880-4_6

1 Introduction

Digital Transformation is a complex process of organizational change that affects the public domain internationally with increasing pervasiveness [1, 2]. In particular, the organization of justice in Italy has been undergoing a profound process of change for some years now, and digitalization is emerging as a key driver toward innovation, reshaping, and modernization of the work processes and services of the Courts.

Digital tools can help courts optimize and refocus internal processes, improve services to users, and democratize access to justice, increasing both employee and citizen engagement, and leveraging scarce financial resources. Digital technologies carry a potential for more accessible, affordable, intelligible, and faster services in the court setting [3].

Digital transformation is more than the introduction of technologies. It is about people being involved in the implementation of technologies and building practices, languages, knowledge, and cultures that allow for further exploration of new digital technologies [4].

In a digital transformation process, in which knowledge is transferred across very different stakeholders and settings, knowledge needs to be translated to make it mutually understandable and relevant [5]. Knowledge translation is required to contextualise the transfer from the source of knowledge to the recipient and interpret the knowledge to be exchanged in a way that is meaningful for the recipient [6]. The case was a digital transformation project triggered by the introduction of the Telematics Civil Process in the Supreme Court of Cassation in Italy, the Italian final court of appeal. Digital governance of the civil process involves the need to adapt to new forms of language and new practices and activities to replace those traditionally carried out by lawyers, judges, and administrative officers/clerks.

Tabrizi et al. [7] observed that digital transformation is not primarily about implementing digital technology but about developing an appropriate strategy, in which the human element plays a key role. We therefore respond to the call to shed more light on the knowledge transfer and knowledge translation related to digital transformation [8] and especially among project team members.

The paper may be located within the emergent knowledge translation literature, in the effort to add to the understanding of project related mechanisms able to foster knowledge translation in an organizational change process activate by a digital transformation. The aim is to understand if an organizational change project could be interpreted as an example of knowledge translation process.

The paper is articulated as follows. First, the reference framework is given in Sects. 2 and 3 presenting our approach to the concepts of digital transformation and knowledge translation. In Sect. 4, the methodology adopted for the empirical study is described. Then, the case study is presented in Sect. 5. Finally, conclusions are drawn in Sect. 6.

2 Digital Transformation and Organizational Change in Public Domain

There is a broad consensus that technology does matter in the current public management reforms [9]. However, as indicated by recent works (e.g., [10]), it seems that the phenomenon of digital transformation differs from past IT-related change and cannot, therefore, be explained entirely using established theoretical models. Recent research portrays digital transformation as an emerging field of scholarly interest for management and organizational researchers, as well as a new research paradigm [1].

Digital transformation seems to have an intricate and encompassing connection to the topic of organizational change, requiring a broader view of and comparison with the literature on innovation and organizational change [11]. Hanelt et al. [1] define digital transformation as organizational change that is triggered and shaped by the widespread diffusion of digital technologies.

Digital transformation in the public sector means new ways of working with stakeholders, building new frameworks of service delivery and creating new forms of relationships [12]. It is not merely transforming analog and manual tools to digital tools, but a broad organizational transition towards new tools, policies, practices, work processes and operations [13].

Mergel et al. [14] defined digital transformation in public sector as: "*A holistic effort to revise core processes and services of government beyond the traditional digitization efforts. It evolves along a continuum of transition from analog to digital to a full stack review of policies, current processes, and user needs and results in a complete revision of the existing and the creation of new digital services*". According to Denhardt and Denhardt [15], the processes of digital transformation in public administration are "complex" phenomena that involve the redesign and management of organizational structures, dynamics, processes, practices, tools and organizational and inter-organizational relations of the stakeholders involved.

Janowsky [16] identified four different steps of digital transformation: *digitization (technology in government), transformation (electronic government), engagement (electronic governance) and contextualization (policy-driven electronic governance).*

The four-stage model is defined on whether the transformation has an internal or external impact and if transformation is or not related to a specific context in terms of sector or geographical space (country or city). Moving from a step to another, the complexity of the transformation process increases, in terms of actors involved and effects on working practice and way of interacting and offering services. While in the first step the main focus is on technology, in the fourth step the pressure is *to responding to the changing needs and aspirations of the society; supporting self-governance for local communities to be able to govern themselves with no or little interference from government* Janowsky [16].

This process is still in progress and requires a great effort from academics and practitioners to understand different dynamics. As stated by Andersson et al. [17]

"digital technologies come with a logic of standardisation, rationalisation, effi-ciency, text-based communication and quantitative judgements; a logic that fits work that is purely calculative rather well. Other types of public sector work, for example social work, comes with a logic of situation specific practices, care, knowl-edge creation, qualitative judgements, and involves the careful and slow interaction with citizens, that embody and to some extent negotiate, the formal rules of the bureaucracy."

Even if it is not clear at all what digital transformation is and what it is not, the analysis of the literature shows that it is a process that involves strategical and orga-nizational dimensions and implies change. In our perspective, it is dynamic and contest specific, so our approach is not discovering why it fails or gets success, but understanding which organizational dynamics take place in a digital transformation experience. As stated by Andersson et al. [17] *"The dynamics of how these changes come about in practice is however not known, and there is thus a need to look more carefully at how the work of public administrators is transformed though the devel-opment and implementation of automated technologies".*

Managerial literature, in fact, has mostly focused on understanding what are the critical success factor enabling digital transformation in the public sector, and except for a few of contributions [14] has not investigated the different practices adopted in diverse public administrations according to an interpretative perspective. Not a great effort was addressed to investigating how different practices take place in different public contexts.

3   Digital Transformation and Knowledge Translation

A number of researchers have dealt with the interfaces of knowledge transfer among individuals engaged in inter-organisational collaborations across different domains of expertise [5, 18]. Specific forms of expertise play an important role in facilitating the coordination and transfer of knowledge across boundaries. The transfer of knowledge is a complex process that depends, to a great extent, on organizations' characteristics, but also on the type of management they adopt [19]. Rajalo and Vadi [20] described boundary-crossing and pragmatic boundary-crossing mechanisms as different practices used to facilitate communication and build a common framework among the partners.

Collaboration between heterogeneous actors from different organizational set-tings involved in a process of digital transformation often implies complex knowl-edge translation acts because each partner has his/her own nomenclature, demands and expectations of innovation [21]. Knowledge translation becomes a (key) glue able foster knowledge transfer [22]. In these settings, translation is a dynamic pro-cess, where each actor operates at the organisational level to produce a specific output (a document, report, video, etc.). This implies adopting others' perspectives and selecting a framework and words that can be easily understood by others.

One of the most critical factors is the creation of an interactional space, where actors work together to overcome their individual and organisational interests and needs and to negotiate and collaborate to achieve a common goal [18]. Establishing this space is vitally important and may need specific effort: every player involved should his/her language to adopt a different framework, moving from his/her "natural environment" [23]. Computer technicians, for instance, often use a more technical-specialist language, and the vocabulary can be hard to understand and share. Similarly, in any public administration and the courts in particular, the staff use its own language and has a particular way of storing and transferring knowledge.

4 Methodology

The case was a digital transformation project triggered by the introduction of the Telematics Civil Process in the Supreme Court of Cassation in Italy.

Three data collection techniques were used: documentary analysis, participant observation and semi-structured interviews with clerks and judges involved in the project team. The data collection was carried out between early July 2019 and December 2021. Issues then emerged naturally from the data [24], rather than the data being fitted to predetermined categories.

Participant observation was the main source of data for the rest of this study. Two of the authors were directly involved in the project team. During their fieldwork, they spent 1 day a week in the Court from 9 a.m. to 1 p.m. Having free access to the Court premises, they could make many formal and informal contacts and become relatively familiar with clerks and judges.

The project was configured in the mode of the so-called research-intervention [25]: from the point of view of the two researchers, it unfolded according to the following two features:

- A close link between theory and practice to configure an epistemology of knowing-transforming and vice-versa
- A participatory approach: in order to produce knowledge for improving organizational practices, it was necessary to pursue active collaboration, at all stages of the research, among all actors involved, rather than attempting to minimize their influence on the research design

The assessing and redesign methodologies adopted can be summarized as follows:

- Appreciative Inquiry Change Management Approach. This is a "participatory" approach to organizational change that is based on collaborative methods of planning, diagnosis (organizational check-up) and intervention, such as Focus Group, Action Planning and Appreciative Inquiry Summit [26].
- Task Technology Fit. The approach allows for the detection and evaluation of the degree to which information technology assists an organizational actor (individual, group, structure) in performing its specific task. The Task Technology Fit

approach wishes to establish the degree of fit between the characteristics of the task that the user of a given technology must perform and the solutions offered by the application or computer system, to support a successful performance [27].

- Stakeholder Analysis [28]. This methodology represented the basis for organizing the information to be acquired during meetings with the various qualified stakeholders, aimed at identifying the opportunities and constraints of organizational change and development within a complex system.
- Organizational Capability Maturity Model. The approach aims at process improvement; its goal is to help the organization improve its performance [29].

5   Case Analysis

5.1   The Telematics Civil Process

The Telematics Civil Process is enabled through the online remote execution of operations—such as document filing, transmission of communications and notifications, consultation of the proceedings status using the registry held by the chancery, consultation of the files and case law—which previously were only available by physically visiting the Court chancery.

The rationale for the introduction of the Telematics Civil Process is to simplify the process requirements for lawyers, magistrates and court clerks. It allows practitioners and offices to exploit the potential of delocalisation and management in dematerialised form of the various procedural activities, as well as remote consultation of telematic files. It is a "systemic" technology, replacing operational practices based on paper-based information exchange, not replaceable and enabling new functions and services. Its systemic characteristic requires strong integration in input–output processes.

The experience of the courts of first and second instance has made clear that it is essential that the process of design and implementation of Telematics Civil Process technology systems is not developed using a purely top-down logic. Instead, it needs to be "built" through a collaborative approach of sharing knowledge, practices and experiences of the various stakeholders involved in the process, both internal and external to the courts. The acquisition of "digital" knowledge and skills, for example, cannot be achieved through mere participation in a training course on software features. It requires effective practice, participation and involvement of people in the assessing and redesign of workflows. Collaborative and organisational learning paths based on the transfer of perspectives and experiences must take into account the fact that any change initiative requires a translation and reinterpretation that looks at the needs, conditions and constraints of the organisational context in which the technological up-grading and change management initiative is designed and implemented [30].

5.2 The Steps of the Project

The project developed by the University of Campania was based on a "research-intervention" approach aimed at developing and implementing design solutions in order to solve real and contingent problems of organizational, institutional and social systems [31] and achieve the following goals/deliverables:

- Organizational proposals for innovation of court services, based on the potential offered by the Telematics Civil Process
- Proposals for the redesign of the relationship between the registry and the magistrate in view of the telematic filing of measures, taking into account the necessary effects on the application of *Massimario* and *Italgiureweb*
- Management proposals in a transitional phase following the launch of digital filings

The project, which began in September 2019 and is still ongoing, is divided into the following three work packages:

- WP1. Survey of the "Task–Technology fit AS IS" of the Supreme Court of Cassation
- WP2. Development and organizational change of Sections, Registry services and other structures of the Supreme Court of Cassation Civil Area as a result of the introduction of the electronic filing of documents following the implementation of the PCT
- WP3. Development and organizational change in support of the Presidents of Section and Councillors of the Civil Area Sections of the Supreme Court of Cassation Civil Area as a result of the launch of the introduction of the magistrate's computer system Desk

At the end of 2021, the project was "located" in WP2.

5.3 Project Development and Translation Tools

This section explains the change management actions and tools activated by researchers that supported knowledge translation processes.

In WP1, the members of the project team carried out a document and desk analysis, and participated to planning meetings and focus groups. The information elaborated was shared preliminarily and informally by means of forms and check lists (shared with the Ministry of Justice). During the focus groups, two of the authors were involved both in leading the discussion and observing; they led participants to formulate opinions on topics collectively recognized as relevant to the Court of Cassation. To begin with, the theme of the discussion was presented, preparing participants for the issues that would be addressed, making them appear as common situations on which they had already been confronted in other occasions and avoiding digressions or misunderstandings about the questions submitted. The observer was involved in taking notes and studying the dynamics and the climate established in the team. In a subsequent phase, the observer shared with the presenter his perceptions for an improved management of the focus groups. The researchers developed a memorandum outlining thoughts that emerged in the focus group that were shared by all participants.

The assessment of the impact of digital systems on the organizational workflow was interpreted by referring to Venkatraman's model [32]. This approach highlights the facilitating role of ICT with reference to the ability to redesign and reconfigure the processes of intra- and inter-organizational activities. The analytical frame of the model focuses on two parameters of observation: the analysis of the impact of digital systems on potential benefits in terms of performance and the level of change of the relationships that link internal activities to those carried out outside the organization. The hypothesis underlying Venkatraman's model is that the benefits related to the introduction of new digital solutions are limited if such solutions are applied without a corresponding change in the way the different activities that define the workflow are implemented and coordinated.

The researchers created an ad hoc visualization tool to illustrate to other team members the results of the analysis carried out through Venkatraman's model. This visualization technique relies on dimensions such as colour, size, shape, texture and visual orientation, affecting the insights derived from the data. The use of pictures, graphs and colours makes it possible to grasp complex relationships between many different factors very quickly, supporting fruitful communication, assessing, and decision-making processes. The analysis showed that the introduction of the Telematics Civil Process requires business process improvement interventions, with a level of change (incremental/radical) linked to the impacts of the technology on the process. In this perspective, such impacts have been "labelled" in different types:

- Type 1: automation of a single operation or activities within a process
- Type 2: change or development of information support functions for the processing of individual operations or activities within a process
- Type 3: integration between different processes
- Type 4: dismissal of the process and reconfiguration of the responsibilities (scope) of the organizational unit of reference

The different processes had been represented in the graphs and figures with different colours. The back office activities of the central clerk's office, for instance, have been identified as having impact type 4 (yellow). The back-office of the central clerk's office—in the jargon common in the offices called *Sala Pietrostefani*—has the function of verifying and arranging the dossier formed by the clerks' front-office, processing the appeals presented by the Attorney General's Office, completing the data entered in the computer system and sending to the Sixth Section the dossiers which the latter is able to handle in a given time. The personnel available consisted of ten employees, two managers and three porters. The activities of the back-office are closely linked to the paper nature of the dossiers and the consequent difficulty in managing the dossiers in the physical space available and the handling due to the high number of legal causes. The back-office gathers registered appeals with all the relevant subsequent acts which, for logistic reasons, after filing are kept in a separate archive by role number and are not immediately included in the file. An in-depth check is then carried out on the presence of all registered acts and on the consistency of the information available in the current computer system. Once the control is completed, the files are passed on to the Sixth Civil Section. With the introduction of the digital civil process, these activities will lose their organizational "meaning": in substance, they will disappear, freeing up human resources for the digital management and control of the judicial proceedings. The awareness of the elimination of this process was shown through the report and the figures constructed by the researchers from the perspective of Venkatraman's model, triggered the discussion among the project team members of how to "reuse" human resources formerly engaged in the *Sala Pietrostefani*.

During WP2, a memorandum of understanding was signed between the Supreme Court, the Ministry of Justice, the Attorney General's Office, and the National Forensic Council. The beginning of an experimental phase in the implementation of the digital process was to set to take place from October 2020, in order to test the technological system, verify the functionality of the revised error codes and that of the acceptance/correction phase by clerks.

During the design and implementation phase of the digital process a critical issues was related to the differences in background and language adopted by the different stakeholders involved in the process. In particular, we refer to the difficulties in "communication" between the computer scientists of the software house that was entrusted with the design of the information system, the Ministry of Justice officials, the court clerks and the judges. Each of these actors was the bearer on the one hand of specific needs (technological, legal, administrative, etc.) and on the other hand, of extremely specialized technical language that was difficult to understand by the other stakeholders. One of the major goals was to develop a set of organizational actions aimed at facilitating data, information, and knowledge transfer among the different groups aimed at integrating viewpoints, needs and ways of working and overcoming resistance to change.

In order to improve the organizational development and technological upgrading, in this phase, the researchers suggested, built and implemented a set of organizational actions/tools (such as a coherent bundle of organizational actions) conceived in a systemic and holistic way. These tools aimed at improving both communication and coordination between the different actors involved (e.g., software house, justice ministry officials, judges, clerks, lawyers' representatives, etc.) also promoting forms of individual and organizational knowledge transfer.

In particular, such organizational actions/tools consisted in:

- Setting up a "leading team". This team promoted the adoption of the organizational measures necessary to support the effective start-up and development of the digital process in the Supreme Court, also through the possible formulation of regulatory changes that may be appropriate as a result of experimentation and during the first phase of implementation. This team also promotes IT training for all those involved (administrative and technical staff, lawyers, magistrates), also through the organization of joint and transversal initiatives among the various institutional actors, for the appropriate sharing and mutual knowledge of all phases (filing of acts by the parties, acceptance by the Registry, consultation of acts and filing of orders by the magistrates). The team is made up of judges and clerks of the Court and representatives of the Minister of Justice

- Setting up a temporary operational working team. An additional operational working team was established, aiming at the effective development of techno-logical solutions and organizational practices based on the opportunities and constraints offered by the software being designed and the organizational char-acteristics of the Supreme Court. This team was designed as a "building block of a social learning system" and its members (designers of the software house, a selected group of court clerks and Minister staff) represented the social "contain-ers" of the skills that constitute these systems. It was an informal organizational entity in which people developed and shared practices, technological/organiza-tional solutions, ways of doing things, languages, as a logical consequence of their involvement in this common activity. The team made a systematic use of meetings and gatherings (also remotely)

- Carrying out training and learning development activities. The implementation of the digital process during the experimentation phase envisaged a modular training activity towards clerks and judges. Organizational training for heads of offices, judges and administrative staff, during implementation, has been carried out through a logic of action learning, i.e. "training-action" aimed at individual, group and organizational development, through concrete experience in which these actors learn with others to work on real problems and reflect on their expe-rience. The modalities through which these training paths have been devel-oped are:

  - Ad hoc video tutorials made by the software house to explain features and procedures of the new software
  - Automated problem solving chatbot for users
  - Interactive webinar sessions in which participants could interact among each other and with the "coordinator" of the seminar (supplier/software developer) through the tools available from videoconferencing systems, dealing with the different functionalities and features of the software (practical demonstration)
  - Help desk for problem solving, aimed at providing technical and/or informa-tive assistance/support to the users

The head of the administrative unit of the Court highlighted:

Only through building interdisciplinary working groups, and interactive webinar sessions were we able to develop a genuine form of dialogue with those who were designing the new information system. Before, it seemed like we were speaking different languages. They were talking about functions, procedures and computer interfaces; we were using exclu-sively legal jargon. Building moments and spaces for translating each other's needs was an essential element in the kick-off of the PCT. The role of facilitators (the researchers involved in the project) was crucial in this regard.

According to a software house manager:

> We couldn't figure out what the real problem was for the clerks to handle telematics filing. We used to have meetings that ended in nothing ... where everyone left slamming the door. Through a simulated session developed in the temporary operational working team, we realized that we needed to add a different filing scheduling function to move forward.

6   Discussion and Concluding Remarks

Digital transformation processes in public administration are complex organizational change interventions [33]. They go well beyond the "simple transition" from paper to digital. Digitization is a complex phenomenon that involves redesigning and managing the organizational arrangements, dynamics, processes, practices, tools, and organizational and inter-organizational relationships of the various stakeholders involved [15].

In the case under scrutiny, the methodologies and practices of change management, supporting the process of digital transformation in the Supreme Court of Cassation, were illustrated.

In fact, change in public administration is linked not only to the innovation of rules and procedures, but also to the management of people, through the adoption of an approach that can be termed as "behavioural" [34]. Manzoni and Angehrn [35], Taylor and Helfat [36] and Zorn [37] emphasize that successful change implementation efforts are as much a function of the ability to manage people interaction and knowledge translation as they are of the adoption of effective technology. The process of translating and transfer knowledge is particularly challenging in the public administration because of the pressure towards process and service innovation.

In the case analysed in this chapter, approaches, methods and tools for change management have been designed in accordance with a logic oriented towards participation, involvement and cooperation of the different organizational actors, aiming at a bottom-up re-design of activities and work processes. Change management includes, in fact, the design and implementation of a holistic system of both hard and soft actions [38], ranging from the redesign of employee tasks and duties to training related to new digital skills, from the modification of the performance appraisal system to the choice of new criteria for staff selection, from interventions on people motivation and involvement to the understanding of how to limit resistance to change and facilitate knowledge translation [39].

Both theoretical and empirical sections made clear that clerks, magistrates and computer technicians have different languages and styles and may fall into the trap of thinking that their knowledge is "correct" [23]. This makes it harder to understand another point of view [21]. Each person is knowledgeable about specific tools and methods and is often suspicious of other perspectives.

The set of actions developed for the management of the organizational change project—from the establishment of focus groups and interdisciplinary working groups to the implementation of interactive webinars, to the deployment of academic researchers in the role of facilitators—are interpreted as a system (a "place") for knowledge translation that facilitated the process of organizational change triggered by the digital transformation. Furthermore, our findings showed how knowledge visualization could be used to foster knowledge translation and sharing among team members. Knowledge visualization is understood as both a collective and interactional process and a systematic approach where different players translate their expertise, share a framework and develop common ground to support assessing and decision-making [8]. In this respect, we also explore how the adoption of knowledge visualization tools may help to support effective knowledge translation.

In our case study we have shown that the project of change itself may act as a knowledge translation mechanism. Such project can therefore be interpreted as the interactional space where different players share the framework and develop a common language. The bottom-up approach pushes participants to adopt organizational tools and languages that in turn become shared assets of the collaboration. This means that both project, as coordination mechanism, and project tools themselves have the potential to become a fruitful interactional space where participants may positively enhance knowledge translation.

The effectiveness of organizational change triggered by a disruptive technology, as widely established in the literature [40, 41], depends not only on the intrinsic characteristics of the new ICT, but also on the ability to develop a coherent and integrated *bundle* of redesign interventions at multiple organizational levels and, more generally, on how knowledge is translated among the different stakeholders involved. Our study had some limitations though, which must be taken into account when evaluating its results. First, we adopted a qualitative approach, therefore results may not be widely generalizable. Second, the case study was set in a specific context that has influenced the outcomes of our analysis.

References

1. Hanelt, A., Bohnsack, R., Marz, D., & Antunes Marante, C. (2021). A systematic review of the literature on digital transformation: Insights and implications for strategy and organizational change. *Journal of Management Studies, 58*(5), 1159–1119.
2. Sidorenko, E. L., Bartsits, I. N., & Khisamova, Z. I. (2019). The efficiency of digital public administration assessing: Theoretical and applied aspects. *Public Administration Issues, 2*, 93–114.
3. Susskind, R. O. C. (2016). *The future of justice.* Oxford University Press.
4. Pasmore, W., Winby, S., Mohrman, S. A., & Vanasse, R. (2019). Reflections: Sociotechnical systems design and organization change. *Journal of Change Management, 19*(2), 67–85.
5. Simeone, L., Secundo, G., & Schiuma, G. (2018). Arts and design as translational mechanisms for academic entrepreneurship: the metaLAB at Harvard case study. *Journal of Business Research, 85*, 434–443.

6. Simeone, L., Secundo, G., & Schiuma, G. (2017). Knowledge translation mechanisms in open innovation: the role of design in R&D projects. *Journal of Knowledge Management, 21*(6), 1406–1429.
7. Tabrizi, B., Lam, E., Girard, K., & Irvin, V. (2019). Digital transformation is not about technology. *Harvard Business Review, 13*, 1–6.
8. Canonico, P., De Nito, E., Esposito, V., Fattoruso, G., Pezzillo Iacono, M., & Mangia, G. (2022). Visualizing knowledge for decision-making in Lean Production Development settings. Insights from the automotive industry. *Management Decision, 60*(4), 1076–1094.
9. Vintar, M. (2010). Current and future public management reforms: Does technology matter? *NISPAcee Journal of Public Administration and Policy, 3*(2), 13–30.
10. Wessel, L., Baiyere, A., Ologeanu-Taddei, R., Cha, J., & Blegind-Jensen, T. (2021). Unpacking the difference between digital transformation and IT-enabled organizational transformation. *Journal of the Association for Information Systems, 22*(1).
11. Poole, M., & Van de Ven, A. (2004). *Handbook of organizational change and innovation.* Oxford University Press.
12. European Commission. (2013). Powering European public sector innovation: Towards a new architecture. Retrieved from https://ec.europa.eu/digital-single-market/en/news/powering-european-public-sector-innovation-towards-new-architecture.
13. Bjerke-Busch, L. S., & Aspelund, A. (2021). Identifying barriers for digital transformation in the public sector. In D. R. A. Schallmo & J. Tidd (Eds.), *Digitalization. Management for professionals.* Springer.
14. Mergel, I., Edelmann, N., & Hauga, N. (2019). Defining digital transformation: Results from expert interviews. *Government Information Quarterly, 36*, 1–16.
15. Denhardt, J. V., & Denhardt, R. B. (2015). *The new public service: Serving, not steering.* Routledge.
16. Janowsky, T. (2015). Digital government evolution: From transformation to contextualization. *Government Information Quarterly, 32*, 221–236.
17. Andersson, C., Hallin, A., & Ivory, C. (2022). Unpacking the digitalisation of public services: Configuring work during automation in local government. *Government Information Quarterly, 39*, 1–10.
18. Canonico, P., De Nito, E., Esposito, V., Pezzillo Iacono, M., & Mangia, G. (2020). Understanding knowledge translation in university–industry research projects: a case analysis in the automotive sector. *Management Decision, 58*(9), 1863–1884.
19. Siegel, D., Veugelers, R., & Wright, M. (2007). Technology transfer offices and commercialization of university intellectual property: Performance and policy implications. *Review Literature and Arts of the Americas, 23*(4), 640–660.
20. Rajalo, S., & Vadi, M. (2017). University-industry innovation collaboration: reconceptualization. *Technovation, 62–63*, 42–54.
21. Sandberg, J., Holmström, J., Napier, N., & Leven, P. (2015). Balancing diversity in innovation networks. *European Journal of Innovation Management, 18*(1), 44–69.
22. Petrilli, S. (2003). Translation and semiosis: introduction. In S. Petrilli (Ed.), *Translation* (pp. 17–37). Rodopi.
23. de Rond, M., & Bouchikhi, H. (2004). On the dialectics of strategic alliances. *Organization Science, 15*, 156–169.
24. Caven, V., Navarro, E., & Diop, M. (2012). A cross-national study of accommodating and 'usurpatory' practices by women architects in the UK, Spain and France. *Architectural Theory Review, 17*(2/3), 365–377.
25. Butera, F. (1980). La ricerca intervento. In P. Bontadini & G. Gasparini (Eds.), *Teoria della organizzazione e realtà italiana: problemi e contributi.* Franco Angeli.
26. Cooperrider, D. L., & Srivastva, S. (1987). *Appreciative inquiry in organizational life, research in organizational change and development.* JAI Press.
27. Goodhue, D. L., & Thompson, R. L. (1995). Task-technology fit and individual performance. *MIS Quarterly, 19*(2).

28. Freeman, R. E. (1984). *Strategic management: A stakeholder approach.* Pitman.
29. Martinez, M., Di Nauta, P., & Sarno, D. (2017). Real and apparent changes of organizational processes in the era of big data analytics. *Studi Organizzativi, 2.*
30. Plesner, U., Justesen, L., & Glerup, C. (2018). The transformation of work in digitized public sector organizations. *Journal of Organizational Change Management, 31*(5), 1176–1190.
31. Burton, R. M., Obel, B., & Hakonsson, D. D. (2015). *Organizational design: A step-by-step approach.* Cambridge University Press.
32. Venkataraman, N. (1994). IT-enabled business transformation: From automation to business scope redefinition. *Sloan Management Review, 35*(2), 73–87.
33. Klijn, E. H. (2008). Complexity theory and Public Administration: what is new? Key concepts in complexity theory compared to their counterparts in public administration. *Public Management Review, 10*(3), 299–317.
34. Hinna, A., Mameli, S., & Mangia, G. (2016). *La pubblica amministrazione in movimento. Competenze, comportamenti e regole.* Egea.
35. Manzoni, J.-F., & Angehrn, A. A. (1997). Understanding organizational dynamics of IT-enabled change: a multimedia simulation approach. *Journal of Management Information Systems, 14*(3), 109–140.
36. Taylor, A., & Helfat, C. E. (2009). Organizational linkages for surviving technological change: Complementary assets, middle management, and ambidexterity. *Organization Science, 20*(4), 718–739.
37. Zorn, T. E. (2003). The emotionality of information and communication technology implementation. *Journal of Communication Management, 7*(2), 160–171.
38. Pezzillo Iacono, M., De Nito, E., Martinez, M., & Mercurio, R. (2017). Exploring the hidden aspect of organizational change: The constellation of controls at a FCA Plant. *Studi Organizzativi, 2.*
39. Liyanage, C., Elhag, T., Ballal, T., & Li, Q. (2009). Knowledge communication and translation—A knowledge transfer model. *Journal of Knowledge Management, 13*(3), 118–131.
40. Eriksson, C. B. (2004). The effects of change programs on employees' emotions. *Personnel Review, 33*(1), 110–126.
41. Orlikowski, W. J. (1996). Improvising organizational transformation over time: A situated change perspective. *Information Systems Research, 7*(1), 63–92.

Group Workshop as a "Human-Centered Approach" for Identification and Selection of Business Processes for Robotic Process Automation

Lars Berghuis, Abhishta Abhishta, Wouter van Heeswijk, and Aizhan Tursunbayeva

Abstract Robotic process automation (RPA) has been rapidly diffusing in organizations to automate monotonous business processes. Nevertheless, only about half of such projects are successful, as organizations struggle to identify simple yet impactful processes. Existing approaches for selecting business processes for RPA include process mining and individual interviews. These have been often charged to be time-consuming, unsystematic, overly complex, and dependent primarily on individual perspectives. In this empirical study, we explore the deployment of group intelligence to select business processes suitable for RPA. We investigate whether and how a group of relevant actors can jointly generate ideas, evaluate them, and select the most salient processes for RPA automation. We draw on the design science to develop a human-centered artifact that fulfills actors' needs—a group workshop for RPA identification and selection—and to assess such artifacts. The workshop incorporates elements of the business process management lifecycle and nominal brainstorming. The workshop is designed by drawing on the recommendations of the existing relevant literature. A real-life group-based RPA identification and selection workshop experiment was conducted with a group of employees of an audit firm located in the Netherlands. A follow-up survey and interviews were carried out with the participants to evaluate the workshop, indicating an overall positive experience and suitability to effectively identify relevant processes. This study proposes a new systematic group approach for identifying and selecting business processes for RPA, which could be applied in a variety of contexts and organizations. It also puts forward a comprehensive agenda for future research and practice.

Keywords RPA · Group · Human-centered · Workshop · Methodology

L. Berghuis (✉) · A. Abhishta · W. van Heeswijk
University of Twente, Enschede, The Netherlands
e-mail: Lars.Berghuis@nl.ey.com

A. Tursunbayeva
University of Naples 'Parthenope', Naples, Italy

© The Author(s), under exclusive license to Springer Nature Switzerland AG 2024
A. Lazazzara et al. (eds.), *Towards Digital and Sustainable Organisations*,
Lecture Notes in Information Systems and Organisation 65,
https://doi.org/10.1007/978-3-031-52880-4_7

103

1   Introduction and Background

Automatization of organizational processes has previously touched primarily on production lines. However, a seminal work by Osborne and Frey [1] predicted that not only repetitive, routine, and monotonous jobs would be automated in the future, but also those that involve knowledge work, such as jobs of accountants and auditors. On one side, these results have been highly debated. On the other, the exponential development of technologies such as Robotic process automation (RPA) and their growing diffusion in organizations to automate monotonous business processes—such as invoice processing, onboarding, or payment reminder notification—make us all take the conclusions of [1] seriously. Nearly 53% of respondents of Deloitte's RPA survey have started their RPA journey already in 2018 and their number was planned to increase to 72% in 2020. Moreover, the report also concluded that if this trend continues, RPA will achieve near-universal adoption within 5 years [2].

RPA is software that permits the automation of tasks previously executed by humans. For example, this software allows, via a script, to let a digital robot access websites and system applications to read, extract or fill in data [3]. The diffusion of RPA in organizations has been driven by such expected benefits as savings on employees' costs and increased employee satisfaction [4]. Furthermore, compared to traditional process automation—which may require substantial software development skills—RPA does not change any underlying organizational information technology (IT) systems, operating solely on the front-end. Whereas traditional process automation often requires developers to add or alter code of programs, such as altering back-end code and writing Application Programming Interfaces (APIs), RPA only requires development within the RPA tool, creating an automation layer on top of existing programs. As such, it does not invade any of the business' IT infrastructure and simplifies implementation [3, 5]. Nevertheless, only about half of such projects are successful, as organizations struggle to identifying simple yet impactful processes that require no "human" interventions, and whose automation can generate business value. For example, Deloitte's survey reported that 63% of 400 respondents did not meet the expected deadline for RPA projects [2], while between 30 and 50% of these failed their projects. One of the main reasons for this was claimed to be difficulties in finding processes fitting the RPA solution [3, 6]. It was also highlighted that RPA is not a solution to each process, and its application to a specific process or task requires a careful analysis of the automation potential including the assessment of potential benefits and risks. The latter includes excessive maintenance or incorrect data processing, which can consequently lead to lengthy and costly implementations, lowered enthusiasm, and missing out on organizational automation opportunities [7].

Existing approaches for selecting business processes for RPA include individual interviews or process mining. The former method drawing on individual perspectives was mentioned as potentially too time-consuming, unsystematic, and/or subject to the human judgment or understanding of what RPA is. The latter approach seems to be a solution to this problem that can contribute to human decision-making by involving algorithms to calculate RPA suitability for a process [8], although this method was also referred to as too complex [9] and thus not suitable for all types of organizations. Process mining and analysis rely on event logs and specific IT skills, which might not be available in all smaller and medium-sized enterprises [10].

This research sets to address the shortcomings of current RPA process identification and selection methods by designing a new approach. To do it, we hypothesize that RPA process identification and selection can draw on group intelligence—e.g., group workshops—where multiple relevant stakeholders can be involved to jointly generate ideas, discuss, evaluate them, and select among these the most suitable process for RPA automation. The specific research question set for this study was "Whether and/or how can a workshop-based process selection method contribute to the identification of suitable business processes for the implementation of RPA?"

It is worthwhile to acknowledge that group workshops have already been suggested as a suitable approach for the identification and selection of RPA processes [11]. However, to the best of our knowledge, neither this study nor any others have tried to verify this proposition empirically, nor did they describe whether or how group workshops can be adopted in organizations for RPA identification or selection.

To design the group-based approach we drew on the design cycle approach, commonly used in information systems and software engineering studies to design human-centered artifacts that fulfill actors' needs and to assess such artifacts, as well as brainstorming techniques diffused in organization studies literature. The artifact designed in this study, drawing on recommendations of these two corpora of literature, is a group workshop for RPA identification and selection. Specifically, the workshop incorporates elements of the business process management (BPM) life-cycle [12] and nominal brainstorming [13]. A real-life group-based RPA identification and selection workshop experiment was conducted with a group of employees of one of the audit firms located in the Netherlands. A follow-up survey was carried out with the workshop's participants to evaluate the workshop. In addition, interviews with experts, both experienced with RPA and auditing, were conducted to evaluate the outcome of the workshop.

In the remainder of this article, we briefly describe the design cycle approach enriched with the brainstorming method that informed the workshop design. We then describe the workshop experiment and evaluation methodology, followed by a presentation of the findings. The article concludes with a discussion of our findings and offers recommendations for future research and practice.

2 Theoretical Framework

This study builds on the design science research commonly used within the information system and software engineering scholars to solve problems or create opportunities by designing software or systems—artifacts—that fulfill the needs of stakeholders [12]. Specifically, design science iteration is performed through (a) Designing an artifact (or treatment) that contributes to the improvement of performance and (b) empirically investigating the performance of such artifact (i.e., validation of a treatment) [12]. The artifact in our study is a group workshop that can lead to the identification and selection of suitable RPA processes for organizations [12].

The design cycle of an artifact includes four phases: "Problem investigation", "Treatment design", "Treatment validation", and "Implementation evaluation" (see Fig. 1). This specific paper reports on the Treatment design and Treatment validation phases, as the former phase has been addressed in a preliminary study that informed this research [14], while the latter is out of the scope of this study.

2.1 Treatment Design

To ensure the systematic approach for the development of the workshop, within the *treatment design phase* we drew on the BPM lifecycle framework [10] often used for optimizing business processes including RPA projects [15]. Although the BPM lifecycle provides technical and processual guidance on the overall phases including process identification, discovery and analysis that process management should involve, it does not reveal potential structures for user/human involvement in these sub-phases. In particular, we observed that it does not indicate whether and how the phases could be executed in a group setting. This knowledge gap will be investigated in this study, addressing questions pertaining to the number of participants, and their experiences or roles that lead to the most effective, efficient, and human-centered approach for identifying processes. To negate present shortcomings, we enriched the BPM framework with the "Brainstorming" method that has been used for decades in social science research [13].

Fig. 1 Design cycle phases

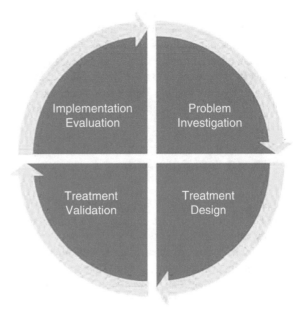

Brainstorming, as proposed by Osborn in 1953, is often used for finding innovative solutions to problems by letting multiple individuals use "the brain to storm a creative problem". The main idea behind brainstorming is that the whole (i.e., the group) is greater than the sum of parts (i.e., individuals). Brainstorming is suitable to evaluate whether products are feasible, reliable, and economically interesting [13]. Thus, it is frequently used in decision-making by managers and practitioners [13].

Overall, the BPM lifecycle provides guidance and tools for identifying and managing business processes through three main sequential phases: *Process Identification*, *Process Discovery* and *Process Analysis*. Meanwhile, brainstorming is comprised of two phases: *Idea Generation* and *Idea Evaluation* [13]. The former coincides with the BPM's identification phase, while the latter aligns with its Discovery and Analysis phases [9]. Thus, we identified brainstorming as a suitable method to be integrated with BPM for RPA process identification and evaluation. There are three primary types of brainstorming including *Standard* (participants have interactive sessions during both brainstorming phases), *Nominal* (participants generate ideas individually during the idea generation phase), and *Electronic* (participants could be fully anonymized via a virtual session) [16]. It has been suggested that the latter two outperform the former approach in terms of the number of ideas as well as their quality [16]. Thus, in our study, we combined these two approaches to benefit from their strengths. Indeed, electronic brainstorming (EBS) was identified as most effective when the group is large (e.g., more than eight group members), while nominal brainstorming (NBS) does not impose restrictions on the number of participants. Moreover, NBS fosters interactive group discussions between participants, in which they can openly communicate ideas, comments, or concerns. Meanwhile, EBS permits participants to attend the workshop virtually, which was imperative as the study was conducted during the lockdown introduced due to the Covid-19 pandemic.

Below we briefly discuss the BPM lifecycle phases recognizing the efforts of previous authors:

Process Identification

This is the phase in which a business problem is posed [10]. It focuses on identifying relevant processes in a business unit, division, or even the whole organization (often based on specific pre-defined criteria) for further discovery and analysis to ultimately be redesigned and implemented. A Process landscape comprises core, management, and support processes dimensions. It is frequently used during process identification to map all processes within an organization, while a Process profile combines specific descriptions (e.g., process name, goals, owner, etc.) about identified processes.

Process Discovery

In this phase, already identified and described (AS-IS) processes are modeled into a visual representation to provide a better understanding of the process including their strengths and weaknesses. Such modeling efforts of business processes have already been applied to RPA implementations [17].

Process Analysis
In this phase, the portfolio of modeled processes is analyzed to determine whether these should be optimized, for example, to reduce their cycle time, operational costs, or error rate. In other words, this phase determines whether processes should be RPA-ed or not. To differentiate between different RPA potentials of each process, we developed, in our preliminary study, a matrix that can help to classify each process into "Limited", "Potential", "Strategic" or "Quick Wins" categories (see Fig. 3 and [14] for discussion).

2.2   Treatment Validation

The *Treatment validation phase* of the Design cycle involves evaluation of the artifact and understanding of whether any adjustment to the artifact needs to be made [12]. To ensure a well-rounded evaluation this need to involve both the validation of the artifact (i.e., workshop), as well as its outcomes (e.g., identified RPA processes). The positive outcome of this evaluation would intend that the artifact is ready for implementation.

3   Methodology

Below we describe our approach to the workshop design, as well as an experiment we run to evaluate it.

The workshop was designed to have two sessions: (1) Focused on the Process identification phase (see Appendix 1) and (2) Focused on Process Discovery, and Process Analysis phases (see Fig. 2 and Appendix 2). The workshops were conducted online (via Microsoft Teams), which permitted digital tools (e.g., Padlet and Draw.io) to be prepared in advance. Considering the recommendations for the duration of the workshop [18], each workshop session lasted for circa 2 h. The workshops were planned to be held in 2 days.

3.1   Treatment Design

Process Identification
Responding to the calls of the previous research [19] and building on the findings of the literature review that informed this study [14], at the beginning of the first workshop participants were first planned to be provided with introductory information on RPA, illustrative examples of RPA, and its potential benefits and opportunities.

Following the brainstorming approach for process identification, two principal roles were envisioned to be present during the workshop: (1) facilitators who

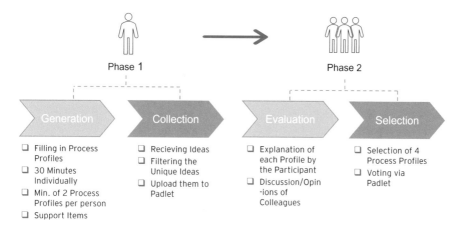

Phase 1 → Phase 2

Generation ➤ **Collection** ➤ **Evaluation** ➤ **Selection**

Generation	Collection	Evaluation	Selection
❑ Filling in Process Profiles ❑ 30 Minutes Individually ❑ Min. of 2 Process Profiles per person ❑ Support Items	❑ Recieving Ideas ❑ Filtering the Unique Ideas ❑ Upload them to Padlet	❑ Explanation of each Profile by the Participant ❑ Discussion/Opin-ions of Colleagues	❑ Selection of 4 Process Profiles ❑ Voting via Padlet

Fig. 2 Integration of NBS with the BPM lifecycle phases

coordinate the session to ensure balanced input and (2) participants who generate ideas and evaluate those of others [13]. The latter was planned to be with the different levels of knowledge and expertise of the processes in concern to increase the number of ideas and their quality [20], such as managers familiar with the strategic aspects of the processes, and employees familiar with their operational side. The workshop design proposed having two facilitators (the first author of this paper, and one of the department managers), and eight invited participants within the department; the recommended number for optimal brainstorming that can enable a flow of ideas and a fluid discussion [16].

At this phase, the participants were envisioned to work individually (e.g., to avoid free-riding) to brainstorm and profile at least two processes for RPA with the help of a process landscape and process criteria tools. The process landscape was developed after interviewing three departmental managers about the core, management, and supporting processes present in the department (see [14] for discussion).

A Padlet was created, where the participants could upload their process profiles (see Appendix 3). These profiles were then planned to be reviewed by the facilitators to eliminate duplicates, while the workshop participants could take a break. Unique process profiles were planned to be explained by their proponents in a facilitated discussion that could resolve any questions. All these processes were then planned to be voted by the workshop participants individually via Padlet to select four processes to pass to the following workshop.

Process Discovery and Process Analysis
In the Process Discovery and Process Analysis phase the shortlisted processes were planned to be evaluated in a group discussion as per the criteria that emerged from the preliminary literature review including their complexity and the potential value added to the business (see [14] for discussion).

The Process Discovery and Process Analysis phase were overall planned to start with a short recap of the first session to refresh the participants' memory and an introduction to Business Process Modelling (via BPMN-R language). Subsequently, each of the shortlisted processes was first planned to be profiled in Draw.io by each of the participants. This is to get the most detailed description of each process and to check whether the participants share their visions for the same processes. As a result, two models of each process profile were envisioned to be created: four profiles re-profiled by eight participants planned for this workshop individually. Eight participants were planned to give all participants sufficient time for proper discussion of their ideas while ensuring an interactive and dynamic session. Each model then was intended to be presented by the "creator", allowing the remaining participants to pose questions and comments. The models were envisioned to be discussed as a group to examine the model completeness and accuracy of the modeled processes.

The final step was planned to be filling the developed in advance RPA prioritization and selection matrix (see Fig. 3). Also, this activity was planned to be conducted as a group. Each participant should give their opinion on where each of the processes should be positioned within the matrix. The objective was to reach a consensus. Therefore, the facilitator was planning to coordinate the discussion in a way that everyone could share their opinion.

All workshop participants were planned to be experts working within the same department (i.e., IT-audit department) at one big audit firm located in the Netherlands with different levels of experience with the business processes of concern. These were supposed to include three staff IT auditors, three senior-IT auditors, and two managers. The tasks include mainly auditing IT processes relevant to the Annual Financial Statement reporting. These processes are generally repetitive and mostly standardized. Thus, the department has already started experimenting with RPA by

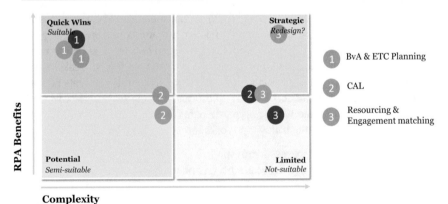

Fig. 3 RPA prioritization and selection matrix designed for the evaluation of processes (mapping of the processes to the matrix by both respondents and RPA experts (blue: respondent 1; dark blue: respondent 2; grey: participants))

rolling them out for two processes and believes that there is much more potential for RPA adoption.

3.2 Treatment Validation

Validation of designed artifacts is a central and important aspect of the design cycle [21]. It is often referred to be an approach to rationalize to stakeholders the effectiveness and benefits of a designed artifact [12]. It is thus widely used in research and practice (e.g., [22]). The artifacts could be evaluated to improve their characteristics and performance (i.e., formative evaluation), as well as to establish a shared understanding of the artifact in various contexts (i.e., summative evaluation) [20].

The former approach was adopted for the evaluation of the workshop in this research. Specifically, treatment validation here was set to: a) evaluate the workshop design; and b) explore how the designed workshop contributed to the identification of RPA suitable processes.

The workshop design was evaluated with the help of the survey designed [22] initially to assess the organizational workshop designed to look for sustainability opportunities. This survey evaluates participants' perspectives on the designed workshop with the help of a 5-point Likert scale (1 = Strongly disagree and 5 = Strongly agree) and identifies potential opportunities in terms of what should be "started", "stopped", "considered" and "continued" to be done in the workshop. The survey considers the participants' workshop acceptance in terms of its "ease of use" and "usability" (i.e., human-centeredness of the workshop). The former refers to whether the different elements within the workshop are clear, easy to apply, and systematic, while the latter aims to investigate whether participants perceived the workshop as effective. This survey was distributed among all workshop participants (n = 6) at the end of the second workshop.

The workshop outcome evaluation was conducted to understand two RPA experts' (from the same IT-audit department) perspectives on the processes selected for automation with the help of the designed workshop. Here the RPA experts were first shown all the Process profiles that resulted from the first workshop, and then their models from the second workshop. Here the experts had to first select the processes they would take to the second workshop, and then map these processes to the RPA prioritization and selection matrix. It is worth noting that during the evaluation, the experts were not given any information on the selection made by the participants. This was done to identify the alignment between the processes selected and their mapping by the workshop participants and the RPA experts. Finally, the experts were interviewed to explore whether the workshop managed to extract useful knowledge from the participants on the processes suitable for RPA following the interview protocol presented in Appendix 4.

4 Findings

Five of the invited experts attended the workshops. Thus, one of the envisioned facilitators also joined as a workshop participant. This role change was made to ensure the interaction during the workshop and the diversity of the participants' profiles. Considering that there were six participants, this brought the number of process profiles from a planned four to three. Two of these were both management and supporting processes. Thus, it was decided to group each junior expert with a senior expert and let them work together on modeling these processes in session 2. Although this is a deviation from the original workshop design, we believe it positively impacted the workshop, as working in couples stimulated the active participation of the involved participants.

4.1 Treatment Design

Process Identification

The goal of this first session was for participants to generate ideas and let them fill process profiles. While some of the participants managed to fill two process profiles, some came up with three or more. This led to a total of 16 process profiles (see Fig. 4).

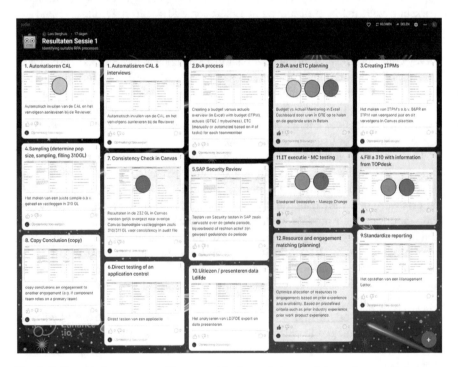

Fig. 4 Padlet with the process profiles created by the workshop participants (orange circles: processes voted by the participants; blue circles: processes voted by respondent 1; red circle: processes voted by respondent 2)

The process profiles were numbered. Similar processes received the same number to recognize their duplicate nature. These brought the number of unique processes to 12. These processes were discussed by the participants for their suitability for RPA based on the criteria included in the process profiles. This was followed by voting to identify the top three most voted options.

Process Discovery and Process Analysis
These top three processes (see Table 1) that were taken to the next phase (i.e., to be modeled using BPMN-R language) included BvA and ETC Planning, Resource and Engagement matching (both Management and Support processes), and Client Assistance Letter Automation (CAL) (Core process).

During the final part of the workshop, participants had to evaluate these processes in terms of their potential for automation, and potential expected benefits and based on this evaluation position them with the help of the RPA prioritization and selection matrix (Fig. 3).

4.2 Treatment Validation

Workshop Design Evaluation
The outcome of the survey illustrates how the workshop was perceived by the workshop participants (see Table 2).

As illustrated in Table 2, with regards to the 'Ease of use' of the workshop, overall, the participants agreed that the designed workshop was easy to use and understandable. This was especially true for the participants' perception of the facilitator's presentation on what RPA is and the process criteria for RPA suitability. Meanwhile, the perceptions of the participants were lower for more technical aspects of the workshop including the application of the process landscape, process profile, and BPMN-R language.

The participants also overall agreed that the designed workshop was effective for RPA selection. Specifically, they found the use of the instruments used during the workshop (e.g., process profile), as well as the brainstorming approach for RPA identification

Table 1 Top three processes selected for the second workshop

Process #	# of votes	Process title	Description
2	6	BvA and ETC Planning	Budget vs. Actual Monitoring and Estimated Time Consumed in an Excel Dashboard by extracting data from time registration and budget application
1	5	CAL	Filling in the client assistance letter automatically
12	3	Resource and Engagement matching (planning)	Optimize allocation of resources to engagements based on employees' prior experience and availability. Based on predefined criteria such as prior industry experience, prior work product experience

Table 2 Survey outcomes

Statement	P1	P2	P3	P4	P5	P6	Mean
Ease of use							
The goal of the workshop was made clear	4	4	5	5	4	4	4.3
I understand what RPA is	4	5	5	5	5	5	4.8
I understand the primary functions of RPA	4	4	5	5	5	4	4.5
I understand the process criteria for RPA suitability	5	4	4	5	5	5	4.7
I understand the process landscape	4	4	4	4	5	4	4.2
The process profile was easy to understand and apply	4	4	3	4	3	4	3.7
The BPMN-R language was easy to understand and to apply	3	4	4	4	4	3	3.7
The steps within the workshop were clear and easy to understand	5	4	4	4	3	4	4.0
The facilitator gave a clear presentation	5	5	4	5	5	4	4.7
Overall, I found the workshop clear	5	5	4	4	5	4	4.5
Mean	4.3	4.3	4.2	4.5	4.4	4.1	
Usability							
The process landscape helped me to identify potential RPA suitable processes	4	3	4	3	4	4	3.7
The brainstorming sessions helped me to think of processes with automation potential	3	4	2	5	4	5	3.8
The process profile was useful to evaluate the process criteria and thus RPA suitability	5	4	3	4	4	5	4.2
I thought the BPMN-R language was useful to evaluate the process criteria and thus RPA suitability	5	4	4	4	4	3	4.0
Overall, I found the workshop to be effective	4	5	4	4	5	5	4.5
Mean	4.2	4	3.4	4	4.2	4.4	
Recommendations							
What should be added to the workshop? (Started)							
What should be removed from the workshop? (Stopped)							
What should be considered within the workshop? (Considered)							
What should be continued? (Continued)							

and analysis to be useful. Meanwhile, the use of BPMN-R was recommended to be continued.

In terms of the good practices that should be added to the workshop design, the participants mentioned having demonstrations of more RPA best practices during the workshop (n = 2), as well as increasing the duration of some parts of the workshop (n = 2) especially for evaluating ideas and modeling of the processes. In terms of the practices to be "stopped" the participants (n = 3) stated that the RPA presentation part was too long for them, as they are "IT minded and have some prior knowledge". The practice to be "continued" included exercises carried out during the workshop such as process modeling with BPMN-R, as well as the use of process profile and prioritization matrix.

Workshop Outcome Evaluation

Figure 4 illustrates the processes voted by the respondents (blue and red circles) compared to the ones voted by the participants (orange circles). The outcome of this evaluation illustrates that both individual experts and workshop participants selected the same process as the absolute top for RPA. Meanwhile, there were some discrepancies both between the two experts and between the experts and workshop participants for the remaining top processes. For example, some processes were generated as potential ideas during the process identification phase (e.g., #11), which the participants did not vote to pass to the process evaluation phase of the workshop. Interestingly, RPA experts referred that this process was being automated at the time when the workshop was conducted, indicating that the participants had missed this idea. There were also processes (e.g., #2) that were new to the RPA experts. Expert interviews also enriched the list of the processes that emerged from the workshop (n = 16) with one additional process such as leaver control (i.e., monitoring of employees leaving the company).

Furthermore, the participants and the experts also mapped similarly the top three shortlisted processes for RPA with a minor variance only for processes 2 and 3 (see Fig. 3), where the participants seemed to be slightly more positive in terms of the business value of some processes (e.g., #3)

5   Discussions and Conclusions

This research proposes a systematic, user-friendly, and human-centered method to identify, select and evaluate organizational processes for RPA that draws on group intelligence. The combination of the BPM lifecycle with the brainstorming technique helped designing a group workshop as an artifact. In this study, we demonstrated that this method can aid organizations in identifying and selecting processes for RPA.

The workshop format was tested with two workshop sessions in a specific context (a service company in the Netherlands). It also experimented with IT-minded people, who are overall open to IT innovations and familiar with most of the instruments used during the workshop (e.g., process modeling via BPMN-R). To fully generalize the findings of this study, the workshop should be examined in companies from different sectors, of different sizes, countries, and -employee roles (e.g., multiple departments). This could be a fruitful avenue for future research.

The designed workshop was applied specifically for RPA process identification, selection, and evaluation. Future scholars might want to assess the workshop's usefulness for assessing the suitability of process technologies other than RPA, for instance, identifying, selecting and evaluating processes where process mining can be adopted. In addition, the effectiveness of the group workshop method could also be compared to other process selection methods (e.g., those focused on individuals). Considering the low number of workshop participants, no reliability test was conducted to check the quality of the data collected (e.g., via a survey). Despite these limitations, we believe the study has important scholarly and practical implications.

Identifying RPA-suitable processes is one of the key challenges for organizations that start their RPA journey [3, 6]. Moreover, the analysis of the processes for RPA has been mostly overlooked in literature. This study contributed to addressing such knowledge gaps. Specifically, we propose a new systematic group approach for identifying and selecting business processes for RPA, which could be applied in a variety of contexts and organizations.

This study also designs an artifact by integrating the BPM lifecycle (specifically, BPM from IT literature) with the brainstorming technique (from social science literature). Previous studies touched upon the potential of group workshops for BPM initiatives, yet without providing a detailed description of how this potential could be achieved [10], for example in terms of workshop structure and ideal group composition for the generation of ideas and their evaluation. Our study provides such a description of both the design of the group workshop artifact and its evaluation in real-world environments, significantly expanding existing knowledge. The research also responds to calls for scholars from different disciplines to design systematic approaches for RPA process identification and selection [8] that enhance the implementation of RPA [7].

From a practical perspective, the detailed descriptions provided in this paper on the workshop design, as well as its implementation, can guide organizations already implementing or eager to launch RPA initiatives by providing a systematic and all-inclusive approach for designing, implementing, and evaluating workshops for their identification and selection. The designed workshop can be tailored to a variety organizations and contexts, both with and without RPA experience. For example, in organizations with fewer IT-skilled employees, more time can be spent on explaining RPA and its potential benefits, and vice versa.

To conclude, numerous businesses today are trying to adopt RPA, yet many initiatives are unsuccessful because organizations struggle to identify RPA-suitable processes. This interdisciplinary study proposes a new methodological and practical method that tackles this important challenge. Future conceptual and empirical interdisciplinary studies could validate the group workshop format to augment its validity and reliability. Such studies could also apply different methodological approaches such as action or ethnographic studies, or longitudinal research to comprehend whether the identified processes were actually automated, as well as to assess the effectiveness of the designed artifact (i.e., both workshop and the relevant processes for RPA identified via such workshop). Moreover, such studies could also explore different techniques for generating ideas and selecting solutions such as the design thinking approach, which has started being frequently used in consulting projects as well as in scholarly investigations [23]. Finally, such studies could also draw on solid theoretical perspectives from information system or social science literature, such as organizing vision perspective or technology frame, which take into account the business value of IT as resulting from stakeholders' efforts to make sense of new technology [24] to the identification and evaluation of the business processes to RPA.

Appendix 1. Session 1: Process Identification: Detailed Description of the Steps Taken (Approximate 2 h)

No.	Step	Time (ca.)	Description
1	Introduction to the Workshop & Session 1	10 min	First of all, a short introduction of the workshop is given to set the general objective of the workshop. During this introduction some background information about the workshop and its goal will be explained. It should be explicitly mentioned that the goal of the workshop is to find out if there are any processes within the department or organization (depending on the context) that can be (partly) automated by RPA. During this step it is also important to inform the participants what benefits the outcome of this workshop might imply for them. For instance, increasing the time employees can spent on more challenging tasks. Lastly, an explanation about the goal of session 1 is given, which is identifying processes and filling them into the Process Profiles

Additional:

• Introduce the facilitators and participants to each other
• Show a short video of a general RPA process to give participants an initial understanding
• Participants can ask questions during the workshop |
| 2 | Explaining Robotic Process Automation | 30 min | During this step a detailed explanation about RPA will be given (e.g., including What RPA is, It's Primary Functions and the process criteria processes should possess in order to be suitable for RPA). In addition, different examples of processes where RPA is being used can be mentioned. For example, the procurement process, creating new customers or the onboarding process. What is most important during this step is to give the participants, i.e. the process experts, a well enough understanding of RPA and the process criteria

Additional:

• If available, some use cases can be shown (video material)
• Primary functions that can be harder to understand should be shortly explained
• All process criteria should be explained and the most important once should be highlighted
• The Business Champion should be capable of answering questions from participants about the capabilities of RPA |

No.	Step	Time (ca.)	Description
3	Exercise: Generating Ideas (NBS)	45 min	During this step, the exercise for the participants is explained as well as the steps that are taken (Generating, Collecting, Evaluating and Selecting). It is important to be very clear about the goal of this exercise as well as its instruction, in order to avoid mistakes. The goal of this exercise is for participants to brainstorm individually (30 min) and fill in processes within the Process Profile. The minimum amount of process profiles filled in by participants should be set to 2, to prevent free riding. A Padlet link will be created and send to the participants to upload their Process Profiles. Lastly, the general brainstorm rules should be mentioned to the participants before the exercise. *Additional*: • Participants will enter breakout rooms within Teams to work individually on their exercise • The facilitators will enter during the exercise different breakout rooms to answer questions from participants • Participants have received via email the Process Profile including the process criteria as well as two tools to support them with the generation of ideas • These two tools are the Process Landscape and the listing of the Primary Functions
4	Break, Collecting and Sorting the Ideas	10 min	Once the participants have uploaded all their process profiles to Padlet, all unique ideas are being sorted by the facilitators. For this reason, it is important to have a facilitator who is familiar with all of the processes that are in scope. He or she must evaluate which of the uploaded processes within Padlet are similar. During this step participants will have a ten-minute break
5	Evaluating Ideas (NBS) and selecting top three	20 min	After the ideas have been collected and sorted, the process profiles will be evaluated and selected by the group. First, each of the unique ideas will be explained shortly by its creator. This explanation should include a short introduction to the process and the reason for thinking it might be suitable for RPA. Once the creator is finished explaining, other participants have the opportunity to ask questions and elaborate on the idea. During this step it is important that participants engage the discussion as this is one of the core elements of the workshop that distinguishes itself from other process selection method
6	Selecting the Ideas by voting	3 min	After each unique idea has been discussed the selection step can take place. During this step, four processes will be selected to the next session. Every participant has to vote for four processes of which they think have the most RPA potential. This voting can be easily done in Padlet. Session 1 is ended once the voting is finished and therefore processes are selected

Appendix 2. Session 2: Process Discovery and Process Analysis: Detailed Description of the Steps Taken (Approximate 2 h)

No.	Step	Time (ca.)	Description
1	Recap	5 min	Before starting with explaining the goal for the second session, a short recap of the results from session 1 will be given. This will help refresh the participants memory. Moreover, the goal of filling in the Process Portfolio can be explained
2	Explanation of BPMN(-R)	20 min	Participants will be introduced to the Business Process Modelling Notation (BPMN), explaining that it's a language consisting out of standard notations to model processes. At the beginning of this step the goal of this modelling should be explicitly explained, such as getting a better understanding of the process and re-evaluating the process criteria. *Additional*: • A use case or other example of a process, where RPA is yet implemented, can be modelled to show as an example • With this modelled example, process criteria can be re-evaluated
3	Exercise: Process Modelling via BPMN(-R)	30 min	After the BPMN(-R) language is clear to the participants, they can start with modelling one of the selected Process Profiles from session 1. Because there are eight participants present, one Process Profile will be modelled by two participants. As a result, a process will be modelled two times. Modelling can be done in www.draw.io. Again, each participant will be put into a breakout room for 30 min *Additional*: • The focus should not be on the correct usage of the BPMN notations, but visualizing the process in a detailed way, so new insights will be obtained • The facilitator can give a demonstration to the participants on how to use Draw.io • Participants will enter breakout rooms within Microsoft Teams to work individually on their exercise • The facilitators will enter different breakout rooms, during the exercise, to answer questions from participants
4	Break	15 min	After time is finished, participants have the opportunity to catch a break for 15 min

No.	Step	Time (ca.)	Description
5	Evaluating the Modelled Processes	25 min	Once the break is finished, participants will join the Teams meeting again to start a discussion about the completeness and accuracy of the modelled processes. Each participant will first share his or her screen to give a short explanation about the model including its different systems, gateways and activities. BPMN-R uses a 'bolt' as a notation that shows the requirement of a certain discussion. These bolts are especially important to evaluate as this might be a difficult step to execute for the robot. The facilitator will furthermore emphasize the importance of re-evaluating the Process Criteria. After each model is explained by its creator, participants can start the discussion by asking questions and comment
6	Positioning processes within the Matrix	10 min	The last step is to fill in the RPA Prioritization and Selection Matrix (i.e., Process Portfolio). This will be done as a group. Participants will give their opinion about where each of the processes should be positioned within the matrix. During this step it is important for the participants to reach a consensus. Therefore, it is the facilitator's task to let everyone share their opinion
7	Concluding	5 min	The facilitator will then thank everyone for their cooperation and effort

Appendix 3. Process Profiles to Be Filled in by Participants

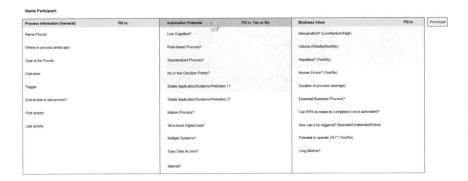

Appendix 4. Interview Protocol for RPA Experts

Introduction of the researcher:

- Explaining the goal of the interview
- Explaining and illustrating the workshop design

Interview questions:

1. Who are you, what is your job title and what experience do you have with RPA?

The researcher shows generated RPA processes, explaining how they are generated and which of the processes are similar, and which are unique.

2. After showing you all the generated processes by the participants, which of these processes do you think have the most potential for RPA and should be taken to the next session?
3. Why do you think that these are the most suitable?
4. Do you think that besides these three processes there are more processes generated by the participants suitable for RPA?
5. Do you think that there are more relevant processes suitable for RPA within the IT-audit department that have not been generated by the participants?

The researcher shows process models created by participants, explaining why and how they are created.

6. Looking at these modeled processes, where would you place the processes on the matrix?
7. Do you think that any of these processes should be initiated for further development?

References

1. Frey, C. B., & Osborne, M. 2013. The future of employment: How susceptible are jobs to computerisation?, Oxford Martin Programme on Technology and Employment. https://www.oxfordmartin.ox.ac.uk/publications/the-future-of-employment/#:~:text=According%20to%20their%20estimates%2C%20about,an%20occupation%27s%20probability%20of%20computerisation.
2. Trefler, A. (2018). The Big RPA Bubble. *Forbes*. Retrieved April 26, from https://www.forbes.com/sites/cognitiveworld/2018/12/02/the-big-rpabubble/#4dc3d91568d9.
3. Van der Aalst, W. M. P., Bichler, M., & Heinzl, A. (2018). Robotic process automation. *Business and Information Systems Engineering, 60*(4), 269–272. https://doi.org/10.1007/s12599-018-0542-4
4. Cooper, L., Holderness, K., Sorensen, T., & Wood, D. A. (2019). Robotic process automation in public accounting. *SSRN Scholarly Paper*. https://doi.org/10.2139/ssrn.3193222
5. Penttinen, E., Kasslin, H., & Asatiani, A. (2018). How to choose between robotic process automation and back-end system automation? In *26th European conference on information systems: Beyond digitization—Facets of socio-technical change, ECIS 2018* (pp. 1–14).
6. Leopold, H., Van der Aalst, H., & Reijers, H. A. (2018). Identifying candidate tasks for robotic process automation in textual process descriptions. *Lecture Notes in Business Information Processing, 318*(January), 67–81. https://doi.org/10.1007/978-3-319-91704-7_5
7. Syed, R., Suriadi, S., Adams, M., Bandara, W., Leemans, S. J. J., Ouyang, C., Arthur, H. M., Van De Weerd, I., Thandar, M., & Reijers, H. A. (2020). Robotic process automation: Contemporary themes and challenges. *Computers in Industry, 115*, 103162. https://doi.org/10.1016/j.compind.2019.103162
8. Wanner, J., Hofmann, A., Fischer, M., Imgrund, F., Janiesch, C., & Geyer-Klingeberg, J. (2020). Process selection in RPA projects—Towards a quantifiable method of decision making. In *40th international conference on information systems, ICIS 2019, November*.

9. Leemans, M., van der Aalst, W. M. P., van den Brand, M. G. J., Schiffelers, R. R. H., & Lensink, L. (2018). Software process analysis methodology—A methodology based on lessons learned in embracing legacy software. In *2018 IEEE international conference on software maintenance and evolution (ICSME)* (pp. 665–674). https://doi.org/10.1109/ICSME.2018.00076

10. Dumas, M., La Rosa, M., Mendling, J., & Reijers, H. A. (2013). Business process management. In *Lecture notes in business information processing* (Vol. 168). https://doi.org/10.1007/978-3-319-04175-9_1

11. Goris, V. (2019). *An assessment of process discovery techniques with the purpose of finding RPA eligible processes.* Master's thesis. University Utrecht Repository. https://dspace.library.uu.nl/handle/1874/384820

12. Wieringa, R. J. (2014). *Design science methodology for information systems and software engineering.* Springer. https://doi.org/10.1007/978-3-662-43839-8

13. Boddy, C. (2012). The nominal group technique: An aid to brainstorming ideas in research. *Qualitative Market Research: An International Journal, 15*(1), 6–18. https://doi.org/10.1108/13522751211191964

14. Berghuis, L. (2021). *Using the wisdom of the crowd to digitalize: Designing a workshop-based process selection method for the identification of suitable RPA processes.* Master's thesis. University of Twente. Retrieved from http://essay.utwente.nl/88768/

15. Flechsig, C., Lohmer, J., & Lasch, R. (2019). Realizing the full potential of robotic process automation through a combination with BPM. In *Lecture notes in logistics* (pp. 104–119). https://doi.org/10.1007/978-3-030-29821-0_8

16. Maaravi, Y., Heller, B., Shoham, Y., Mohar, S., & Deutsch, B. (2020). Ideation in the digital age: Literature review and integrative model for electronic brainstorming. *Review of Managerial Science.* https://doi.org/10.1007/s11846-020-00400-5

17. Agaton, B., & Swedberg, G. (2018). *Evaluating and developing methods to assess business process suitability for robotic process automation.* Master's thesis. Chalmers University of Technology and University of Gothenburg. Chalmers Open Digital Repository. Retrieved from http://publications.lib.chalmers.se/records/fulltext/255664/255664.pdf, https://odr.chalmers.se/bitstream/20.500.12380/255664/1/255664.pdf

18. Lorentz Centre. (2021, June 15). Virtual workshops. Retrieved from https://www.lorentzcenter.nl/virtual-workshops.html.

19. Slack, N., & Brandon-Jones, A. (2019). Process technology. In *Operations management* (9th ed., pp. 246–275). Pearson Education.

20. Paulus, P. B., Kohn, N. W., Arditti, L. E., & Korde, R. M. (2013). Understanding the group size effect in electronic brainstorming. *Small Group Research, 44*(3), 332–352. https://doi.org/10.1177/1046496413479674

21. Venable, J., Pries-Heje, J., & Baskerville, R. (2016). FEDS: A framework for evaluation in design science research. *European Journal of Information Systems, 25*(1), 77–89. https://doi.org/10.1057/ejis.2014.36

22. Geissdoerfer, M., Bocken, N. M. P., & Hultink, E. J. (2016). Design thinking to enhance the sustainable business modelling process—A workshop based on a value mapping process. *Journal of Cleaner Production, 135*, 1218–1232. https://doi.org/10.1016/j.jclepro.2016.07.020

23. Brown, T. (2008). Design thinking. *Harvard Business Review.* https://hbr.org/2008/06/design-thinking.

24. Palas, M. J. U., & Bunduchi, R. (2021). Exploring interpretations of blockchain's value in healthcare: A multi-stakeholder approach. *Information Technology & People, 34*(2), 453–495. https://doi.org/10.1108/ITP-01-2019-0008

Striving to Become Agile in the Public Sector: A Context Theory Perspective

Tobias Kautz and Robert Winter

Abstract With an increasing number of digitalization initiatives in the public sector, public shared service providers that deliver and steering bodies that orchestrate the realization of those initiatives are under pressure to become agile, i.e., to adopt agile activities, principles, and an agile mindset. This study investigates challenges and corresponding mitigation measures of scaled agile transformations of such organizations. Based on data gathered through Action Research based multiple case studies and drawing on context theory, it identifies obstacles related to the political, environmental, and internal context as well as transformation management itself. Among them are siloed actions and individual interests, IT legacy, complexity of customer requirements, insufficient resources, no shared vision, low professionalization, and a missing holistic picture. Value stream thinking, architectural thinking, successful pilot projects, constructive criticism, and a culture of failure are suggested as countermeasures. The identified obstacles and measures fit well into and extend the findings from a systematic literature review. Our contribution is to contextualize and extend insights and recommendations related to the large-scale agile transformation of public shared service providers and steering bodies that both serve multiple customers, i.e., other public sector organizations. Further research can quantitatively test the measures, develop maturity models for them, or identify obstacle-measure-patterns. Practitioners receive insights that should also contribute to a more successful transformation of the public sector in the benefit of society and economy.

Keywords Public sector · Large scale agile transformation · Context theory

T. Kautz (✉) · R. Winter
Institute of Information Management, University of St. Gallen, St. Gallen, Switzerland
e-mail: tobias.kautz@unisg.ch; robert.winter@unisg.ch

© The Author(s), under exclusive license to Springer Nature
Switzerland AG 2024
A. Lazazzara et al. (eds.), *Towards Digital and Sustainable Organisations*,
Lecture Notes in Information Systems and Organisation 65,
https://doi.org/10.1007/978-3-031-52880-4_8

1 Introduction

Being used to non-fragmented, digital services that can be consumed anywhere and anytime, citizens and private companies nowadays expect the same comfort from the public sector. For the providers of these services (e.g., government agencies), these expectations led to numerous *digitalization initiatives* aimed at enhancing service efficiency and quality [1]. To make delivery of such services more efficient or enable them at all, (political) leadership of the public sector implement strategic measures such as the involvement of citizens and other stakeholders in service design and delivery [1] or macro-organizational changes such as creating new, dedicated agencies [2]. Another measure is the reformation of existing organizations such as state-owned, independent (i.e., not being just the IT department for one agency) digital service providers. Given the radical change in the needs of their customers (i.e., government agencies), these are thus required to undergo a more fundamental, enterprise-wide *digital transformation*, i.e., altering their business model, value creation and organizational culture [1, 3]. Another type of public organization undergoing reformation is the establishment or development of steering bodies that take responsibility for coordinating sector-wide digitalization efforts. Both types of organizations now operate in environments that are increasingly characterized by "VUCA" [4] so that a sequential, traditional approach of service (and software) development and its governance appears to be not sufficient anymore.

To enable successful operations in such environments and reacting to rapidly changing user expectations, organizations strive to be more agile. *Being agile* can be understood as adopting agile principles, agile values, and an agile mindset comprised of customer centricity, continuous learning and improvement, taking on accountability, embracing uncertainty, and ensuring trust and collaboration [5, 6]. These values and principles can also contribute to *enterprise agility*, that characterizes organizations that are efficient and effective in reacting to changes through sensing, seizing and transforming capabilities [7], which are helpful in a VUCA environment [8]. Adopting agile methodology, i.e., *doing agile*, can be considered as an intermediary step to being agile [6] and has become popular among private sector IT organizations [9]. Also, it is increasingly adopted in public sector IT organizations [10, 11]. Scaling agile might create challenges on its own (cf., e.g., [12]), and for the public sector additional challenges are likely to arise through its specific context.

We focus our research on public shared service providers (PSSPs). These are now expected to initiate and manage their agile transformations, especially after the push in digitalization due to COVID-19 [13, 14]. However, their aim of generating revenue with the other public organizations (their service customers) and staying in business might be endangered as their transformation not only poses a risk to stability of operations, but also may highlight organizational knowledge or capability gaps. Likewise, executives of the steering bodies are required to align project and portfolio management with agile principles and values. However, an unsuccessful implementation of agile principles and values could prevent them from reaching their aims regarding the optimal allocation of investments/resources, the continuous delivery of new systems and services, and as well risk their personal standing.

Thus, the explorative research presented in this paper aims to answer the following research questions:

1. Which obstacles arise when public organizations involved in the digitalization of the public sector aim to become agile on a scaled level?
2. Which preliminary measures promise to address these obstacles?

We define *obstacle* in the context of this study as "something that impedes progress or achievement" [15], which is in this case becoming agile, and *measure* as "a step planned or taken as a means to an end" [16], i.e., to mitigate these obstacles. For this study, we understand public sector as collection of all authorities, agencies, departments, and state-owned companies. They all provide the abovementioned services to citizens and firms. In other words, it is what is commonly understood as 'the state'. *Public organization* refers to organizations that are part of this collection. *Involved in the digitalization of the public sector* should indicate that they do not only contribute to the digitalization of only one client organization, but to multiple ones that might also be dispersed over different levels of administration (local, province/state-level, country-level). The PSSPs and steering bodies comply with this definition.

The remainder of this paper is structured as follows: After briefly reviewing the relevant literature, the methodology will be explained. The results are then presented and discussed before a conclusion is made.

2   Literature Review

2.1   *Conceptual Foundations*

Agile

Agile *methodologies* can be defined as a "documented collection of policies, processes, and procedures" ([17], p. 803) to develop software in an agile manner, i.e., with the characteristics of "iterative development and a focus on interaction, communication, and the reduction of resource-intensive intermediate artifacts" ([18], p. 12). While these usually focus on the team-level, *agile frameworks* extend these through practices on technology governance and on management level [19]. In the software engineering context, *principles* have been defined as "a first and fundamental statement of the discipline worded in a prescriptive manner in order to guide action, that can be verified in its consequences" ([20], p. 4). Thus, they are more abstract than the prescriptions made by methodology. The principles can be based on *values*, which can be defined as "beliefs about what is right and wrong and what is important in life" [21]. A *mindset* can be understood as "a set of attitudes or fixed ideas that somebody has" [22], which might also include adopted values and principles. Given the more fundamental and projectable nature of principles, values and mindset, the adoption of those is more related to being agile. Transformation can be understood as "a complete change in somebody/something" [23]. We understand agile transformation as the change from non-agile to agile principles and values, aiming also to develop an agile mindset, that can be—but does not necessarily need to be—accompanied by the replacement of non-agile methodologies through agile ones. The aspect of large-scale relates to "the usage of agile [...] in large multi-team settings" ([12], p. 3). These multiple teams refer to internal teams of the PSSPs that deliver digital services to customers, or the teams involved in the endeavors steered by the steering body, that deliver digital solutions to the public sector. For the purposes of this study, scaling agile should also imply changes on the program level, i.e., not just adopting agile methodology or principles across all projects, but also change and define new coordination and management mechanisms on at least program, if not also enterprise-wide level.

Obstacles

In the reviewed literature, identified obstacles (or challenges) are—if at all— abstracted or aggregated based on their common theme (cf. Sect. 2.2). However, to enable systematic analysis and presentation in this study, a context—management—performance perspective [24] is adopted. Considering context, i.e., "environmental forces or organizational characteristics at a higher level of analysis that affect a focal behavior in question" ([25], p. 156), is seen as a valuable approach in management [26] and also public administration research [24]. It has also been applied for the similar research problem of digital service teams in government [27] and for the related research field of project governance [28], and also plays an important role in other organization-related studies (cf. Sect. 2.2). "Management" in this case is the transformation management, executed by the transformation management team (i.e., a team comprised of top management executives and/or employees directly associated with them). The *Theory of Context* by O'Toole and Meier [24] poses that the impact of management efforts (e.g., the performance) is affected by the political, environmental and internal context of a (public) organization. Based on that theoretical lens, the allocation of identified obstacles in this study will be done according to these context spheres—or to the management effort, i.e., for 'faults' that can be attributed to the transformation management team itself. Therefore, context theory also facilitates to identify obstacles whose elimination might be easier and possible on a shorter term, while others require middle- to long-term changes in the bureaucratic and political system.

Measures

In similar studies, specific theoretical lenses have been applied to derive and analyze measures such as control mechanisms [29] or Normalization Process Theory [30]. However, given the exploratory nature of this study, a very specialized ex-ante analysis framework is not considered as useful. Fuchs and Hess [12] intend to draw on socio-technical systems theory to analyze actions (i.e., measures), but then realize, "[h]owever, some actions [...] can be viewed in the light of multiple socio-technical dimensions since they are general and can, for instance, be performed to address diverse challenges" ([12], p. 11). Thus, as this theory is not appropriate to distinguish between different types of measures, it is not valuable for their presentation in this paper. Accordingly, measures identified in literature and this study are only clustered content-wise without a specific theoretical lens.

2.2   Related Work

When conceptualizing the research problem, different and more or less distant and projectable streams of prior research can be identified. The first, most generic one, comprises studies focusing on the role of context in organizational transformations, without focusing on the public sector. Another stream are studies looking at organizational transformations and the associated challenges (i.e., obstacles) in the public sector in general, and—following from our theoretical lens—with a special emphasis on context. Then, the introduction of agile methodology and principles can be considered, both with regards to the unscaled (i.e., project) and scaled (i.e., program, organization) level. For the latter, it is insightful to consult the literature on the challenges of agile transformations in the private sector. It should be noted, however, that a projectability issue arises here, given the different contexts of private and public organizations.

The Role of Context in Organizational Change
The role of considering (multiple levels of) context for studying organizational change has long been recognized [31]. Context-related aspects such as the need for change given by the environment, trust and consensus orientation, and organizational structure were found to be an important facilitator of organizational change capacity [32]. Similarly, Jansson [33] emphasizes the social context creating particularities that could also affect change success.

Organizational Transformations and Their Challenges in the Public Sector
In an often cited article (over 1600 citations on Google Scholar at the time of writing of this paper), Fernandez and Rainey [34] review the literature to identify eight success factors for organizational change in the public sector: validation and communication of the need for change, existence of a change strategy, internal support, top management commitment, support by political leaders and externals, adequate resources, and institutionalization and comprehensiveness of the change. Tangi, Janssen, Benedetti and Noci [35] investigate the related concept of digital government transformation using structural equation modeling to identify obstacles such as organizational barriers or lack of support.

The Role of Context in Organizational Transformations in the Public Sector
Coming to the studies highlighting the role of context in transformation-related fields in the public sector, Pedersen [36] reviews the literature to report 14 individual challenges in four dimensions that are—besides organizational challenges and transformational ability—contextual pressure and challenges, e.g., outside forces

fostering to undergo a digital transformation or the degree of technical integration between public sector organizations. Drawing also on contingency theory, Andrews, Beynon and McDermott [37] use contextual variables, among them size, complexity, autonomy, and personnel structure, to explain the intensity of organizational capabilities (i.e., the ability to coordinate resources and activities to reach goals/ achieve a high performance). van der Voet [38] studies the shape of cutback strategies based on the context spheres proposed by O'Toole and Meier [24].

Agile Organizational Transformations and Their Challenges in the Public Sector

As agile transformations are at the core of this research, prior studies were identified through a systematic literature review using the *Business Source Complete* database from *EBSCO* and supplementary *Google Scholar*, where the first five pages of the latter were considered, respectively. Using *Atlas.ti*, the challenges and measures were systematically extracted from the sources and clustered either by context factors or by common theme, respectively, after the projects were conducted. This enabled the unbiased identification of possible new challenges and measures, while also facilitating the presentation in this and the discussion in a later section. The identified clustered obstacles are summarized in Table 1.

The identified clustered *measures* are: Conducting change management, implementing stepwise change, providing education, fostering changes at client, gaining leadership support, revising regulations and prescriptions, altering decision making practices, introducing management information systems, and restructuring teams.

Agile Organizational Transformations and Their Challenges in the Private Sector

Fuchs and Hess [12] who appear to be the authors that have most recently investigated the challenges of scaled agile transformations holistically, identify six categories of challenges regarding the correct method application, technological environment, organization, culture, organization's members' abilities, and motivations of these.

The literature review has two important implications. First, that there might be aspects such as management support [10, 12, 34, 39] that are considered relevant in all research streams and, although not specific for our research problem, are important for the successful large-scale agile transformation. Second, it has shown that there might be a research gap with respect to studying—in the public sector—agile transformations on an organizational level (cf. also [11]) and of organizations that serve multiple client organizations. Thus, it seems adequate to investigate this issue using the methodology presented in the next section.

Table 1 Obstacle clusters for agile adoption identified in literature with column structure drawing on the Theory of Context by O'Toole and Meier [24]

Political context	Environmental context	Internal context	Management approach
• Emphasis on individual interests • Lack of trust	*Complexity:* • 'Business' complexity • Legacy systems • Inherent complexity in adopting agile *Munificence:* • Insufficient management support (time & resources) • Inadequate customer support	*Goals:* • Ambidextrous goals *Centralization:* • Inappropriate culture • Immature leadership *Professionalization:* • Lack of own personnel • Missing competences	• Missing management methods • Missing guidelines for teams • Inappropriate guidelines

3 Methodology

3.1 Case Organizations

To answer the research question, a multiple case study leveraging Canonical Action Research (CAR) was conducted at three public sector organizations in Switzerland. Two of them where PSSPs that provide IT services (e.g., business applications) to multiple public agencies. These PSSPs were not customer centric and efficient enough in delivery to implement digitalization effectively and efficiently. Thus, they aimed at adopting agile values and principles and also explicitly considered to implement the Scaled Agile Framework® [40]. One of the three studied organizations (in the following *SteerOrg*) is not a regular provider of shared services but is one of the organizations charged with orchestrating sector-wide digitalization efforts as a steering body. It was in the need for a new program governance and project management approach due to frequent changes of project scope, time, and budget. This new approach should embrace agile values and principles, where adopting agile methodology was considered as one option to achieve this.

3.2 Canonical Action Research Approach

The research project was conducted in the form of Action Research projects in context of consulting engagements commissioned by respective executives of the organizations. Especially with a research team with consulting background, the research and consulting modes of inquiry do not contradict each other, but instead can facilitate access to issues of high relevance for organizations [41]. AR seemed to be suitable, as a deep understanding of the (political) context of the transformation projects needed to be achieved and trustful relationships with the organizations' employees to be established to reveal feelings and fears that might have been hidden to 'normal' outside researchers. Within AR, CAR appeared appropriate as is not only one very widely followed approach [42], but also has certain distinctive characteristics that were needed in the project and are summarized by Baskerville and Wood-Harper [43]: An *iterative process* was required to jointly advance the understanding of the researchers of a complex, dynamic phenomenon as well as the mutual understanding of researchers and practitioners. A *rigorous structure* of the projects was needed to comply with the expectations of the practitioners as well as a *collaborative involvement* to facilitate building of trust and emphasize mutual learning, promoting concrete solutions from the researcher. Last, *organizational development* was the primary goal, since enhancing the collaboration within the transformation team and employees in general was intended. This is also reflected in CAR theory, following a situational feature—action—outcome structure [42], which is especially useful as it answers both of the research questions.

3.3 Data Collection and Analysis

The selection of the cases reflected a *common process* design, which means that the same focal phenomenon of obstacles encountered during a scaled agile transformation was investigated in different organizations to enhance generalizability [44]. While the organizations were all involved in the conceptualization, building and realization of digital services in the public sector, they differed, e.g., in terms of the concrete service portfolio, their clients (while overlaps might exist), organization size, management composition and background. This design could be especially helpful to identify generalizable obstacles in the political and environmental context. Data collection was based on semi-structured interviews and secondary documents, data analysis on thematical analysis supported by different frameworks as shown in Table 2.

The choice of the interviewees was done in alignment with the clients and reflected the dynamic problem and organizational understanding. Interviewees were asked for their assessment of the transformation endeavor's progress in general, received role-specific questions, and were able to raise and elaborate issues not already mentioned but of importance for them. In addition, secondary documents comprising the organizational foundations and the transformation endeavors itself were analyzed. Data analysis as well mirrored the evolving problem understanding, where different frameworks have been applied within each case, starting from a standardized framework to an individualized refinement of that or a self-developed one. Where applicable, the interview questionnaires evolved analogously, first being constructed based on the standardized frameworks and then on the challenges becoming clearer and current pressing topics.

Table 2 Data sources and analysis frameworks/techniques per case

	Data sources	Frameworks and techniques for data analysis
PSSP 1	• 3+ semi-structured interviews, partly repetitive (i.e., same employees) with regular employees and top management • Vast of internal documents	• Digital TransformationOrchestrator (DTO) [45] • DTO (refined)
PSSP 2	• 20+ semi-structured interviews, partly repetitive, with employees at multiple hierarchy levels • Vast of internal documents	• DTO • Supplementary coding, self-developed framework
SteerOrg	• 10+ semi-structured interviews with team of SteerOrg and clients • Vast of internal documents	• DTO • Supplementary coding • Digital government strategy themes

4 Results

4.1 Identified Obstacles

Political Context

All organizations operated in a context that was characterized by a *high separation of power* and an *adversarial decision process* (i.e., with no final binding decision for all) between the stakeholders that needed to be involved into decision making [24]. Given the Swiss *federal* structure, some organizations were also faced with stakeholders on *multiple levels of government* [24]. This became apparent through the mirroring of political power (with regards to, e.g., budget, number of users) of the customer organizations to their weight in the decision-making process. Related to this, it was not possible to override these individual interests or enforce decisions against their wills even if this would have maximized the utility of the customer base as a whole. This context resulted in siloed actions and the pursuit of individual interests. Siloed actions were taken by teams of the delivering units or projects, while individual interests were emphasized especially in strategic discussions. Both was reinforced through the *hierarchical structure* [24] of some organizations. This does not contribute to becoming agile which is reliant on a collaborative mindset and quick decision making [5, 46].

Environmental Context

The environmental context of all organizations was characterized through a *high turbulence and complexity* [24]. Demands and requirements changed fast, intensified through COVID-19. The high complexity resulted from a heterogeneous IT legacy landscape, where IT systems were often monolithic and created a strong reliance on third parties or vendors. *Munificence* [24] in terms of the budget and resource equipment was insufficient. At the same time, a commitment of the customer organizations would have been necessary to replace the legacy systems. However, *social capital* [24] was found to be high in at least one organization, given the Swiss tradition of self-organizing small groups. In concrete, this implied the collaboration between some forerunners that joined forces to carry out digitalization projects on their own, which might later be adopted by other customer organizations. The highly complex and monolithic IT systems do not contribute to becoming more agile with its emphasis on the fast roll-out of solutions that immediately add value while reacting to shifts in requirements (as opposed to slow and intermediate changes to systems to enable the release of new features for end users). The low munificence generally limits the investments in new, agile-ready tools, business applications, and experts. The Swiss tradition of self-organizing small groups, in contrast, shares the same values (e.g., accountability and collaboration) as the agile mindset.

Internal Context
The internal context was marked by multiple, competing *goals* [24]. In concrete, this was manifested in a needed yet missing shared vision about the future business and IT architecture. Except for (some part of) of the leadership of these organizations, *professionalization* [24] was low (e.g., due to the reliance on externals) and only started to evolve through the hiring of new people with experience in digitalization. Given the self-steering teams and individuals dependent to base their decisions on a common vision, the absence of such can be considered not to promote becoming agile. The low professionalization also potentially hinders becoming agile as existing team members need to undergo a difficult change process.

Management Approach
Additional obstacles were not related to the context, but to the transformation management approach. Here, a missing holistic and differentiated big picture (in the heads of the transformation management teams and in the change communication) became apparent. First, the relationships between services, processes, and IT systems (e.g., with regards to the service portfolio and service delivery structure, introduction of new software tools and corresponding process redesign) were not sufficiently considered. Second, and partly as a consequence, dependencies between projects and workstreams were not transparent or ignored, e.g., by developing processes and the service portfolio separately. Third, the understanding of the customer was—at least in the beginning—very narrow, i.e., there was no separation between the concept of an organization as a customer, between dedicated roles within the customer organization (such as procurement or management), and between the actual user and the customers' customers (i.e., the citizens and firms). Next to creating general inefficiencies and difficulties with regards to the structuring of the transformation endeavors, this also promoted thinking in silos than emphasizing collaboration.

4.2   Measures Proposed in All Cases

Value Stream Thinking and Architectural Thinking

To enable a comprehensive understanding of the as-is and to be-state of the own and (reference) client organization, more holistic frameworks were suggested drawing on the value stream idea [47], the DTO [45] and the Business Engineering methodology [48]. The frameworks were customized based on the communication needs within the AR projects but shared distinctive features. They put the needs of the customers' customer at the highest level, which then influenced the interrelated strategy, processes, and IT systems of the customer organizations (or the public sector in general with regards to SteerOrg) which then should influence the own strategy, processes, and IT systems of the PSSPs and SteerOrg. On the one hand, this was intended to enable the transformation management to better steer the projects and work streams and to identify synergies and dependencies. On the other, change communication should be improved through showing reasons for and consequences of the internal change to stakeholders. Besides tackling the obstacle of not having such a big picture specifically, the framework also helps to break up monolithic systems and to spot commonalities and differences in individual customer interests. Moreover, it makes it easier to identify works of the above-mentioned forerunners that might be re-used. It could also even directly promote enterprise agility through identifying the areas where change might occur (e.g., demands or new technologies) and highlight where resources need to be reconfigured (e.g., processes or IT systems) to quickly adapt to this change.

(Successful) Pilot Projects

Next, it was proposed to initiate pilot projects that quickly deliver results in the form of either design work for the transformation of the own organization—or functionality to customers. These should bring together all relevant internal stakeholders. This contributes to the mitigation of the obstacles through a 'tangible' implementation of the relationships and dependencies that were formerly ignored—and to the replacement of legacy systems. It furthermore promotes being agile directly through customer centricity (in terms of prototypes brought quickly to the customers) and through the building of trust between the stakeholders involved in the project as well as between the customers and the project team and its corresponding organization in general.

Constructive Criticism and Culture of Failure

Constructive criticism, i.e., an open and respectful criticism accompanied by ideas how to improve the situation, was also recommended. This comprised highlighting that a change needs to take place (because otherwise, e.g., costs would rise dramatically) and which decisions are required by political decision makers to enable the necessary change. As a corresponding measure, a culture of failure should be established to not being 'abolished' when either communicating these past failures or making considerably 'small' errors in the future. This could contribute to eliminating legacy systems through getting investment funding and the chance for a protype-based (cf. pilot projects), somehow risky replacement of those. It can contribute to being agile directly through an emphasis on continuous learning and improvement as well as the embracement of uncertainty.

4.3   Towards an Integrated Model

Abstracting the findings presented in Sects. 4.1 and 4.2 leads to the consolidated model visualized in Fig. 1. As outlined in the introduction, the types of organizations that are in focus of this research operate in a VUCA environment, e.g., regarding customer demands. This is also reflected in the different context spheres of the transformation initiatives described in the figure based on the context characteristics proposed by O'Toole and Meier [24], which were identified as obstacles in the previous sections. It should be noted that the context spheres are interrelated, e.g., that a fragmentation of actors in the political context promotes an environmental context which is, for instance, characterized by a high information systems complexity, which in turn makes room for competing goals, for example, whether to invest into the legacy systems of immature customers or realize new digital solutions with more mature customers. Both the 'old', non-agile organization as well as the transformation initiative's organization (e.g., programs, projects) are located within these context spheres. The transformation initiative transforming the non-agile organization into an agile one is obstructed by obstacles related to the management approach and to the different context spheres. The measures presented in Sect. 4.2 were suggested to mitigate the negative impact of the obstacles. As this effect relies on the elimination or at least reduction of context features (e.g., models from value stream and architectural thinking break up complexity) and adaption of the management approach, this constitutes an indirect effect on being agile. In addition, the measures also have a direct effect on being agile, because they embrace agile principles, values, and/or mindset, like the architectural models facilitate achieving a common vision and customer-centric thinking. This also marks an indirect effect on enterprise agility, which was presented as the ultimate goal of becoming agile in Sect. 1. The measures could also have a direct effect on enterprise agility through enhancing its associated capabilities, like the holistic models contribute to, e.g., sensing capabilities as they provide a set of entities which must be monitored for change. Last, the measures are also related internally—value stream thinking and architectural thinking support identifying pilot projects, which are based on a culture of failure allowing to take appropriate risks in those.

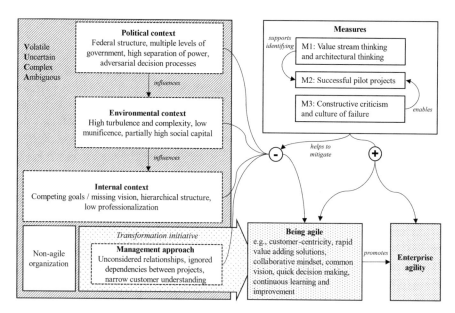

Fig. 1 Visualization of findings drawing on the Theory of Context by O'Toole and Meier [24]

5 Discussion and Conclusion

5.1 Interpretation of the Findings with Regards to the Previous Literature

The findings concerning the political context fit well into the existing literature that reports, concerning the separation of power, an emphasis on individual interests (e.g., [49, 50]) and relatedly a lack of trust (e.g., [39, 49]). This could be common for the public sector and other complex, decentral organizations. Regarding the environmental context and the complexity and turbulence of requirements, e.g., Hong and Kim [51] note that opposed to private companies, governments target only one, but very heterogenous customer group. Complexity with regards to IT legacy has also been identified in several studies (e.g., [11, 52]). Munificence in terms of the release of resources and commitment by senior management is also found to be insufficient (e.g., [10, 53, 54]), also indicating the generalizability of the findings. The same applies for a lack of customer commitment (e.g., [55]). Coming to the internal context, competing goals and an unclear vision seem to not have been previously reported in an agile context. This might be related to the specific selection of cases that have multiple organizational customers as opposed to previous studies, primarily looking at agile transformation of teams within an agency. While it could be easier to align on a common vision within an organization, bringing multiple agencies to a common vision appears to be more difficult. Professionalization, however, has been recognized as an issue, either with an emphasis on the dependency on specific persons [53] and consultants [56] or missing competences (e.g., [10, 53, 55]). This might also be a common property of public sector organizations. Concerning the management approach, the missing holistic and differentiated picture appears not to have been found in prior research. The discovery might again relate to the research design that focused on large-scale transformations and did not focus on just the implementation of frameworks but becoming agile and thus general business model aspects and value creation were more considered. However, given that this was found in all cases with their respective management teams of different educational and professional backgrounds, this might be a preliminary generalizable insight.

Somewhat corresponding to this novel finding, value stream thinking and architectural thinking as a measure could also not be identified in previous literature. However, thinking in value streams might also not be found in literature because this is less relevant in studies not looking at scaled agile transformations and for studies that investigate scaled agile transformations it is an implied pre-condition. In contrast, the need for pilot projects has been recognized before [30, 49, 56]. The last proposed measure, constructive criticism and culture of failure, was only mentioned by Hong and Kim [51] proposing risk-friendly monitoring and rewarding systems. Again, this might be related to this study focusing on large-scale transformations, as risk taking is more an issue when deciding which projects to start and thus less relevant on an intra-project-level. Moreover, as Hong and Kim [51] investigate the phenomenon of becoming an agile government, this might be more associated with the focus of this study.

5.2 *Implications for Practice*

With this work, practitioners, i.e., the management of PSSPs and of steering bodies as well as political leaders, receive an overview of obstacles that need to be removed to pave the way for such organizations to be agile. Moreover, a set of preliminary measures is proposed that can be further detailed out, implemented, and tested. The integrated model presented in Sect. 4.3 especially indicates that every measure targeted at the reduction of obstacles needs to consider the interrelated nature of the context spheres. Furthermore, it is recommendable that practitioners do 'foundational' work (value stream/architectural thinking and constructive criticism/failure culture) first before approaching pilot projects. Now, the question arises whether, under which circumstances, and how long the findings and recommendations can be generalized. While differences with regards to properties of these PSSPs such as the specialty of the service portfolio, the independence and regulation (with regards to, e.g., the selection of customers, prescription of services to be offered, budget control) and the intent to realize a profit might exist, similar problems might be faced by executives within PSSPs from multiple federal levels, countries and even from similar organizations from the private sector. The situation for steering bodies can be seen analogously, while the differences there might relate to aspects such as budget, responsibilities, or the authority to issue binding directives. But even independent of this projectability, understanding agile transformations of PSSPs and associated risks is of high social relevance. Cost increases/efficiency losses due to unsuccessful transformations reduces the budget—depending on the financing mechanism of these organizations—that is available for other public investments. Issues regarding stability and security of operations could have negative impacts on economic and social life. The first argument holds true for the steering bodies as well. As many PSSPs are forced to stay in business due to regulatory constraints, avoiding dependence on private companies and the specialized services they offer, even in the long term it could not be assumed that 'the market' and private companies as a replacement will ensure an efficient and reliant service delivery. At the same time, the efficiency gains expected from adopting agile methodology create a grand chance. Naturally, the steering bodies as a management overhead will be relevant as soon as any form of orchestration and coordination of local efforts is desired.

5.3   Limitations and Future Research

Every study has limitations, and the project at hand is no exception. First, the sample size is quite small and having at least an additional steering body would have enabled further abstraction from case-specifics. Second, while the conduction of the research alongside regular consulting engagements has deepened the insights, this might have created a selection bias towards organizations where many and/or significant obstacles occur. Third, the usage of context theory as an analytical lens and the case selection has resulted in most findings being related to the political and environmental context, as the cases share only a few commonalities on the management approach, given their yet quite different 'business model'.

Besides addressing these limitations, future research could more systematically study the impact of the proposed measures through a quantifiable operationalization of the concept of being agile and measuring improvements at relevant organizations after the measures have been implemented. Considering the identified obstacles, these could be defined more differentiated, e.g., through developing stage models, or in the case of the measures, maturity models. Regarding the linkages between the obstacles and measures identified in this and previous research, these could be studied quantitatively in a higher number of organizations (e.g., the proposed integrated model could serve as the basis for a structural equation modeling). This would also allow identifying patterns, which does not seem to have been done in the existing literature.

References

1. Mergel, I., Edelmann, N., & Haug, N. (2019). Defining digital transformation: Results from expert interviews. *Government Information Quarterly, 36*(4), 1–16.
2. Clarke, A. (2019). Digital government units: what are they, and what do they mean for digital era public management renewal? *International Public Management Journal, 23*(3), 358–379.
3. Verhoef, P. C., Broekhuizen, T., Bart, Y., Bhattacharya, A., Dong, J. Q., Fabian, N., & Haenlein, M. (2021). Digital transformation: A multidisciplinary reflection and research agenda. *Journal of Business Research, 122*, 889–901.
4. Bennett, N., & Lemoine, G. J. (2014). What a difference a word makes: Understanding threats to performance in a VUCA world. *Business Horizons, 57*(3), 311–317.
5. van Manen, H., & van Vliet, H. (2014). Organization-wide agile expansion requires an organization-wide agile mindset. In A. Jedlitschka, P. Kuvaja, M. Kuhrmann, T. Männistö, J. Münch, & M. Raatikainen (Eds.), *15th international conference on product-focused software process improvement, PROFES 2014, LNCS* (Vol. 8892, pp. 48–62). Springer.
6. Horlach, B., & Drechsler, A. (2020). It's not easy being agile: Unpacking paradoxes in agile environments. In *Agile processes in software engineering and extreme programming—Workshops, LNBIP* (Vol. 396, pp. 182–189). Springer.
7. Teece, D., Peteraf, M., & Leih, S. (2016). Dynamic capabilities and organizational agility: Risk, uncertainty, and strategy in the innovation economy. *California Management Review, 58*(4), 13–35.
8. Klimenko, R., Winter, R., & Rohner, P. (2019). Designing capability maturity model for agile transformation excellence. In: *MCIS2019 proceedings* (pp. 1–9).
9. Edison, H., Wang, X., & Conboy, K. (2021). Comparing methods for large-scale agile software development: A systematic literature review. *IEEE Transactions on Software Engineering*, 1–23.
10. Vacari, I., & Prikladnicki, R. (2015). Adopting agile methods in the public sector: A systematic literature review. In: *27th international conference on software engineering and knowledge engineering proceedings* (pp. 1–6).
11. Mohagheghi, P., & Lassenius, C. (2021). Organizational implications of agile adoption: A case study from the public sector. In *ESEC/FSE 2021: Proceedings of the 29th ACM joint meeting on European software engineering conference and symposium on the foundations of software engineering* (pp. 1444–1454). Association for Computing Machinery.
12. Fuchs, C., & Hess, T. (2018). Becoming agile in the digital transformation: The process of a large-scale agile transformation. In *ICIS 2018 Proceedings* (pp. 1–17).
13. Gabryelczyk, R. (2020). Has COVID-19 accelerated digital transformation? Initial lessons learned for public administrations. *Information Systems Management, 37*(4), 303–309.
14. Agostino, D., Arnaboldi, M., & Lema, M. D. (2020). New development: COVID-19 as an accelerator of digital transformation in public service delivery. *Public Money & Management, 41*(1), 69–72.
15. Obstacle Definition & Meaning. Last retrieved May 19, 2022, from https://www.merriam-webster.com/dictionary/obstacle.
16. Measure Definition & Meaning. Last retrieved May 19, 2022, from https://www.merriam-webster.com/dictionary/measure.
17. Chan, F. K. Y., & Thong, J. Y. L. (2009). Acceptance of agile methodologies: A critical review and conceptual framework. *Decision Support Systems, 46*(4), 803–814.
18. Cohen, D., Lindvall, M., & Costa, P. (2004). An introduction to agile methods. *Advances in Computers, 62*, 1–66.
19. Theobald, S., Schmitt, A., & Diebold, P. (2019). Comparing scaling agile frameworks based on underlying practices. In R. Hoda (Ed.), *Agile processes in software engineering and extreme programming—Workshops, LNBIP* (Vol. 364, pp. 88–96). Springer.

20. Séguin, N., Tremblay, G., & Bagane, H. (2012). Agile principles as software engineering principles: An analysis. In C. Wohlin (Ed.), *Agile processes in software engineering and extreme programming 13th international conference, XP 2012, LNBIP* (Vol. 111, pp. 1–15). Springer.
21. Definition of value noun from the Oxford Advanced Learner's Dictionary. Last retrieved May 19, 2022, from https://www.oxfordlearnersdictionaries.com/definition/english/value_1?q=value.
22. Definition of mindset noun from the Oxford Advanced Learner's Dictionary. Last retrieved May 19, 2022, from https://www.oxfordlearnersdictionaries.com/definition/english/mindset?q=mindset.
23. Definition of transformation noun from the Oxford Advanced Learner's Dictionary. Last retrieved May 19, 2022, from https://www.oxfordlearnersdictionaries.com/definition/english/transformation?q=transformation.
24. O'Toole, L. J., & Meier, K. J. (2014). Public management, context, and performance: In quest of a more general theory. *Journal of Public Administration Research and Theory, 25*(1), 237–256.
25. George, J. M., & Jones, G. R. (1997). Organizational spontaneity in context. *Human Performance, 10*(2), 153–170.
26. Bamberger, P. (2008). From the editors: Beyond contextualization: Using context theories to narrow the micro-macro gap in management research. *Academy of Management Journal, 51*(5), 839–846.
27. Mergel, I. (2019). Digital service teams in government. *Government Information Quarterly, 36*(4), 1–16.
28. Kiselev, C., Winter, R., & Rohner, P. (2020). Project success requires context-aware governance. *MIS Quarterly Executive, 19*(3), 199–211.
29. Westermann, F. (2019). *A Balancing Act: Defining a control-oriented approach to public sector agility*. Master thesis. Delft University of Technology. Retrieved from http://resolver.tudelft.nl/uuid:d8b03c83-d4e8-4288-9287-fa3c4eb7dc91.
30. Carroll, N., Bjørnson, F. O., Dingsøyr, T., Rolland, K. H., & Conboy, K. (2020). Operationalizing agile methods: Examining coherence in large-scale agile transformations. In M. Paasivaara & P. Kruchten (Eds.), *Agile processes in software engineering and extreme programming—Workshops, LNBIP* (Vol. 396, pp. 75–83). Springer.
31. Pettigrew, A. M., Woodman, R. W., & Cameron, K. S. (2001). Studying organizational change and development: Challenges for future research. *The Academy of Management Journal, 44*(4), 697–713.
32. Soparnot, R. (2011). The concept of organizational change capacity. *Journal of Organizational Change Management, 24*(5), 640–661.
33. Jansson, N. (2013). Organizational change as practice: A critical analysis. *Journal of Organizational Change Management, 26*(6), 1003–1019.
34. Fernandez, S., & Rainey, H. G. (2006). Managing successful organizational change in the public sector. *Public Administration Review, 66*(2), 168–176.
35. Tangi, L., Janssen, M., Benedetti, M., & Noci, G. (2021). Digital government transformation: A structural equation modelling analysis of driving and impeding factors. *International Journal of Information Management, 60*, 1–10.
36. Pedersen, K. (2018). E-government transformations: challenges and strategies. *Transforming Government: People, Process and Policy, 12*(1), 84–109.
37. Andrews, R., Beynon, M. J., & McDermott, A. M. (2016). Organizational capability in the public sector: A configurational approach. *Journal of Public Administration Research and Theory, 26*(2), 239–258.
38. van der Voet, J. (2019). Organizational decline and innovation in public organizations: A contextual framework of cutback management. *Perspectives on Public Management and Governance, 2*(2), 139–154.

39. Bolhuis, W. T. C. (2021). *How can (large scale) agile be effectively adopted and scaled up in Dutch public sector organisations.* Master thesis. University of Twente. Retrieved from http://purl.utwente.nl/essays/88539.
40. SAFe 5 for Lean Enterprises. Last retrieved May 19, 2022, from https://www.scaledagile-framework.com/safe-for-lean-enterprises/.
41. Davison, R. M., & Martinsons, M. G. (2007). Action research and consulting. In N. Kock (Ed.), *Information systems action research* (pp. 377–394). Springer.
42. Davison, R. M., Martinsons, M. G., & Kock, N. (2004). Principles of canonical action research. *Information Systems Journal, 14*(1), 65–86.
43. Baskerville, R., & Wood-Harper, A. T. (1998). Diversity in information systems action research methods. *European Journal of Information Systems, 7*(2), 90–107.
44. Eisenhardt, K. M. (2020). What is the Eisenhardt method, really? *Strategic Organization, 19*(1), 147–160.
45. Schröder, D., Kiselev, C., Rohner, S., Kautz, T., & Rohner, P. (2022). Entwicklung, Einsatz und Wirkung des Digital Transformation Orchestrator. *Controlling, 34*(1), 59–64.
46. Drury, M., Conboy, K., & Power, K. (2012). Obstacles to decision making in Agile software development teams. *Journal of Systems and Software, 85*(6), 1239–1254.
47. Value Streams. Last retrieved May 19, 2022, from https://www.scaledagileframework.com/value-streams/.
48. Winter, R. (2010). Organisational design and engineering—Proposal of a conceptual framework and comparison of business engineering with other approaches. *International Journal of Organizational Design and Engineering, 1*(1&2), 126–147.
49. Onwujekwe, G., & Weistroffer, H. (2019). Agile development in bureaucratic environments: A literature review. In M. Themistocleous & P. R. da Cunha (Eds.), *15th European, Mediterranean, and Middle Eastern Conference, EMCIS 2018, LNBIP* (Vol. 341, pp. 316–330). Springer.
50. Ghimire, D., Charters, S., & Gibbs, S. (2020). Scaling agile software development approach in government organization in New Zealand. In *ICSIM '20: Proceedings of the 3rd international conference on software engineering and information management* (pp. 100–104). Association for Computing Machinery.
51. Hong, K. P., & Kim, P. S. (2020). Building an agile government: Its possibilities, challenges, and new tasks. *Halduskultuur: The Estonian Journal of Administrative Culture and Digital Governance, 21*(1), 4–21.
52. Bjørnson, F. O., Vestues, K., & Rolland, K. H. (2017). Coordination in the large: A research design. In *XP '17: Proceedings of the XP2017 scientific workshops* (pp. 1–5). Association for Computing Machinery.
53. Lappi, T., & Aaltonen, K. (2017). Project governance in public sector agile software projects. *International Journal of Managing Projects in Business, 10*(2), 263–294.
54. Mantovani Fontana, R., & Marczak, S. (2020). Characteristics and challenges of agile software development adoption in Brazilian Government. *Journal of Technology Management & Innovation, 15*(2).
55. Patanakul, P., & Rufo-McCarron, R. (2018). Transitioning to agile software development: Lessons learned from a government-contracted program. *The Journal of High Technology Management Research, 29*(2), 181–192.
56. Ylinen, M. (2021). Incorporating agile practices in public sector IT management: A nudge toward adaptive governance. *Information Polity, 26*(3), 251–271.

Analysing the Bottom-Up Approach to Develop Organisational Culture in Virtualised Organisations

Irene Pescatore ⓘD, Filomena Pagnozzi ⓘD, and Gilda Antonelli ⓘD

Abstract Due to the processes of the virtualisation of work, organisations are facing profound transformations which are also changing their organisational culture. The mainstream academic literature defines organisational culture in terms of shared meaning i.e., patterns of belief, symbolism, rituals, and mythology, which evolve and function as a source of cohesion for an organisation (Glaser et al. Management Communication Quarterly 1(2):173–198, 1987). Therefore, it argues that organisational culture develops within organisations through a top-down approach (Shepherd and Sutcliffe. The Academy of Management Review 36(2):361–380, 2011). However, as emerging technologies and the virtualisation of work have brought about substantial change (Großer and Baumöl. International Journal of Information Systems and Project Management 5(4):21–35, 2022), it is necessary to redefine the concept of organisational culture. Considering the different approaches to organisational culture, the present research aims at analysing how it is formulated within virtualised organisations (Atkinson and Sohn. TESOL Quarterly 47, 2013) that have several peculiarities both in terms of organisational designs and soft competencies (Autor et al. The Quarterly Journal of Economics 118(4):1279–1333, 2003; Autor. The changing task composition of the US Labor Market: An update of Autor, Levy, and Murnane (2003)—David Autor. ScholarSite, Inc., 2013; Grundke et al. Which skills for the digital era? Returns to skills analysis. OECD, 2018; Bissola et al. Journal of Product Innovation Management 31, 2014). Despite the increasing prevalence, this aspect has received little attention within academia. We will analyse the bottom-up perspective through the lenses of Sociotechnical and Complexity theories (Bednar and Welch. Information Systems

---

I. Pescatore (✉) · F. Pagnozzi
DEMM, University of Sannio, Benevento, BN, Italy
e-mail: ipescatore@unisannio.it; filomena.pagnozzi@unisannio.it

G. Antonelli
Economics Department, D'Annunzio University, Pescara, Italy

Management Department, WSB University, Gdansk, Poland
e-mail: gilda.antonelli@unich.it

A. Lazazzara et al. (eds.), *Towards Digital and Sustainable Organisations*,
Lecture Notes in Information Systems and Organisation 65,
https://doi.org/10.1007/978-3-031-52880-4_9

141

Frontiers 22(2):281–298, 2020; Kuhn. 9. The essential tension: Tradition and innovation in scientific research. In The essential tension. University of Chicago Press,
pp 225–239. 2011; Bauman. Liquid modernity. Polity, 2000), as well as compare
academic and grey literature to highlight the need for a change in the mainstream
approach to organizational culture.

Keywords Organisational culture · Virtual team · Emerging technologies ·
Socio-technical theories · Complexity theory

1   Introduction

The use of emerging technologies, as well as the spread of COVID-19, has caused
profound changes in organisational management, activities, and decision-making.
One of the most important issues arising from these changes concerns workers due
to the increasing virtualisation of the workplace, with often-mandatory remote
working vacating fixed physical office spaces. Therefore, within many organisations, it is becoming more and more frequent to use the term virtual team, which in
the present literature does not have a unique definition. There are researchers who
define the virtual team in terms of the implementation of new technologies and
telecommunication to promote coordination and cooperation [1], others in terms of
groups of workers operating from different geographical locations [2], and those
who, on the other hand, define virtual teams as relevant organisational groups to
support infrastructural evolution [3]. Technology is the most relevant factor that
characterises a successful virtual team. However, it is important to consider another
fundamental element, the organisational culture, that differentiates organisations or
teams from others. As for the virtual team, there are many definitions of organisational culture within academic literature. Mainstream scholars define organisational
culture as a top-down process originating from management and implemented, or
even imposed, upon an organisation [4–6]. Therefore, in this case, the culture of an
organisation is associated exclusively with the values, principles, and beliefs of
management [7–9]. The adoption of a bottom-up approach to organisational culture
ensures the active participation of workers in the decision-making process, as well
as encourages shared principles and values between employees, who build a working environment themself. To develop a bottom-up organisational culture within a
virtualised and dynamic organisation, it is necessary that workers develop specific
competencies which have become essential in recent years. Some studies demonstrate that a bottom-up approach to organizational culture is a particularly influential contribution that contrasts with the mainstream view of organisational culture
with an innovative vision [10–13]. This new approach is supported by some recent
theories, such as Socio-Technical and Complexity theories. These emerging theories, which are generally used in computer-based IT research, can also be applied to

the study of organisational management. Because of emerging technologies, COVID-19, and the virtualisation of work environments, organisations need to be flexible and dynamic [14]. According to Socio-technical theory, organisations can be described as sets of technical and social subsystems that jointly create value and innovation [9] while according to Complexity theories, they are complex systems, made by a multiplicity of relationships inside and outside the organisation itself [15–17]. Considering these definitions, a new vision of organizational culture can be asserted: culture is no longer created according to a verticalised pattern, but workers assume a primary role in defining it through their input and shared values [18–20]. There are few studies, both in academic and grey literature, that consider the bottom-up approach of organizational culture in virtualised organisations which apply Socio-technical and Complexity theories.

2 The Organisational Culture

Since the late twentieth century, culture has assumed a fundamental role in organisations. Many definitions of organisational culture have been proposed in academic literature. In the mid-1900s, psychologists and sociologists introduced the concept of climate into organisations, highlighting its influence on organisational lives [21]. The terms climate and culture were subsequently used interchangeably until the 1970s [22]. However, since the mid-1970s researchers have given greater importance to the concept of organisational culture and its definition [23]. Schein [24, p. 111] was the first scholar to formally define organisational culture as "*a pattern of shared basic assumption which has been discovered, developed or invented by a specific group as it learns to manage with issues of external adaptation and internal integration, which is effective enough to be considered valid and, therefore, to be taught to new team members as a correct way to perceive, think and feel about reframing problems*". Soon after, other scholars introduced new elements to define organisational culture. Pettigrew [25] introduced anthropological concepts such as symbolism, mythology, and rituals that could be used in the organisational analysis as tools to foresee culture; Hofstede et al. [9], on the other hand, highlighted the importance of shared values, beliefs, and practices amongst members [26]. Lastly, amongst the earlier definitions of organisational culture (Table 1), Wagner [5] introduced the concept of organisational culture as a method to influence the beliefs and behaviors of an organisation's members.

All these definitions refer to the dissemination of organisational culture according to a top-down approach [4]. Moreover, many mainstream scholars affirmed that organisational culture and all the components that characterise it, start from the organisation's leaders and managers that are at the top of the organisational chart. All the other members who are in the lower part of the chart absorb such values and principles, which influence their behaviors and practices [6]. However, organisational culture does not depend only on factors considered by mainstream researchers [27]. The organisational culture must be strongly shared by all members of an

Table 1 Earlier definitions of organisational culture

Authors	Definition
Schein (1990)	Culture is a pattern of shared basic assumption which has been discovered, developed or invented by a specific group as it learns to manage with issues of external adaptation and internal integration, which is effective enough to be considered valid and, therefore, to be taught to new team members as a correct way to perceive, think and feel about reframing problems
Pettigrew (1989)	Culture is the system of publicly and collectively accepted meanings operating for a given group at a given time. This system of terms, forms, categories, and images interpret people's situations themselves. Moreover, the results of the concept of culture I have in mind are symbol, language, ideology, belief, ritual, and myth
Hofstede (1984, 1990)	Culture is the collective programming of the mind that distinguishes the members of one group or category of people from others
Alvesson (2002)	Culture is regarded as a more-or-less cohesive system of meanings and symbols, in terms of which social interaction takes place. Social structure is regarded as the behavioral patterns to which the social interaction itself gives rise
Wagner (2005)	An informal, shared way of perceiving life and membership in the organisation that binds members together and influences what they think about themselves and their work

Source: Authors' elaboration

organisation and, as such, should also consider the needs, wishes, and well-being of workers [11]. Due to emerging technologies and continuous changes in organizations, also organizational culture definition may be updated. By pursuing a Socio-technical approach, organisational culture became a fundamental element to ensure organisations' success because social and technical aspects converge to achieve the same goal and, therefore, these are greatly influenced by the culture and values of the organisations' members [28]. Furthermore, analyzing organisational culture through the lenses of Complexity theory it seems really in line with modern organisational structures. According to this theory, an organisation is defined as complex when it represents a system, in which it is important to ensure the balance between all the internal and external agents. These elements need to be strongly interconnected, differentiate, in constant evolution, and have to have fragile, permeable and indistinct boundaries [29]. According to Complexity theory, the organizational culture needs to be generated by the feedback exchanged by agents. Therefore, the top-down approach is abandoned altogether in favour of a bottom-up approach [30]. Moreover, organisational culture can be developed using a bottom-up approach if members have specific competencies, acquired from experience and training, which are consistent with organisational values and strengthen them [31].

3 Virtualised Organisations and Organisational Culture

Due to the COVID-19 pandemic, organisations have been pushed to adopt and implement a process of virtualisation of work. This process, not entirely new, has allowed organisations to leap forward at least 10 years, especially in some areas of

Europe such as Italy. Two years later in 2019, this process has become a widespread reality. *"Virtual organizations are defined as a temporary collection of enterprises that co-operate and share resources, knowledge, and competencies to better respond to business opportunities"* [32, p. 1]. Virtualisation, thanks to the use of emerging technologies, establishes a new way of working that leads to rethink, redesign, and manage spaces, processes, and people using flexibility, agility, and dynamism. The virtualisation of work involves the adoption of four principles: working without fixed time and place; guiding employees towards the achievement of results and managing their work with full autonomy; free access and use of knowledge, experiences, and ideas; and flexible working relationships. Technology, therefore, is certainly one of the determining factors that favor the process of virtualisation and digital transformation of organisations being able to act in a determined manner on different variables such as the quality of work and productivity. However, technology, while being a determining variable, is the only one that affects the process of virtualisation of organisations and their way of working. In highly virtualized environments employees experience greater autonomy and responsibility and interaction is developed and implemented through new ways of communicating [33]. Thus, organisations can create and develop virtual teams with talented people who have the right skills to succeed in a complex, dynamic and global economy.

There is no unique definition of a virtual team; it can be defined as *"groups of collaborators dispersed geographically and/or from an organisational point of view that are assembled using a combination of telecommunications and information technology to perform an organisational task"* [1, p. 17]. Morrison-Smith and Ruiz [3] believe that they are now fundamental organisational units to support the evolving and increasingly globalised social and economic infrastructure. Some scholars define virtual teams as *"a group of people interacting through interdependent tasks guided by a common purpose and working across space, time, and organisational boundaries"* [34, p. 18] using modern and advanced information and communication technologies. However, some researchers believe that the virtual term indicates collaboration in teams working whilst never meeting face to face [35, 36]. More recently, Bell and Kozlowski [37] identified virtual teams as working arrangements where team members are geographically dispersed, have limited face-to-face contact, and work interdependently with electronic media to achieve common goals. Kirkman and Mathieu [38] believe that the physical dispersion of team members can in no way be considered the only distinguishing feature of virtual teams because, team members, can be placed and work both on different continents and in the same buildings. Virtual teams, in line with virtualised organizations, are characterized by distinctive features such as the total lack of traditional organisational boundaries of time and space, the use of technology to communicate [39, 40] and flexibility. The organisational culture not only influences the effectiveness with which organisations implement these processes [41] but also shapes the behavior of the members of the organisation [42]. The virtualisation of organisations involves the adoption of a more agile and flexible organisational culture focused on the enhancement of people and their skills. In this perspective, the organisational change, due to the adoption of processes of virtualisation and digitalisation of work, entails the need to adopt a more involved organisational culture with greater commitment and active participation of employees.

4   The Bottom-Up Approach to Culture

In many organisations, the top-down approach dominates the organisational culture. In general, management is characterised by planning, organisation, command, coordination, and control [43]. In their studies, Kim and Arnold [44] created a hierarchical model that outlines a useful process to determine priorities, action plans, production objectives, and the choice of performance improvement programs. The top-down process is described by scholars as the planned coordination of intentions and actions to achieve specific results imposed by a central authority. According to Pressman and Wildavsky [45], adopting a top-down perspective the power, the decisions, the processes, and the hierarchical structure are strongly centralized. The top-down approach is based on a direct instruction and control structure, however, situations, where perfect control exists, can be very difficult to achieve.

The bottom-up approach follows a completely reverse process that starts from the bottom. Using this approach, organisations adopt a culture that involves the base of the organisation by providing less weight in the decision-making process to managers, especially in change management [46]. Lipsky [47] for example, adopts a bottom-up perspective according to which power becomes decentralized. The implementation of the processes takes place through networks of actors such as stakeholders or local employees (so-called "street bureaucrats"). The adoption of a bottom-up approach entails that the strategies are not totally determined by the top, but employees have a shared responsibility in defining them. The advantages of a bottom-up culture include: active participation of employees in decision-making processes and greater autonomy; active sharing of company values; greater motivation and employee empowerment; increased creativity and proactivity at lower levels of the organization; and creation of a greater added value of employees in carrying out their duties thanks to a culture based on continuous feedback.

Furthermore, the adoption of a bottom-up approach to reinforce culture clearly highlights the Socio-technical character of change in organisations and adherence to participatory forms of management. This change is not defined and imposed by the top management but rather emerges from the positive qualities and abilities of the organisation and all its members [12]. Hartl [13] conducted a qualitative analysis based on the study of eleven business cases each characterised by different organisational cultures. All organisations needed to address organisational change in the context of digital transformation. The authors demonstrated that it is important to adopt a dynamic, bottom-up approach to change through the involvement and active participation of all members in all processes from the definition of goals to the creation of a co-development and specific co-values for the entire organisation. The adoption of a bottom-up approach to culture implies the participation at every level of all the members of the organisation encouraging a greater identification and responsibility of the members towards the organisation to which they belong. Therefore, it is necessary to involve human resources in all phases of the decision-making process, from the development of the vision to the implementation and its diffusion, especially in those processes that have as object a change.

5 Discussion

The common thread that requires change within virtualised organisations is essentially based on two important variables: technology and its relationship with humans. These elements involve a radical change in the production system which has a huge impact on the organisational, economic, and social system. Not surprisingly, technological improvements and social changes are profoundly transforming the ways and methods of work in modern organisations. Therefore, emerges the need to adopt a Socio-technical perspective centred on work systems that include both the machine and interaction between people and machines [48]. Mohr and van Amelsvoort [49, p. 2] defined the Socio-technical approach as: "[…] *the participatory and multidisciplinary study and improvement of how workplaces, individual organisations, networks, and ecosystems function internally and in relation to their environmental context, with particular attention to the mutual interactions of the entity's value creation processes*". A Socio-technical system is represented by two interdependent and complementary sub-systems [50]: a technical subsystem (composed of technologies, means, tools, and know-how) identified by the activities, processes, and technology that allow the transformation of inputs into outputs to generate value for all stakeholders; a social subsystem made up of people, the relationships that are created, and the organisational structure. Pasmore [51] introduces a third variable, arguing that every organization is made up of people, a technical system and the environment. People use tools and knowledge with the aim of producing goods and/or services used by consumers or users (the latter are part of the external environment of the organization). Therefore, a correct balance between the three systems is necessary in order to make an organization more effective. A modern Socio-technical approach centred on the person does not consider the technical and social subsystems as distinct and separate but as integrated and capable of generating co-value and creating innovation. More recent academic literature suggests analysing the internal functioning of organisations by considering the environmental context of individual processes, roles, organisational units, networks, and ecosystems [49]. The adoption of a socio-technical approach can foster a deeper understanding of the cultural and organisational change processes of virtualised organisations operating in highly digitised environments [52].

In order to spread bottom-up approaches to organisational culture, it is necessary to analyse innovative theories. Amongst these, it is important to consider Complexity theories. The profound technological, organisational, social, and political transformations are generating complex systems to be managed in different fields, mathematical, biological, organisational, etc. [53–55]. This is the reason why Complexity theories enable innovative ways to examine and theorise organisational activities [56, 57] organisation design [58], and organisational culture [59]. Complexity theory arises in contrast to some mainstream theories' assumptions. The latter is based on Newton's approach, which argued that astral bodies were determined by linear mechanical laws and causalities [60], as well as the Cartesian analytical approach, in which each problem can be divided into different parts and recomposed to generate the final solution of the whole phenomenon [61, 62]. Otherwise, the emerging paradigm of Complexity theory does not assume that causality is based on mechanical operations. In particular, the contribution of these theories allows us to analyse social systems and organisations as heterogeneous systems, where causes and effects are influenced by a variety of factors and actors that are both internal and external to its tighter boundaries. Indeed, Complexity theory is relevant because nowadays organisations are complex and multifaced and need to consider not only the internal environment (workers' well-being, the work-life balance, the relationship between members of an organisation, the economic and financial satisfaction, etc.) but also the external environment, considering the management of all the elements that are not under the direct control of the organization itself. Manson, one of the leading researchers of Complexity theories, stated that "*complexity research concerns how complex behavior evolves or emerges from relatively simple local interactions between system components over time*" [63, p. 38]. According to his study, it is necessary to leave the static view of organisations, to introduce a challenging vision based on change and transformation. Moreover, an organisation is defined as a complex system because complexity is synonymous with "putting together different interdependent factors" and, therefore, finding a balance between all the elements that build and influence an organisation [17]. In other words, the complexity consists in the multiplicity of relationships to be managed both inside and outside organisations. Considering the internal environment and relationships, which are those that mainly affect the organisational culture [64], these must be flexible, dynamic, and adaptive to different situations. Anyway, Complexity theories strengthen the bottom-up approach to the spread of organisational culture, despite the diversity of perceptions, ideas, culture, and behaviors amongst members of organisations [20]. In Complexity theories, the organisational culture is developed through feedback, which are the opinions and proposals exchanged by members of organisations. Feedback, whether positive or negative, is fundamental, as it represents mechanisms that strengthen balances in complex systems [18, 65]. While negative feedback is more common in traditional organisations that favor stability in static situations [19, 66–68]; positive feedback is typical of organisations capable of seeking balance in situations of change. In addition, positive feedback promotes stability even in situations of change, such as those that organisations face constantly. Therefore, if the mainstream paradigm of a dominant organisational culture that starts from the top is completely abandoned, it would be possible to foster greater connectivity among the members of the organisation [18] and, consequently, create a bottom-up organisational culture that effectively reflects the principles, values, and decisions of the entire organisation.

To deal with this more innovative approach to create organizational culture it is crucial to reflect on employees' competencies. *"Competence is an underlying characteristic of a person, which results in effective and/or superior performance in a job"* [69, p. 8]. Overall, competencies can be described as a set of skills, attitudes, and knowledge [31]. For organisations to succeed in such a dynamic and ever-changing market, members need to develop specific competencies which are acquired through training, or previous experiences and knowledge [70]. Furthermore, previous studies have demonstrated that the possession by the workers of some specific competencies and the culture and shared values of an organization are inter-related [71]. Mainstream studies affirm that organisational culture develops based on the competencies, beliefs, values, and behaviors of the leaders and managers of an organisation [72] and the specific strategic policies that are implemented to grow them. Otherwise, the organisational culture could be developed from the bottom-up, by utilising the workers' competencies. Some of the most related competencies to organisational culture are communication, creativity, cooperation, and personal initiative [73–76]. To develop an organisational culture using the bottom-up approach, an efficient communication strategy between members represents one of the most important factors. Emerging technologies and the use of new software, and social media are important tools to develop communication between employees [77]. Socialisation can also create shared values and therefore a well-valued organisational culture. Helmerich et al. [78] demonstrate that the use of digital tools has increased the associative power amongst workers, thanks to the exchange of knowledge, teamwork, the acquisition of new information, and activities carried out independently. Therefore, the use of digital tools promotes cohesion among all workers as it guarantees equal opportunities for acquiring knowledge, skills, and experience [79]. Therefore, virtualisation processes have generated an intensification in the use of collaborative tools and applications which are useful for horizontal, vertical, and transversal communication, workflow management, as well as the sharing of documents and multimedia files related to projects and tasks amongst members [80]. Efficient communication generates strong cooperation between the members of an organisation. Working in groups and creating cohesion facilitates the achievement of work goals and the exchanging of ideas, learning from the experiences and practices of others, as well as time-sharing. In addition, cooperation in an organisation ensures the creation of a high-performance working environment based on trust and compliance, both financially and organisationally [81]. Moreover, considering the deep transformations that organisations are undergoing, cooperation is useful to create digital platforms in virtual teams for networking, the diffusion of knowledge and project management [82], as well as for improving performance [83]. Through cooperation between members, it is also possible to make strategic, operational decisions and, therefore, develop an organisational culture. On the other hand, successful cooperation is fostered by the strong personal initiative of team members. Everyone should feel like an important part of the team and, therefore, should actively participate in decision-making processes and carry out different activities: this is truer in successful virtual teams [84]. Furthermore, personal initiative is an important competence for creating a bottom-up organisational culture, referring to particularly proactive behaviors of workers who, in turn, can influence organisational decisions and culture. Moreover, to be able to influence the organisational culture, workers must be creative. Creativity, which is closely related to innovation, is relevant for finding solutions to complex issues in an alternative way to foster cooperation, as well as finding relationships and similarities between seemingly unrelated things. In modern organisations, creativity needs to be developed both individually and on a team level. Many studies demonstrate that collective creativity is more effective than individual creativity [85] and that there is also a link between the proactivity of a team, and the individual and collective creativity of team members [86]. In addition, promoting creativity and innovation at the collective level, especially in virtual teams, allow observing and understanding of how efficiently address all the challenges that the external environment produces [76]. Therefore, it emerged how the substantial change of the organisations in terms of emerging technologies and virtualisation can also impact the organisational culture, which can be developed and diffused using a bottom-up approach, starting from the workers' values, ideas, beliefs, behaviors, and competencies.

6   Conclusion

Organisational culture is one of the fundamental elements to ensure the success of every organisation and assumes an even more determined role in highly virtualised organizations. The use of emerging technologies and the introduction of remote working has not only led to organisations adapting to new ways of work based upon the different management of spaces, processes, and employees in virtual teams but also to the adoption of an organisational culture based on shared values and participation. Kim et al. [12] showed how decentralised organisations implement more bottom-up actions than more centralised organisations. With this perspective, our research proposes to adopt a bottom-up organisational culture in virtualised workspaces, in which well-being, needs, values and competencies play a fundamental role and then criticises the top-down approach supported by most mainstream theories. The bottom-up approach implies the involvement and active participation of all members of an organisation in decision-making and in the value-creation process. This type of culture can be implemented through the use of specific competencies, as mentioned above, obtained through experience and continuous training in line with organisational values [31]. However, we believe that this approach is not suitable for all types of organisations as there is no "one best way". This aspect emerged also in the literature. Some authors suggest the use of a combined approach that implies the adoption of a top-down and bottom-up approach, especially in highly flexible, agile, and dynamic contexts. The adoption of a combination of the two approaches involves on the one hand a clear definition of objectives, guarantees the directionality of the change and careful action planning (top-down) while success is guaranteed due to the active participation (bottom-up) of all the members of the organisation [13]. Our research, being a theoretical contribution, could be developed empirically through quantitative analysis in actual organisations in order to straighten the implications proposed. Further future studies can be carried out in this direction.

References

1. Townsend, A. M., DeMarie, S. M., & Hendrickson, A. R. (1998). Virtual teams: Technology and the workplace of the future. *Academy of Management Executive, 12*, 17–29.
2. DeSanctis, G., & Monge, P. (1999). Introduction to the special issue: Communication processes for virtual organizations. *Organization Science, 10*(6), 693–703.
3. Morrison-Smith, S., & Ruiz, J. (2020). Challenges and barriers in virtual teams: A literature review. *SN Applied Sciences, 2*(6), 1096.
4. Shepherd, D. A., & Sutcliffe, K. M. (2020). Inductive top-down theorizing: A source of new theories of organization. *The Academy of Management Review, 36*(2), 361–380.
5. Wagner, B. G. (2005). A Study on the influence of characteristics of organizational culture to the work performance. *The International Journal of Accounting and Business Society, 13*(2), 51–67.
6. Tohidi, H., & Jabbari, M. M. (2012). Organizational culture and leadership. *Procedia - Social and Behavioral Sciences, 31*, 856–860. https://doi.org/10.1016/j.sbspro.2011.12.156
7. Glaser, S. R., Zamanou, S., & Hacker, K. (1987). Measuring and Interpreting organizational culture. *Management Communication Quarterly, 1*(2), 173–198. https://doi.org/10.1177/0893318987001002003
8. Hofstede, G. (1984). *Culture's consequences: International differences in work-related values.* Abridged ed. Sage Publications.
9. Hofstede, G., Neuijen, B., Ohayv, D. D., & Sanders, G. (1990). Measuring organizational cultures: A qualitative and quantitative study across twenty cases. *Administrative Science Quarterly, 35*, 286-316. https://doi.org/10.2307/2393392
10. Atkinson, D., & Sohn, J. (2013). Culture from the Bottom-upBottom-up. *TESOL Quarterly, 47.* https://doi.org/10.1002/tesq.104
11. Sinclair, J., & Collins, D. (1994). Towards a quality culture. *International Journal of Quality & Reliability Management, 11*(5), 19–29. https://doi.org/10.1108/02656719410062849
12. Kim, Y.H., Sting, F.J., & Loch, C. H. (2014).Top-down, bottom-up, or both? Toward an integrative perspective on operations strategy formation. *Journal of Operations Management, 32*(7–8), 462–474.
13. Hartl, E. (2019). A Characterization of Culture Change in the Context of Digital Transformation. In: *25th Americas Conference on Information Systems, Proceedings of the 25th Americas Conference on Information Systems* (AMCIS 2019), Cancún, Mexiko.
14. Großer, B., & Baumöl, U. (2022). Virtual teamwork in the context of technological and cultural transformation. *International Journal of Information Systems and Project Management, 5*(4), 21–35. https://doi.org/10.12821/ijispm050402
15. Kuhn, T. S. (2011). The essential tension: tradition and innovation in scientific research. In *The Essential Tension: Tradition and Innovation in Scientific Research,* 225–239. University of Chicago Press. https://doi.org/10.7208/9780226217239-010
16. Bauman, Z. (2000). *Liquid modernity. Polity,* Cambridge.
17. Morin, E. (1999). *Seven complex lessons in education for the future.* Paris: United Nations Educational, Scientific and Cultural Organization.
18. Anderson, P. W. More is different. *Science, 177*(4047), 393–396. https://doi.org/10.1126/science.177.4047.393
19. Mitleton-Kelly, E. (2003). Ten principles of complexity and enabling infrastructures. Chapter 2 In *E. Mitleton-Kelly (Ed.), Complex systems and evolutionary perspectives on organizations.* The application of Complexity theory to organizations. Elsevier Science.

20. Latta, G. F. (2020). A complexity analysis of organizational culture, leadership, and engage-ment: Integration, differentiation, and fragmentation. *International Journal of Leadership in Education, 23*(3), 274–299. https://doi.org/10.1080/13603124.2018.1562095
21. Lewin, K., Lippitt, R., & White, R. K. (1939). Patterns of aggressive behavior in experimen-tally created «social climates». *The Journal of Social Psychology, 10*, 271–299. https://doi.org/10.1080/00224545.1939.9713366
22. Schneider, B., Ehrhart, M. G., & Macey, W. H. (2013). Organizational climate and culture. *Annual Review of Psychology, 64*(1), 361–388. https://doi.org/10.1146/annurev-psych-113011-143809
23. Bellot, J. (2011). Defining and Assessing Organizational Culture. *Nursing Forum, 46*(1), 29–37. https://doi.org/10.1111/j.1744-6198.2010.00207.x
24. Schein, E. H. (1990). Organizational culture. *American Psychologist, 45*(2), 109–119. https://doi.org/10.1037/0003-066X.45.2.109
25. Pettigrew, A. M. (1989). On studying organizational cultures. *Administrative Science Quarterly, 24*(4), 570. https://doi.org/10.2307/2392363
26. Alvesson, M. (2002). *Understanding Organizational Culture.* SAGE Publications Ltd. https://doi.org/10.4135/9781446280072
27. Mei, X., Iannacchione, B., Stohr, M. K., Hemmens, C., Hudson, M., & Collins, P. A.(2017). Confirmatory analysis of an organizational culture instrument for corrections. *The Prison Journal, 97*(2), 247–269. https://doi.org/10.1177/0032885517692831
28. Little, R. G. (2005). Organizational culture and the performance of critical infrastruc-ture: Modeling and simulation in socio-technological systems. *Proceedings of the 38th Annual Hawaii International Conference on System Sciences, 63b.* https://doi.org/10.1109/HICSS.2005.477
29. De Toni, A. F. (2011). Teoria della complessità e implicazioni manageriali: Verso l'auto-organizzazione. *Sinergie Italian Journal of Management, 81*, 57–96.
30. Mitleton-Kelly, E. (2006). A Complexity approach to co-creating an innovative environment. *World Futures The Journal of General Evolution, 62*(3).
31. Lauro, S. D. (2021).Alignment and misalignment between employees' competencies and orga-nizational values. *In: 21st Workshop dei docenti e dei ricercatori di Organizzazione aziendale, WOA. Genova.*
32. Nami, M. R. (2008). Virtual organizations: An overview. *International Conference on Intelligent Information Processing (IIP: Intelligent Information Processing)* IV, 211–219. https://doi.org/10.1007/978-0-387-87685-6_26.
33. Cascio, W. F. (2000). Managing a virtual workplace. *Academy of Management Perspectives,14*(3), 81–90.
34. Lipnack, J., & Stamps J. (2000). *Virtual Teams—Reaching Across Space,Time, and Organizations with Technology.* John Wiley & Sons, New York.
35. Davison C., S., & Ward, K. (1999). *Leading international teams.* McGraw-Hill, London
36. Jarvenpaa, S.L., Knoll, K., & Leidner, D. E. (1998). Is anybody out there? Antecedents of trust in global virtual teams. *Journal of Management Information Systems,14*(4), 29–64.
37. Bell B., S., & Kozlowski, S. W. J. (2002). A typology of virtual teams: Implications for effec-tive leadership. *Group & Organization Management, 27*(1), 14–49.
38. Kirkman, B. L., & Mathieu, J. E. (2005). The Dimensions and antecedents of team virtuality. *Journal of Management, 31*(5), 700–718.
39. Geber, B. (1995). Virtual teams. *Training, 32*(4), 36–42.
40. Townsend, A. M., DeMarie, S. M., & Hendrickson, A. R. (1996). Are you ready for virtual teams?. *HR Magazine, 41* (9), 122–126.
41. McDermott, C. M., & Stock, G. N. (1999). Organizational culture and advanced manufactur-ing technology implementation. *Journal of Operations Management 5*, 521–533.
42. Zheng, W., Yang, B., & McLean, G. N. (2010). Linking organizational culture, structure, strat-egy, and organizational effectiveness: mediating role of knowledge management. *Journal of Business Research, 63*(7), 763–771.
43. Fayol, H. (1949). *General and Industrial Management.* Pitman, London.

44. Kim, J. S., & Arnold, P. (1996). Operationalizing manufacturing strategy: An exploratory study of constructs and linkage. *International Journal of Operations & Production Management, 16*(12), 45–73.

45. Pressman, J., & Wildavsky, A. (1973). *Implementation. How Great Expectations in Washington are Dashed in Oakland; or why it's Amazing that Federal Programs Work at all, This Being a Saga of the Economic Development Administration as Told by Two Sympathetic Observers who Seek to Build Morals on a Foundation of Ruined Hopes.* Berkeley, CA: University of California Press.

46. Beer, M. (2001). How to develop an organization capable of sustained high performance: Embrace the drive for results-capability development paradox. *Organizational Dynamics, 29*(4), 233–47.

47. Lipsky, M. (1980). Street-level bureaucracy: Dilemmas of the individual in public services. New York: Russell Sage Foundation. *Politics & Society, 10*(1), 116–116. https://doi.org/10.1177/003232928001000113

48. Bednar, P. M., & Welch, C. (2020). Socio-technical perspectives on smart working: Creating meaningful and sustainable systems. *Information Systems Frontiers, 22*(2), 281–298. https://doi.org/10.1007/s10796-019-09921-1

49. Mohr, B. J., & van Amelsvoort, P. (2016). *Co-creating humane and innovative organizations: Evolutions in the practice of socio-technical system design.* Portland ME: Global STS-D Network Press.

50. Cuel, R., Ravarini, A., Ruffini, R., & Varriale, L. (2021). Smart working in Italian public administration: A socio-technical approach. *Electronic Journal of Management, 3*.

51. Pasmore, W. A. (1988). *Designing effective organizations: The sociotechnical systems perspective.* New York: John Wiley and Sons.

52. Kling, R., & Lamb, R. (1999). IT and Organizational change in digital economies: A sociotechnical approach. *Computers and Society, 29*(3), 17–25.

53. Whitehead, A. N. (1925).*Science and the Modern World*, New York, Macmillan.

54. Von Neumann, J. (1966). Theory of self-reproducing automata. University of Illinois Press. Urbana and London.

55. Lewin, R. (1992). *Complexity: Life at the Edge of Chaos.* New York: MacMillan Publishing Company.

56. Black, J., & Edwards, S. (2000). Emergence of virtual or network organizations: Fad or feature. *Journal of Organizational Change Management, 13*, 567–576. https://doi.org/10.1108/09534810010378588

57. Maguire, S., & Mckelvey, B. (1999). Complexity and management: Moving from fad to firm foundations. *Emergence 1.* https://doi.org/10.1207/s15327000em0102_3

58. Levinthal, D., & Warglien, M. (1999). Landscape design: Designing for local action in complex worlds. *Organization Science - ORGAN SCI 10*, 342–357. https://doi.org/10.1287/orsc.10.3.342

59. Frank, K. A., & Fahrbach, K. (1999). Organization culture as a complex system: Balance and information in models of influence and selection. *Organization Science, 10*(3), 253–277. https://doi.org/10.1287/orsc.10.3.253

60. Styhre, A. (2002). Non-linear change in organizations: Organization change management informed by complexity theory. *Leadership & Organization Development Journal, 23*, 343–351. https://doi.org/10.1108/01437730210441300

61. Cartesio, R. (2002). *Discorso sul metodo. Testo francese a fronte (Testi a fronte).*

62. Cartesio, R. (2003).*Le passioni dell'anima: Testo francese a fronte*, Milano: Bompiani. Tradotto da Salvatore Obinu.

63. Manson, S., M. (2001). Simplifying complexity: a review of Complexity theory. *Geoforum 32*(3), 405–414.

64. Holland, J. H. (1992). Complex adaptive systems. *Daedalus, 121*(1), 17–30.

65. Anderson, P. W. (1999). Complexity theory and organization studies. *Organization Science: A Journal of the Institute of Management Sciences, 10*(3).

66. Arthur, W. B. (1990). Positive feedbacks in the economy. *Scientific American, 262*(2), 92–99.
67. Arthur, W. B. (1999). Complexity and the economy. *Science, 284*(5411), 107–109. https://doi.org/10.1126/science.284.5411.107
68. Mitleton-Kelly, E. (2005). Designing a new organization: A complexity approach. *In: European Conference on Research Methods in Business and Management Studies (ECRM)*, Paris.
69. Boyatzis, R. E. (1982). *The competent manager - a model for effective performance*. Willey, New York.
70. Zdonek, I., Podgórska, M., & Hysa, B. (2017). The competence for project team members in the conditions of remote working. *Foundations of Management, 9*, 213–224. https://doi.org/10.1515/fman-2017-0017
71. Gorenak, M., & Ferjan, M. (2015). The influence of organizational values on competencies of managers. *E+M Ekonomie a Management, 18*, 67–83. https://doi.org/10.15240/tul/001/2015-1-006
72. D'Espagnat, B., Deal, T. E., & Kennedy, A. A. (1982). *Corporate cultures: The rites and rituals of corporate life*. Basic Books.
73. Autor, D. H., Levy, F., & Murnane, R. J. (2003). The skill content of recent technological change: An empirical exploration. *The Quarterly Journal of Economics, 118*(4), 1279–1333. https://doi.org/10.1162/003355303322552801
74. Autor, D. (2013). The Changing Task Composition of the US Labor Market: An Update of Autor, Levy, and Murnane (2003) - David Autor. ScholarSite, Inc. 25 aprile 2022, (2013). https://www.scholarsite.io/
75. Grundke, R., Marcolin, L., Nguyen, T., & Squicciarini, M. (2018). W*hich skills for the digital era? Returns to skills analysis*. https://doi.org/10.1787/9a9479b5-en
76. Bissola, R., Imperatori, B., & Trinca Colonel, R. (2014). Enhancing the creative performance of new product teams: An organizational configurational approach. *Journal of Product Innovation Management, 31*. https://doi.org/10.1111/jpim.12101
77. Lauro, D. S., Tursunbayeva, A., & Antonelli, G. (2019). How nonprofit organizations use social media for fundraising: A systematic literature review. *International Journal of Business and Management, 14*, 1. https://doi.org/10.5539/ijbm.v14n7p1
78. Helmerich, N., Raj-Reichert, G., & Zajak, S. (2021). Exercising associational and networked power through the use of digital technology by workers in global value chains. *Competition & Change, 25*(2), 142–166. https://doi.org/10.1177/1024529420903289
79. Wilkin, C. L., De Jong, J. P., & Rubino, C. (2018). Teaming up with temps: The impact of temporary workers on team social networks and effectiveness. *European Journal of Work and Organizational Psychology, 27*(2), 204–218. https://doi.org/10.1080/1359432X.2017.1418329
80. Antonelli, G., Agrifoglio, R., Bissola, R., Buonocore, F., Cuel, R., Curzi, Y., De Molli, F., Lauro, S. D., Di Virgilio, F., Fabbri, T., Flamini, G., Imperatori, B., Metallo, C., Mochi, F., Montanari, F., Neri, M., Palumbo, R., Paolino, C., Pompa, L., … Zifaro, M. (2023). Il futuro del lavoro si chiama "smart working"? Riflessioni e prospettive. *Prospettive in Organizzazione*, 1–45.
81. Lopes, M., & Soares, A. E. (2014). The influence of social network on psychological safety. *Journal of Industrial Engineering and Management JIEM, 7*(5), 995–1012. https://doi.org/10.3926/jiem.1115
82. Dossena, C., & Mochi, F. (2020). Smart Working: opportunità o minaccia? La parola ai professionisti. *Prospettive in Organizzazione, 13*, 1–5.
83. Baruch, Y., & Lin, C. P. (2012). All for one, one for all: Coopetition and virtual team performance. *Technological Forecasting and Social Change, 79*(6), 1155–1168.
84. Blackburn, R., Furst, S., & Rosen, B. (2003). Building a winning virtual team. *Virtual Teams That Work: Creating Conditions for Virtual Team Effectiveness*, 95–120.
85. Hargadon, A., & Bechky, B. (2006). When collections of creatives become creative collectives: A field study of problem solving at work. *Organization Science, 17*. https://doi.org/10.1287/orsc.1060.0200
86. Xu, X., Jiang, L., & Wang, H.-J. (2019). How to build your team for innovation? A cross-level mediation model of team personality, team climate for innovation, creativity, and job crafting. *Journal of Occupational and Organizational Psychology, 92*(4), 848–872. https://doi.org/10.1111/joop.12277

What Is New About e-Human Resource Management? Deepening Through a Bibliometric Analysis

Daria Sarti, Teresina Torre, and Stefano Za

Abstract The purpose of this study is to map the conceptual structure of the body of knowledge regarding the research field named e-Human Resource Management, with the aim of depicting an updated picture and contributing to a better understanding of this stream. The research develops a bibliometric analysis of 184 articles resulting from the search, following two steps. First, the analysis of descriptive performance indicators identifies the main traits of the debate on e-HRM, in terms of publications, productive countries, as well as the publication's impact of the target journals, number of citations per country and most cited articles in the dataset. Then, the study performs a co-word analysis to deepen the conceptual structure of the dataset. The results highlight a growing and spread academic interest in this research topic, especially in the recent few years, which confirms the usefulness of monitoring its evolution. It offers a basis to deepen how this interest is presented. The bibliometric analysis reveals that there are different streams of research in which the e-HRM debate is developed. Seven clusters were identified. Firstly, there is the predominant cluster covering the main issues (effectiveness, IoT, innovation), theories (TAM) and research methodology (SEM) within the domain. As well, other clusters highlight specific areas of interest. For example: the e-HRM in SMEs, the peculiar role of technology in managing personnel, the role of HR department. This paper contributes to the field by providing an examination of the current state of the art of research on e-HRM as well as identifying the current areas of speculation in

D. Sarti (✉)
Department of Economics and Management, University of Florence, Florence, Italy
e-mail: daria.sarti@unifi.it

T. Torre
Department of Economics and Business Studies, University of Genoa, Genova, Italy
e-mail: teresina.torre@economia.unige.it

S. Za
Department of Management and Business Administration, University "G. d'Annunzio", Pescara, Italy
e-mail: stefano.za@unich.it

A. Lazazzara et al. (eds.), *Towards Digital and Sustainable Organisations*,
Lecture Notes in Information Systems and Organisation 65,
https://doi.org/10.1007/978-3-031-52880-4_10

the literature and may offer some suggestions for future development in the perspective of the new trends in HRM.

Keywords e-HRM · Electronic human resource management · Bibliometric analysis · Co-occurrences · Co-words analysis

1 Introduction

In a paper published by Hay Group in 2002 focusing on e-human resource as a new source of value creation, authors introduced a challenging and central question such as: "*to e or not to e?*". Arguing their answer, they highlighted that the true point in this request was not the alternative suggested, but it was "when" the "e" would become inevitable. Indeed, exactly 20 years ago, they suggested that Human Resources Departments had to become "digital", that they had to turn towards a more technological model to play their role, because through the potential of technologies they would become abler to put more attention to the strategical perspective of the companies and develop appropriate operational tasks accordingly to their expectations. It is in this context that the concept of e-HRM – introduced and formalized some decades before the publication of the paper we are referring to (early e-HRM studies began appearing around 1995, as Strohmeier [1] underlines)—has relevantly increased. The transfer to a computer or to intranet-internet networks of some of the people management activities (through e-HR solutions) or web-based human resources [2] is so redefining the ways in which companies manage relationships with their people, even from the organizational point of view, as well as from the technological point of view. This trend towards digitalization has been reinforced during the pandemic we lived in in the last years and has involved the field of the human resource management, attracting new attention on e-HRM by companies, which have tried to redefine the way the electronic dimension influences people management and have introduced and enlarged the usage of specific electronic tools, not always doing this in the right order but seizing the opportunity to reflect on the changes required. Indeed, as it has been underlined, "*if organizations do not have a strong HRM system to begin with, they should not implement e-HRM: it will fail*" [3], p. 99).

The favorable context and the relevance of the topic (the importance of people in organization is continuously underlined so as their appropriate management) suggest the usefulness of proposing an updated state of the art in this area of research. Many reviews have been run during the years by renowned scholars, devoted to studying this topic and representing authorities in the field. Of course, we started from these works, appreciating their contribution, and were intrigued by the possibility to verify the updated situation with regard to the scientific interest to deepen knowledge. Indeed, the most recent of these reviews dates back to 2017 [cfr. 3]. We think that the evolution e-HRM is living is so quick and follows unexpected paths, that it could be useful to make the point now; so, our aim is to make order in a dynamic field. Moreover, it is arguable that contributions have been published coherently with the evidence that this field of research is evolving due to its intrinsic nature, which combines classic management and information system. Indeed, many and different research areas have shown their interest towards this peculiar field, which has always been considered as an intersection one among HR and IT. By the way, it has been highlighted that "*the field of the intersection of HRM and information technology is dynamic*" [4 , p. 633]), suggesting that it could be interesting continuing in following research development. Previous reviews concentrate on the definition of e-HRM, suggesting it as an umbrella expression under which trying to propose an appropriate and strong one, discussing in depth the nature of e-HRM and the differences with traditional HRM, introducing attention towards value potential of technologies in HRM and the factors affecting the e-HRM adoption and its consequences.

The goal of this study is to explore the current state of the art of research in the field of e-HRM, developing a bibliometric review literature so to take a revised picture of the current body of research, a precise and objective conceptual structure of the discipline, help to discover key cluster and catch new elements, which have been considered in the meantime as characterising it, and offer stimuli for a renewed attention to it. At the best of our knowledge, no other study on e-HRM has been developed using this approach. This methodology is precious because it introduces a systematic, transparent and reproducible review process, improving the quality of reviews and allowing the researchers to map the research field without subjective bias, concentrating the attention on the relationship between different concepts present in the research on the topic. This is our research question: how can research on e-HRM be described from a quantitative point of view and how relevant is its effect on the academic community interested in understanding if e-HRM is present or not in people management in organizations?

In this perspective, the focus is put on the whole process of human resource management and the electronic way it is run and not on single specific activities and processes—such as e-recruitment, e-training and so on—even if specific care has been devoted to them by scholars, coherently with practices conducted in companies.

The paper is organized as follows. Section 2 introduces the methodology and the literature search protocol. Section 3 describes the results of our bibliometric analysis, while Sect. 4 offers a global picture of the main topic emerging from the dataset so to focus on the meaning and the evolution e-HRM represents in HRM field. The final section contains a short summary of the results and some reflections; limitations and indications for future developments conclude the paper.

2   Research Method

This paper embraces a bibliometric approach and investigates the evolutionary path, through the years, of the academic literature on the phenomenon of e-HRM [5]. This kind of analysis uses a quantitative approach to describe, evaluate and monitor published research. This method is precious to introduce a systematic, transparent and reproducible review process, improving the quality of reviews and allowing the researchers to map the research field without subjective bias [6]. Bibliometric methods have two purposes: performance analysis, which investigates the research and publication performance; science mapping, which points to find the structure and dynamics of the field under investigation [6, 7].

For bibliometric studies, the literature selection is crucial to ensure validity and consistency of the study. We adopted a three-step research protocol [8] to select the literature and analyze the results, as shown in Fig. 1. First, we chose the database containing bibliometric data and filtered the core document set. Once the dataset was identified (184 publications), the refining stage was performed by cleaning and standardizing some fields of the corpus. The data analysis carried out two research outcomes:

1. The examination of descriptive performance indicators (descriptive analysis); and
2. The conceptual structure of the dataset, exploring the main issues debated in the corpus through a co-word analysis and adopting social network analysis tools (bibliometric analysis).

We used R and the bibliometric package to perform the bibliometric analysis [9, 10].

The co-word analysis allowed us to define a comprehensive overview of the current body of research, a precise and objective conceptual structure of the subject under investigation and helped us to identify some key clusters [11]. The co-word analysis is a content analysis technique, and it assumes that keywords are a meaningful representation of the content of an article [12] and allow the researchers to understand the conceptual structure of the research field examined. Further, it permits finding the main concepts treated, and it represents an effective strategy to describe the interaction between different areas of research [7]. The co-word

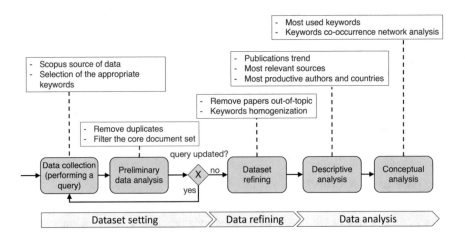

Fig. 1 Research protocol (adapted by [8])

analysis uses co-occurrence patterns, which are paired items in the corpus of a set of articles, to identify the relationships between the two concepts in the area of research [13].

2.1 Data Collection and Refinement of Results

The first step involved a comprehensive research through a wide research query with Scopus. The choice for Scopus is due to the extensive documentation as an all-inclusive bibliographic data source. It has proven reliable and, in some respects, even better than other data sources such as the Web of Science [14, 15].

The research query selection process began with a literature review of the cornerstone papers related to e-HRM (as suggested by authors using this method, see for example [16]. After several interactions aiming to define a research query as broadly as possible to catch all possible papers, the resulting query was:

TITLE-ABS-KEY ("virtual HRM" OR "Web based HRM" OR "Electronic HR" OR "electronic HRM" OR "e-HR" OR "e-HRM" OR "HR information system" OR "HRIS")

We performed a full search of the selected terms in titles, abstracts and keywords. This step generated a total of 1026 contributions. The second step consisted in restricting the search by considering only peer-reviewed journal articles (709) published in English (682). As a result, the sample consisted of 682 articles.

To ensure that all out-of-topic papers were identified, we started performing a manual refinement of the dataset by reading the title, abstract, and keywords of the 682 papers. By an initial screening of the papers, we realized that many articles in the dataset were from different research domains (e.g., Medicine, Oncology, material, and physical science). We apprehended that the acronym HRIS is widely used in medicine with different meanings to indicate different phenomena such as "High-risk Individuals", "Heat-Related Illnesses", "Reductase Inhibitors", "Health Risk Indexes". Still, the same acronym is also used with different meanings in other research domains, such as: "High Refractive Index Species" in optical, material and physical science, and "High-resolution images" in Computer Studies. Therefore, we decided to update our previous query by omitting HRIS from the list of terms to find. Moreover, we excluded the consideration of the index keywords (keywords automatically assigned to each paper by the platform) from our search since we noted they were not aligned with the paper's content. For this reason, we searched the terms only in the title, abstract and authors' keywords. The final query retrieved 385 documents. The analysis of the resulting dataset to ensure that all out-of-topic papers was taken up. A new manual refinement of the title, abstract, and author' keywords of the 385 documents in dataset was carried out. To reduce subjectivity biases, two authors carried out this analysis independently of the other by agreeing in advance on the inclusion/exclusion criteria [17–19].

In this phase, also we excluded several papers because they still belong to completely different disciplines, such as the Cardiovascular and Medical domains. At the end of this process, the sample was composed of 184 articles.

The following step consists of the cleaning one to homogenize keywords used in the articles. As a result, all the keywords that indicated the same topic were replaced with a unique word. Two researchers performed this analysis separately, and the results were compared to arrive at a final shared agreement and to consider our dataset ready for the analysis.

3   Descriptive Bibliometric Analysis

The bibliometric analysis is presented in four subsections: the number of publications by year, the most cited papers and the average number of citations in a specific year, journals publishing activity, and publishing activity by country.

3.1   Publication by Year

According to Fig. 2, the papers investigating e-HRM appear in the research literature for 25 years (the first paper was published in 1997). This evidence is coherent with previous reviews that state the increasing adoption of e-HRM from the late 1990s [1, 3]. During the time period research in the field increases. However, the publication trend shows irregularity, with steady growth in some years: in descending order by number, 2019 is the most prolific (with 28 articles published), then 2021 (19 articles), 2013 (17 articles), and 2020 (15 articles). On the other hand, some negative trends are evident in the years 2008 (1 article; −83% decrease compared to the previous year), 2012 (2 articles; −78% decrease compared with the previous year), 2017 (6 articles; −54% decrease compared to the previous year) and 2020 (15 articles; −reduction of 54% compared to the previous year). However, the overall trend shows growth until 2019. As for 2022, it is important to report that we consider only the first 5 months of the year since we gathered data until May 30th: considering the data of this first period it seems that the topic collects a significant interest.

3.2   Citations by Years and Most Cited Papers

The number of citations is a good way to accurately depict the relevance of the papers published in a specific field [20]. Table 1 presents the most cited articles in our sample (we consider those receiving at least 50 citations). The number of citations indicated the paper popularity of each paper and the influence it plays on the

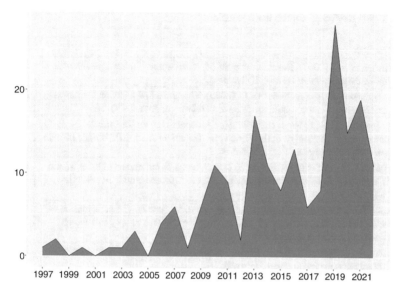

Fig. 2 Number of publications per year (since 1997)

community interested in the field. The first place is occupied by Strohmeieir (2007), which reached 250 citations. Then, we find Lengnick-Hall (2003), with 182 citations, and Boundarouk (2009) with 152.

A large number of the most cited papers are reviews together with a good proportion of papers which are focused on empirical studies.

3.3 Journals Publishing Activity

Table 2 shows that the most prolific journal is *The International Journal of Human Resource Management* (IJHRM), which collects 20 out of the total 117 papers in our dataset, followed by *Employee Relations* (ER) with 11 papers. According to ABS, both are in the "Human Resource Management and Employment Studies" field of studies. The former ranks 3 and the latter 2. In Table 2, we consider the journals, which published at least two papers on our topic, but there is a long list where one article appeared. These represent around 64% of the entire sample. From our analysis reported in Table 2 it emerges that studies analyzing our topic of interest are mainly published in journals focusing (mainly) on Business, Management and Accounting (12 out of 29), social science (7 out of 29), Decision Sciences (2 out of 29), Engineering (2 out of 29), Art and Humanities (1 out of 29), Economics (1 out of 29), Energy (1 out of 29), Agricultural and Biological Sciences (1 out of 29), Computer Science (1 out of 29), Psychology (1 out of 29).

At the same time, there is a wide variation in the "reputation" of journals publishing studies on this topic. They range from a maximum of 22.6 citation score for the

Table 1 The most cited articles in the sample

#	Article Title	Total citations
1	Strohmeier, S. (2007). Research in e-HRM: Review and implications. *Human resource management review*, *17*(1), 19–37.	250
2	Lengnick-Hall, M. L., & Moritz, S. (2003). The impact of e-HR on the human resource management function. *Journal of labor research*, *24*(3), 365.	182
3	Bondarouk, T. V., & Ruël, H. J. (2009). Electronic Human Resource Management: challenges in the digital era. *The International Journal of Human Resource Management*, *20*(3), 505–514.	152
4	Marler, J. H., & Fisher, S. L. (2013). An evidence-based review of e-HRM and strategic human resource management. *Human resource management review*, *23*(1), 18–36.	124
5	Ruel, H. J., Bondarouk, T. V., & Van der Velde, M. (2007). The contribution of e-HRM to HRM effectiveness: Results from a quantitative study in a Dutch Ministry. *Employee relations*.	109
6	Parry, E., & Tyson, S. (2011). Desired goals and actual outcomes of e-HRM. *Human resource management journal*, *21*(3), 335–354.	108
7	Bondarouk, T., Parry, E., & Furtmueller, E. (2017). Electronic HRM: four decades of research on adoption and consequences. *The International Journal of human resource management*, *28*(1), 98–131.	90
8	Voermans, M. and van Veldhoven, M. (2007), "Attitude towards E-HRM: an empirical study at Philips", *Personnel Review*, 36 (6), 887–902.	89
9	Panayotopoulou, L., Vakola, M., & Galanaki, E. (2007). E-HR adoption and the role of HRM: Evidence from Greece. *Personnel Review*, *36*(2), 277–294.	87
10	Parry, E. (2011). An examination of e-HRM as a means to increase the value of the HR function. *The International Jour*nal of Human Resource Management*, *22*(05), 1146–1162.	87
11	Marler, J. H., & Parry, E. (2016). Human resource management, strategic involvement and e-HRM technology. *The International Journal of Human Resource Management*, *27*(19), 2233–2253.	82
12	Marler, J. H. (2009). Making human resources strategic by going to the Net: reality or myth?. *The International Journal of Human Resource Management*, *20*(3), 515–527.	76
13	Strohmeier, S. (2009). Concepts of e-HRM consequences: a categorisation, review and suggestion. *The International Journal of Human Resource Management*, *20*(3), 528–543.	74
14	Florkowski, G. W., & Olivas-Luján, M. R. (2006). The diffusion of human-resource information-technology innovations in US and non-US firms. *Personnel Review*.	71
15	Gueutal, H. G. (2009). A Guest Editor's introduction: Special issue on Electronic Human Resource Management and the Future of Human Resource Management. *Journal of Managerial Psychology*, *24*(6), 482.	71
16	Strohmeier, S. (2013). Employee relationship management—Realizing competitive advantage through information technology? *Human Resource Management Review*, *23*(1), 93–104.	66

(continued)

Table 1 (continued)

# Article Title	Total citations
17 Bell, B. S., Lee, S. W., & Yeung, S. K. (2006). The impact of e-HR on professional competence in HRM: Implications for the development of HR professionals. *Human Resource Management, 45*(3), 295–308.	65
18 Bondarouk, T., & Brewster, C. (2016). Conceptualising the future of HRM and technology research. *The International Journal of Human Resource Management, 27*(21), 2652–2671.	65
19 Olivas-Lujan, M. R., Ramirez, J., & Zapata-Cantu, L. (2007). E-HRM in Mexico: adapting innovations for global competitiveness. *International Journal of Manpower, 28*(5), 418–434.	65
20 Bondarouk, T. V., & Ruël, H. J. (2009). Electronic Human Resource Management: challenges in the digital era. *The International Journal of Human Resource Management, 20*(3), 505–514.	59
21 Bondarouk, T., & Ruël, H. (2013). The strategic value of e-HRM: results from an exploratory study in a governmental organization. *The International Journal of Human Resource Management, 24*(2), 391–414.	54
22 Lin, L. H. (2011). Electronic human resource management and organizational innovation: the roles of information technology and virtual organizational structure. *The International Journal of Human Resource Management, 22*(02), 235–257.	54
23 Tansley, C., & Newell, S. (2007). Project social capital, leadership and trust: A study of human resource information systems development. *Journal of Managerial Psychology*.	54
24 Yusliza, M. Y., Othman, N. Z., & Jabbour, C. J. C. (2017). Deciphering the implementation of green human resource management in an emerging economy. *Journal of Management Development*.	51
25 Hooi, L. W. (2006). Implementing e-HRM: The readiness of small and medium sized manufacturing companies in Malaysia. *Asia Pacific Business Review, 12*(4), 465–485.	50

"Journal of Strategic Information Systems" in the area of Decision Making to a minimum of 0 in Energy and Business, Management and Accounting.

It is interesting noticing that the "Journal of Strategic Information Systems" represents the main valuable and recognized source in the domain of IT and Decision Making and it enlivens the debate in an area of research other than the prevailing one in the HRM with four articles that are all concentrated in the same volume issued in 2013, thus making us wondering if in the specific discipline the debate has suffered a setback and is stuck at 10 years ago.

Table 2 further indicates the metrics of each source to evaluate the impact and productivity of any published document, such as the h-index, g-index, and m-index. The h-index measures the impact and productivity of researchers' publications. The g-index and m-index are basically the modified versions of h-index. The g-index shows articles information with higher citations in a dataset. Thus, it is always equals to or higher than the h-index. The m-index provides the h-index on yearly basis starting form the first publication. The analysis in Table 2 depicts that almost

Table 2 Most recurring Journals (N = 117)

#	Journal	Scopus Subject areas	H index	G index	M index	Total Citations	Number of publications	First publication year	Last publication year
1	International Journal of Human Resource Management	Business, Management and Accounting: Industrial Relations, Business, Management and Accounting: Organizational Behavior and Human Resource Management, Business, Management and Accounting: Business and International Management, Business, Management and Accounting: Strategy and Management, Business, Management and Accounting: Management of Technology and Innovation	15	20	0.789	995	20	2004	2021
2	Employee Relations	Business, Management and Accounting: Industrial Relations, Business, Management and Accounting: Organizational Behavior and Human Resource Management	10	11	0.625	268	11	2007	2021
3	International Journal of Manpower	Business, Management and Accounting: Organizational Behavior and Human Resource Management, Business, Management and Accounting: Management of Technology and Innovation, Business, Management and Accounting: Strategy and Management	3	7	0.187	84	7	2007	2022
4	Human Resource Management Review	Business, Management and Accounting: Organizational Behavior and Human Resource Management, Psychology: Applied Psychology	5	6	0.312	479	6	2007	2021
5	European Journal of International Management	Social Sciences: Education, Business, Management and Accounting: Business and International Management, Business, Management and Accounting: Organizational Behavior and Human Resource Management	4	5	0.307	46	5	2010	2013

#	Journal	Scopus Subject areas	H index	G index	M index	Total Citations	Number of publications	First publication year	Last publication year
6	Human Resource Management Journal	Business, Management and Accounting: Organizational Behavior and Human Resource Management	5	5	0.192	179	5	1997	2021
7	Asian Social Science	Arts and Humanities: General Arts and Humanities, Economics, Econometrics and Finance: General Economics, Econometrics and Finance, Social Sciences: General Social Sciences	3	4	0.3	22	4	2013	2016
8	International Journal of Scientific and Technology Research	Social Sciences: Development, Business, Management and Accounting: Management of Technology and Innovation, Engineering: General Engineering	1	1	0.333	2	4	2020	2020
9	Journal of Strategic Information Systems	Decision Sciences: Information Systems and Management, Business, Management and Accounting: Management Information Systems, Computer Science: Information Systems	4	4	0.4	55	4	2013	2013
10	Personnel Review	Business, Management and Accounting: Organizational Behavior and Human Resource Management, Psychology: Applied Psychology	4	4	0.235	286	4	2006	2016
11	International Journal of Advanced Science and Technology	Energy: General Energy, Computer Science: Computer Science: General Computer Science, Engineering: General Engineering	1	1	0.25	3	3	2019	2019

(continued)

Table 2 (continued)

#	Journal	Scopus Subject areas	H index	G index	M index	Total Citations	Number of publications	First publication year	Last publication year
12	International Journal of Data and Network Science	Social Sciences: Communication, Computer Science: Computer Networks and Communications, Computer Science: Information Systems, Computer Science: Computer Science Applications, Computer Science: Artificial Intelligence, Computer Science: Software	2	3	2	14	3	2022	2022
13	International Journal of Human Resources Development and Management	Business, Management and Accounting: Organizational Behavior and Human Resource Management	2	3	0.105	9	3	2004	2020
14	Human Resource Management	Business, Management and Accounting: Organizational Behavior and Human Resource Management, Psychology: Applied Psychology	2	2	0.105	103	2	2004	2006
15	Human Resource Management International Digest	Business, Management and Accounting: Organizational Behavior and Human Resource Management	0	0	0	0	2	2011	2013
16	Human Resources for Health	Social Sciences: Public Administration, Medicine: Public Health, Environmental and Occupational Health	2	2	0.25	18	2	2015	2015
17	International Journal for Quality Research	Engineering: Industrial and Manufacturing Engineering, Decision Sciences: Management Science and Operations Research, Engineering: Safety, Risk, Reliability and Quality	1	1	0.5	1	2	2021	2021

#	Journal	Scopus Subject areas	H index	G index	M index	Total Citations	Number of publications	First publication year	Last publication year
18	International Journal of Business Information Systems	Decision Sciences: Information Systems and Management, Business, Management and Accounting: Management of Technology and Innovation, Business, Management and Accounting: Management Information Systems	2	2	0.153	9	2	2010	2012
19	International Journal of Human Capital and Information Technology Professionals	Business, Management and Accounting: Management of Technology and Innovation Computer Science: Computer Science (miscellaneous)	1	1	0.25	3	2	2019	2021
20	International Journal of Innovative Technology and Exploring Engineering	Engineering: Civil and Structural Engineering Computer Science: General Computer Science Engineering: Electrical and Electronic Engineering: Mechanics of Materials	1	1	0.2	1	2	2018	2019
21	International Journal of Recent Technology and Engineering	Business, Management and Accounting: Management of Technology and Innovation Engineering: General Engineering	0	0	0	0	2	2019	2019
22	International Journal of Technology and Human Interaction	Computer Science: Information Systems Computer Science: Human–Computer Interaction	2	2	0.153	7	2	2010	2010

(continued)

Table 2 (continued)

#	Journal	Scopus Subject areas	H index	G index	M index	Total Citations	Number of publications	First publication year	Last publication year
23	International Journal on Emerging Technologies	Agricultural and Biological Sciences: Agricultural and Biological Sciences (miscellaneous)Business, Management and Accounting: Management of Technology and Innovation Engineering: Engineering (miscellaneous)	1	2	0.25	4	2	2019	2019
24	Journal of Asian Finance, Economics and Business	Economics, Econometrics and Finance: Finance Economics, Econometrics and Finance: Economics and Econometrics Business, Management and Accounting: Management Information Systems	1	2	0.333	4	2	2020	2021
25	Journal of Managerial Psychology	Psychology: Social Psychology Business, Management and Accounting: Organizational Behavior and Human Resource Management Decision Sciences: Management Science and Operations Research Psychology: Applied Psychology	2	2	0.125	125	2	2007	2009
26	Prabandhan: Indian Journal of Management	Business, Management and Accounting: General Business, Management and Accounting	2	2	0.222	6	2	2014	2019
27	Problems and Perspectives in Management	Social Sciences: Law Social Sciences: Sociology and Political Science Social Sciences: Social Sciences (miscellaneous)Business, Management and Accounting: Business and International Management Business, Management and Accounting: General Business, Management and Accounting Decision Sciences: Information Systems and Management	1	1	0.076	2	2	2010	2014

#	Journal	Scopus Subject areas	H index	G index	M index	Total Citations	Number of publications	First publication year	Last publication year
28	Public Personnel Management	Social Sciences: Public Administration Business, Management and Accounting: Organizational Behavior and Human Resource Management Business, Management and Accounting: Management of Technology and Innovation Business, Management and Accounting: Strategy and Management	2	2	0.095	46	2	2002	2014
29	Worldwide Hospitality and Tourism Themes	Social Sciences: Development Environmental Science: Management, Monitoring, Policy and Law Business, Management and Accounting: Tourism, Leisure and Hospitality Management	2	2	0.153	23	2	2010	2018

all the most recurring sources have also a higher productivity and impact based on the h-index, g-index, and m-index. Anyway, from the table it emerges also an interest in e-HRM across the fields. Finally, Table 2 provides information about the total citations of each source and the first and last publication year of a contribution in each source.

3.4   Publishing Activity by Country

E-HRM seems to be a topic discussed worldwide, as suggested by the list of 37 countries obtained considering the affiliation of the 389 authors in the dataset. Figure 3 shows the output attained considering the "most productive country by volume".

In detail, Fig. 3 distinguishes papers where the authors are from the same county (Single Country Publication—SCP) and papers whose authors come from different countries (Multiple Country Publication—MCP). The paper written by authors with a multi-country configuration is associated with the corresponding author's country. Based on this analysis, publications on *e-Human Resource Management* come mainly from the USA and UK, with 18 and 17 publications, respectively. These two countries are followed by The Netherlands (11 papers), India (10 papers), China, Germany, and Malaysia (8 papers), and Finland and Italy (5 papers). It is interesting

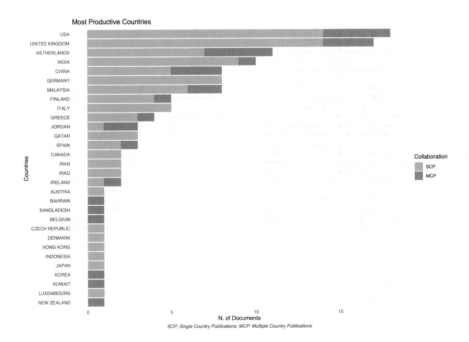

Fig. 3   Most productive countries

to note that according to the MCP, The Netherlands, China, Jordan and Ireland seem to be the most collaborative countries. Regarding this aspect, caution is necessary. Indeed, it could be observed that some habits by scholars may influence the result. For example, it is custom that scholars who have an international career continue in using that affiliation even if they come back to their effective nationality, so suggesting a multi-country collaboration which is not such.

The figure reveals that some countries do not present collaborations (e.g., Germany, Italy, and Canada). In contrast, countries such as Bahrain and New Zealand have a single publication that has been produced in collaboration with other countries.

Interestingly, there is no correspondence between the number of articles published in each country, the total citations, and the average article citations. The analysis proves that the USA are the most productive country and present the largest number of citations. However, the average article citations are higher for The Netherlands (59.1) and Germany (57.2) compared to that of the USA (50.7), suggesting that the most relevant considered analysis and reflections are developed in European countries, where some of the respected author live and study. For the UK, the average citation is even lower (22.9).

4 The Main Topics Investigated in the Dataset

To explore the most relevant topics discussed in the papers composing our dataset, we analyzed the most recurring keywords used by authors. This analysis provides some interesting insights regarding the nature of the discussion on the e-HRM and gives us the possibility to examine which focus papers present in our dataset have.

In detail, the analysis is articulated in the following two parts:

1. the trend of the most used keywords which are 42—we considered those which have at least 3 citations, so that this allows us to select an appropriate set ok keywords to describe the topic discussed in the dataset;
2. the authors' keywords co-occurrences.

4.1 Top Most Used Keywords

This analysis starts with the distribution of the most used keywords defined by the authors over the years (Fig. 4). *Electronic Human Resource Management* is the most frequent keyword with 32 occurrences, followed by *Human Resource Management* with 27 occurrences and *Human Resource Information Systems* with 22 occurrences. *Information technology, e-Human Resources, E-Recruiting, Strategic Human Resource Management, Communication Technologies,*

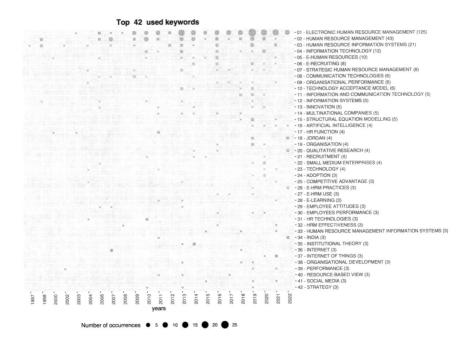

Fig. 4 The main 42 keywords used in the dataset over the years

Organizational Performance, *Technology Acceptance Model* are the other keywords in the top ten with more than 6 occurrences (12, 10, 8, 6, 6, 6, 6, respectively).

The frequency of the keywords does not appear regular in the figure and at the same time it seems to be intensified for some of the keywords in specific periods. Newer focus in the e-HRM context, such as "Organizational Development", "Employees performance", "HRM effectiveness", "Artificial Intelligence", "E-Recruiting", "TAM", "Structural Equation Modeling" and "Qualitative research" are relatively new with no publications that date back more than 10 years. Considering the three most frequent keywords, we can observe that *Electronic Human Resource Management* was first used in 2003 and has been used more frequently used after 2011, while *Human Resource Information Systems* presents a number of frequencies a little higher in 1998 and was used from 1997 with a trend characterized by some peaks in the years 2016 and 2019 to date. Information technology was first mentioned among the keywords of the articles in the dataset in 2010 with a trend characterized by some peaks in the years 2013, 2016 and 2020 to date. This is coherent with the evolution put in evidence by authors studying the field according to their disciplinary affiliation, which emphasizes the phenomenon (multidisciplinary by nature) from the subjective point of view.

4.2 Authors' Keywords Co-occurrences

The analysis of the connections among the main topics discussed in our dataset can provide further interesting insights. Starting from the 42 most recurring authors' keywords, co-occurrences network was created (as shown in Fig. 5).

In the graph, the keywords are the nodes, while the tie means that two of them are mentioned together in the same publication (generating in such a way a co-occurrence); the thickness of the tie reflects the number of contributions in which the pair appears, so that the thicker the tie, the more frequent the association. On the basis of their connections, it is possible to recognize seven clusters:

1. Cluster 1, which includes the following five keywords: communication technologies, institutional theory, multinational companies, qualitative research, recruitment. Starting from these keywords it seems that there is a first cluster of papers debating the use of online communication for performing recruitment activities, adopting a qualitative research approach (see Fig. 6);
2. Cluster 2, which comprises the following six keywords: artificial intelligence, e-human resources, e-learning, e-recruiting, organizational development, social media. Considering these keywords, we can suggest that the main topic of this cluster could be related to operational and technical aspects of e-HRM specifically related to single areas of the HRM (e.g. e-learning, e-recruitment) and specific technologies (e.g., artificial intelligence and social media);
3. Cluster 3, which is formed by all the papers that cite the following 19 keywords: e-HRM practices, e-HRM use, electronic human resource management, employees' performance, HRM effectiveness, human resource management, human resource management information systems, India, information and communication technology, information systems, information technology, innovation, internet, IoT, Jordan, Organization, Strategy, Structural Equation Modeling, Technology Acceptance Model. It seems that this cluster is mainly related to papers debating the adoption of different kinds of digital technologies in the HRM context, with a particular focus on performance and effectiveness. The keywords contained in this cluster are more numerous than those of the other clusters, and from a first reading, they seem consistent with each other. We could therefore speculate that this cluster represents a more relevant one than the others.
4. Cluster 4, which is defined by the relationships between the following two keywords: hr. function and resource-based view. The main topic of this cluster could be focused on the specific hr. function within the company and its key role in managing the strategic resource that human resources are;
5. Cluster 5, which includes four keywords; these are: adoption, employee attitudes, performance and small medium enterprises. The main topic of this cluster could be focused on the adoption of the e-HRM in the small-medium sized companies highlighting the concepts of employee attitudes and performance as well and suggesting a peculiar interest for smaller companies, where it is arguable more difficult to move towards the use of e-HRM tools;

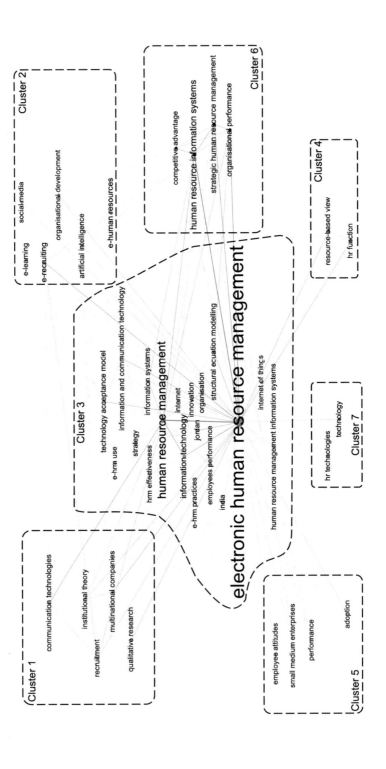

Fig. 5 Authors' keywords co-occurrence

Fig. 6 Our representation of the main clusters' topics

6. Cluster 6, which is composed by four keywords, namely: competitive advantage, human resource information systems, organizational performance, strategic human resource management. We can assume that the main topic of this cluster could be focused on the adoption of e-HRM as strategic, with may lead to positive outcomes arising from the introduction and implementation of human resource information systems;

7. Cluster 7, which includes two keywords, that are: HR technologies and technology. The main topic of this cluster could be focused on technology and their introduction to manage hr.

5 Conclusions, Limitations, and Further Research

This paper aims to propose a picture of current research on e-HRM, considering that this field is expected to be a hot topic in human resource management and that is continuously and rapidly evolving by effect of the technological evolution and the adaptative usage of related tools to the new organizational requests. Moreover, previous reviews are by consequence and by definition provisional, even if they remain precious references for those aiming to study the evolution of human resource management and the role played by IT system in supporting it.

All of the available reviews contribute to enter the object and the scope of such a complex and multifaced field and examine it from different points of view following researchers' interest. These reviews in general share the list of search keywords (e-HRM, electronic HRM, digital HRM, virtual HRM, HRIS and so on), but present specific focuses which complement the possibility of deepening this phenomenon. We can summarize their contributions following their chronological order. For example, Strohemeir [1] develops a conventional review of finding concerning e-HRM consequences, offering a configuration-based framework to study its multi-level nature. Bondarouk and Ruel's review [21] focuses on e-HRM definition, integrating four elements: content, implementation, targeted users and consequences. Van Geffel and colleagues [22] privilege the literature in the information system field, demonstrating that research focused on post-implementations issues, while Marler and Fisher [23] run an evidence-based review searching for evidence with regard to the relationship between e-HRM and strategic HRM, concluding that more empirical studies are required. Ruel and Bondarouk [4] focus on the challenges e-HRM has to face and underline the undervaluation of the complexity shown by the project developed in this field. Wirtky et alii [24] concentrate on the impact of IT on HRM, underlying that there is considerable unaddressed value potential of IT in HRM. Bondarouk and colleagues [3] propose a framework, where factors affecting adoption of e-HRM and consequences are summarized.

In this paper, we take another path, proposing a bibliometric method, convinced that it offers another complementary contribution. We aim at describing the existing literature on e-HRM, taking into account any paper using this label, without discussing which definition has been chosen but considering what the object of interest is. To achieve this goal, we performed our analysis on a sample of 184 articles, as result of the selective process according to protocol, articulated in two steps. First, we performed a descriptive bibliometric analysis; secondly, we identified the main topics of our dataset through a co-word analysis.

The results of the descriptive analysis highlight a growing academic interest in this research topic, confirmed by observing the progressive increase in the number of publications over time. This is evident also in recent times, in which the pressure towards digitalization has been revamped in general and also by scholars in this field. As well, a number of new focus (e.g. "Employees performance", "HRM effectiveness", "Artificial Intelligence", and "Qualitative research") emerge in the last 10 years showing a fertile and fermenting ground. It is suggested that the discipline mainly concerned on the topic, and which has higher recognition is the Business and Management domain, particularly journals in the field of "Human Resource Management and Employment Studies" while the debate in the IT domain seems suffering a setback. By analyzing the most recurring authors' keywords of our dataset, it is possible to identify groups of papers covering the topic of e-HRM from different perspectives. Specifically different cluster were found. Some of them were specifically focused on the setting of application of e-HRM, i.e. SMEs with specific concern with employees' attitudes (cluster 5), and MNCs recruitment practices through communication technologies (cluster 1). Cluster 6 studies e-HRM from a strategic point of view, while cluster 7 focus on the technology and its role in managing HR. Cluster 2 encompasses studies of activities and tools for e-HRM, cluster 4 is interested in the role of HR function in managing people in an e-HRM perspective. Cluster 3 is the prevalent one gathering the most relevant contributions in e-HRM: we could consider it as the *mainstream* cluster, since it is related to the most significant and emerging issues (effectiveness, IoT, innovation), theories (TAM) and research methodology (SEM) in the field. In general, it seems to us that this area represents the most potentially fruitful one to deepen our research interest with the right balance between theoretical perspective (which reinforces the construct understanding) with practical one (which represents the interest by effective interest by companies). The emerging balance between theory and practice represents an unexpected result. Indeed, this result is in contrast with previous evidence emerging from other literature reviews which suggest that studies in this area have a "non-theoretical character" [1] thus leading authors to claim to adopt a more theoretical perspective [3].

The present study has both theoretical and practical implications. From a theoretical perspective, it contributes to the existing literature providing useful insights on the worldwide evolution of interest and on the focus researches have privileged offering contributions to the comprehension of the frameworks scholars use. Especially through a bibliometric literature review a new revised perspective was offered to scholars focusing on this topic.

From a practical standpoint, our research addresses the current focuses and stimulates attention by HR managers on the large horizon covered by e-tools.

This work also presents limitations. The current study focused on papers published only in journals index on Scopus. To enrich our dataset, it could be interesting to also consider Web of Science or selected international conference proceedings. Conference proceedings could present new emerging trends that have not been addressed in the journal papers. We limited our investigation to authors' keywords only. It would be interesting to develop the research also entering the content so to also consider those paper in which e-HRM appears in relationship to other topics.

As for future research, considering current prior results and following previous studies (e.g., Bondarouk et al. [3]), we will consider enlarging the keywords included in the present study taking into consideration other keywords such as digital HR or Digital human resource management.

Also, a more in-depth analysis of the literature will be granted, in the next step of the research, by the adoption of a Systematic Literature Network Analysis [25, 26] combining a computational literature review [27] to further provide the authors with a deeper understanding on the development of studies in the topic. As well, the analysis will be further developed by assigning the selected studies to each cluster and analyzing their content accordingly in order to better support the description of the clusters and provide further insights on the subject.

References

1. Strohmeier, S. (2007). Research in e-HRM: Review and implications. *Human Resource Management Review, 17*(1), 19–37.
2. Walker, A. J. (Ed.). (2001). *Web based human resources*. Mc Graw Hill.

3. Bondarouk, T., Parry, E., & Furtmueller, E. (2017). Electronic HRM: Four decades of research on adoption and consequences. *The International Journal of Human Resource Management, 28*(1), 98–131.
4. Ruël, H., & Bondarouk, T. (2014). E-HRM research and practice: Facing the challenges ahead. In *Handbook of strategic e-business management* (pp. 633–653). Springer.
5. Castriotta, M., Loi, M., Marku, E., & Naitana, L. (2019). What's in a name? Exploring the conceptual structure of emerging organizations. *Scientometrics, 118*(2), 407–437.
6. Zupic, I., & Cater, T. (2015). Bibliometric methods in management and organization. *Organizational Research Methods, 18*(3), 429–472.
7. Cobo, M. J., Lopez-Herrera, A. G., Herrera-Viedma, E., & Herrera, F. (2011). Science mapping software tools: review, analysis, and cooperative study among tools. *Journal of the American Society for Information Science and Technology, 62*(7), 1382–1402.
8. Za, S., & Braccini, A. M. (2017). Tracing the roots of the organizational benefits of IT services. In S. Za, M. Drăgoicea, & M. Cavallari (Eds.), *Exploring services science. IESS 2017. Lecture notes in business information processing.* Springer.
9. Aria, M., & Cuccurullo, C. (2017). Bibliometrix: An R-tool for comprehensive science mapping analysis. *Journal of Informetrics, 11*(4), 959–975.
10. Cuccurullo, C., Aria, M., & Sarto, F. (2016). Foundations and trends in performance management. A twenty-five years bibliometric analysis in business and public administration domains. *Scientometrics, 108*(2), 595–611.
11. Za, S., Pallud, J., Agrifoglio, R., & Metallo, C. (2020). Value co-creation in online communities: A preliminary literature analysis. *Exploring Digital Ecosystems, LNISO, 33*, 33–46.
12. Callon, M., Courtial, J. P., Turner, W. A., & Bauin, S. (1983). From translations to problematic networks: an introduction to co-word analysis. *Social Science Information, 22*(2), 191–235.
13. Cambrosio, A., Limoges, C., Courtial, J. P., & Laville, F. (1993). Historical scientometrics? Mapping over 70 years of biological safety research with coword analysis. *Scientometrics, 27*(2), 119–143.
14. Zhu, J., & Liu, W. (2020). A tale of two databases: The use of web of science and scopus in academic papers. *Scientometrics, 123*, 321–335.
15. Harzing, A. W., & Alakangas, S. (2016). Google Scholar, Scopus and the Web of Science: A longitudinal and cross-disciplinary comparison. *Scientometrics, 106*, 787–804.
16. Caputo, A., Marzi, G., Pellegrini, M. M., & Rialti, R. (2018). Conflict management in family businesses: A bibliometric analysis and systematic literature review. *International Journal of Conflict Management, 29*(4), 519–542.
17. Keupp, M. M., Palmié, M., & Gassmann, O. (2012). The strategic management of innovation: A systematic review and paths for future research. *International Journal of Management Reviews, 14*(4), 367–390.
18. Denyer, D., & Neely, A. (2004). Introduction to special issue: innovation and productivity performance in the UK. *International Journal of Management Reviews, 5-6*(3/4), 131–135.
19. Tranfield, D., Denyer, D., & Smart, P. (2003). Towards a methodology for developing evidence – Informed management knowledge by means of systematic review. *British Journal of Management, 14*(3), 207–222.
20. Baier-Fuentes, H., Merigó, J. M., Amorós, J. E., & Gaviria-Marín, M. (2019). International entrepreneurship: A bibliometric overview. *International Entrepreneurship and Management Journal, 15*(2), 385.
21. Bondarouk, T. V., & Ruël, H. J. (2009). Electronic Human Resource Management: Challenges in the digital era. *The International Journal of Human Resource Management, 20*(3), 505–514.
22. Van Geffen, C., Ruël, H., & Bondarouk, T. (2013). E-HRM in MNCs: What can be learned from a review of the IS literature? *European Journal of International Management, 7*(4), 373–392.
23. Marler, J. H., & Fisher, S. L. (2013). An evidence-based review of e-HRM and strategic human resource management. *Human Resource Management Review, 23*(1), 18–36.

24. Wirtky, T., Laumer, S., Eckhardt, A., & Weitzel, T. (2016). On the untapped value of e-HRM: A literature review. *Communications of the Association for Information Systems, 38*(1), 2.
25. Colicchia, C., & Strozzi, F. (2012). Supply chain risk management: A new methodology for a systematic literature review. *Supply Chain Management: An International Journal, 17*(4), 403–418.
26. Strozzi, F., Colicchia, C., & Creazza, A. (2017). Literature review on the "Smart Factory" concept using bibliometric tools. *International Journal of Production Research, 55*(22), 6572–6591.
27. Antons, D., Breidbach, C. F., Joshi, A. M., & Salge, T. O. (2021). Computational literature reviews: Method, algorithms, and roadmap. *Organizational Research Methods*, 1–32.

Part II
Platforms and Ecosystems

Designing Reputation Mechanisms for Online Labor Platforms: An Empirical Study

Alexandre Bagnoud, Lena-Marie Pätzmann, and Andrea Back

Abstract Reputation mechanisms are commonly used on digital platforms to reduce information asymmetry, increase trust, and facilitate transactions between users. Despite extensive research on the design challenges of such mechanisms, the specificities of online labor platforms, like the evolution of skills or the heterogenous context in which transactions take place, are not fully addressed in the current literature. Thus, this work aims at determining how to design suitable reputation mechanisms for online labor platforms. The research follows the Action Design Research approach and is conducted in cooperation with the providers of the online labor platform "Scrambl.". First, a synthesizing analysis of design features of state-of-the-art reputation mechanisms of a sample of 21 existing online labor platforms is conducted. Second, a systematic literature review is performed along with ten semi-structured interviews with potential users of Scrambl. to identify and evaluate relevant design requirements. Seven design requirements emerge from this work, which may serve as a guideline for researchers and practitioners in the labor market industry to design adequate reputation mechanisms.

Keywords Reputation mechanism · Online labor platform · Design · Trust · Information asymmetry

1 Introduction

Driven by the democratization of the internet, digital platforms and ecosystems have been thriving in the last two decades [1, 2]. The most well-known types are e-commerce platforms and marketplaces such as eBay, Airbnb, or Booking.com. These digital platforms are only effective if there is a certain level of trust between

A. Bagnoud (✉) · L.-M. Pätzmann · A. Back
Institute of Information Management, University of St. Gallen, St. Gallen, Switzerland
e-mail: lena-marie.paetzmann@unisg.ch; andrea.back@unisg.ch

A. Lazazzara et al. (eds.), *Towards Digital and Sustainable Organisations*,
Lecture Notes in Information Systems and Organisation 65,
https://doi.org/10.1007/978-3-031-52880-4_11

the different parties, which can be particularly challenging to reach in an online environment [3]. Reasons for this are that transactions on digital platforms are usually anonymous, geographically dispersed, and not recurrent [4–6]. In order to combat these challenges and increase trust between the different parties, digital platforms and ecosystems often have reputation mechanisms in place (e.g., eBay [4]). They allow users to evaluate each other publicly and build reputation based on past transactions, thus encouraging them to perform effectively and removing those with bad intentions in order to foster trust for future trades [3, 4]. The design and effects of such reputation mechanisms have been widely researched during the last two decades (e.g., [4, 7, 8]), and it is proven that beside fostering trust between users, these mechanisms also lead to higher payoffs for sellers or buyers [6, 9–13]. Despite the large number of papers on this topic, a recent study reveals that it is still not clear for platform providers how they should design reputation mechanisms [7]. In addition, most studies around this topic are conducted based on mechanisms used by traditional platforms or marketplaces like eBay or Airbnb (e.g., [6, 8, 10, 12]). However, other types of platforms emerged over the years, such as those active on online labor markets, which remain largely underrepresented in the academic literature. Online labor platforms are becoming a popular way to find job opportunities, as it was estimated in 2016 that around 10.1% of the of the U.S. workforce were employed through such platforms [14]. Because of their unique characteristics, online labor platforms may require reputation mechanisms that differ from the common ones [15]. In cooperation with the providers of the online labor platform "Scrambl." (hereafter named "practitioners"), this paper aims to analyze this topic more deeply and develop design knowledge to help providers of online labor platforms in the design process of their reputation mechanisms.

Researchers claim that online labor platforms are different from many other types of platforms. For instance, unlike platforms like eBay or Airbnb, where the products or services offered are standardized and have a quality that remains consistent, platforms like Scrambl. involve the rating of people or firms whose skills or characteristics may vary over time [15]. Also, since organizations and workers have close contacts with each other during projects, the reputation mechanisms on online labor platforms may be influenced by empathy and social ties, which is usually not the case on other types of platforms [16, 17]. Therefore, researchers are of the opinion that the design features of the reputation mechanisms of other kinds of platforms cannot be replicated, as they may not fully suit the specificities of online labor markets [15–17].

The question of how to design reputation mechanisms for online labor platforms has not fully been answered by researchers yet. First, most studies on reputation mechanisms are centered around traditional platforms like auction or accommodation marketplaces, or review platforms [6]. The specificities of online labor markets are therefore rarely fully addressed in these papers (e.g., [4, 5, 7, 8]). Second, the synthesizing analyzes available of the design features of existing reputation mechanisms do not consider online labor platforms [7]. Thus, it remains unclear how the reputation mechanisms of online labor platforms are currently designed and whether they are comparable to those of traditional online marketplaces. Third, several examples in the literature show that designing reputation mechanisms can be delicate. For instance, major platforms like eBay or Airbnb had to redesign their mechanisms over time to correct flaws and increase their efficiency in reducing the information asymmetry between users [4, 8, 18]. In fact, a recent study confirms that providers of digital platforms still lack a clear understanding on how to design effective reputation mechanisms on their own [7]. Therefore, there is a need for a synthesis of design requirements emerging from theory and validated by practice that could guide platform providers in the design of their reputation mechanism.

Based on these research gaps and in order to solve the practitioners' problem, the research question is defined as follows:

How should reputation mechanisms of online labor platforms be designed to reduce information asymmetry and increase trust between users?

In order to answer this question, a framework based on the Action Design Research (ADR) approach is followed, allowing the consideration of the organizational context of the type of platforms in question [19, 20]. First, a synthesizing analysis of state-of-the-art reputation mechanisms of online labor platforms is performed using a morphological box, which allows to compare them to those of other types of platforms and understand if and how they differ from each other. Then, a systematic literature review is performed to synthesize design requirements discussed in literature, which are validated by ten semi-structured interviews with practitioners and end-users.

The results contribute to literature by bringing further evidence on how to design reputation mechanisms by looking at a type of platform absent from similar analyzes. The identification of design requirements for reputation mechanisms on online labor platforms does not only synthesize different elements discussed in former studies, but also takes into account the perspective from practitioners and end-users who confirm their relevance and add some nuance to their definition, which should help practitioners to design adequate reputation mechanisms.

The paper is organized as follows. The next section provides a short theoretical background on online labor platforms and reputation mechanisms. Section 3 revolves around the methodology used in this study. The results are presented in Sects. 4 and 5 discusses their implications for researchers and practitioners. A conclusion is finally drawn in Sect. 6 along with the limitations of this paper.

2 Theoretical Background

2.1 Online Labor Platforms

The purpose of online labor platforms is to match buyers (i.e., organizations) and sellers (i.e., workers) of professional services [6]. Therefore, these platforms are two-sided and must also deal with two-sided information asymmetry [6]. An important distinction must be made between crowdsourcing platforms, such as

Amazon Mechanical Turk, and online labor platforms, such as Scrambl. In the former, crowd workers are usually low-skilled and perform low-paid homogenous and repetitive tasks that can easily be rated and that do not require a broad set of skills. In the latter, workers are high-skilled and perform heterogeneous tasks that are difficult to rate and that may require workers to develop their skills further over time to adapt to new trends [15]. Because of the fundamental differences between these two types of platforms, they also require distinct reputation mechanisms. Therefore, this paper only considers online labor platforms.

Online labor markets differ from other common marketplaces in various aspects and may therefore require reputation mechanisms that are tailored to their specificities. For instance, traditional marketplaces are rather static as the quality evaluated by users is assumed to remain more or less constant over time [15]. This is why, in this context, a reputation score based on a simple average of the overall ratings given over time may work well. By contrast, online labor markets are dynamic and multidimensional. The workers' skills evolve over time, as they may learn new skills through education, improve their current skills through experience, or lose some skills because they do not use them for some time. Therefore, an evaluation given today may not be predictive of a worker's performance 6 months later [15]. Another difference is that the context in which the services are performed and the tasks themselves are highly heterogenous [15]. Heterogeneity is also a result of the fact that workers may decide to apply for new types of tasks that they never performed before [21]. Platforms such as eBay, Amazon, or Airbnb usually do not face such highly heterogenous environments, and their reputation mechanisms may thus not be fully suitable for online labor markets. Furthermore, transactions on online labor platforms are about services and projects that are carried out over an extended period of time (a few days, weeks, or even months). Such projects may involve regular communication between the parties to discuss the tasks, the goals, the expectations, or the progress. The greater closeness resulting from these social interactions may lead to a feeling of empathy or social pressure that may affect the feedback given. For instance, the leniency issue may increase due to the fact that a user does not want to harm their counterparty with whom they built ties over the course of the project [16, 17]. This, in turn, may increase the issue of inflation of positive feedback on online labor platforms [17]. By contrast, platforms like eBay, Amazon, or Airbnb usually lead to one-off transactions between anonymous users who have very limited contact (if any at all) with each other. Another difference between traditional marketplaces and online labor platforms is the fact that the latter involve the exchange of so-called "credence goods" or "experience goods", namely services whose quality cannot be judged before the purchase and is still difficult to evaluate even after they have been performed [16, 21]. Therefore, organizations face higher risks when buying services, and they may not have the expertise required to judge the true quality of a service [22]. Because of this uncertainty, organizations may tend to give lenient feedback.

2.2 *Reputation Mechanisms*

Reputation can be defined as "the conditional probability that an individual will behave in a certain manner based on what is generally said or believed about that individual's character or standing" [23, 24]. Reputation stands in a triadic relationship with trust and trustworthiness [25]. An individual's trustworthiness is a trait that emerges when other people place trust in that individual. Reputation is then an expression of the level of an individual's trustworthiness and acts as a reference that may influence a person's decision to trust that individual or not [24]. In order to leverage the triadic relationship between trust, trustworthiness and reputation, most providers of online platforms have implemented some sort of reputation mechanisms. Reputation mechanisms are defined as "mechanisms that collect, distribute, and aggregate feedback about participants' past behavior" [26].

Reputation mechanisms may serve two different roles [27]. In the case of moral hazard, reputation mechanisms act as a sanctioning device: They motivate users to behave in an honest way in order to avoid any punishment in the form of negative feedback [27]. When it comes to adverse selection, reputation mechanisms have a signaling role. Feedback about the quality of past transactions helps people to make a sound judgment on whether a user or product corresponds to their needs, thus increasing transparency between the users [27].

Several empirical studies confirm the positive effects of the use of reputation mechanisms, such as an increase in the average payoffs, a higher probability of being trusted and entering transactions, or higher price premiums for sellers with a good reputation [6, 9–13, 24]. However, the design of such mechanisms can be cumbersome, as several challenges must be considered when choosing design features. First, platforms usually rely on users' intrinsic motivation to use their reputation mechanism [11]. However, leaving feedback incurs rating costs for users, such as time, and does not provide any direct return to the evaluator [7]. Therefore, it is important to consider the incentives that can be given to users to use a reputation mechanism. Second, inflation and polarization of ratings are common challenges on reputation mechanisms. Inflation relates to the situation where an extremely high percentage of the ratings provided is positive, whereas polarization refers to the situation where only very positive or very negative experiences are reported [7, 28, 29]. These challenges are usually due to lenient ratings, retaliation, or collusion and manipulation, and are relevant to all types of platforms, including online labor platforms [4, 16, 24, 30–32]. The reputation mechanisms' design plays a big role in the apparition or tackling of these challenges, as the case studies of eBay or Airbnb prove it [4, 8, 18, 31]. Therefore, it is key to consider them carefully in every design decision.

3 Methodology

3.1 Research Framework

This paper is a design-oriented study that follows the Action Design Research approach, which is a research method particularly suitable for information systems research as it is centered around the creation of artifacts through multiple iterations [19, 20]. ADR takes into account the role of the organizational context and its impact on the development of artifacts, which should happen in a co-creation process between the researchers, the practitioners, and the end-users [20]. Because this research project is conducted in cooperation with the providers of the platform Scrambl., it is deemed important to consider the organizational context as a key element in the development of artifacts and to include the practice partners in the different iterations.

The general research framework used in this paper is depicted in Fig. 1. The aim of this study is to explore and better understand the problem domain, namely whether the reputation mechanisms of existing online labor platforms have design features that are similar or different than those of other types of marketplaces, and whether practitioners and end-users have unique expectations when it comes to the design of reputation mechanisms on online labor platforms. Thus, it has a problem-centered entry point and focuses on the diagnosis stage, as it ends with the creation of a diagnosis artefact, i.e., the definition and validation of design requirements [19].

Three iterations are performed. First, a synthesizing analysis of the design features of state-of-the-art reputation mechanisms of a sample of online labor platforms is performed. Design features "capture the technical specifics of the solution and are specific artifact capabilities" [33]. The aim is to compare the results of this analysis with those of other types of platforms to identify potential differences in their design. Second, a systematic literature review is carried out to gather design requirements for reputation mechanisms that are discussed in literature and that are relevant for online labor markets. In this research approach, design requirements are defined as "generic

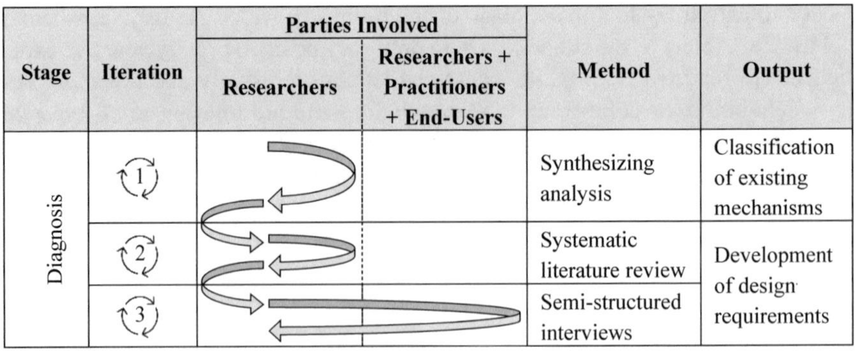

Stage	Iteration	Parties Involved		Method	Output
		Researchers	Researchers + Practitioners + End-Users		
Diagnosis	1			Synthesizing analysis	Classification of existing mechanisms
	2			Systematic literature review	Development of design requirements
	3			Semi-structured interviews	

Fig. 1 Research framework

requirements that should be met by any artifact aiming to create a solution for the underlying problem class" [33]. The results are then validated in the third iteration, where semi-structured interviews are conducted with practitioners and end-users. At the end of each iteration, the results are evaluated and discussed with the practitioners, and the learnings are incorporated in the next iteration [19].

3.2 Synthesizing Analysis

Selection Process Initially, the practitioners provided the researchers with a list of 17 online platforms that they consider as potential competitors of Scrambl., clustered in three categories based on their respective target group: freelancers, students, and no specific target group. In order to increase the sample size, the search engine Google.com was used to look for other similar online labor platforms that were not included in the list provided. Only platforms covering the Swiss and/or US markets were considered. This search led to 32 additional platforms that were added to the sample, reaching a total of 49 platforms in the initial sample. Based on this sample, a formal check was conducted to verify if all platforms could be accessed without any limitation that may hinder the analysis of a potentially existing reputation mechanism. Where needed, dummy accounts were created for an organization and/or a worker in order to access all the features of the platforms. In the case of 15 platforms, the creation of an account required either to make a payment to access the platform, to provide official documents for identity or firm verification, or to set up a phone call with the platform provider. As undertaken in a similar study, these platforms were excluded from the sample as their reputation mechanisms could not be accessed without causing too many implications [7]. Then, the 34 remaining platforms were checked for the existence of a reputation mechanisms. 13 platforms did not possess a reputation mechanism at the time of the analysis and were therefore excluded from the sample as well. The remaining 21 platforms form the final sample for the synthesizing analysis.

Data Analysis In order to analyze the design of the reputation mechanisms of the sampled platforms in a systematic and structured manner, the researchers use the "morphological box of feedback mechanisms" created in a similar study [7]. While all elements of the original model are kept, the morphological box is developed further to analyze additional design features that are not considered in the initial version. For instance, the morphological box used in this paper is structured based on the generic process (GP) of reputation mechanisms, namely "collecting feedback", "computing", and "presenting reputation" [34]. This tackles the lack of consideration of the reputation mechanisms' computation method in former studies, which is an important feature that can be designed in different ways [7]. To conduct the actual analysis, the researchers visit each platform sampled and write down the design features used in their reputation mechanism. The individual observations are then aggregated, and the results are presented in the morphological box in absolute and relative terms.

3.3   Systematic Literature Review

The literature review is designed and conducted based on the four-phases approach described in [35]. Phase 2 and phase 3 are described below (i.e., *Selection Process* and *Data Analysis*).

Selection Process   The selection of the articles relevant for the systematic literature review follows a three-step process adapted from a former study and is summarized in Fig. 2 [36].

Step 1: Selection of Keywords   Reputation mechanisms are often referred to as reputation systems, feedback mechanism, or feedback systems. To take into account the interchangeability of these expressions, the initial search string defined is ("feedback" OR "reputation") AND ("mechanism*" OR "system*"). It is then refined by adding further keywords. Only articles considering reputation mechanisms in the context of digital platforms or marketplaces are of interest. Therefore, the search string is extended with ("market*" OR "platform*") AND ("digital" OR "online"). In order to restrict the results further, a last group of keywords is added, namely ("trust" OR "design" OR "freelanc*" OR "labo*r"), as the articles should focus on platforms related to the labor market in general or specifically to freelancers (like Scrambl.), or as they should discuss the design or trust topics around such platforms. The search is restricted to the title, abstract, and keywords of the articles in the databases, as the aim is to only find papers that have reputation mechanisms as their main focus.

Step 2: Selection of Databases   Because the topic of reputation mechanisms has its roots in different academic fields, such as economics (information asymmetry and game theory), marketing (consumer behavior), business innovation (platform business models), or information systems (computation), the search is carried out on

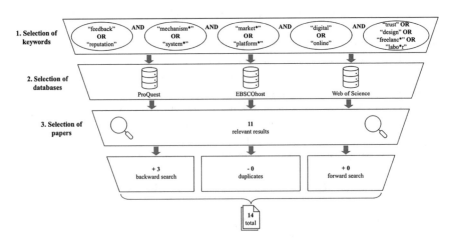

Fig. 2 Three-Step Paper Search and Selection Process (adapted from [36])

databases that cover multiple journals at the same time instead of performing a journal-specific search. The databases selected are ProQuest, EBSCOhost, and Web of Science. Filters are applied to the results to only keep peer-reviewed articles, thus ensuring a high quality. Furthermore, only papers that were published from 2010 onwards are kept, thus ensuring a high relevance as the literature shows that early reputation mechanisms evolved and were redesigned several times before 2010 [4, 18, 26]. The search leads to a total of 2762 results over the three databases.

Step 3: Selection of Papers In order to select relevant articles, the titles, abstracts and keywords of the results from step 2 are scanned. First, and because of the high quantity of results, only papers stemming from journals with a rating of A+, A, B, or C according to the VHB-Jourqual3 list are kept. Papers that do not have the design of reputation mechanisms on online platforms as their main focus are excluded. Before selecting an article, the authors systematically eliminate duplicates, which results in eleven relevant articles. Second, and to include potentially highly relevant articles that were published before the year 2010 or in journals with a lower rating, backward search and forward search are applied. Three papers are added from backward search, and zero from forward search, to reach a total of 14 relevant articles.

Data Analysis The analysis and synthesis of the selected articles is performed in a concept-centric manner [37]. In a first step, a conceptual content analysis is performed [38]. The aim of this method is to examine text material to uncover the presence of concepts as well as their frequency and importance. For this purpose, the techniques of open, axial, and selective coding are used. Coding is performed manually using the software ATLAS.ti. For the open coding process, each article is read individually. Words or sentences that relate to potential design requirements are tagged and assigned to emerging constructs [39]. For the axial coding process, these constructs are organized into potential relationships to differentiate conditions from actions, interactions, and consequences. Selective coding is then used to identify key concepts and to relate the constructs to them. Following the approach used in another paper, each key concept corresponds to a design requirement relevant for reputation mechanisms on online labor platforms [34]. All the key concepts are reported in a concept matrix, whose columns represent the uncovered design requirements, and whose rows show the articles in which they appear [40]. The concept matrix provides a clear overview of the results of the literature review and facilitates the comparison with the results from the semi-structured interviews.

3.4 Semi-Structured Interviews

Selection Process Three groups of interviewees are identified, namely organizations, workers, and practitioners. An interview guideline was prepared for each of these groups based on four thematical blocks, namely: (i) introduction, (ii) questions about reputation mechanisms in general, (iii) questions about reputation mechanisms on online labor platforms, (iv) conclusion [41]. Both the researchers and the practitioners were actively involved in the sampling of potential interviewees. Overall, ten interviewees were recruited. The organization contacts were selected by the practitioners directly. The main criteria for the selection were the interviewees' familiarity with the platform Scrambl. and their ability to cover the perspective of the organizations on the platform. This group of interviewees includes four men and one woman of different ages, two of which work in a large organization, one is the recent founder of a start-up, and two are serial entrepreneurs. The workers were recruited by the researchers. Four persons accepted to be interviewed: three women and one men of different ages who study at three different universities and in two different academic fields. One just started her studies, two are in their last semester, and the last one graduated the year before and counts as a young professional. To cover the practitioners' point of view, Scrambl.'s Chief Operating Officer is interviewed.

Data Analysis To analyze the interviews' transcripts, a conceptual content analysis is performed in the same way as for the systematic literature review. One difference is that for the open coding process, the key concepts identified during the literature review are used as pre-defined codes in order to facilitate the comparison between the findings from theory and those from practice. However, further codes may also emerge in case interview participants mention constructs that are not discussed in literature. The key concepts identified as relevant design requirements are again reported in a concept matrix [40], which is subsequently compared to the one that emerged from the literature review in order to validate the design requirements or uncover potential differences.

4 Results

4.1 Synthesizing Analysis of Existing Mechanisms

The absolute and relative frequencies of the design features of the reputation mechanisms observed on the 21 online labor platforms sampled are shown in Table 1. The relative frequencies are calculated for each design feature individually. Because the values are rounded, it can be that the sum of the relative frequencies may not always lead to a perfect 100%.

Overall, the results are very similar to those observed on other types of platforms [7]. One fundamental difference is that one third of online labor platforms have two-sided reputation mechanisms, i.e., mechanisms that allow bidirectional feedback, which is significantly higher than the 3% observed on other types of platforms [7]. When it comes to computation, which is an element that is not present in prior analyzes, it can be observed that most online labor platforms use human-based methods, while a few implemented a hybrid method [10]. Nine platforms compute the score by

Table 1 Frequency of design features within the sampled mechanisms (adapted from [7])

GP	Design Feature	Specification					
Collecting Feedback	Reciprocity	One-sided (worker to organization) 4 (19%)		One-sided (organization to worker) 10 (48%)		Two-sided 7 (33%)		
	Submission restriction	None 1 (5%)			Voluntarily after transaction 20 (95%)			
	Query method	Qualitative 3 (14%)			Qualitative and quantitative 18 (86%)			
	Content	Rating + Comment 14 (67%)		Comment 2 (10%)		Multiple / Other 5 (24%)		
	Submission category	Overall rating 14 (67%)	Three categories 2 (10%)	Four categories 2 (10%)		Six categories 2 (10%)	Thirteen categories 1 (5%)	
	Scale level	None 3 (14%)		1 1 (5%)		2 1 (5%)	5 16 (76%)	
Computing	Method	None 2 (10%)		Human-based 15 (71%)		Hybrid 4 (19%)		
	Measure	None 2 (10%)	Average of ratings 9 (43%)	Sum of positive ratings 1 (5%)		Sum of endorsements 1 (5%)	Multiple 8 (38%)	
Presenting Reputation	Feedback evaluation	Not possible 15 (71%)		Reply from rated user 3 (14%)		Mark as helpful 3 (14%)		
	Certification / badge	None 8 (38%)	Verified user 3 (14%)	Top rated user 3 (14%)		Others 3 (14%)	Multiple 4 (19%)	
	Context	None 10 (48%)	Project description 2 (10%)	Pictures of project 2 (10%)		User's role 2 (10%)	Multiple 5 (24%)	
	Identity	None 1 (5%)	Anonymous or pseudonyms 11 (52%)	Name disclosure 4 (19%)		Mixed 5 (24%)		
	Filter	None 16 (76%)	User type 1 (5%)	Skills involved 1 (5%)		Multiple 3 (14%)		
	Sorting	None 16 (76%)		Multiple 5 (24%)				
	Symbol	None 3 (14%)		Stars 16 (76%)		Thumbs 2 (10%)		
	Color	None 3 (14%)	Yellow 11 (52%)	Black 3 (14%)	Green 2 (10%)	Orange 1 (5%)	Grey 1 (5%)	

simply averaging the ratings, and eight use multiple measures to calculate a user's reputation. Regarding the presentation of reputation, one difference that can be noticed is that online labor platforms tend to use stars and the color yellow more often than other types of platforms, which use a broader set of symbols and colors [7].

To close this iteration, the results are evaluated with the practitioners, who confirm that the distribution of the specifications of the different design features are in line with their expectations.

4.2 Design Requirements

Systematic Literature Review The concept matrix depicted in Table 2 summarizes the results of the systematic literature review. In total, seven design requirements for reputation mechanisms on online labor platforms were identified in theory, namely: *robust, convenient, informative, accurate, sensitive, transparent,* and *dynamic*. A definition of these requirements according to theory is provided in Table 3. Most design requirements are discussed in several papers and seem to be broadly recognized. One requirement, *dynamic*, is mentioned in only one paper, which, however, focuses on online labor platforms and their specificities [15]. Because of the underrepresentation of this type of platforms in academic literature on reputation mechanisms, it may be that other authors never suggested this requirement because they never considered the specificities of such platforms. Therefore, this design requirement is included in the concept matrix and its relevance is to be evaluated through the semi-structured interviews with practitioners and end-users.

Table 2 Concept matrix for design requirements from theory (adapted from [40])

Refs.	Concepts / Design requirements						
	Robust	Convenient	Informative	Accurate	Sensitive	Transparent	Dynamic
[4]				X			
[6]			X				
[7]		X	X	X	X	X	
[15]			X	X			X
[16]			X				
[18]			X				
[23]	X			X	X		
[27]			X		X		
[32]	X					X	
[34]	X					X	
[42]		X					
[43]	X	X			X		
[44]					X		
[45]		X					

Table 3 Validation of the design requirements identified

Design requirements	Definitions according to theory	Definitions according to practice
Robust	Prevent all sorts of attacks and malicious behaviors such as fake ratings, frauds, collusions, unfair ratings, manipulations, etc.	Prevent all sorts of attacks and malicious behaviors such as fake ratings, frauds, collusions, unfair ratings, manipulations, etc.
Convenient	Minimize their costs for users such as time and effort through a simple mechanism easy to understand, use, and maintain.	**Motivate users** and minimize their costs such as time and effort through a simple mechanism easy to understand, use, and maintain.
Informative	Providing pertinent details that signal the users' characteristics and quality and that help to differentiate them.	Providing pertinent details that signal the users' characteristics and quality and that help to differentiate them **in a positive manner**.
Accurate	Ensure a high predictive power of the reputation by reducing subjectivity.	Ensure a high predictive power of the reputation by reducing subjectivity **and providing enough context**.
Sensitive	Reflect promptly the changes in users' quality and behavior and sanction users that do not meet defined quality requirements.	Reflect promptly the changes in users' quality and behavior and sanction users that do not meet defined quality requirement **in a mild way.**
Transparent	Provide users with means to check the input data and understand the computation that leads to the reputation displayed.	Provide users with means to check the input data and understand **the basic principles** of the computation that lead to the reputation displayed.
Dynamic	Consider the heterogenous and fast evolving environment and adapt the reputation based on a given context.	Consider the heterogenous and fast evolving environment and adapt the reputation based on a given context.

Semi-Structured Interviews The insights gathered from the interviews confirm that the seven design requirements identified in the systematic literature review correspond to the needs from practice. No further design requirement was uncovered. However, while there is an overlap between theory and practice, some nuances in the definitions of these requirements emerged from the interviews. The definitions of the requirements evaluated and reformulated according to practice are listed in Table 3.

For instance, when it comes to *convenience*, both a practitioner and a worker explain that the reputation should not only be simple to use, as described in the literature, but also provide incentives to use it.

Regarding the *informativeness* of reputation mechanisms, interview participants emphasize the fact that it should be slightly different on online labor platforms to account for the fact that it involves the rating of people. Two organizations and a worker express their wish for an *informative* mechanism that differentiate users in a positive manner, rather than separating "good" from "bad" users.

Concerning *accuracy*, several interviewees mention that they want as much context as possible when consuming feedback, i.e., they want to have great detail about the situation in which the transaction took place and the two parties who took part in the transaction. That way, they can better understand how *accurate* the rating is and how relevant it is to them.

While interview participants agree that reputation mechanisms should be *sensitive* and act as a sanctioning device, they express their fear that a high *sensitivity* on online labor platforms may have heavy consequences on workers' future job perspectives. For instance, a worker explains that a project may go wrong for reasons that are independent of them, and a bad rating may have unfair negative consequences on that worker's future job prospects. Due to this, three workers request that the *sensitivity* of the reputation mechanisms on online labor platforms should be mild.

When it comes to *transparency*, users seem to attach less importance to it than it is discussed in the literature. Some interviewees mention that a basic *transparency* of the mechanism is important to them, however, they also explain that a full *transparency* of the computation method is not a main requirement for them.

Finally, the interview participants confirm that *robustness* and *dynamism* are important design requirements, which they define in the same way as in theory.

The results in Table 3 are reflected with the practitioners, who agree that the refined definitions from practice better suit the specificities of online labor platforms.

5   Discussion

As explained in the theorical background, the characteristics of online labor platforms differ from traditional digital platforms and marketplaces. Therefore, practitioners and researchers expect that these platforms require reputation mechanisms that are tailored to their specificities, but it is unclear how they should be designed.

The synthesizing analysis of the reputation mechanisms of a sample of online labor platforms complements a recent study that contains a similar analysis on other types of online platforms and tackles the general underrepresentation of online labor platforms in literature on this topic [7]. It also addresses the lack of consideration of the design of the reputation mechanisms' computation in that former study, which is an essential component of such mechanisms. By comparing the results with those of that similar paper, it can be observed that, in general, the design features of the mechanisms of online labor platforms do not differ substantially from those of the mechanisms of other types of platforms [7]. This result seems surprising as it goes against the hypothesis made in this paper. However, as reported by researchers, platform providers tend to replicate the reputation mechanisms of well-known platforms like Amazon or eBay, as they are believed to be the common standard and as it speeds up the implementation [7]. This theory may explain the similarities between the design features of the different types of platforms despite their respective specificities. One fundamental difference to note and which contributes to research on this topic is that online labor platforms tend to use double-sided reputation mechanisms more often, and thus there seems to be a higher need for bidirectional trust building on this type of platform.

As it is not possible to derive from the synthesizing analysis alone if reputation mechanisms on online labor platforms should be designed differently, the hypothesis is further tested by identifying design requirements. From the seven requirements that emerge from the systematic literature review (i.e., *robust, convenient, informative, accurate, sensitive, transparent,* and *dynamic*), one, *dynamic*, appears in only one paper that focuses on online labor platforms. The semi-structured interviews conducted with practitioners, organizations and workers confirm that these design requirements generally match with the needs and expectations from practice. However, the interview participants bring additional nuance in the definition of the design requirements by mentioning aspects that are usually not always clearly stated in the literature. For instance, they define a *convenient* mechanism as a mechanism that provides them with incentives to use it, and they want to have context around the ratings available on the mechanism to increase its *accuracy*. Because online labor platforms involve the evaluation of individuals, they expect a positive differentiation of the users and require a mild *sensitivity* in order to limit the detrimental consequences of negative ratings on a worker's chances on the job market. Finally, although they consider *transparency* as relevant, the interview participants seem to attach less importance to it than what is mentioned in literature. These findings address the lack of consideration of online labor platforms and of the point of view from the practice in former studies, as they confirm the need for *dynamic* reputation mechanisms and bring important nuances in the definition of broadly accepted design requirements when it comes to online labor platforms. They also contribute to existing work by providing a synthesis of all design requirements instead of discussing only a selection of them as done in former studies, thus providing practitioners with a comprehensive overview of the requirements to consider when designing their mechanism.

To sum up, the results confirm the hypothesis that online labor platforms require different reputation mechanisms. The design requirements that emerged from theory and practice answer the research question by giving general indications on how the reputation mechanisms of online labor platforms should be designed and where they need to differ from those of other types of platforms. Future research should dive deeper to understand which design features should be used by online labor platforms to develop reputation mechanisms that fulfil the design requirements identified in this paper.

6   Conclusion

The aim of this paper was to understand how reputation mechanisms for online labor platforms should be designed, hypothesizing that the specificities of this type of platforms would require different mechanisms than traditional ones. Two artifacts emerge from this study, namely a morphological box stemming from the synthesizing analysis of the reputation mechanisms of existing online labor platforms, and a list of design requirements with their definition according to theory and practice. The synthesizing analysis shows that the reputation mechanisms of existing online labor platforms do not differ significantly from other mechanisms. However, the validation of the seven design requirements identified in the systematic literature review with practitioners and end-users unveils that they do have requirements that differ slightly from those defined in the literature, largely due to the specificities of online labor platforms.

By using several sources of data, this paper contributes to theory by confirming that the design requirements generally discussed in academic literature are relevant in practice, and by bringing additional nuance in their definition in the context of online labor markets. The synthesizing analysis also contributes by providing knowledge on the current design of reputation mechanisms on online labor platforms.

From a practical perspective, this paper gives providers of online labor platforms a list of design requirements evaluated with end-users that should be fulfilled when designing their reputation mechanisms. This should help to design reputation mechanisms that better suit their own organizational context instead of replicating mechanisms from other platforms.

This paper is subject to certain limitations. First, despite the fact that the methodology used (ADR) is focused on the development of artifacts by taking into account the organizational context, it must be acknowledged that the design requirements were evaluated in cooperation with a single platform, namely Scrambl. Therefore, the organizational environment considered in this paper is limited to the point of view of these practitioners and potential users of that platform. Second, the semi-structured interviews conducted with users and practitioners to identify the design requirements emerging from practice are based on a relatively small sample for each group (1 practitioner, 4 workers, 5 organizations). Although the insights gathered do not differ significantly between the interview participants, it must be acknowledged that they cannot be claimed to be representative of all users of online labor platforms. Third, the synthesizing analysis of the reputation mechanisms of existing online labor platforms looks only at the frequency at which each individual design feature appears. Future research could dive deeper and analyze if some patterns can be observed when it comes to the combination of different design features at the same time.

References

1. Zhang, T., Agarwal, R., & Lucas, H. C. (2011). The value of it-enabled retailer learning: Personalized product recommendations and customer store loyalty in electronic markets. *MIS Quarterly, 35*(4), 859–881.
2. Hou, J., & Blodgett, J. (2010). Market structure and quality uncertainty: A theoretical framework for online auction research. *Electronic Markets, 20*(1), 21–32.
3. Sutherland, W., & Jarrahi, M. H. (2018). The sharing economy and digital platforms: A review and research agenda. *International Journal of Information Management, 43*, 328–341.

4. Bolton, G. E., Greiner, B., & Ockenfels, A. (2013). Engineering trust: Reciprocity in the production of reputation information. *Management Science, 59*(2), 265–285.
5. Tadelis, S. (2016). The economics of reputation and feedback systems in E-commerce marketplaces. *IEEE Internet Computing, 20*(1), 12–19.
6. Moreno, A., & Terwiesch, C. (2014). Doing business with strangers: Reputation in online service marketplaces. *Information Systems Research, 25*(4), 865–886.
7. Steur, A. J., & Seiter, M. (2021). Properties of feedback mechanisms on digital platforms: An exploratory study. *Journal of Business Economics, 91*(4), 479–526.
8. Fradkin, A., Grewal, E., & Holtz, D. (2021). Reciprocity and unveiling in two-sided reputation systems: Evidence from an experiment on Airbnb. *Marketing Science, 40*(6), 1013–1029.
9. Ba, S., & Pavlou, P. A. (2002). Evidence of the effect of trust building technology in electronic markets: Price premiums and buyer behavior. *Management Information Systems Quarterly, 26*(3), 243–268.
10. Bajari, P., & Hortaçsu, A. (2003). The winner's curse, reserve prices, and endogenous entry: Empirical insights from eBay auctions. *The Rand Journal of Economics, 34*(2), 329–355.
11. Bolton, G. E., Katok, E., & Ockenfels, A. (2004). How effective are electronic reputation mechanisms? An experimental investigation. *Management Science, 50*(11), 1587–1602.
12. Melnik, M. I., & Alm, J. (2002). Does a seller's eCommerce reputation matter? Evidence from eBay auctions. *The Journal of Industrial Economics, 50*(3), 337–349.
13. Thompson, S., & Haynes, M. (2017). The value of online seller reputation: Evidence from a price comparison site: The value of online seller reputation. *Managerial and Decision Economics, 38*(3), 302–313.
14. Scully-Russ, E., & Torraco, R. (2020). The changing nature and organization of work: An integrative review of the literature. *Human Resource Development Review, 19*(1), 66–93.
15. Kokkodis, M. (2021). Dynamic, multidimensional, and skillset-specific reputation systems for online work. *Information Systems Research, 32*(3), 688–712.
16. Bolton, G. E., Kusterer, D. J., & Mans, J. (2019). Inflated reputations: Uncertainty, leniency, and moral wiggle room in trader feedback systems. *Management Science, 65*(11), 5371–5391.
17. Filippas, A., Horton, J. J., & Golden, J. M. (2019). *Reputation inflation* (NBER Working Paper No. 25857). National Bureau of Economic Research.
18. Ye, S., Gao, G., & Viswanathan, S. (2014). Strategic behavior in online reputation systems: Evidence from revoking on eBay. *MIS Quarterly, 38*(4), 1033–1056.
19. Mullarkey, M. T., & Hevner, A. R. (2019). An elaborated action design research process model. *European Journal of Information Systems, 28*(1), 6–20.
20. Sein, M. K., Henfridsson, O., Purao, S., Rossi, M., & Lindgren, R. (2011). Action design research. *MIS Quarterly, 35*(1), 37–56.
21. Kokkodis, M., & Ipeirotis, P. G. (2016). Reputation transferability in online labor markets. *Management Science, 62*(6), 1687–1706.
22. Yoganarasimhan, H. (2013). The value of reputation in an online freelance marketplace. *Marketing Science, 32*(6), 860–891.
23. Jøsang, A., Ismail, R., & Boyd, C. (2007). A survey of trust and reputation systems for online service provision. *Decision Support Systems, 43*(2), 618–644.
24. Rice, S. C. (2012). Reputation and uncertainty in online markets: An experimental study. *In-formation Systems Research, 23*(2), 436–452.
25. Keser, C., & Späth, M. (2021). The value of bad ratings: An experiment on the impact of distortions in reputation systems. *Journal of Behavioral and Experimental Economics, 95*, 1–11.
26. Resnick, P., Zeckhauser, R., Friedman, E., & Kuwabara, K. (2000). Reputation systems. *Communications of the ACM, 43*(12), 45–48.
27. Dellarocas, C. (2005). Reputation mechanism design in online trading environments with pure moral hazard. *Information Systems Research, 16*(2), 209–230.
28. Lafky, J. (2014). Why do people rate? Theory and evidence on online ratings. *Games and Economic Behavior, 87*, 554–570.
29. Resnick, P., & Zeckhauser, R. (2002). Trust among strangers in internet transactions: Empirical analysis of eBay's reputation system. In M. R. Baye (Ed.), *The economics of the internet and E-commerce* (Vol. 11, pp. 127–157). Emerald Group Publishing Limited.

30. Dellarocas, C. (2000). Immunizing online reputation reporting systems against unfair ratings and discriminatory behavior. In *Proceedings of the 2nd ACM conference on electronic commerce* (pp. 150–157).

31. Dellarocas, C., & Wood, C. A. (2008). The sound of silence in online feedback: Estimating trading risks in the presence of reporting bias. *Management Science, 54*(3), 460–476.

32. Luca, M., & Zervas, G. (2016). Fake it till you make it: Reputation, competition, and yelp review fraud. *Management Science, 62*(12), 3412–3427.

33. Chanson, M., Bogner, A., Bilgeri, D., Fleisch, E., & Wortmann, F. (2019). Blockchain for the IoT: Privacy-preserving protection of sensor data. *Journal of the Association for Information Systems, 20*(9), 1274–1309.

34. Sänger, J., Richthammer, C., & Pernul, G. (2015). Reusable components for online reputation systems. *Journal of Trust Management, 2*(5), 1–21.

35. Snyder, H. (2019). Literature review as a research methodology: An overview and guidelines. *Journal of Business Research, 104*, 333–339.

36. Engel, C., & Ebel, P. (2019). Data-driven service innovation: A systematic literature review and development of a research agenda. In *Proceedings of the 27th European Conference on Information Systems (ECIS)*, Stockholm & Uppsala, June 8–14.

37. Schryen, G. (2015). Writing qualitative IS literature reviews—Guidelines for synthesis, interpretation, and guidance of research. *Communications of the Association for Information Systems, 37*(12), 286–325.

38. Recker, J. (2021). *Scientific research in information systems: A beginner's guide* (2nd ed.). Springer Nature Switzerland AG.

39. Bortz, J., & Döring, N. (2006). *Forschungsmethoden und Evaluation: für Human- und Sozialwissenschaftler*. 4. überarb. Aufl. Springer Medizin Verlag.

40. Webster, J., & Watson, R. T. (2002). Analyzing the past to prepare for the future: Writing a literature review. *MIS Quarterly, 26*(2), xiii–xxiii.

41. Bogner, A., Littig, B., & Menz, W. (2014). *Interviews mit Experten: Eine praxisorientierte Einführung*. Springer Fachmedien.

42. Dellarocas, C. (2010). Online reputation systems: How to design one that does what you need. *MIT Sloan Management Review, 51*(3), 33–38.

43. Lin, I.-C., Wu, H.-J., Li, S.-F., & Cheng, C.-Y. (2015). A fair reputation system for use in online auctions. *Journal of Business Research, 68*(4), 878–882.

44. Lumeau, M., Masclet, D., & Penard, T. (2015). Reputation and social (dis)approval in feedback mechanisms: An experimental study. *Journal of Economic Behavior and Organization, 112*, 127–140.

45. Pavlou, P. A., & Gefen, D. (2004). Building effective online marketplaces with institution-based trust. *Information Systems Research, 15*(1), 37–59.

Additive Manufacturing as Game Changer Technology in the Manufacturing Sector: The Business Model's Renewal

Patrizia Accordino (ID)**, Raffaella Coppolino** (ID)**, and Elvira Tiziana La Rocca** (ID)

Abstract Additive manufacturing (AM) allows creating a product by adding the material layer by layer until achieving an end piece rather than using traditional technologies. The goal is to produce objects deriving from electronic data thanks to 3D printing—the most known form of AM—or other technologies. It increases the digitalization of manufacturing activities stimulating them in investing in innovative requirements and leading to major changes in the business ecosystem. It offers significant advantages allowing industries to optimize their processes, reducing the components required and the related costs. Furthermore, the capability to customize products positively affects the costs, the distribution, the market, inventories, and services related. AM can help the environment due to the potential in reducing the life cycle of materials, energy and water consumed by optimizing processes and could avoid the waste of resources. Significant benefits, strongly supported by tax and financial incentives and advantages, concern the supply chain processes and productive industries which reshore from developing to emerging countries subverting the recent opposite trend and often shifting production to the local context. AM proposes a new manufacturing concept, increasing the speed and flexibility of production. This stimulates firms to be more resilient to pivot from one component to another and promote a different balance changing the relationship with the customer and creating new and dynamic connections. This study contributes to understanding how the AM change the way firms create and capture value. Based on our findings, we identify several opportunities to encourage further advances in this area.

Keywords Additive manufacturing · Business model · Roboze

P. Accordino · R. Coppolino · E. T. La Rocca (✉)
University of Messina, Messina, Italy
e-mail: elviratiziana.larocca@unime.it

© The Author(s), under exclusive license to Springer Nature Switzerland AG 2024
A. Lazazzara et al. (eds.), *Towards Digital and Sustainable Organisations*, Lecture Notes in Information Systems and Organisation 65, https://doi.org/10.1007/978-3-031-52880-4_12

1   Introduction

Additive Manufacturing (AM) can be considered a game-changing method of production over the years in many sectors, such as aerospace, automotive, engineering,
medical, etc. [1]. Specifically, 3D Printing technology can be a game-changer for
logistics suppliers [2–4]. To take advantage of these new technological possibility's
potential, some innovative design methods are required for facing the increased
digitization, the greater demand for highly skilled workers, the importance of data
security, and the possible reshoring of some production back to Europe [5].

Several studies have analyzed the phenomenon from different perspectives, starting from technical studies on the changes in production processes, up to the strategic and managerial implications.

Our research intends to contribute to the existing literature by investigating a
case study on game-changing technologies as potentially competitive tools of future
value in the new economy era and by underling which are the main critical success
components for creating, delivering, and capturing value for firms and their
stakeholders.

With all the above in mind, this paper aims at investigating the role of AM in the
renewal of the business model focusing the attention on the way digital technologies
allow involving consumers in value-adding activities in an open innovation approach
[6] and, at the same time, permit the decentralization and localization of production
[7] activating a closed-loop flow of materials, so promoting a circular economy [8].

To try to answer the research question *"how does the AM change the way firms
create and capture value?"*, we perform an explorative qualitative analysis based on
a single case study, represented by an innovative Italian startup operating in the 3D
printing industry. Several reasons support our choice. Firstly, in the AM innovative
firms have shaped business logic that cannot be understood according to existing
types of business models. Secondly, the business models of innovative startups can
be more disruptive than those of incumbents, who can make incremental changes
just to realize options related to the new digital technologies, tools, and platforms.
Indeed, innovative startups develop and implement a set of activities, which differ
from those of a well-established company. In addition to this, innovative startups
and SMEs are strongly supported by the Government in the field of financing and
taxation as well as in the specific sector of additive manufacturing.

The paper is organized as follows. Section 2 presents the literature background
of AM. Section 3 describes some methodological aspects concerning the research
context, the selected case study, research design, and data collection. Section 4
shows the results and discussions of this study. Theoretical and managerial implications, limitations and further research directions are developed in the last section.

2 Literature Background on AM

AM is a general term that indicates all technologies based on the dispersed-accumulated forming principle [9]. It consists of the process due to which it is possible to create a product by adding the material layer by layer until achieving an end piece rather than using traditional subtractive technologies by removing it [10]. The basic goal is producing objects deriving from 3D models or different electronic data thanks to 3D printing—the most known form of additive manufacturing—or other technologies. Starting from a computer-generated file, an object could be reproduced in physical form through an overlay of different layers of material that thus give shape to the virtually designed object. The material used is several, from plastic to metals, ceramics, glass, even edible materials and new thermoplastic materials in carbon tubes and fibres that are constantly being developed [11].

The new opportunity offers enormous significant advantages [12]. First, those linked with products. Indeed, enabling the development, modification, and optimization of the design process, allows many industries to optimize their processes and configure their products creating a fast prototype and directly reducing the number of components required for an application and the related costs [4]. Furthermore, while traditional components are complex and require multiple production steps, due to the innovative technology, the assembly of products is extremely simplified since it often allows to achieve it in a single piece, avoiding labour-intensive components.

In addition to this, the capability to customize and tailor products according to the customer's wishes modifying them easily and in a short time without the need of reconfiguring machines and production lines and quickly delivering solutions to customers positively impacts the costs, the distribution, the market, inventories—that undergo a significant decrease concerning stock level, raw materials, and the final product [13]—and services related.

Concretely, additive manufacturing can help the environment due to the potential in reducing the life cycle of materials, energy and water consumed by optimizing processes and could avoid the waste of resources. Moreover, some products could be repaired and reused rather than replaced [14].

But the most impressive benefits are those concerning the supply chain processes and integration [15, 16], less susceptible to delays and less reliant on transportation infrastructure. Furthermore, reducing costs directly impacts the budget of the firms, workers, and the surroundings.

Relevant consequences concern the location of the production since it could impact the market stimulating to reshore productive industries from developing to emerging countries subverting the recent opposite trend and often shifting production to local or regional contexts [17].

Finally, owing to the need for continuous and effective dialogue between devices, machines, and robots, it increases the digitalization of manufacturing activities stimulating them in investing in innovative requirements.

As a result, it leads to major changes in the business ecosystem, enabling firms to compete within the global economy, significantly involving a growing number of different actors. To be precise, the organizational framework of additive manufacturing is complex; indeed, some firms are directly involved in the development and production while others are only devoted to integrating components and software. Further companies are material providers. Then there are the firms that simply apply and integrate the technology every day, in the fields of healthcare, aerospace, automotive, defense, and consumable goods including food. At least, there are also knowledge and education institutions implementing academic research on the topics and different platforms and networks connecting firms with potential customers [18].

Paying attention to the other side of the medal, additive manufacturing proposes a new manufacturing concept, by encouraging customers in promoting the self-creation of products [19, 20]. Therefore, increasing the speed and flexibility of production could provoke disruption in the supply chains. This necessity of flexibility stimulates firms to be more resilient to changes in demand quickly respond and pivot from one component to another and promote a different balance by coordinating within and across supply chains, changing the relationship with the customer and creating new and dynamic connections [21, 22].

All those aspects could affect financing methods and taxation [23]. Consequently, a lot of firms may not access easily financing methods supporting this kind of technology. Therefore, additive manufacturing could be encouraged by government programs that overcome such common market failures. Indeed, several countries provide addressed incentives such as tax breaks and grants and other leverage opportunities that help reduce operational costs, attract customers, and increase competitiveness in the field of innovation. In countries in which Governments have set up this kind of policy, the tax credit is often qualified as Research and Development opportunity, available for companies developing new or improved products, processes and/or software.

Additive manufacturing creates also problems concerning the intellectual property of the digital files and the authorization of its use, rather than in its manufacture, transport and point of sale. It is widely known that the Organisation for Economic Cooperation and Development (OECD) is developing new models for the taxation of digital services and intangible value, including those contained in digital files. This may affect the transfer pricing of the multinational groups in the case in which they have to involve vendors in other tax jurisdictions […] [24].

Finally, additive manufacturing could impact the taxation of goods and services. Indeed, generally, countries levy taxes on raw materials or at intermediate stages when value is created, while other taxes like value-added taxes or goods and service taxes are entirely applied to consumption.

It is important to notice that firms involved in the additive manufacturing field are, initially, innovative startups whose development is concretely favoured by European Union. Indeed, many countries like Italy provide tax incentives for investors and, also consistent tax and financial advantages for innovative startups.

3   Design and Method

This section presents the research context, focused on the challenges that emerge from the adoption of additive manufacturing as a game-changer in the way firms create and co-create value. Then, we examine an anecdotal case study, explaining the data collection process.

3.1   The Research Context

Often in times of crisis, new trends emerge, able to overcome dark times thanks to creative thinking and the innovations that come from it. Resilience seems to be the keyword in this historical moment in which pandemics and wars lead to a deep profound crisis. Nevertheless, to be resilient it is often necessary to find the "keystone" to turn a need into an opportunity. Consequently, we can often observe the pivoting phenomenon in several young companies [25–27] as well as the role of game-changer played by people and/or technologies [28, 29].

On another hand, business model innovation has been widely examined in literature as a key to business success ([6, 30, 31]). In particular, with the growing awareness of the importance of sustainability, attention has increasingly focused on innovative business models that were harbingers of economic and social sustainability, as well as environmental, and that would lead companies towards an increasingly circular economy [32, 33].

The evolution of studies on business models related to additive manufacturing highlights the presence of incremental development paths alongside disruptive changes, whether they are open or closed [34] (see also [35, 36]).

VOSviewer software was applied to achieve the relationships and identify the co-occurrence pattern of the keywords used by the authors of the scientific documents [37] retrieved on Scopus and Wos, having as research string ["additive manufacturing" and "business model*"].

The overlay visualization (in Fig. 1) underline how the interest on the subject has involved scholars from different research fields. In fact, if in a first time the interest was on specific issues related to production, such as *product development, rapid prototyping* and *CAD*, over the years, studies on issues relating to the business system and the full sustainability of strategic choices relating to *industry 4.0, circular economy, environmental impact* have multiplied.

Starting from these assumptions, the basic idea of the paper is to analyse the role of game-changer played by additive manufacturing in defining and implementing the business model, trying to answer the question: *how does the AM change the way firms create and capture value?*

To do so, we conduct a desk analysis to identify an anecdotal case that could be a pilot study for highlighting emerging peculiarities in the field [38].

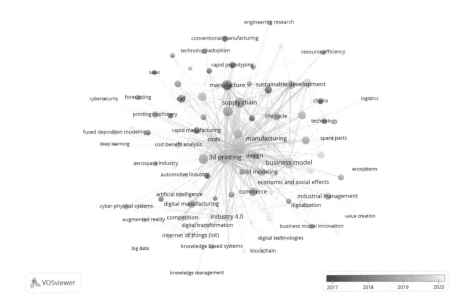

Fig. 1 Overlay visualization (min. occurence: 5; weights: links; scores: time since pubblication)

3.2 Data Collection

To explore the role of additive manufacturing as a game-changer, we start performing an internet search on additive manufacturing and its several forms, and we focus our attention on 3D printing. Inside the https://www.3dprintingbusiness.directory/ we find 6359 companies *involved in the entire 3D printing industry workflow*. Among these companies, we pinpoint the attention on Italian AM companies (for example, Lima Corporate—in the medical field-, Avio Aero—for the design, production and manutention of components for civil and military aeronautics—, Sisma and DWS—in the dental and jewellery segments—) and particularly on Roboze, one of the two Italian firms in the ranking of the 100 'Technology Pioneer' companies drawn up by the World Economic Forum.

To understand this "contemporary phenomenon within its real-life context" [39], an analysis of this anecdotal case was conducted in two steps. In the first one, we visit the website to gather information about the firm and its way to present itself. In the second step, with a snowball sample technique [40], we analyze the articles on Italian media and on the blogs and the sites where were news and/or interviews on Roboze and its CEO and other managers. In this phase, more than 250 documents/ videos are examined for gathering information about this scale-up [41], to highlight the way AM transforms how firms create, deliver, capture and exchange value [33].

3.3   The Sample

Roboze is the Apulian scaleup market leader in the 3D printing sector for super polymers. It designs and manufactures 3D printers for industrial manufacturers and offers digital services for extreme applications.

Starting in 2013 from the founder's intuition Alessio Lorusso, this startup history is full of passion and perseverance. Roboze was born in an Apulian mechanical workshop. In the beginning, its founder installed the precision gears of a workshop machine tool inside the 3D printer. Then working on engineering and materials science, Roboze has developed particularly performing materials, such as thermoplastic polymers and carbon fiber reinforced PEEK for metal replacement applications.

Today Roboze is an international scaleup that, with 3D printing, is revolutionizing the supply chain and subverting production management. Its patent is all over the world.

Roboze operates in several countries, indeed, it has offices in Italy and in the United States, and has recently inaugurated its headquarters in Houston, employing hundreds of people. One of the investors, is Federico Faggin, the inventor of the microchip and the touchscreen, who was also a member of the advisory board since August 2018.

Alessio Lorusso in his company has obtained awards and recognitions as illustrated in Table 1.

Recently, in the EIT Digital Challenge 2020, Roboze entered among the 20 finalist scaleups from all over Europe. In addition to this, it actively takes part in events, conferences, and fairs to communicate effectively with its partners, and current and potential customers, such as at the end of May 2022, Roboze Day in Germany, a 3D printing event for companies that want to transform their production in an efficient, digital, and sustainable way. Finally, in June, APS Meetings 2022, in Lyon, and FMW 2022, in Rimini.

4   Findings and Discussion

In the contest outlined, the company under investigation is exponentially growing riding and driving the wave of digital technologies to become a driver of change in the manufacturing sector. Roboze has expanded its range of action becoming highly competitive. Its business model proposes to switch from delocalized mass production to a customized one in the place of need [42]. This could solve the weakness of current supply chains in geographic areas of the world.

Roboze has ambitious growth programs, also for the recruitment of people considered a key value, starting with those involved in research and development to all the members of the team that deals with international development [43].

From our desk analysis, we have identified several critical success factors briefly described as follows.

Table 1 Roboze: main data and facts

Foundation	2013
Headquarters	Bari (Apulia, Italy) Houston (Texas, USA)
CEO and Founder	Alessio Lorusso
Technology	beltless technology patented 3D printing technology
Peculiarity	Roboze develops the most accurate 3D printing technology in the world. It specializes in super materials, i.e., polymers which, due to their thermal, mechanical, and chemical properties, can replace metals in extreme environments.
Industries	Aerospace, Energy, Manufacturing Processes, Mobility & Transportation, Defense, Education & Research, Product Development, Medical Devices, Chemical Industry
Materials	Helios™PEEK 2005, Carbon PEEK, PEEK, Carbon PA, ULTEM™ AM9085F, PP, Flex-TPU, PC—LEXAN™ EXL AMHI240F, FUNCTIONAL-NYLON, Strong-ABS
Awards	
2018	EY award for the best startup of the year.
2018	Forbes included Alessio Lorusso among the 30 most influential and innovative Under 30 in Europe in the Industry category.
November 2020	EIT Digital Challenge among the 20 finalist scaleups from all over Europe
December 2020	Italian Mechatronics Award Roboze is the most innovative startup with a special mention.
May 2022	Awarded as Technology Pioneer by World Economic Forum
Investors	
Equiter Spa—Intesa Sanpaolo	Banking groups in Europe and through its VC firm Equiter Spa, it selects and invests in the most promising high-tech firms.
NovaCapital	Financial holding and investment company
Lagfin	The holding company of Campari Group.
Alfredo Altavilla	Industrial leaders, President of ITA Airways, advisor CVC fund
Boris Collardi	Leader in the financial sector
Federico Faggin	Revolutionized history by co-inventing the microprocessor
Diego Piacentini	Top manager in the High Tech and Supply Chain sector, he has held top positions in Apple and Amazon.
Luigi de Vecchi	Chairman EMEA at Citi, he is an international finance guru
Alain Harrus	Expert in industrial manufacturing processes with a background in Physics and years of VC experience in Silicon Valle
Stefano Bernardi	Co-founder and partner of Semantic Ventures and full-time investor of future-tech societies
Andrea Dusi	CEO of Treccani Futura, enhancement of technological issues
Andrea Guerra	Manager with international experience
Roberto Ferraresi	Long-time investor and current CEO of The Equity Club
Luca Giacometti	Senior positions (GE Capital), Galileo SPAC founder (Nasdaq)
Denis Faccioli	CEO of Tecres, a leading company in biomedical technologies

Source: www.roboze.com

4.1 Infrastructure

Roboze technology relies on hardware and software scalable and flexible, in addition to performance and reliability guaranteed by the integrated control platform.

It implements the "Manufacturing as a Service" model allowing additive manufacturing centers for goods close to the point of use known. This model affects positively the production and procurement costs of a company.

With a digital warehouse rather than having physical warehouses, companies can reduce their inventory costs by producing with Roboze industrial additive manufacturing systems, on-demand, and just-in-time.

In addition to this, Roboze, in a perfect reshoring trend, decided to maintain one of the two Headquarters in Bari, which has a strategic geographical position and keep local businesses connected to the rest of the world physically and technologically due to the availability of fully comprehensive digital services. Indeed, thanks to several multinational companies established in Bari, since the Nineties, the competitiveness of the Apulian district has increased [44].

In this context, the business model is aimed at developing scale-up solutions through collaborations with like-minded individuals, companies, and investors [30] that allow small companies to adopt innovative solutions, making them globally competitive through an organizational design focused on mass customization and new kind of learning [7, 45].

4.2 Offer

Roboze 3D printers' innovation presents two key points:

- high precision and replicability of the pieces on a large scale.
- the use of new generation composite materials.

Roboze has developed the 3D printing technological ecosystem dedicated to *metal replacement,* allowing the replacement of metals in many applications with great advantages in terms of lightness, mechanical strength, workability, and chemical resistance.

The platform allows customized production for each individual customer all over the world, reducing time and costs for manufacturing companies.

The 3D system aims to satisfy production needs and optimize waste, thanks to the demand and just-in-time production.

Today's market has become increasingly competitive, and companies are relying on AM methods to increase their speed, and efficiency, and to achieve quality for their end-users. Roboze meets this need with a fully equipped industrial automation PLC (programmable logic controller) developed in partnership with the B&R of ABB Group. Main advantages regard remote-control management, simple maintenance, reliability, complete design freedom to produce specific parts, and availability of components when a firm needs them. This technological ecosystem integrates 3D printing into customized industrial parts production that fits into production systems by ensuring quality standards, process repeatability, and control.

Thanks to Roboze's innovative technologies, mass production can turn into customization and traditional manufacturing must modify its industrial processes to meet customer needs.

4.3 Customers

Roboze technology has thousands of customers, including many of the major industry leaders such as the US Army, Leonardo, General Electric, Airbus, Bosch, Honeywell, Dallara Automobili, Iveco, and Formula 1 teams.

Many companies are adopting recent technologies to innovate their warehouses and to achieve greater flexibility in the supply chain. A crucial aspect of customizing production is to reduce the time to market. Traditional methods do not allow flexibility and cannot be adapted continuously to new applications.

In addition to the large global corporations, Roboze is also active in the transport sector: in a few hours, the 3D printers can produce the spare parts of the railway trains to maintain the Trenitalia fleet, thus avoiding waste and a long keeping of spare parts in FS warehouses.

In the medical field, Roboze is studying an innovative technology of materials capable of reproducing prostheses within the human body that promote cell regeneration.

Then there is another particularly key area, the New Space Economy: Roboze is working on new materials that will help reduce weight thus increasing the efficiency of space travel.

Furthermore, the circular economy of Roboze allows to recover even after years the pieces that are not needed and, starting from these scraps, the company can create a new material. A process to the advantage of environmental sustainability.

4.4 Tax and Financial Viability

Roboze's economic and financial indicators are extremely interesting. In 2017 Roboze achieved revenues of one million euros (+84% compared to 2016) and a net profit of 0.2 million (+500%), with a turnover quadrupled. Exports for 69%, with a presence in all distribution channels in the EMEA area, India, and South Korea.

Roboze has closed its first seed investment round in 2018, obtaining three million euros. The project was evaluated and approved by Equiter, for developing Roboze's research laboratories in Bari and thus expanding its line of 3D printers. It has been the first company in which the RIF Fund invests, dedicated to research and innovation in the southern regions of Italy [46].

Earlier this year Roboze announced the obtaining of further investments from the best family offices and world-renowned top managers. This additional fundraising will accelerate Roboze's growth in the USA enhancing especially the research activity in its Italian R&D center where the scaleup is building a new chemical laboratory.

Thus, Roboze can boast of having a pool of prestigious international investors that believe in its vision and in the change of a production paradigm that its technology is enabling in the manufacturing companies of the world, replacing metals, and producing parts without wasting raw materials.

Therefore, incentives offered to investors in the form of deductions from their income and to firms, such as hyper-amortization, tax credit on costs incurred as part of an R&D project, and other facilitating tools-incentivize, stimulate companies to increase investments aimed at adopting solutions such as those signed Roboze. Indeed, in Apulia, there are two Special Economic Zones (SEZ) designed to encourage investments by Italian and foreign companies, by creating favourable conditions for the setting up of new businesses thanks to a series of tax incentives such as grants or tax credits, in case of interventions in the field of infrastructure, technology including and fast-track procedures.

In 2018, Roboze received a 3,000,000 € grant based on "equity and quasi-equity" and 2,400,000 € came from the EU's European Regional Development Fund through the Italian Operational Program "Research and Innovation" 2014–2020.

The company had a turnover of 3.5 million euros in 2019 and in the COVID period, 3D printing had a key contribution so despite the lockdowns Roboze has grown in triple figures. Thanks to the fact that it has become essential to produce components locally, the global supply chain has been modified due to the health crisis [47].

Roboze intends to grow exponentially. With the pandemic, the revolution in operational processes is urgent for companies of all sizes and sectors and additive printing is essential both to make the production process more effective but also to solve logistical problems and have a positive impact on the environment.

In synthesis, the analysis shows that the main push of AM to renew the business model is related to the possibility of remaining small sized by focusing the organizational design on collaborations with suppliers and customers that push towards mass customization and new forms of learning and Research. This peculiarity also allows you to take advantage of the incentives relating to economic and environmental sustainability of which the AM is a harbinger in both production and logistics.

5 Conclusions and Implications

The present study represents a first-desk analysis with a specific focus on the impact of game-changing technologies on the firm business model in the manufacturing sector. We identify several critical success factors for creating, delivering, and capturing value for firms and their stakeholders.

Roboze's technology suggests the key relevance of moving to just-in-time and on-demand customized production in the place of need. Producing only when there is a need, where there is demand, and making customized components for the customer who places the order, are new significant advantages offered by AM in line with the main literature ([4, 12]). By doing so, the company can propose a better service to the customer, and a greater intrinsic value to the product. As explained in some studies [13, 14, 16], printing what a company wants, where and when it wants, leads to shorter and simpler supply chains, localized production and distribution models that allow benefits such as savings on logistics costs, reduction of energy consumption and inventory costs. Relying on additive manufacturing centers affects the optimization of operating and maintenance costs of machines. The 3DP service allows for more effective production processes. This model offers economic benefits and sustainability improvements. Companies can use digital drawings to produce spare parts on-demand and on-site. Producing just what is needed can minimize inventory waste and reduces the amount of unsold finished products.

Our findings have several managerial and theoretical implications. It allows to understand how the AM can be a great managerial tool to face the increasingly dynamic business environment. Managers should catch these opportunities offered by new technologies and use them for the development of their business models. By moving to the various underlined components, they should be able to differentiate their business model from the competitors and take advantage. For companies the main challenge is an accurate planning to prepare, to promote and to execute the new projects through the game-changing technologies.

Furthermore, even more in this period in which the economic system is looking for sustainable business models, companies should focus their attention on efficiency and growth. Producing where there is a specific demand, rather than moving goods around the world, therefore translates into a benefit for the environment and for warehouse management costs and creates new highly skilled jobs. Entire supply chains are reorganizing to produce with a "local value chain" [48]. Also, the COVID emergency has placed the focus on technology and has made industries understand that it is time for a change. In the last 50 years, there has been a strong offshoring trend and global companies have brought production to low-cost countries, such as India, and China. The pandemic is changing the Value Chain model that has characterized the global economy for decades and it has highlighted the strategic importance of the transition from delocalized mass production to local tailor-made production. It is like a breaking point, demonstrating the importance of shortening traditional global supply chains. On-site production translates into a reduction in transport costs and a reduction in CO_2 emissions.

In addition to this, tax incentives and other financial advantages offered to innovative startups and SMEs and to the firms involved in 3D printing could represent an enabling factor. On the other side, problems linked with the intellectual property of the digital files and the authorization, the taxation of digital services and intangible value and those linked with transfer pricing and Vat are still being analyzed by the international institutions involved. Indeed, new rules are generally planned to be implemented by 2023 [49]. In any case, the possible consequences could be addressed by government intervention by bridging the gap deriving from the reduction of revenues otherwise to increasing tax rates [50].

This research presents some limits that can be interesting opportunities for future research. First, the study is based on a single case study, therefore, it is not possible to generalize the findings. Our conclusions are based on a desk analysis built on secondary data. However, the results open new research directions based on primary data, in fact, qualitative analyzes could investigate, through in-depth interviews, the decision-making processes and the antecedents in the growth paths of innovative digital startups and SMEs involved in additive manufacturing.

References

1. Beyer, C. (2014). Strategic implications of current trends in additive manufacturing. *Journal of Manufacturing Science and Engineering, 136*(6), 064701. (8 pages). https://doi.org/10.1115/1.4028599
2. Arbabian, M. E., & Wagner, M. R. (2020). The impact of 3D printing on manufacturer–retailer supply chains. *European Journal of Operational Research, 285*(2), 538–552. https://doi.org/10.1016/j.ejor.2020.01.063
3. Chen, L., Cui, Y., & Lee, H. L. (2021). Retailing with 3D printing. *Production and Operations Management, 30*(7), 1986–2007. https://doi.org/10.1111/poms.13367
4. Li, X., Li, Y., Cai, X., & Shan, J. (2016). Service channel choice for supply chain: Who is better off by undertaking the service? *Production and Operations Management, 25*(3), 516–534. https://doi.org/10.1111/poms.12392
5. Fernández-Macías, E., Hurley, J., Peruffo, E., Storrie, D., Poel, M., & Packalén, E. (2018). *Game changing technologies: Exploring the impact on production processes and work.* Eurofound. Retrieved 31 May 2022, from https://policycommons.net/artifacts/1845334/game-changing-technologies/2590800/. CID: 20.500.12592/qztk30
6. Chesbrough, H. (2010). Business model innovation: Opportunities and barriers. *Long Range Planning, 43*(2–3), 354–363. https://doi.org/10.1016/j.lrp.2009.07.010
7. Ben-Ner, A., & Siemsen, E. (2017). Decentralization and localization of production: The organizational and economic consequences of additive manufacturing (3D printing). *California Management Review, 59*(2), 5–23.
8. Despeisse, M., Baumers, M., Brown, P., Charnley, F., Ford, S. J., Garmulewicz, A., et al. (2017). Unlocking value for a circular economy through 3D printing: A research agenda. *Technological Forecasting and Social Change, 115*, 75–84. https://doi.org/10.1016/j.techfore.2016.09.021
9. Cozmei, C., & Caloian, F. (2012). Additive manufacturing flickering at the beginning of existence. *Procedia Economics and Finance, 3*, 457–462. https://doi.org/10.1016/S2212-5671(12)00180-3

10. Achillas, C., Tzetzis, D., & Raimondo, M. O. (2017). Alternative production strategies based on the comparison of additive and traditional manufacturing technologies. *International Journal of Production Research, 55*(12), 3497–3509. https://doi.org/10.1080/00207543.2017.1282645

11. Huang, S. H., Liu, P., Mokasdar, A., & Hou, L. (2013). Additive manufacturing and its societal impact: A literature review. *International Journal of Advanced Manufacturing Technology, 67*, 1191–1203. https://doi.org/10.1007/s00170-012-4558-5

12. Mellor, S., Hao, L., & Zhang, D. (2014). Additive manufacturing: A framework for implementation. *International Journal of Production Economics, 149*, 194–201. https://doi.org/10.1016/j.ijpe.2013.07.008

13. Ghadge, A., Karantoni, G., Chaudhuri, A., & Srinivasan, A. (2018). Impact of additive manufacturing on aircraft supply chain performance. *Journal of Manufacturing Techology Management, 29*(5), 846–865. https://doi.org/10.1108/JMTM-07-2017-0143

14. Rejeski, D., Zhao, F., & Huang, Y. (2018). Research needs and recommendations on environmental implications of additive manufacturing. *Additive Manufacturing, 19*, 21–28. https://doi.org/10.1016/j.addma.2017.10.019

15. Oettmeier, K., & Hofmann, E. (2016). Impact of additive manufacturing technology adoption on supply chain management processes and components. *Journal of Manufacturing Technology Management, 27*(7), 944–968. https://doi.org/10.1108/JMTM-12-2015-0113

16. Rinaldi, M., Caterino, M., Fera, M., Manco, P., & Macchiaroli, R. (2021). The impact of additive manufacturing on supply chain design: A simulation study. *Procedia Computer Science, 180*, 446–455. https://doi.org/10.1016/j.procs.2021.01.261

17. Moradlou, H., & Tate, W. (2018). Reshoring and additive manufacturing, world review of intermodal. *Transportation Research, 7*(3), 241–263. https://doi.org/10.1504/WRITR.2018.10014280

18. Van der Zee, F., Rehfeld, D., & Hamza, C. (2015). *Open innovation in industry including 3d printing*. European Union. Last accessed 06/2022, from https://www.europarl.europa.eu/activities/committees/studies.do?language=EN

19. Rogers, H., Baricz, N., & Pawar, K. S. (2016). 3D printing services: Classification, supply chain implications and research agenda. *International Journal of Physical Distribution and Logistics Management, 46*(10), 886–907. https://doi.org/10.1108/IJPDLM-07-2016-0210

20. Tziantopoulos, K., Tsolakis, N., Vlachos, D., & Tsironis, L. (2019). Supply chain reconfiguration opportunities arising from additive manufacturing technologies in the digital era. *Production Planning and Control, 30*(7), 510–521. https://doi.org/10.1080/09537287.2018.1540052

21. Attaran, M. (2017). Additive manufacturing: The most promising technology to alter the supply chain and logistics. *Journal of Service Science and Management, 10*(03), 189–206. https://doi.org/10.4236/jssm.2017.103017

22. Pour, M. A., Zanardini, M., Bacchetti, A., & Zanoni, S. (2016). Additive manufacturing impacts on productions and Logistics systems. *IFACPapersOnLine, 49*(12), 1679–1684. https://doi.org/10.1016/j.ifacol.2016.07.822

23. Schlimgen, J. R. (2010). Virtual world, real taxes: A sales and use tax adventure through second life starring Dwight Schrute. *Minnesota Journal of Law, Science and Technology, 11*(2), 877–899.

24. Gómez Requena, J. A. (2018). Tax treaty characterization of income derived from cloud computing and 3D printing and the Spanish approach. *Intertax, 46*(5), 408–421.

25. Chaparro, X. A. F., & de Vasconcelos Gomes, L. A. (2021). Pivot decisions in startups: A systematic literature review. *International Journal of Entrepreneurial Behavior and Research, 27*(4), 884–910.

26. Hampel, C. E., Tracey, P., & Weber, K. (2020). The art of the pivot: How new ventures manage identification relationships with stakeholders as they change direction. *Academy of Management Journal, 63*(2), 440–471.

27. McDonald, R., & Gao, C. (2019). Pivoting isn't enough? Managing strategic reorientation in new ventures. *Organization Science, 30*(6), 1289–1318.

28. Hendershott, T., Zhang, X., Zhao, J. L., & Zheng, Z. (2021). FinTech as a game changer: Overview of research frontiers. *Information Systems Research, 32*(1), 1–17.
29. Stylos, N., & Zwiegelaar, J. (2019). Big data as a game changer: How does it shape business intelligence within a tourism and hospitality industry context? In M. Sigala, R. Rahimi, & M. Thelwall (Eds.), *Big data and innovation in tourism, travel, and hospitality* (pp. 163–181). Springer.
30. Bocken, N. M., Short, S. W., Rana, P., & Evans, S. (2014). A literature and practice review to develop sustainable business model archetypes. *Journal of Cleaner Production, 65*, 42–56.
31. Osterwalder, A., & Pigneur, Y. (2013). Designing business models and similar strategic objects: the contribution of IS. *Journal of the Association for Information Systems, 14*(5), 237–244.
32. Bocken, N., & Snihur, Y. (2020). Lean Startup and the business model: Experimenting for novelty and impact. *Long Range Planning, 53*(4), 101953.
33. Geissdoerfer, M., Pieroni, M. P., Pigosso, D. C., & Soufani, K. (2020). Circular business models: A review. *Journal of Cleaner Production, 277*, 123741.
34. Savolainen, J., & Collan, M. (2020). How additive manufacturing technology changes business models? - Review of Literature. *Additive Manufacturing, 32*, 101070.
35. Friedrich, A., Lange, A., & Elbert, R. (2022). How additive manufacturing drives business model change: The perspective of logistics service providers. *International Journal of Production Economics, 249*, 108521.
36. Matos, F., Godina, R., Espadinha-Cruz, P., & Matos, M. F. (2021). Additive manufacturing technology: Designing new business models. In *Proceeding of the 17th European Conference on Management, Leadership and Governance (ECMLG)*, pp. 296–304.
37. van Eck, N. J., & Waltman, L. (2014). Visualizing bibliometric networks. In Y. Ding, R. Rousseau, & D. Wolfram (Eds.), *Measuring scholarly impact: Methods and practice* (pp. 285–320). Springer International Publishing.
38. Eisenhardt, K. M., & Graebner, M. E. (2007). Theory building from cases: Opportunities and challenges. *Academy of Management Journal, 50*(1), 25–32.
39. Yin, R. K. (1984). *Case study research: Design and methods.* Sage.
40. Biernacki, P., & Waldorf, D. (1981). Snowball sampling: Problems and techniques of chain referral sampling. *Sociological Methods & Research, 10*(2), 141–163.
41. Kozinets, R. V. (2002). The field behind the screen: Using netnography for marketing research in online communities. *Journal of Marketing Research, 39*(1), 61–72. https://doi.org/10.1509/jmkr.39.1.61.18935
42. Zanetti, F. (2021). Back to the future. La storia di Roboze, startup che ha brevettato una tecnologia innovativa di stampa 3D in grado di realizzare anche i componenti di un treno. *FS News.* Retrieved in date 30 May 2022 from https://www.fsnews.it/it/focus-on/innovazione/2021/10/15/roboze-bari-alessio-lorusso-intervista.html#:~:text=La%20storia%20di%20Roboze%2C%20startup,i%20componenti%20di%20un%20treno&text=A%20soli%2017%20anni%2C%20nel,la%20scienza%20e%20la%20tecnologia. Last accessed 06/2022
43. Abirascid E. (2020). *Roboze, la scaleup che porta la rivoluzione della stampa 3D alle PMI Startup Business.* Last accessed 2022/05/05, from https://www.startupbusiness.it/roboze-la-scaleup-che-porta-la-rivoluzione-della-stampa-3d-alle-pmi/105828/
44. Florio, M., Pellegrin, J., & Sartori, E. (2014). *Research intensive clusters and regional innovation systems: A case study of mechatronics in Apulia, Working Papers 201403.* CSIL Centre for Industrial Studies. https://www.csilmilano.com/docs/WP2014_03.pdf
45. Jordan, J. M. (2019). Additive manufacturing ("3D printing") and the future of organizational design: Some early notes from the field. *Journal of Organization Design, 8*(1), 1–7.
46. Millionaire Redazione. (2018). *La startup Roboze chiude un round da 3 milioni di euro.* Retrieved in date 30 May 2022 from https://www.millionaire.it/la-startup-roboze-chiude-un-round-da-3-milioni-di-euro/. Last accessed 06/2022.
47. Impresacity Redazione: Roboze, la scale-up che rivoluziona la produzione industrial. (2021). Retrieved in date 30 May 2022 from https://www.impresacity.it/news/24664/roboze-la-scale-up-che-rivoluziona-la-produzione-industriale.html

48. Econopoly: Reshoring, alcune ipotesi sugli effetti della pandemia. Il Sole 24 Ore. June 1. (2021). Last accessed 06/2022, from https://www.econopoly.ilsole24ore.com/2021/06/01/reshoring-globalizzazione-pandemia/
49. OECD. *Statement on a two-pillar solution to address the tax challenges arising from the digitalisation of the economy*, October 2021. https://www.oecd.org/tax/beps/statement-on-a-two-pillar-solution-to-address-the-tax-challenges-arising-from-the-digitalisation-of-the-economy-october-2021.pdf
50. Flynn, C. The questions executives should ask about 3D printing. *Harvard Business Review*, April 19 (2016). https://hbr.org/2016/04/the-questions-executives-should-ask-about-3d-printing

Raising Environmental Alerts in the Arctic Region by Analyzing Pollution Data from Sentinel 5p

Achille Ciappa, Marco Corsi, Chiara Francalanci, Paolo Giacomazzi, and Tommaso Terenghi

Abstract The paper presents the results of an analysis of a 3-year time series of pollution data from the European Satellite Sentinel 5p, with a focus on the identification of peaks of pollution in the Arctic region. This research contributes to the literature with a methodology for the automatic identification and geolocation of anomalous peaks of pollution, potentially indicating new or intensifying human activity, either industrial or commercial. A step increase in human activity could indicate new human settlements, growing ship traffic, or other forms of exploitation of the natural resources in the Arctic region, which, in turn, could be an indication of a growing environmental risk. While previous research mostly focuses on drawing accurate pollution maps, in our work we have designed an algorithm to identify peaks of pollution and, thus, eliminate pollution areas that do not represent an indication of a change in human activity, both on land and at sea. Our methodology has been tested in five areas of interest in the Arctic region. Results show how Sentinel 5p data can be effectively used for a large-scale, continuous monitoring of areas of interest, both on land and at sea. Our algorithm has identified roughly 200 peaks per year in the considered areas, highlighting the sources of pollution and indicating growing human activity in locations that are in fact generally considered at risk. Further work will be conducted in the ARCOS project to build a complete, longitudinal dataset of pollution peaks to be released as open data.

Keywords Environment · Pollution · Alerting · Arctic

A. Ciappa · M. Corsi
eGeos, Rome, Italy
e-mail: achille.ciappa@e-geos.it; marco.corsi@e-geos.it

C. Francalanci (✉) · P. Giacomazzi · T. Terenghi
Politecnico di Milano, Milan, Italy
e-mail: chiara.francalanci@polimi.it; paolo.giacomazzi@polimi.it;
tommaso1.terenghi@mail.polimi.it

© The Author(s), under exclusive license to Springer Nature
Switzerland AG 2024
A. Lazazzara et al. (eds.), *Towards Digital and Sustainable Organisations*,
Lecture Notes in Information Systems and Organisation 65,
https://doi.org/10.1007/978-3-031-52880-4_13

1   Introduction

The paper presents the results of an analysis of a 3-year time series of pollution data from the European Satellite Sentinel 5p, with a focus on the identification of peaks of pollution in the Arctic region. This research effort has been performed as part of the activities of the ARCOS project, aimed at designing a platform to identify and monitor environmental and security problems in the Arctic. This research contributes to the ARCOS project objectives with a methodology for the automatic identification and geolocation of anomalous peaks of pollution, potentially indicating new or intensifying human activity, either industrial or commercial. A step increase in human activity could indicate new human settlements, growing ship traffic, or other forms of exploitation of the natural resources in the Arctic region, which, in turn, could be an indication of a growing environmental risk.

There exist several research studies (see Sect. 2) and actual services that measure pollution across the Arctic region. While previous research mostly focuses on drawing accurate pollution maps, in our work we have designed an algorithm to identify peaks of pollution and, thus, eliminate pollution areas that do not represent an indication of a change in human activity, both on land and at sea. Previous research works mainly looking at historical data. The analysis of historical data is typically targeted to the assessment of pollution levels, with the goal of monitoring the impact of environmental conditions on the quality of life (human or wild) or on business (with objectives of compliance, facility management or security). Most of these services are based on a network of hardware sensors that need to be installed, connected and managed. Instances of these services are Clarity (clarity.io), Aeroqual (aeroqual.com), and envea (envea.com). This type of services represents the bulk of the market, but they cannot be used to monitor large areas (their typical reach is a building, a plant or specific areas in a city). In this respect, our research is innovative, as it is based on satellite data that are available without a need for installation of a new network of sensors, which is always expensive and seems feasible on a much smaller scale compared to satellite data.

Pollution maps based on Satellite data are provided by Copernicus Marine Service. These maps represent a reference to assess pollution levels and trends, especially when addressing environmental issues. However, Copernicus does not provide a service to monitor human activity, perform change detection and raise alerts. The real-time monitoring and alerting mechanism represent a fundamental distinctive feature of our work.

More specifically, our goal is to identify plumes of pollution (time sequence of moving pollution clouds) and reconduct them to their geographical source to favor interpretation. Sources are named and located based on an in-depth desk analysis aimed at building a static map of the Arctic by integrating information from multiple sources, including Open Street Map, Marine Traffic, Ship Next, Wikipedia, Twitter, Facebook and several blogs specialized on Arctic-related topics. The map includes over 500 locations. Alerts can be positioned on a map, equipped with a classification of the points of interest which includes oil&gas and research stations that are not included in standard maps of the Arctic.

It is well known that pollution data have a number of advantages:

- Sentinel 5p pollution data are free to use.
- They can be used to monitor large areas.
- They can be used to monitor any type of land and sea area, with no dependency and the land recognition and classification capabilities of specific tools.
- Pollution is difficult to disguise and can be identified and measured even in zones where human settlements are difficult to see with imaging techniques.

This opens up opportunities to use this type of data to continuously monitor large areas and raise alerts, as opposed to inspecting a small area upon a user input/ request as per the typical use case addressed by existing services. From this perspective, it should be noted that our outputs could represent a natural complement to the more traditional data processing chain supporting human activity monitoring, by providing an efficient and low-cost mechanism to identify the geographical zones where there is an ongoing peak of activity and then use other types of data for an in-depth and focused inspection limited to those zones. This addresses a current issue of monitoring large areas, such as the Arctic, with the goal of identifying new and potentially unexpected human activities, targeting the needs of institutional organizations interested in understanding various trends, including environmental issues, natural resources exploitation, political influence, and security.

The presentation is organized as follows. Section 2 reviews the state of the art, with a focus on previous research exploiting Sentinel 5p data. Section 3 presents our approach to data analysis, providing a short description of the system that has been designed as part of the ARCOS project. Section 4 summarrizes empirical results and discusses the main findings. Conclusions are finally drawn in Sect. 5.

2 State of the Art

Data from Sentinel 5p have been broadly studied, as they provide several advantages, including their free availability, their update frequency (thanks to the satellite's capacity to cover the whole globe at least daily), and a relatively high spatial resolution (5.5 × 3.5 km) enabling a variety of applications (e.g. [1–6]). They are also particularly suitable to explore environmental issues and, in fact, have been found to have superior performance compared to traditional optical multi-spectral satellite data [1]. For example, NO_2 data retrieved by Sentinel-5p have been found to support a more effective detection of local steel enterprises compared to MODIS data [1]. In addition to this, Sentinel 5p pollution data have been found to have a better correlation with monthly productivity levels of steel enterprises. This indicates not only the possibility to identify human activity, but also the quality and dependability of results.

Recently, Sentinel 5p data have been used to measure the impact of restrictions implemented to control the spread of Covid-19 on pollution. In [2], authors have measured NO_2 levels in the Shandong Province of China, observing a clear improvement of air quality due to a reduction of human travel and production activities. Authors indicate that pollutants are also correlated with meteorological data (temperature, humidity, wind, etc.), showing interesting directions to triangulate Sentinel 5p data with other data, when available, to validate results. Other studies have used Sentinel 5p data to measure the impact of heating on pollution (NO_2, CO, and SO_2) in urban areas, identifying a significant increase of all pollutants in the winter season [3]. In [4], authors show a positive correlation between NO_2 concentration and acute respiratory infection symptoms in children based on data collected in the Demographic and Health Survey (DHS) in Senegal, reinforcing the significance of Sentinel 5p data when used in combination with other sources of data.

With respect to previous studies, our goal is to identify *peaks* of pollution in a large area, without any precise indication of the locations to be monitored. Our approach is potentially interesting, as we can use peaks of pollutions to unveil new human settlements or an intensifying human activity in unexpected locations. However, it introduces new challenges related to the detection and geolocation of peaks of pollution.

A recent study [5, 6] has tackled the issue of geolocating pollution plumes generated by ships, with a focus on the Arctic region (North and Baltic Sea). Their goal is to provide an automated tool aiding the enforcement of more demanding NO_2 emission requirements for ships operating in the North and Baltic Sea, come into effect in 2021, by assessing pollution based on Sentinel 5p data. Their main problems are (1) the identification of pollution plumes generated by a ship moving in the open sea and (2) the correct association between plumes and ships. Regarding the first problem, authors propose a multivariate plume segmentation method based on the spatial properties of ships, corrected with geographical wind data. Their results show that their method significantly improves threshold-based baselines. Moreover, the NO_2 levels of the segmented plumes are found to have a high correlation with values of ships' emission potential. However, the association between plumes and ships is performed using AIS (Automatic Identification System) data, without a mechanism to geolocate plumes based on geographical information from Sentinel 5p only. This limitation has a considerable impact on the economic scalability of their method (AIS data are not free) and on the ability to use their approach to monitor large areas.

We borrow from this study the idea of expanding plumes to ensure the inclusion of each plume's emission point by replacing the value of pollution in a pixel with the maximum value in the surrounding region, as further explained in Sect. 3. This plume expansion mechanism mitigates the pollution dispersion effect of wind; the drawback is that the area that can be identified as pollution source is broader and, thus, less precise. We further this reference study [5, 6] by (1) designing an algorithm to identify peaks of pollution and, thus, eliminate plumes that do not represent an indication of a change in human activity, both on land and at sea and (2) taking into account seasonality to define a baseline of pollution enabling peak detection depending on arctic seasons. For this purpose, we need a 30 day time window to identify pollution sources. The next section presents the methodology that we have designed to fulfil these objectives.

3   Methodology

3.1   Choice of Pollutants and Data Retrieval

Among the pollutants available from TROPOMI based on Sentinel-5P satellite data, we focus on Nitrogen Dioxide (NO_2), as it is released into the atmosphere by the combustion of fuel with a relevant concentration for only few hours. Since the objective of the ARCOS project is to monitor changes in human activity, other types of pollutants (CO, CH_4) would be less effective, as they are more persistent, concealing peaks of pollution. We make a distinction between stratospheric and tropospheric NO_2, in order to determine the true contribution of human activities to NO_2 pollution levels, that can be accurately identified using tropospheric data (Tropomi allows the separate download of stratospheric and tropospheric NO_2 concentration data, via Sentinel Hub API [7]).

3.2   Image Preparation

Image data retrieved via Sentinel Hub must be processed and cleaned to obtain the correct information that can be used to identify pollution sources and perform time-series analysis. First, images must be filtered, discarding those that contain too many missing values (>25%) or those that contain too many equal values (>75%). Non-discarded images further processed by means of polynomial interpolation, as follows (see Fig. 1). The matrix representing an image is divided into N sub-matrices and, using an iterative algorithm, for each sub-matrix, only one pixel is considered. The value of the remaining pixels is estimated by applying polynomial interpolation on the data points composed by each pixel in the same relative position of each sub-matrix. Finally, the final matrix that represents a single time frame of a day is calculated as the mean value across interpolated matrices.

The resulting images are then de-noised (see Fig. 2). For each hourly image, quantiles are calculated and daily quantiles are computed as the mean value across hourly quantiles. Each pixel value of the images is then denoised by rescaling its position in the hourly quantile range according to the value of the daily quantile. This methodology brings the values of each daily image close to the most likely real value while maintaining the information on pollution peaks, called plumes.

At this point, the hourly images are normalized to remove the Background Pollution Intensity (BPI) component (Fig. 3). The maximum value of the BPI is identified through a histogram-threshold based method. Using this approach, each pixel in the image is classified into one out of two categories (background and plume), according to the position of its value in the value frequency histogram. The maximum value of the BPI is subtracted from the value of each pixel classified as plume, while the value of pixels classified as background are set to 0.

Fig. 1 Filling missing values with interpolation, Sabetta port May 10, 2021.

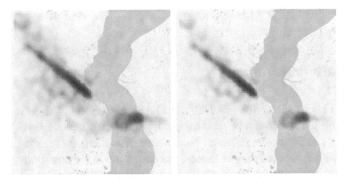

Fig. 2 Denoising images, Sabetta port, March 29, 2021

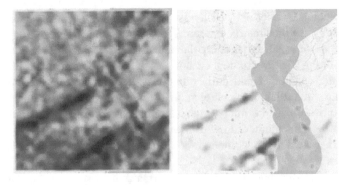

Fig. 3 Removing background pollution intensity, Sabetta port, October 25, 2021

The previously described methodology is applied to all hourly images. One daily image is then created, in which the value of each pixel is calculated as the mean value of the pixels in the same position across all hourly images. The overall result of this procedure is one clean, de-noised, and normalized image per day showing information on pollution plumes, which represent the input necessary to identify peaks of pollution and locate their source, as described in the next sections.

3.3 Pollution Source Detection

Since Nitrogen Dioxide emissions are highly volatile, wind conditions can cause significant daily variations in NO_2 concentration. Intuitively, plumes generated from the same source should ideally intersect at the point of emission, but if the emission is not continuous and the plume is moved by the wind, they may not intersect. Consequently, the pollution source would not be identified. To prevent these phenomena, a plume expansion filter is applied to each daily image, similar to [5, 6]. This filter replaces the value of a pixel with the highest value of surrounding pixels. This expands plumes and ensures that they intersect at the emission point. It should be noted that this process reduces the precision with which the source is identified, as it leads to the identification of an intersection region as opposed to a point. We apply this procedure to each daily image and data is used to generate a frequency map of the sources, represented in a 100×100 pixel matrix. In this way, it is possible to determine which points represent sources of pollution, based on three criteria: point frequency, land distance, and edge proximity.

Seasonality is also taken into account, as NO_2 emissions are not constant over time since some areas may be more active at certain times of the year. To analyze the trend of NO_2 emissions in an area of interest, we use a moving average based on all daily images in a given time window, as opposed to using a mean value calculated on an entire year. We have set the extension of the time window to 30 days (see Fig. 4).

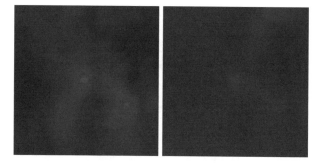

Fig. 4 Image aggregation, Sabetta port, March 20, 2021, obtained (from left to right) with 30–200 days mean, showing how seasonality has a strong influence on the identification of pollution sources

3.4   Image Conversion to Single Band

To simplify subsequent analyses, daily images are converted to single-band images. This is a standard procedure enabling grey-scale visualization without altering the information contained within the images. After conversion, NO$_2$ peak levels and their geolocation can be visualized on a map, as shown in the figures below.

We use the concept of luminance, defined as the intensity of light emitted from a surface per unit area. In our context, luminance represents the intensity of light emitted from any color in an image. We calculate luminance for each pixel contained in each daily image, thus creating a single-band daily image, in which each pixel contains the corresponding luminance value. The calculation of luminance for each pixel was at first done following the specifications provided by W3C [8], but better results were obtained using a more experimental method [9] that maintains the characteristics of the original image with greater precision. For each pixel, R, G, and B values are extracted and then luminance is calculated as:

$$Luminance_{pixel} = \sqrt{0.299 \cdot R^2 + 0.587 \cdot G^2 + 0.114 \cdot B^2}$$

Once luminance is computed, a single-band version of the daily image can created. Figure 5 shows on the left, the daily image generated for Sabetta port (Russia) and on the right the single-band counterpart. It can be noted how the information contained in the original image are perfectly transposed in the grayscale one.

3.5   Image Filtering and Peak Identification

Not all daily images contain pollution peaks and, consequently, images are filtered to extract a subset of images containing peaks. This process is organized in four steps:

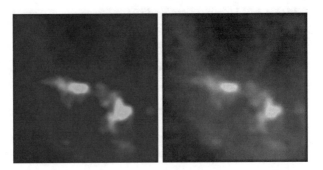

Fig. 5 Original (left) and single-band (right) images (Sabetta port, Russia, March 23, 2021)

1. For each image, the pixel with the highest value of luminance is considered. If this pixel has a luminance lower than a hard threshold set to 160 (luminance ranges between 0 and 255, and 160 represents a really low value corresponding to a very dark pixel on a greyscale), the image is discarded, as it is very unlikely to contain significant pollution peaks.
2. Remaining images are analyzed to identify clusters of pixels with a high value of luminance (the CV2 library of OpenCV has been used for this analysis [10, 11]). Specifically, pixels with a low value of luminance (between 0 and 127) are set to 0, while other pixels are set to 1. Then pixels marked with 1 are clustered. Ideally, each cluster should correspond to a peak.
3. However, some images contain clusters covering a very large area. We exclude images with clusters larger than a threshold number of pixels (the threshold has been empirically set to 400). A large cluster is likely to be associated with the so called artifacts, that is sets of pixels with a very high level of luminance due to an error in remote sensing devices.
4. Finally, images with a high number of clusters are discarded as they contain a chaotic distribution of high levels of NO_2 levels, probably due to atmospheric factors (see right-side image in Fig. 6). This procedure calculates the coordinates of the center of each cluster [12], corresponding to the coordinates of a pollution peak. Then, images with a number of peaks greater than twice the number of plumes (see Sect. 3.5) are discarded, while remaining images are included in the output.

3.6 Event Stream Generation

Peaks are identified on a continuous basis, generating an event stream containing the following information: date, location name, pollutant, coordinates of peaks contained in the image and related intensities. The intensity of a peak is calculated as the mean value of luminance within a square of 10 pixels centered in each cluster's center.

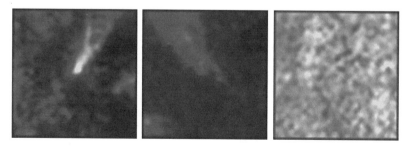

Fig. 6 Sample images with a useful peak (left), no clusters (center), too many clusters (right). Images refer to Sabetta port, February 25, April 3, and September 3, 2021 (from left to right)

4 Results

4.1 Findings

NO$_2$ peak detection has been carried out in 200 km × 200 km areas centered in the locations of Murmanks, Sabetta Port, Vostok Oil Project (Sever Bay), Tiksi, Diomede (Bering Strait) [13–16]. The central coordinates and size of these areas are shown in Table 1.

Peak detection has been carried out in the years 2019, 2020, and 2021. For each year, and for each area, an event stream is produced (Sect. 3.6), where an event is defined as a NO$_2$ pollution peak in a location inside the area. The number of discovered events per year is reported in Fig. 7.

The number of pollution peaks depends on many factors, including general weather conditions, as well as local weather and location-specific human activities. Remarkably, the two areas with the largest number of events (Murmansk and Sabetta) show a decrease of NO$_2$ peaks in 2021. This, among other (local) factors, could be associated with the sequence of a lower-than-average arctic sea-ice extent in 2020 [9], followed by a higher-than-average arctic sea-ice extent in 2021 [17].

L'impianto a Sabetta si chiama YAMAL LNG, quello di fronte si chiama ARCTIC LNG2, se puo essere utile.

Table 1 coordinates and size of the areas where NO$_2$ peak detection has been carried out

Area name	Latitude	Longitude	Size
Diomede	65.758333	−168.951667	200 km × 200 km
Murmansk	68.970556	33.075	200 km × 200 km
Sabetta	71.264765	72.060155	200 km × 200 km
Sever Bay	72.880278	80.883611	200 km × 200 km
Tiksi	71.65	128.8	200 km × 200 km

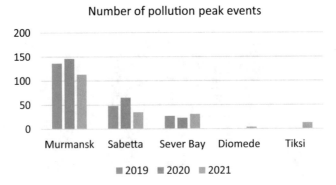

Fig. 7 Number of NO$_2$ pollution peak events for the selected areas, in the years 2019, 2020, 2021

Figure 8 shows the locations of NO_2 peak events in the Sabetta Port area, for 2021. Besides the obvious peak at the Sabetta port site (this site is called Yamal LNG), a second peak (labeled B) has been observed close to the opposite side of the strait (this site is called ARCTIC LNG2), and a third peak in the middle of the strait, north of Sabetta. Peak B is not surprising, because it is well known that there are significant human activities close to the location of the peak. Peak C can be explained by the fact that a large number of ships cross the strait in the north-south direction, as it is confirmed by AIS data on ship movements. A large concentration of ships can raise a NO_2 peak event.

The Sabetta peak, and peak B, can be observed, for example, in Fig. 9, showing the NO_2 pollution map on February 2, 2021. Peak C, in the middle of the strait, can be observed in Fig. 10.

Figure 11 shows the locations of NO_2 peak events in the Murmansk area, in year 2021. There are many peak locations, as in the Murmansk area there is an intense human and industrial activity, as well as sea transportation.

Tiksi is a small town of about 5000 people, located on the shore of the Buor-Khaya Gulf of the Laptev Sea, close to delta of the Lena River. An isolated NO_2 peak has been registered in the year 2020 close to the town, which is also a commercial port (Fig. 12). It is worth noting that no NO_2 peaks have been registered in Tiksi in the years 2019 and 2020.

The Diomede Islands (Fig. 13) is a group of two islands in the middle of the Bering Strait. In the area centered in the Diomede Islands, NO_2 peaks have been observed in the location of Port Clarence, on the East (Alaskan) side of the Bering Strait).

Figure 14 shows the Nos peak event locations in the Sever Bay area. Sever Bay is the main seaport in Vostok Oil cluster, that is scheduled to deliver 25 million tons of oil by year 2024.

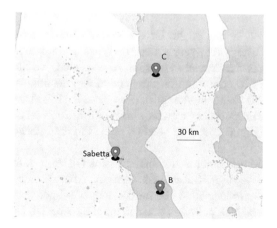

Fig. 8 Locations of NO_2 peak events in the Sabetta Port area, year 2021

Fig. 9 NO$_x$ peak event in Sabetta Port, and peak B, on February 20, 2021

Fig. 10 NO$_2$ peak event in the middle of the Sabetta strait, on February 24, 2021

4.2 Discussion

The criterion for the selection of the locations for our analysis has been to evaluate sites/areas in the arctic characterized by an intense industrial activity, or infrastructural development, or naval transportation. Overall, we have found peaks of pollution where we expected to find them, with few exceptions that will be discussed in this section.

The Sabetta Port is one of the largest Russian Arctic ports, situated on the Yamal peninsula. The port is very active and it has a strategic importance for the development of gas-rich Yamal Peninsula. As expected, we have systematically detected peaks of NO$_2$ pollution on the Sabetta Port location (Fig. 8, "Sabetta" peak). We have also found another peak (Fig. 8, peak "B") at the opposite side of the strait, and this is consistent with the current infrastructural development in the area. In the same Figure, peak "C" can be related to the intense naval activity in the strait.

Sever Bay is an important location in the Vostok Oil Project, that unites the largest deposits in the north of Krasnoyarsk Territory. After reaching its full capacity, the project is set to produce 50 to 100 million tons of oil per year. As expected, we have detected several NO$_2$ pollution peaks in the area, especiall close to the location of Dikson, the main port terminal (Fig. 14).

In the Murmansk area (Fig. 11), we find an NO$_2$ peak close to Teriberka, where there are two large hydroelectric power plants at the mouth of the river. We have

Fig. 11 Locations of NO$_2$ peak events in the Murmansk area, year 2021

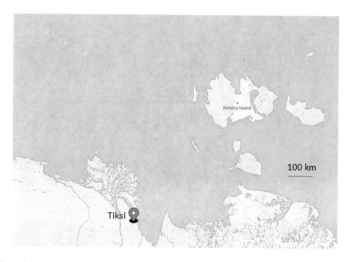

Fig. 12 Locations of NO$_2$ peak events in the Tiksi area, year 2021

found other peaks in the area of the Rybachy Peninsula that can't be explained with the available data, and further analysis is required.

The peak in the location of Tiksi (Fig. 12) is expected, as the activity of this seaport is significant, and also involved in oil activity.

In the Bering Strait we have examined an area centered in the Diomede islands (Fig. 13). We have found a NOs peak in the Clarence Port area. Clarence port is a very small location and the presence of a peak in this location requires further analysis.

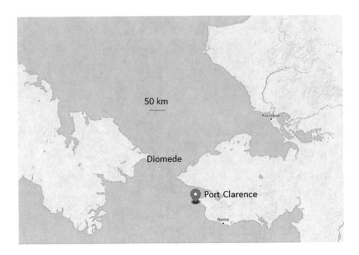

Fig. 13 Locations of NO$_2$ peak events in the Diomede area, year 2021

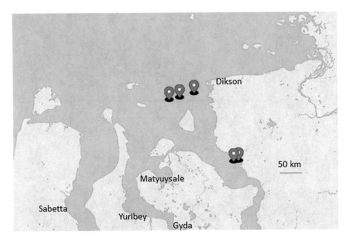

Fig. 14 Locations of NO$_2$ peak events in the Sever Bay area, year 2021

5 Concluding Remarks

The goal of this research is to design a methodology for the automatic identification and geolocation of anomalous peaks of pollution, potentially indicating new or intensifying human activity. Empirical testing is based on the analysis of a 3-year time series of pollution data from the European Satellite Sentinel 5p. Findings indicate that these data can be effectively used to identify peaks of pollution and geolocate their sources in a relatively small area. This suggests that our approach can be used to monitor large areas, providing a low-cost mechanism to spot the zones where there is an ongoing peak of activity and then use other types of data that are not free, but have greater spatial definition to perform a focused inspection limited to those zones.

As noted before, the majority of the peaks that we have identified in our testing is located in well-known risk zones. However, we have also identified a significant number of peaks located in positions that are not among those generally recognized as risky from an environmental or security point of view. As part of our future work, we aim at releasing our results as open data to favor continuous monitoring and collaborative interpretation of results with domain experts. This will allow us to improve the quality of our results, define usage processes, and ultimately understand how our results can help the work of policy makers and define policy recommendations.

Acknowledgements This work was funded by the European Commission H2020 project ARCOS "Arctic Observatory for Copernicus SEA Service" under project No. 101004372. This work expresses the opinions of the authors and not necessarily those of the European Commission. The European Commission is not liable for any use that may be made of the information contained in this work.

References

1. Yuan, Z., et al. Ground Pollution Source Target Detection Based on Modis and Sentinel-5P Products. *2021 IEEE International Geoscience and Remote Sensing Symposium IGARSS, 2021*, 7275–7278. https://doi.org/10.1109/IGARSS47720.2021.9553073
2. Xing, H., Zhu, L., Chen, B., et al. (2022). Spatial and temporal changes analysis of air quality before and after the COVID-19 in Shandong Province, China. *Earth Science Informatics.* https://doi.org/10.1007/s12145-021-00739-7
3. Ayoobi, A. W., Ahmadi, H., Inceoglu, M., et al. (2022). Seasonal impacts of buildings' energy consumption on the variation and spatial distribution of air pollutant over Kabul City: Application of Sentincl—5P TROPOMI products. *Air Quality, Atmosphere and Health, 15,* 73–83. https://doi.org/10.1007/s11869-021-01085-9
4. Kawano, A., Kim, Y., Meas, M., et al. (2022). Association between satellite-detected tropospheric nitrogen dioxide and acute respiratory infections in children under age five in Senegal: Spatio-temporal analysis. *BMC Public Health, 22,* 178. https://doi.org/10.1186/s12889-022-12-577-3
5. Kurchaba, S., van Vliet, J., Meulman, J. J., Verbeek, F. J., & Veenman, C. J. (2021). Improving evaluation of NO2 emission from ships using spatial association on TROPOMI satellite data. In *Proceedings of the 29th International Conference on Advances in Geographic Information Systems (SIGSPATIAL '21)* (pp. 454–457). Association for Computing Machinery, New York, NY. doi:https://doi.org/10.1145/3474717.3484213
6. Kurchaba, S., et al. (2022). *Supervised segmentation of NO2 plumes from individual ships using TROPOMI satellite data.* arXiv preprint arXiv:2203.06993.
7. Sentinel Hub. Documentation. https://docs.sentinel-hub.com/api/latest/
8. Darel Rex Finley. (2006). *HSP color model — Alternative to HSV (HSB) and HSL.* https://alienryderflex.com/hsp.html
9. https://www.arcus.org/sipn/sea-ice-outlook/2020/post-season
10. OpenCV. *Image processing: Structural analysis and shape descriptors.* https://docs.opencv.org/3.4/d3/dc0/group__imgproc__shape.html

11. OpenCV. *K-means clustering in OpenCV.* https://docs.opencv.org/4.x/d1/d5c/tutorial_py_kmeans_opencv.html
12. MDN Web Docs. (2022). *Web accessibility: Understanding colors and luminance.* https://developer.mozilla.org/en/docs/Web/Accessibility/Understanding_Colors_and_Luminance
13. Wan, Z., Nie, A., Chen, J., Ge, J., Zhang, C., & Zhang, Q. (2021). Key barriers to the commercial use of the Northern Sea Route: View from China with a fuzzy DEMATEL approach. *Ocean and Coastal Management, 208,* 105630. https://doi.org/10.1016/j.ocecoaman.2021.105630
14. Port of Sabetta, Yamal Peninsula. (2013). https://www.ship-technology.com/projects/-port-sabetta-yamal-peninsula-russia
15. Staalesen, A. (2021). *Tanker embarks on first ever mid-winter voyage on Northern Sea Route.* https://thebarentsobserver.com/en/arctic-lng/2021/02/tanker-embarks-first-ever-mid-winter-voyage-northern-sea-route
16. Rosneft starts building new oil terminal in Taimyr. (2021). https://arctic-lio.com/rosneft-starts-building-new-oil-terminal-in-taimyr/
17. https://www.arcus.org/sipn/sea-ice-outlook/2021/post-season

Nexus Between Carbon Emissions, FDI, Oil Prices, Economic Growth and Exports in Italy: Empirical Evidence from ARDL-Based Bounds and Wavelet Coherence Approaches

Aamir Javed (iD) **and Agnese Rapposelli** (iD)

Abstract Over the last few decades, most countries' rapid industrialization, population growth, rising energy consumption and lifestyle changes have increased the threat of global warming. In this context, this study examines the relationship between carbon emissions, economic growth, foreign direct investments, oil price, energy consumption and exports in Italy by using yearly data for the period 1970–2019. For this purpose, we first apply the Autoregressive Distributed Lag (ARDL) model; then we employ the wavelet coherence technique in order to check the causality among these variables. The novelty of this approach is that it ascertains the short-run and long-run correlation and causality among the variables simultaneously at different time periods and frequencies. Our findings show that the impact of foreign direct investments on carbon emissions is positive and statistically significant both in short and long-run which supports the pollution heaven hypothesis in Italy. Our results also reveal that the relationship between energy consumption and carbon emission is positive and statistically significant. Furthermore, the study also examines the validity of EKC hypothesis. The findings of ARDL shows that the relationship between economic growth and carbon emission is inverted U-shaped curve, thus providing evidence of the validity of Environmental Kuznets Curve (EKC) hypothesis.

Keywords Carbon emissions · Economic growth · ARDL model · Wavelet coherence technique

A. Javed
Department of Management and Business Administration, "G.d'Annunzio" University of Chieti-Pescara, Pescara, Italy
e-mail: aamir.javed@studenti.unich.it

A. Rapposelli (✉)
Department of Economic Studies, "G.d'Annunzio" University of Chieti-Pescara, Pescara, Italy
e-mail: agnese.rapposelli@unich.it

A. Lazazzara et al. (eds.), *Towards Digital and Sustainable Organisations*,
Lecture Notes in Information Systems and Organisation 65,
https://doi.org/10.1007/978-3-031-52880-4_14

233

1 Introduction

Over the last few decades, most countries' rapid industrialization, population growth, rising energy consumption and lifestyle changes have increased the threat of global warming. Carbon dioxide (CO_2) emissions are thought to be the primary source of the greenhouse effect. The relationship between CO_2 emissions and economic growth has been extensively researched since 1990. With greenhouse gas emissions (GHGs) and the impact of climate change at the forefront of policy debates, a plethora of literature on the determinants of CO_2 emissions has emerged. The majority of studies examine the Environmental Kuznets Curve (EKC) hypothesis, which states that as countries develop, CO_2 emissions rise initially but then fall after a tipping point [1].

In 1992, during the Earth Summit in Brazil, the importance of climate change was recognized globally. To illustrate the relationship between real growth and pollution, Grossman and Krueger [2] developed the Kuznets environmental curve hypothesis. While environmental pollution is a global issue and the planet is exposed to risks resulting from deterioration of environmental quality, the primary responsibility for rescuing the planet from these threats falls on the countries that are the primary emitters of GHGs. Among the most popular GHGs is carbon dioxide, and the main emitters are China, the USA, India, Russia, Japan, and Germany emitting 27.52%, 14.81%, 7.26%, 4.68%, 3.18%, and 2.0% respectively. The success of global attempts to reduce global CO_2 emissions largely relies on the dedication of these primary emitters.

Environmental degradation has been a source of concern for many researchers. The countries that had signed the climate change pact realized in the mid-1990s that stronger rules were required to minimize CO_2 emissions. The Kyoto Protocol, which established legally binding carbon reduction targets for developed countries, was adopted in 1997. The Kyoto Protocol's second era began on 1st January 2013 and finished in 2020. The European Union (EU) and its 28 member states are among the 38 countries that have signed up. The second period is covered by the Doha (Qatar) amendment, where the participating countries are committed to reduce their emissions at a level that is at least 18% lower than it was in 1990. In this period, the EU was committed to reduce CO_2 emissions at a level that is 20% lower than 1990s levels.

According to the European Commission's 2009 and 2010 climate energy package, the 2020 climate energy package aims to make Europe a highly energy-efficient, low-carbon economy by reducing EU greenhouse gas emissions by 20% and increasing the share of EU energy consumption produced from renewable resources to 20% by 2020. In order to meet the 2020 targets, Italy has ratified the Kyoto Protocol and adopted various European energy initiatives into Italian law, such as the European emission trading scheme, the white certificates scheme, financial incentives, and the legislative framework for increasing energy efficiency. Italy has some indigenous production of oil and natural gas, but both oil and gas production will progressively decline in the coming years.

According to studies published by the Intergovernmental Panel on Climate Change (IPCC), global warming induced by human activity has led average temperatures to rise by about 1 °C since the beginning of the industrial era. Severe weather events, rising water rates, the loss of Arctic Ocean ice, and other negative consequences have all been observed as a result of the recent 1 °C global warming. If pollution continues to rise at its current rate, temperature rises induced by climate change would reach 1.5 °C between 2030 and 2052. Thus, nations have begun to develop action plans not only for social and economic development, but also for mitigating climate change. As a result, at the 2015 UN General Assembly, a 15-year plan of action known as the 2030 Agenda for Sustainable Growth, comprised of 17 Sustainable Development Goals (SDGs) and agreed upon by all United Nations (UN) member states, was developed. According to a 2019 SDG report, global warming is the most important area for intervention (SDG13).

Despite the fact that many developing countries place less emphasis on energy consumption due to technological and financial constraints, most developed countries have gradually relied on renewable energy more than ever before. Energy is, without a doubt, the most important driver of economic growth, whether in developed or developing countries. However, most of the energy is generated by using conventional energy sources such as oil, coal, and gas. These fuels emit massive amounts of greenhouse gases, which have been linked to climate change and global warming in recent decades.

In this context, and given the still open debate in literature, this work aims at providing a further contribution by verifying empirically the following research hypothesis for Italy:

H_1: the relationship between economic growth and carbon emissions might have inverted U-shape.
H_2: high energy consumption increases carbon emissions.
H_3: foreign direct investments show a positive association with carbon emissions.
H_4: exports might have significant positive effect on CO_2 emissions.

Based on the above, this study examines the relationship between carbon emissions, economic growth, foreign direct investment, oil price, energy consumption and exports in Italy by using yearly data for the period 1970–2019. For this purpose, we first apply the Autoregressive Distributed Lag (ARDL) model; second, we employ the wavelet coherence technique in order to check the causality among the variables considered.

The rest of the paper is structured as follows. Section 2 introduces the data and discusses the methodology used, Sect. 3 presents the results obtained and Sect. 4 concludes the paper.

2 Data and Methodology

2.1 Data

This study uses annual time-series data for Italy from 1970 to 2019. The dependent variable is carbon emission (metric tons per capita), while the independent variables are the following ones: gross domestic product (constant 2010 US$) per capita, foreign direct investments (the inflow of foreign direct investments per capita), oil price (cured oil price per barrel), exports of goods and services (constant 2010 US$) per capita, energy consumption per capita (million tons oil equivalent) and oil prices (measured in dollars per barrel). The data related to CO_2 emissions, gross domestic product, foreign direct investments and exports are retrieved from the World Development Indicator database. The data related to oil price and energy consumption have been taken from UNCTID and British Petroleum Statistical Review, respectively. We take the natural logarithm of all the variables under investigation in order to eliminate the presence of heteroscedasticity (Table 1).

2.2 Autoregressive Distributed Lag Model (ARDL)

The primary objective of this study is to verify the existence of EKC hypothesis and to examine the casual linkages between carbon emissions (CO_2), economic growth (GDP), foreign direct investment (FDI), oil price (OP), energy consumption (EC) and exports (EXP) in Italy.

The empirical model we used in this study is specified as follows:

$$LNCo2_t = \beta_0 + \beta_1 LNGDP_t + \beta_2 LNGDP_t^2 + \beta_3 LNFDI_t + \beta_4 LNOP_t + \delta_5 EC_t + \delta_6 EXP_t + \mu_t$$

(2.1)

Table 1 Descriptive statistics

	LCO$_2$	LGDP	LFDI	LOP	LEC	LEXP
Mean	1.920	10.296	4.212	3.171	4.740	3.108
Median	1.915	10.386	4.308	3.245	4.720	3.108
Max.	2.106	10.552	6.615	4.695	4.912	3.450
Min	1.662	9.780	0.435	0.191	4.541	2.719
Std. dev.	0.116	0.230	1.646	1.026	0.097	0.195
Skewness	−0.170	−0.828	−0.315	−0.975	0.259	−0.108
Kurtosis	2.104	2.407	2.088	4.260	2.050	2.146
Jarque-Bera	1.915	6.450	2.455	11.230	2.339	1.617
Probability	0.039	0.293	0.004	0.274	0.262	0.446
Obs	50	50	50	50	50	50

where $LNCo2_t$ denotes the logarithm of per capita carbon emissions, $LNGDP_t$ is the logarithm of per capita GDP, $LNGDP_t^2$ denotes the square term of per capita GDP, $LNFDI_t$ is the logarithm of FDI, $LNOP_t$ is the logarithm of oil prices, $LNEC_t$ is the logarithm of per capita energy consumption, $LNEXP_t$ is the logarithm of exports, μ_t is the error term and t denotes the time period. As per the EKC hypothesis, the relationship between economic growth and the square term of economic growth the square term of per capita GDP and should be inversely U-shaped curve. So, if the coefficient value of economic growth is positive, and the square term of economic growth is negative then the EKC hypothesis is proved to valid in case of Italy.

In this study we applied the ARDL bounds testing approach developed by Pesaran et al. [3] to examine the cointegration between CO_2 emissions, GDP, FDI, OP, EC and EXP. The Unrestricted Error Correction Model (UECM) for the ARDL bounds testing approach is given as follows:

$$
\begin{aligned}
\Delta lnCO2_t = {} & \beta_0 + \sum_{i=1}^{p}\beta_1 cnC02_{t-1} + \sum_{i=1}^{p}\beta_2 \Delta lnGDP_{t-1} + \sum_{i=1}^{p}\beta_3 lnGDP_{t-1}^2 \\
& + \sum_{i=1}^{p}\beta_4 \Delta lnFDI_{t-1} + \sum_{i=1}^{p}\beta_5 \Delta lnOP_{t-1} + \sum_{i=1}^{p}\beta_6 \Delta lnEC_{t-1} \\
& + \sum_{i=1}^{p}\beta_7 \Delta lnEXP_{t-1} + \lambda_1 \Delta lnC02_{t-1} \qquad + \lambda_2 \Delta lnGDP_{t-1} \\
& + \lambda_3 lnGDP_{t-1}^2 + \lambda_4 \Delta lnFDI_{t-1} + \lambda_5 \Delta lnOP_{t-1} \\
& + \lambda_5 \Delta lnOP_{t-1} + \lambda_5 \Delta lnOP_{t-1} + \varepsilon_t
\end{aligned}
\tag{2.2}
$$

where β_0 denotes the constant term, Δ is first difference operator, ε_t denotes the error term, β_1 to β_7 and λ_1 to λ_7 represents the long-run and short-run coefficients, respectively. The appropriate lag lengths p can be determined by using the Akaike Information criterion (AIC) and Schwarz Bayesian Criterion (SBC). In order to examine the long-run cointegration between CO_2 emissions, GDP, FDI, OP, EC, and EXP, the first step of the ARDL bounds testing approach is to compare the computed value of F-statistics with the upper and lower critical bounds values of Pesaran et al. [3] or Narayan [4].

After confirming the long-run interlinkages among the variables, the short-run dynamics are estimated by error correction model (ECM) proposed by Engel and Granger [5]. The short-run coefficients and the coefficient of error correction term are estimated by incorporating the ECM into ARDL framework specified as follows:

$$
\begin{aligned}
\Delta lnCO2_t = {} & \beta_0 + \sum_{i=1}^{p}\beta_1 \Delta lnC02_{t-1} + \sum_{i=1}^{p}\beta_2 \Delta lnGDP_{t-1} + \sum_{i=1}^{p}\beta_3 lnGDP_{t-1}^2 \\
& + \sum_{i=1}^{p}\beta_4 \Delta lnFDI_{t-1} + \sum_{i=1}^{p}\beta_5 \Delta lnOP_{t-1} + \beta_6 \Delta lnEC_{t-1} \\
& + \beta_7 \Delta lnEXP_{t-1} + \theta ECT_{t-1} + \varepsilon_{t-1}
\end{aligned}
\tag{2.3}
$$

where θ is the coefficient of the error correction term θECT_{t-1} shows the speed of adjustment towards long-run equilibrium.

2.3 Wavelet Coherence Approach

In order to capture the causality and correlation simultaneously among the time series variables the study deployed the wavelet coherence approach. The technique was initially presented by Goupillaud et al. [6]. The study used the ADF and PP unit root tests to investigate the integration order of CO_2 emissions, GDP, oil price, FDI, EC and exports as a preliminary test. The Zivot-Andrews unit root test were also used to confirm the structural breaks in the variables. Concerning the main objectives of the study, the research analyzed the time- frequency domain dependency between CO_2 emissions and other explanatory variables by employing the R program's wavelet coherence approach.

The primary innovation of wavelet coherence is that the method combines both times—domain causality with frequency- domain causality. It is well known and widely agreed that when there is structural break in a time series, traditional causality tests produce inaccurate results. Therefore, this allows the present study to capture the short and long run casual links between CO_2 emissions, GDP, oil price, FDI, EC, and exports in Italy so wavelet coherence avoid this issue. Economic indicators are likely to be non-stationary at level but stationary at first difference. Indeed, the key issue with the standalone frequency domain technique, more formally known as the Fourier transformation, is that by depending just on the frequency domain, information from the time domain is completely omitted [7]. To avoid these problems the study applied Granger's wavelet-based causality check. The Δ wavelet approach, which is the part of the Morlet wavelet system, is used in current study.

The ϖ is represented by Eq.(2.4) underneath:

$$\varpi\left(t\right) = \pi^{-\frac{1}{4}} e^{-i\varpi t} e^{-\frac{1}{2}t^2}$$

(2.4)

where portrays the frequency used on the restricted time-series. As stated by Adebayo [8] and Kalmaz and Kirikkaleli [9], there is indeed a time transition to the time–frequency domain that corresponds to the wavelet change. ϖ is transformed; thus, it progressed into ϖk:

$$\varpi_{k,f}\left(t\right) = \frac{1}{\sqrt{h}}\varpi\left(\frac{t-k}{f}\right), k, f \in \mathbb{R} f \neq 0$$

(2.5)

$P(t)$ is the time series data that is incorporated. Consequently, Eq. (2.6) shows the function of continuous wavelet:

$$\varpi_p\left(k,f\right) = \int_{-\infty}^{\infty} p\left(t\right) \frac{1}{\sqrt{f}} \varpi\left(\overline{\frac{t-k}{f}}\right) dt$$

(2.6)

According to Adebayo and Kirikkaleli [10], when the coefficient ϖ is added to the equation, Eqs. (2.7) and (2.8) are regenerated:

$$p(t) = \frac{1}{C_{\varpi}} \int_0^{\infty} \left[\int_{-\infty}^{\infty} |wp(a,b)|^2 \, da \right] \frac{db}{b^2}$$

(2.7)

To captures the vulnerability of CO_2 emissions, GDP, oil price, FDI, EC and exports, the wavelet power spectrum (WPS) is illustrated as follows:

$$WPS_p(k,f) |W_p(k,f)|^2$$

(2.8)

The cross-wavelet transformation (CWT) method converted the time-series variable in Eq. (2.8) into Eq. (2.9):

$$W_{pq}(k,f) = W_p(k,f) \overline{W_q(k,f)}$$

(2.9)

where $W_p(k,f)$ and $W_q(k,f)$ stand for the two time-series, and squared wavelet coherence is represented in Eq. (2.10):

$$R^2(k,f) = \frac{\left| S\left(f^{-1} W_{pq}(k,f) \right) \right|^2}{S\left(f^{-1} |W_p(k,f)|^2 \right) S\left(f^{-1} |W_q(k,f)|^2 \right)}$$

(2.10)

If the $R^2(k, f)$ value approaches one, it indicates that the time series indicators are connected or that there is a causal relationship between the time series variables at a specific frequency, which is surrounded by a black line and colored red. Furthermore, whenever $R^2(k, f)$ approaches zero, it indicates that there is no evidence of correlation or causality between the two time series variables, despite the fact that $R^2(k, f)$ does not provide any comprehensive information on the symbol of the interaction. As a result, Torrence and Compo [11] devised a method for identifying distinctions in wavelet coherence by employing deferral signs in the wavering of two-time sequences. The equation for the developed wavelet coherence is the following one:

$$\phi_{pq}(k,f) = \tan^{-1} \left(\frac{L\left\{ S\left(f^{-1} W_{pj}(k,f) \right) \right\}}{O\left\{ S\left(f^{-1} W_{pj}(k,f) \right) \right\}} \right)$$

(2.11)

where L and O represent an imaginary operator and a real part operator, respectively.

3 Results and Discussion

Before analyzing the long-run and short-run dynamics between the variables it is important to examine the stationarity properties of the time-series data. To this purpose we apply the Augmented Dicky Fuller and Philips Perron unit root tests proposed by Dickey and Fuller [12] and Philips and Perron [13]. Our results indicate that all the variables are non-stationary at level and become stationary at first differences. This implies that all the variables are integrated at I(1). We also applied the Zivot and Andrews structural break unit root test to capture the structural break in the data series. The result of this test also indicates that all variables are integrated at I(1).

3.1 ARDL Results

We examine the long run cointegration among the variables by applying the ARDL bound testing approach developed by Pesaran et al. [3]. Table 2 presents the results of the cointegration test. The results indicate that all the variables are integrated, since the calculated value of F-statistics is higher than the lower bound and upper bound critical value at 1% level of significance. Hence, the null hypothesis of no cointegration against the alternative hypothesis is rejected at 1% level of significance. This confirms the existence of long-run relationship between CO_2 emissions, GDP, FDI, OP, EC and EXP. This finding sets the way for the estimation of long-run and short-run estimates.

Long-Run Results After confirming the long-run relationship between CO_2 emissions and the regressors considered, we investigate the long-run and short-run impacts of GDP, FDI, OP, EC and EXP on CO_2 emissions. Table 3 reports the estimated outcomes of the long-run relationship between CO_2 emissions and its determining factors. The long-run results show that the impact of economic growth (per capita income) on per capita carbon emissions is positive and statistically significance at 1% level of significance. This implies that a 1% increase in per capita income increases per capita carbon emissions by 14.89%. Further,

Table 2 ARDL bound test estimates

F-bounds test statistics		Null Hypothesis: no levels relationship		
		Significance	I(0)	I(1)
Optimal lag-length	(3,3,3,2,3,3,2)	10%	1.99	2.94
F-statistics	12.791***			
K	6	5%	2.27	3.28
		2.50%	2.55	3.61
		1%	2.88	3.99

Note: ****, ***, ** and * show significance at 1, 2.5, 5 and 10% level respectively

Table 3 ARDL long-run results and diagnostics tests

Dependent variable	Regressors	Coefficients	Std. error	t-statistics
LCO$_2$	LGDP	14.891	3.879	3.839***
	LGDP-SQ	−0.740	0.192	−3.852***
	LFDI	0.039	0.007	5.271**
	LOP	−0.027	0..008	−3.289***
	LEC	0.525	0.170	3.085**
	LEXP	0.081	0.038	2.138*
Diagnostic tests				
R-sq		0.998		
Adj. R-sq.		0.985		
Normality		3.708(0.157)		
Serial- Corre.		0.986(0.473)		
Hetero.		0.703(0.776)		
ARCH		0.019(0.889)		
CUSUM		Stable		
CUSUM-sq		Stable		

Note: ****, ***, ** and * show significance at 1, 2.5, 5 and 10% level respectively

our results explain that the impact of square term of economic growth on per capita carbon emissions is negative and statistically significance at 1% level of significance suggesting that a 1% increase in per capita income decreases per capita carbon emissions by 0.74%. Our results confirm the validity of EKC hypothesis in Italy. This empirical finding is consistent with other studies, such as Esteve and Tamarit [14] and Sephton and Mann [15] on Spain, Tiwari et al. [16] on India, Fosten et al. [17] on UK, Iwata et al. [18], Shahbaz et al. [19] and Can and Gozgor [20] for France; on the contrary, Mutascu et al. [21] challenge the validation of the EKC hypothesis and show that the EKC is not present in the case of France.

The results show that the impact of FDI on per capita carbon emission is positive and statistically significant at 1% level of significance meaning that a 1% increase in FDI increases the carbon emissions by 0.03%. Moreover, we find that the relationship between oil price and per capita carbon emission is negative and statistically significant at 1% level of significance. This suggests that a 1% increase in oil price reduces the carbon emissions by 0.027%. Our findings also show that the impact of per capita energy consumption on per capita carbon emission is positive and statistically significant at 5% level of significance. This means that a 1% increase in energy consumption increases per capita carbon emissions by 0.52%. This empirical finding is in line with Iwata et al. [18] for France, Saboori et al. [22, 23] for Malaysia, Al-Mulali et al. [24] for Vietnam and Shahbaz et al. [19] for the US. Finally, in case of exports the outcomes reveal that the export has significant and positive impact on per capita carbon emissions meaning that a 1% increase in exports enhance the per capita carbon emission by 0.08%.

Short-Run Results   The short-run estimates of the ARDL model are presented in Table 4. The results explain that the relationship between economic growth and per capita carbon emissions is positive and statistically significant at 1% level, while the relationship between square term of economic growth and per capita carbon emissions is negative. These results confirm for Italy the validity of the EKC hypothesis for short run. This result is in line with Cetin et al. [25] for Turkey, Boluk and Mert [26] for Turkey, Farhani et al. [27] for Tunisia, Boutabba [28] for India and Acaravci and Ozturk [29] for Italy and Denmark.

In line with long-run ARDL estimates the relationship between foreign direct investment and per capita carbon emission is positive and statistically significant at 5% level of significance, suggesting that 1% increase in FDI enhance the per capita carbon emission by 0.01% in short run. The results reveal that there exist a negative and significant relationship between oil price and per capita carbon emissions at 1% level of significance. This indicates that a 1% increase in oil price reduces the carbon emissions by 0.04%. The results also show that energy consumption has a positive and significant impact on per capita carbon emissions implying that 1% increase in energy consumption rises by 0.66%. This finding is in line with Cetin et al. [25] for Turkey, Shahbaz et al. [30] for Tunisia, Shahbaz et al. [31] for Pakistan, Pao and Tsai [32] for Brazil, Russia and China. Our results also confirm that the impact of exports on per capita carbon emissions is positive and significant at 5% level of significance, thus implying that exports enhance per capita carbon emissions in the short run. Furthermore, the coefficient value of the error correction term ECT_{t-1} is negative and statistically significant at 1% level of significance. This finding also confirms the existence of long-run cointegration between the variables and explains that any divergence from short-run to long-run is corrected by 36.1% yearly.

Finally, we perform several diagnostics test to check the stability of the model. The results of serial-correlation, normality and heteroscedasticity tests are listed in Table 3. The estimated model passes all the diagnostics tests, thus confirming to be good and fit. Further, we apply the CUSUM and CUSUM Square tests proposed by Brown et al. [33], which confirm the stability of long-run coefficients.

Table 4   ARDL short-run results

Dependent variable	Regressors	Coefficients	Std. error	t-statistics
LCO$_2$	LGDP	35.528	4.012	8.855***
	LGDP-SQ	−1.713	0.198	−8.638***
	LFDI	0.010	0.001	6.915**
	LOP	−0.041	0.006	−7.075***
	LEC	0.663	0.078	8.458***
	LEXP	0.071	0.026	2.768**
	Coint. Eq. (−1)	−0.361	0.318	−11.351***

Note: ****, ***, ** and * show significance at 1, 2.5, 5 and 10% level respectively

3.2 *Wavelet Coherence Approach Results*

Figure 1 a–e demonstrates the wavelet coherence between CO_2 emissions and its determinants—CO_2 and oil price (a), CO_2 and GDP growth (b), CO_2 and exports (c), CO_2 and FDI (d), CO_2 and energy consumption (e)—in Italy for the period 1971-2019. In accordance with Adebayo and Beton Kalmaz [10], Kalmaz and Kirikkaleli [9] and Pal and Mitra [7], the time is displayed on the horizontal axis

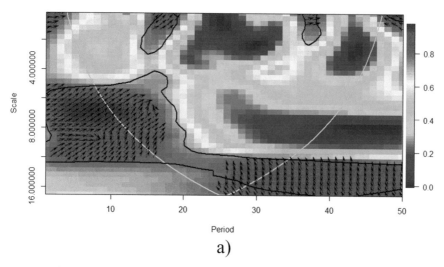

a)

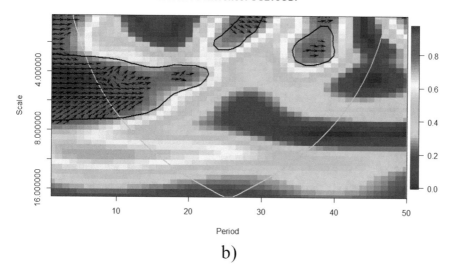

b)

Fig. 1 Wavelet coherence approach results

Wavelet Coherence: CO2vsExports

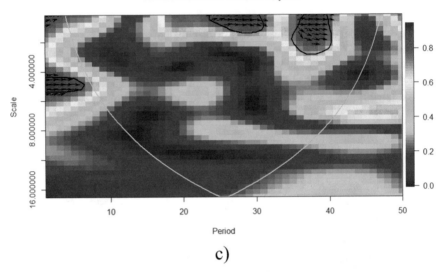

c)

Wavelet Coherence: CO2vsFDI

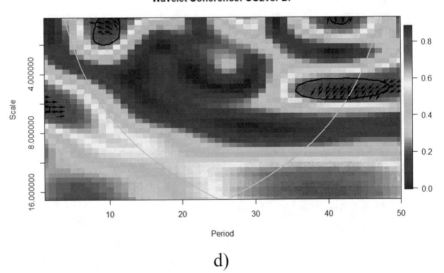

d)

Fig. 1 (continued)

while the vertical axis shows the frequency (the lower the frequency, the higher the scale); periods 0–4, 4–8 and 16 and above represent the short term, medium term and long term, respectively. When analyzing wavelet coherence, the white line shows the cone of influence or impact area that will be used for interpretation. On the right side of the figures, the color scale describes the strength of the correlation. The red color implies high correlations between time-series indicators, whereas the

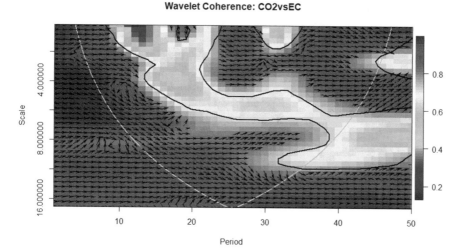

Fig. 1 (continued)

blue color indicates lower dependence between the series. Furthermore, the thick black shapes in figures are calculated based on the Monte Carlo simulation which shows 5% level of significance. The arrows in the wavelet coherence portray the direction of causality and correlation between examined series. A zero-phase difference means that the two-time series move together on a particular scale. Arrows point to the right (left) when the time series are in phase, indicating that they move in the same direction (anti-phase, indicating that they move in opposite directions). Arrows pointing to the bottom right or top left indicate that the first variable is leading, while arrows pointing to the top right or bottom left show that the second variable is leading.

This approach, developed from econophysics, gives information concerning the time and frequency domains, capturing the correlation and causality between CO_2 and the indicators at the same time. Hence, the present study allows short-term, medium-term and long-term correlation and causality between CO_2 emissions and the explanatory variables considered. No relationship between the two time-series is defined in Fig. 1 as cold (blue) color, whilst evidence of connection is represented by warmer (red) color. In Fig. 1a at different scales (different frequencies) between 1978 and 1988 the rightward arrows show the positive and significant correlation between CO_2 emissions and oil price in short and medium term. In addition, between 1995 and 2005 (long term) the leftward arrows show a negative correlation between CO_2 emissions and oil price. Moreover, a leftward upward arrow indicates that oil price causes CO_2 emissions in Italy. In Fig. 1b, at different scales between 1973 and 2015 there is a proof of rightward arrows in short and medium term indicating positive correlation between CO_2 emission and economic growth. Additionally, the rightward and upward arrows indicate that GDP leads CO_2 emission in Italy. In

Fig. 1c, no evidence of correlation is found between CO_2 emissions and exports between 1974 and 1993 at different scale and different frequencies. However, between 1994 and 2010 the rightward arrows depict a positive and significant correlation between CO_2 and exports. Additionally, the rightward downward arrows represent that CO_2 causes exports and there is unidirectional causality. In Fig. 1d, at different scales between 1972 and 1982 the arrows faced the left-hand side which depicts a negative correlation between CO_2 emissions and FDI. Furthermore, between 2005 and 2010 the leftward downward arrows illustrate that CO_2 causes FDI. In Fig. 1e at different scales between 1974 and 2016 in short medium and long term there is evidence of rightward arrows which present a positive and significant correlation between CO_2 emissions and energy consumption. In the same era, the rightward downward arrows show that CO_2 emissions cause energy consumption. Furthermore, there is unidirectional causality running from energy consumption to CO_2 emissions. This finding underlines the importance og energy consumption as a predictor of CO_2 emissions in Italy.

4   Conclusion

This study examines the relationship between carbon emissions, economic growth, foreign direct investment, oil price, energy consumption and exports in Italy by using yearly data for the period 1970-2019.

The results of the ARDL bounds testing approach provide evidence of long-run cointegration among the variables at 1% level of significance in Italy. Our findings show that the impact of FDI on carbon emission is positive and statistically significant both in short and long-run which supports the pollution heaven hypothesis in Italy. Our results also reveal that the relationship between energy consumption and carbon emission is positive and statistically significant. Furthermore, the study also examines the validity of EKC hypothesis. The findings obtained by ARDL model show that the relationship between economic growth and carbon emission is an inverted U-shaped curve. This provides evidence about the validity of EKC hypothesis.

Finally, we employed the wavelet coherence technique in order to check the causality between CO_2 emissions, economic growth, FDI, OP, energy consumption and exports. The novelty of this approach is that it ascertains the short-run and long-run correlation and causality among the variables simultaneously at different time periods and frequencies.

References

1. Grossman, G. M., & Krueger, A. B. (1995). Economic growth and the environment. *The Quarterly Journal of Economics, 110*(2), 353–377.

2. Grossman, G. M., & Krueger, A. B. (1991). *Environmental impacts of a North American free trade agreement.* NBER Working Paper 3914, National Bureau of Economic Research.
3. Pesaran, M. H., Shin, Y., & Smith, R. J. (2001). Bounds testing approaches to the analysis of level relationships. *Journal of Applied Econometrics, 16*(3), 289–326.
4. Narayan, P. K. (2005). The saving and investment nexus for China: Evidence from cointegration tests. *Applied Economics, 37*(17), 1979–1990.
5. Engle, R. F., & Granger, C. W. (1987). Co-integration and error correction: Representation, estimation, and testing. *Econometrica: Journal of the Econometric Society,* 251–276.
6. Goupillaud, P., Grossmann, A., & Morlet, J. (1984). Cycle-octave and related transforms in seismic signal analysis. *Geoexploration, 23*(1), 85–102.
7. Pal, D., & Mitra, S. K. (2017). Time-frequency contained co-movement of crude oil and world food prices: A wavelet-based analysis. *Energy Economics, 62,* 230–239.
8. Adebayo, T. S. (2021). Testing the EKC hypothesis in Indonesia: Empirical evidence from the ARDL-based bounds and wavelet coherence approaches. *Applied Economics Journal, 28*(1), 78–100.
9. Kalmaz, D. B., & Kirikkaleli, D. (2019). Modeling CO_2 emissions in an emerging market: Empirical finding from ARDL-based bounds and wavelet coherence approaches. *Environmental Science and Pollution Research, 26*(5), 5210–5220.
10. Adebayo, T. S., & Beton Kalmaz, D. (2020). Ongoing debate between foreign aid and economic growth in Nigeria: A wavelet analysis. *Social Science Quarterly, 101*(5), 2032–2051.
11. Torrence, C., & Compo, G. P. (1998). A practical guide to wavelet analysis. *Bulletin of the American Meteorological Society, 79*(1), 61–78.
12. Dickey, D. A., & Fuller, W. A. (1979). Distribution of the estimators for autoregressive time series with a unit root. *Journal of the American Statistical Association, 74*(366a), 427–431.
13. Phillips, P. C., & Perron, P. (1988). Testing for a unit root in time series regression. *Biometrika, 75*(2), 335–346.
14. Esteve, V., & Tamarit, C. (2012). Threshold cointegration and nonlinear adjustment between CO2 and income: The environmental Kuznets curve in Spain, 1857–2007. *Energy Economics, 34*(6), 2148–2156.
15. Sephton, P., & Mann, J. (2013). Further evidence of an environmental Kuznets curve in Spain. *Energy Economics, 36,* 177–181.
16. Tiwari, A. K., Shahbaz, M., & Hye, Q. M. A. (2013). The environmental Kuznets curve and the role of coal consumption in India: Cointegration and causality analysis in an open economy. *Renewable and Sustainable Energy Reviews, 18,* 519–527.
17. Fosten, J., Morley, B., & Taylor, T. (2012). Dynamic misspecification in the environmental Kuznets curve: Evidence from CO2 and SO2 emissions in the United Kingdom. *Ecological Economics, 76,* 25–33.
18. Iwata, H., Okada, K., & Samreth, S. (2010). Empirical study on the environmental Kuznets curve for CO2 in France: The role of nuclear energy. *Energy Policy, 38*(8), 4057–4063.
19. Shahbaz, M., Solarin, S. A., Hammoudeh, S., & Shahzad, S. J. H. (2017). Bounds testing approach to analyzing the environment Kuznets curve hypothesis with structural beaks: The role of biomass energy consumption in the United States. *Energy Economics, 68,* 548–565.
20. Can, M., & Gozgor, G. (2017). The impact of economic complexity on carbon emissions: Evidence from France. *Environmental Science and Pollution Research, 24*(19), 16364–16370.
21. Mutascu, M. (2016). A bootstrap panel Granger causality analysis of energy consumption and economic growth in the G7 countries. *Renewable and Sustainable Energy Reviews, 63,* 166–171.
22. Saboori, B., Sulaiman, J., & Mohd, S. (2012). Economic growth and CO2 emissions in Malaysia: A cointegration analysis of the environmental Kuznets curve. *Energy Policy, 51,* 184–191.
23. Saboori, B., Sulaiman, J., & Mohd, S. (2016). Environmental Kuznets curve and energy consumption in Malaysia: A cointegration approach. *Energy Sources, Part B: Economics, Planning, and Policy, 11*(9), 861–867.

24. Al-Mulali, U., Saboori, B., & Ozturk, I. (2015). Investigating the environmental Kuznets curve hypothesis in Vietnam. *Energy Policy, 76,* 123–131.
25. Cetin, M., Ecevit, E., & Yucel, A. G. (2018). The impact of economic growth, energy consumption, trade openness, and financial development on carbon emissions: Empirical evidence from Turkey. *Environmental Science and Pollution Research, 25*(36), 36589–36603.
26. Bölük, G., & Mert, M. (2015). The renewable energy, growth and environmental Kuznets curve in Turkey: An ARDL approach. *Renewable and Sustainable Energy Reviews, 52,* 587–595.
27. Farhani, S., Chaibi, A., & Rault, C. (2014). CO2 emissions, output, energy consumption, and trade in Tunisia. *Economic Modelling, 38,* 426–434.
28. Boutabba, M. A. (2014). The impact of financial development, income, energy and trade on carbon emissions: Evidence from the Indian economy. *Economic Modelling, 40,* 33–41.
29. Acaravci, A., & Ozturk, I. (2010). On the relationship between energy consumption, CO2 emissions and economic growth in Europe. *Energy, 35*(12), 5412–5420.
30. Shahbaz, M., Khraief, N., Uddin, G. S., & Ozturk, I. (2014). Environmental Kuznets curve in an open economy: A bounds testing and causality analysis for Tunisia. *Renewable and Sustainable Energy Reviews, 34,* 325–336.
31. Shahbaz, M., Hye, Q. M. A., Tiwari, A. K., & Leitão, N. C. (2013). Economic growth, energy consumption, financial development, international trade and CO2 emissions in Indonesia. *Renewable and Sustainable Energy Reviews, 25,* 109–121.
32. Pao, H. T., & Tsai, C. M. (2010). CO2 emissions, energy consumption and economic growth in BRIC countries. *Energy Policy, 38*(12), 7850–7860.
33. Brown, R. L., Durbin, J., & Evans, J. M. (1975). Techniques for testing the constancy of regression relationships over time. *Journal of the Royal Statistical Society: Series B (Methodological), 37*(2), 149–163.

Optimal Selection of Sustainable Energy Mix to Achieve Energy Security in Italy: A Fuzzy SWOT Approach

Feroz Khan ⓘ and Agnese Rapposelli ⓘ

Abstract The ever-increasing global warming around the world are subjecting the countries to transition towards cleaner technologies. In the energy sector, the countries are moving towards the adoption of renewable energy resources. However, becoming fully dependent on the use of renewable energy resources is still a challenge due to several technological, socio-political, economic and environmental aspects. These challenges have become even more evident due to problems such as the COVID-19 pandemic and the Russia-Ukraine war. The European Union (EU), particularly Italy has suffered considerably because the country was highly dependent on the import of natural gas from Russia to meet its energy demands. Therefore, to tackle this challenge and achieve energy security in Italy in a more sustainable manner, this research aims to select the most optimal mix of energy among the existing technologies in the country. For this purpose, the study uses a strategic decision-making tool known as fuzzy SWOT approach to evaluate seven energy technologies based on a set of 13 sustainability factors. The fuzzy set theory has been employed to address the possibility of uncertainty during the decision-making process. The technologies that possess the most strengths and opportunities would be considered the most suitable for its adoption, whereas the ones facing weaknesses and threats in the country would be avoided.

Keywords Sustainable development · Energy mix · Energy security · Fuzzy SWOT approach

F. Khan
Department of Management and Business Administration, "G.d'Annunzio" University of Chieti-Pescara, Pescara, Italy

A. Rapposelli (✉)
Department of Economic Studies, "G.d'Annunzio" University of Chieti-Pescara, Pescara, Italy
e-mail: agnese.rapposelli@unich.it

© The Author(s), under exclusive license to Springer Nature Switzerland AG 2024
A. Lazazzara et al. (eds.), *Towards Digital and Sustainable Organisations*, Lecture Notes in Information Systems and Organisation 65, https://doi.org/10.1007/978-3-031-52880-4_15

1 Introduction

The production and consumption of energy of any country have a strong interaction with the GDP growth because it reflects the social and economic activities of that country. This means, an increase in GDP growth leads to an increase in energy demand [1]. However, if the source of the energy production is not clean it is going to have a detrimental impact on the environment. Most of the energy generated around the world comes from fossil fuels such as oil, coal and gas, which are depleting with time. It is also an additional economic burden for a country that imports such fuels to meet its energy demands. To address this problem, countries around the world are shifting towards the usage of renewable energy resources to attain the goals developed by United Nations [2]. However, a transition towards a more decarbonized energy sector would require development of appropriate policy measures and energy mix tailored to the conditions of the region in question [3].

The EU is still largely dependent to cater its energy supply through the use of fossil fuels. The greatest part of the mix is oil which accounts for 90%, whereas around 60% of it is natural gas. These fuels are largely imported from Russia [4]. To reduce the delivered cost of electricity, governments are inclined to give subsidies which becomes an additional burden on the economies. The greatest number of subsidies are given by the middle east and North Africa amounting to 33% and 21% respectively in 2020 which is followed by Europe which allocated a subsidy of 10% in the same year [5]. Apart from the financial constraints associated with the usage of fossil fuels, there are also harmful environmental effects. Around 35% of the total GHG emissions in the EU comes from the energy sector, the biggest share of which is carbon dioxide (CO_2) [6].

According to the targets proposed in the Paris agreement of 2015, it is suggested that 85% of the energy should come from renewable resources by the year 2050 [7]. The EU is an important entity when it comes to economic development, therefore achieving a low carbon economy is considered to be of considerable importance. The aforementioned goal is achieved through reduced energy bills, GHG emissions and less reliance on the import of fossil fuel for energy generation [8]. According to the Pars agreement, the EU intends to raise its GHG emissions reduction targets by 40% till 2030 and become almost completely carbon neutral i.e., to attain a reduction of around 80–95% of emissions by 2050 [9]. For this purpose, the EU have set targets to achieve a renewable share of 74% by the year 2030 along with a complete phase-out of the use of coal for energy generation by the same year [10].

Italy being a founding member of the EU has the third largest economy in the continent with a GDP of $2.058 trillion [11]. Italy produces 24% of its domestic power consumption requirements as compared to 42.5% of production by its peers in the EU. Thus, this puts the country on the 24th position when it comes to energy self-sufficiency with respect to the 27 other countries in the EU [12]. For a comparative analysis on energy autonomy, Germany has a rating of 35% whereas, France has an energy self-efficiency rating of 53%. However, when it comes to the renewable energy, Italy scores better than its counter parts in the EU. For example, the country meets 17.4% of its energy demand from renewable energy as compared to the EU average of 15.5%, ranking it ahead of Germany and France but behind Sweden and Latvia [13]. However, Italy is aiming to meet 55% of its renewable energy mix by 2030, whereas countries like Germany, Netherland and Spain are aiming for the 75% mark [14]. The energy demand of Italy has been constant from the year 2015 to 2020 ranging between 324 TWh and 331 TWh. However, due to COVID-19 there was a decrease in demand by 6.3% bringing it to 307 TWh. In 2021, Italy saw a surge in energy attributing to a rise of 8% with respect to 2020 [15]. The pandemic also had a retarding effect when it comes to the increase in the installation of renewable energy resources due to several structural weaknesses. These obstacles had more to do with long waiting time for the authorization of new plants deployment, land disputes, and lack of consensus [16].

The threat to energy security to Italy had become graver due to the recent conflict between Russia and Ukraine because the country was heavily reliant on the import of natural gas from Russia through Ukraine. Today, around 50% of the electricity in Italy is generated from natural gas as opposed to 37% in 2000 [17]. The disruption in inexpensive supply of natural gas in Italy is subjecting EU to diversify its supply for natural gas, increase energy efficiency and foster its deployment of renewable energy resources through a program known as REpowerEU [18]. The current crises have subjected Italy to roll back to the usage of coal to meet its short-term energy demands. A gas-to-coal switching can potentially reduce the import of 30 bcm of Russian gas for EU. In this case, Italy is rolling back to the functioning of its coal power plants, which accounts for about 4% of the energy generation in the country even though the country had planned to phase-out the use of coal by the year 2025 [19]. Amidst of all this, the prices of wholesale electricity in Italy have almost tripled in the last two years which has made renewable energy deployment such as new offshore wind and solar power more economical [20]. Rolling back to the usage of nuclear power for Italy is also not on the table in the present times because it is abandoned since the Chernobyl accident. Although it is considered to be a more sustainable and suitable alternative to fossil fuels [21].

The aim of this research is to provide a facilitating framework by which Italy can achieve energy security in a more sustainable manner. For this purpose, the study analyses existing power generating technologies in the countries based on the metrics of socio-political, economic, environmental and technical aspects. These metrics were considered based on conducting an extensive literature review and with the help of experts. The methodology employed in this case is a quantitative decision-making approach known as fuzzy SWOT approach. The SWOT methodology can be used to assess or evaluate both quantitative and qualitative measures. It is a managerial tool which was developed based on the grand strategy matrix. The methodology divides factors into four categories of strength, weaknesses, opportunities and threats. This approach helps in identifying strengths and opportunities which could be adopted to attain maximum advantages, while threats and weaknesses can be reduced in order to minimize losses [22]. The usage of fuzzy set theory in this case is employed to capture uncertainty or ambiguity while taking assessment from the experts. The employed technique would help assess the seven existing power generating technologies in Italy based on metrics of sustainability. This as a result would facilitate us to provide the most sustainable mix of energy to achieve energy security in Italy.

The article is organized as follows. Section 2 reviews the literature, Sect. 3 describes the data collection and the methodology used, Sect. 4 discusses the results and gives the conclusion.

2 Literature Review

A shift towards the use of reliable, affordable and modern energy mix as suggested by the seventh goal of the SDGs would require countries around the world to shift towards cleaner energy mix. For both developed and developing countries, it has been found that as opposed to non-renewable sources, the use of renewable energy sources paves way towards sustainable development [2]. Analyzing 24 OECD countries from 1980 to 2014 it has been found that the use of renewable energy sources reduces ecological footprint [23]. However, a transition towards clean energy sources would have to tackle the factors of economic complexities and technological innovation associated with the shift which has been analyzed through studying 28 OECD countries over the course of 1990 to 2014 [24]. The role of public acceptance in adopting a particular energy technology into the energy mix plays an important role. This is evident in the case of Greece in which the public prefers renewable energy resources such as wind and solar power for the purpose of protecting the environment. However, willingness to pay for such technologies is fostered by factors such as energy subsidies, education and state support [25]. Despite all of this, the EU is still largely dependent on the use of fossil fuels [26].

To achieve a more sustainable energy sector in Italy, researchers focus more on the use and adoption of renewable energy technologies fostering a way towards a more decentralized energy systems network [27]. However, a complete phase-out of coal, oil and gas does not seem to be a practical option especially in the short-term phases. Ignoring the possibility of using oil, coal and gas would hinder and mislead the policy makers to determine and adopt the right energy mix [28]. Transitioning towards the use of renewable energy systems in Italy would in fact reduce the GHG emissions, however, it does not reduce the overall energy consumption which makes the notion of energy efficiency and consumption an important subject [29]. The country being highly reliant on the use of fossil fuel has a good potential of generating electricity from hydro power, solar, wind and geothermal. However, a more sustainable alternative to fossil-based energy systems is hydro and solar power-based systems. In fact, solar based power systems in this case are found to be a more substitutable option [30]. In contrast to the previous study, biomass and solar energy does not have a significant effect on energy security [31]. Most of the countries in EU like Italy still depends on the import of energy to meet its energy demands which potentially might be a threat to the energy security of these countries.

Therefore, increasing the technological efficiency of the current renewable systems should be enhanced with the help of knowledge spillover among such countries [32].

The methodologies employed to determine energy mix in the context of Italy includes the portfolio theory. The aim of this research was to determine the profitability associated with five renewable energy systems alternatives i.e., solar, wind, geothermal, hydel, and biomass. The results of the study are more inclined towards the installation of the mix of small power systems including hydro and wind. To determine the optimal energy-mix the research suggests that future studies should use multi-criteria decision analysis to evaluate energy technologies based on criteria involving economic, environmental and technological aspects [33]. Such multi criteria decision making tools have been employed to evaluate the renewable energy systems in Pakistan based on criteria involving economic, environmental, technical, and socio-political aspects. In this case, the study employs fuzzy AHP and qualitative SWOT approach to tackle the problem at hand. The results of the study indicate wind energy to be the most suitable alternative for renewable energy alternative in the country [34].

Moreover, the qualitative PESTLE and SWOT approach are used to assess renewable energy resources in Malaysia. For this purpose, the study uses semi-structured interviews with experts to identify the strengths, weaknesses, opportunities and threats of introducing renewable energy systems in the country [35]. However, the current study is based on the recent crises of energy security in Italy in the wake of Russia-Ukraine war. To achieve energy security in the country in a more sustainable manner, the study aims to gauge existing power energy systems that includes both renewable and non-renewable alternatives that previous studies miss. To achieve this goal the study uses a fuzzy quantitative decision-making tool known as the fuzzy SWOT approach to analyze the energy alternatives based on sustainability criteria. The aim of employing the fuzzy set theory in this case is to address any type of uncertainty or ambiguity during the data collection process [36].

The fuzzy SWOT approach has also been recorded for developing strategies to eradicate energy crises in developing country [37]. It has also been employed to formulate or prioritize pavement management policies for airfields based on technical, financial and reliability criteria [38]. Moreover, its usage has been recorder for sustainable river basin management based on the social, environmental, technical and economic aspects [39]. Factors contributing to the export of tile and ceramic industry have been ranked using the same approach [40]. The fuzzy SWOT approach has been further employed in the development of strategies for solar energy production in an emerging economy [41]. The quantitative fuzzy SWOT approach proposed for this study has been used for supplier selection and order allocation problem [42]. It has also been used to assess and select sustainable electric vehicles to effectively transition towards green mobility [43]. Lastly, it has been used to select most sustainable waste management technologies to valorize agricultural waste to transition towards the circular bioeconomy approach [44].

3   Data Collection and Methodology

The goal of this study is to evaluate a total of seven sources of power generating technologies and determine the most optimal energy mix based on the metrics of sustainability. For this purpose, the study uses a strategic decision-making approach known as fuzzy SWOT approach. The seven power generating technologies are assessed based on a set of internal and external factors. The internal factors consist of strengths and weaknesses which can be controlled, whereas the external factors are characterized by opportunities and threats and are considered to be uncontrollable. The list of internal and external factors in this case are determined based on the metrics of sustainability. These metrics include technical, socio-political, economic and environmental aspects.

For secondary data collection, the SCOPUS database was used. The keywords used in this case were "sustainable energy mix", "optimal selection of sustainable energy mix in Europe", "factors effecting cleaner energy production", "Energy security during the Russia-Ukraine conflict", "Importance of energy security in Italy during the COVID-19 pandemic", "sustainable energy transition in Europe", "sustainability indicators for achieving energy security in Italy". The first search included a total of 90 documents. This was followed by the application of filters. Firstly, articles ranging from the year 2010–2022 were considered. The type of documentation included articles, conference paper, review, and books. The discipline or subject area chosen were energy, environmental sciences, business management and accounting, and economics econometrics and finance. After the application of the aforementioned filters the number of documents came down to 64. These documents were further analyzed through studying the respective topic headings and abstract of each article. This as a result helped remove all the irrelevant and false positive articles bring the total number of documents down to 25. The resultant documents were then thoroughly analyzed to identify the list of factors or criteria that would help to analyze the seven energy alternatives. From this exercise a total of 20 sustainability factors or criteria were adopted which were then further discussed with a panel of experts. The panel consisted of three energy experts. The role of the experts was to shortlist or determine the most crucial sustainability factors for evaluating the seven energy alternatives along with removing any type of redundancy between the list of criteria. Their other role was also to segregate the list of factors into internal and external factors. Finally, through the employment of a mini-Delphi approach the most repeated factors from the experts were shortlisted into a list of total 13 internal and external criteria which are presented in Table 1.

The next step in the data collection process was assess the seven energy alternatives based on the internal and external criteria. For this purpose, a questionnaire is sent to experts in a private electricity company in Italy. The company is called Renexia which was founded in 2011. The company has expertise in the deployment of wind and solar energy. It works in the areas of development, design, construction and management of plants. The questionnaire was developed using google forms. In

Table 1 Sustainability criteria for evaluating alternatives

		Related Literature
Sustainable aspects	*Internal criteria*	
Technical	**C1.** On-grid access	[45–47]
	C2. Storage systems	[48–50]
Socio-political	**C3.** Supportive government polices	[51–53]
	C4. Social acceptance	[54–56]
	C5. Jobs creation	[57–59]
	External criteria	
Environmental	**C6.** Land requirements	[60–62]
	C7. Greenhouse gas emissions	[63–65]
Economic	**C8.** Delivered/unit cost of electricity	[52, 66, 67]
	C9. Capital cost	[68–70]
	C10. Cost of operations and management	[71–73]
Technical	**C11.** Capacity factor	[74–76]
	C12. Technological maturity	[77–79]
	C13. Resource availability	[80–82]

Table 2 Fuzzy five-point Likert scale (Source: Khan et al. [83])

Linguistic variables	Associated numbers
Very Low	(1,1,3)
Low	(1,3,5)
Medium	(3,5,7)
High	(5,7,9)
Very High	(7,9,9)

the first part of the questionnaire the decision-makers are asked to allocate significance to the list of internal and external criteria by using a five-point fuzzy Likert scale (Table 2). Subsequently, this is followed by the evaluation of the seven energy alternatives based on the internal and external criteria using the same scale.

3.1 Fuzzy Set Theory

The criteria and alternatives considered in this study were evaluated by a group of experts belonging to the energy sector. There is an intrinsic possibility of ambiguity when allocating significance to the set of criteria and alternatives. To address this problem, Lotfi Zadeh in 1965 came up with the fuzzy set theory [84]. Below are the steps and equations given for a better understanding of how the method works.

For example, let's suppose "C" is a set having the member function (x), then the fuzzy set with the ordered pair becomes:

$$D = \{(x, \mu b(x)) \quad x \in C \tag{1}$$

In Eq. (1), D is a fuzzy set which has a membership function x. The function ranges from $[0, 1]$ and having all real numbers. For avoid complexity, the study uses the fuzzy triangular membership function. The triangular membership function along with three distance variables denoted by (q, r, s), showcasing lower, mean and upper bounds is presented with the help of Fig. 1.

The range and membership associated with the fuzzy numbers is given in Eq. (2):

$$\mu_b(x) = \begin{cases} (x-q)/(r-q) & q \le x \le r \\ (u-x)/(s-r) & r \le x \le s \\ 0 & otherwise \end{cases} \tag{2}$$

The values q, r, s are all real numbers showcasing significance on the order of $q < r < s$. The values achieved at "s" produces the most probable data i.e. $\mu a(x) = 1$; the values of x at "q" gives the least expected value i.e. $\mu a(x) = 0$. The uncertainty in the data is depicted by the distance between the lower and upper bounds. A lower degree of interval between $[q, s]$ indicates lower amounts of fuzziness in the data and vice versa. The distance between two fuzzy triangular numbers is denoted by Eq. (3).

$$d(\alpha, \beta) = \sqrt{\left(\frac{1}{3}\right)\left[q - q'\right]^2 + \left[r - r'\right]^2 + \left[s - s'\right]^2} \tag{3}$$

3.2 Fuzzy SWOT Approachss

The fuzzy SWOT approach employed in this study is a quantitative decision-making method used to evaluate the seven-energy alternative based on the metrics of sustainability. The associated steps and equations are the following ones [42–44]:

Step 1. The first step corresponds to the selection and determination of alternatives that needs to be evaluated based on the SWOT matrix.

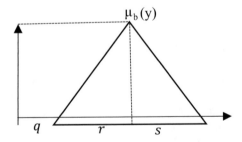

Fig. 1 Fuzzy triangular membership function

Step 2. The evaluation of the alternatives requires the determination of the right set of internal and external criteria. The internal criteria consist of strengths and weaknesses which are controllable, whereas the external criteria consist of opportunities and threats which are uncontrollable.

Step 3. This step involves the assessment of criteria and alternatives by the decision makers. In this case, a five-point fuzzy Likert scale is used for assessment purposes.

Step 4. The data collected as a result of Step 3 in the form of linguistic variables is transformed into its respective fuzzy numbers using Table 1. An average is taken of all the responses using Eq. (4).

$$W_{ij} = \frac{1}{K}\left[w_{ij}^1 + w_{ij}^2 + \ldots + w_{ij}^k\right] \tag{4}$$

The variable K in Eq. (4) represents the number of respondents, whereas (j = 1, 2 ... n) represents the number of alternatives. Moreover, (i = 1, 2 ..., n) represents the criteria's number.

Step 5. In this study, the centroid method has been used for defuzzification of the triangular numbers [85].

$$(q + r + s)/3 \tag{5}$$

Step 6. For the unification of the scale, the process of normalization is done for both the internal and external criteria. In this case, Eq. (6) can be used for the normalization of cost criteria, whereas Eq. (7) can be employed for normalizing benefit criteria. This followed by the attaining the aggregated weights of alternatives which is achieved by multiplying the normalized weights of criteria with the alternatives. Finally, the benchmarking values are achieved by taking the average of all the internal and external criteria.

$$N_{ij(c)} = \frac{\min_j w_{ij}}{w_{ij}} \tag{6}$$

$$N_{ij(b)} = \frac{w_{ij}}{\max_j w_{ij}} \tag{7}$$

where i = 1, 2, ..., n and j = 1, 2, ..., n.

4 Conclusion

The increase in global warming and the depletion of natural resources are subjecting countries around the world to shift towards cleaner energy production. Developed countries like the EU have set targets to achieve these SDGs and are at the forefront in the adoption of these new technologies. To attain these goals, countries like Italy have set their targets for the years 2030 and 2050. However, due to certain impediments these targets seem to be somewhat impractical. These impediments primarily correspond to the recent COVID-19 pandemic and the ongoing Russia and Ukraine war. Italy is among the largest importer of natural gas from Russia, but due to the conflict the country is unable to meet its energy demands in a more sustainable manner. To cater to this problem, a more sustainable energy mix for the country needs to be developed. However, the development of such a mix would require to mix several technical, social-political, economic and environmental factors. To address this gap, this study uses a strategic decision-making tool known as the fuzzy SWOT approach to evaluate seven existing power generating technologies in Italy based on a set of 13 sustainability factors. These factors have been divided into internal and external factors. Internal factors are those that consists of strengths and weaknesses, whereas external factors consist of opportunities and threats. The factors are then further identified based on benefit and cost criteria. Those technologies that have more strengths and opportunities would be considered suitable for its early adoption, whereas those facing threats and weaknesses would be considered as nonviable. The results of the study would be further justified from the help of the secondary literature which would help in the provision of policy recommendations to the respective stakeholders.

References

1. Rahman, Z. U., Khattak, S. I., Ahmad, M., & Khan, A. (2020). A disaggregated-level analysis of the relationship among energy production, energy consumption and economic growth: Evidence from China. *Energy, 194*(1), 116836.
2. Güney, T. (2019). Renewable energy, non-renewable energy and sustainable development. *International Journal of Sustainable Development and World Ecology, 26*(5), 389–397.
3. Papadis, E., & Tsatsaronis, G. (2020). Challenges in the decarbonization of the energy sector. *Energy, 205*(1), 118025.
4. Kemfert, C. (2019). Green deal for Europe: More climate protection and fewer fossil fuel wars. *Intereconomics, 54*(6), 353–358.
5. Parry, I., Black, S., & Vernon, N. (2021). *Still not getting energy prices right: A global and country update of fossil fuel subsidies*. International Monetary Fund.
6. Karmellos, M., et al. (2021). A decomposition and decoupling analysis of carbon dioxide emissions from electricity generation: Evidence from the EU-27 and the UK. *Energy, 231*(1), 120861.
7. Siksnelyte, I., & Zavadskas, E. K. (2019). Achievements of the European union countries in seeking a sustainable electricity sector. *Energies, 12*(12), 2254.
8. Su, W., Zhang, D., Zhang, C., & Streimikiene, D. (2020). Sustainability assessment of energy sector development in China and European Union. *Sustainable Developement, 28*(5), 1063–1076.
9. Jäger-Waldau, A., Kougias, I., Taylor, N., & Thiel, C. (2020). How photovoltaics can contribute to GHG emission reductions of 55% in the EU by 2030. *Renewable and Sustainable Energy Reviews, 126*(1), 109836.

10. Pietzcker, R. C., Osorio, S., & Rodrigues, R. (2021). Tightening EU ETS targets in line with the European Green Deal: Impacts on the decarbonization of the EU power sector. *Applied Energy, 294*(1), 116914.
11. IMF. (2022). *World economic outlook database.* International Monetary Fund.
12. CMS. (2015). *Electricity law and regulation in Italy.* CMS.
13. Rotondi, F., & Salzano, G. (2021). *Italy is lagging its European Union peers on energy autonomy.* Bloomberg.
14. IEA. (2020). *Energy statistics.* IEA.
15. Brown, S. (2021a). *Gas-reliant Italy lags behind in Europe's race to renewables.* Ember.
16. International Trade Administration. (2020). *Italy - Country Commercial Guide.* International Trade Administration.
17. Speak, C. (2022). *Italy announces plan to end reliance on Russian gas by 2025.* The Local.
18. European Commission. (2022). *Questions and answers on REPowerEU: Joint European action for more affordable, secure and sustainable energy.* European Union.
19. Bianchi, M., & Raimondi, P. P. (2022). *Russian energy exports and the conflict in Ukraine: What options for Italy and the EU?* Instituto Affari Internazionali.
20. Brown, S. (2021b). *Italy's deployment of wind and solar has stagnated.* Ember Global Electricity Review.
21. Bersano, A., et al. (2020). Evaluation of a potential reintroduction of nuclear energy in Italy to accelerate the energy transition. *The Electricity Journal, 33*(7), 106813.
22. Arslan, O., & Er, I. D. (2008). SWOT analysis for safer carriage of bulk liquid chemicals in tankers. *Journal of Hazardous Materials, 154*(1), 901–913.
23. Destek, M. A. (2020). Renewable, non-renewable energy consumption, economic growth, trade openness and ecological footprint: Evidence from organisation for economic Co-operation and development countries. *Journal of Cleaner Production, 242*(1), 118537.
24. Doğan, B., Driha, O. M., Lorente, D. B., & Shahzad, U. (2021). The mitigating effects of economic complexity and renewable energy on carbon emissions in developed countries. *Sustainable Development, 29*(1), 1–12.
25. Ntanos, S., et al. (2018). Public perceptions and willingness to pay for renewable energy: A case study from Greece. *Sustainability, 10*(3), 687.
26. Martins, F., Felgueiras, C., & Smitková, M. (2018). Fossil fuel energy consumption in European countries. *Energy Procedia, 153*(1), 107–111.
27. Colasante, A., D'Adamo, I., & Morone, P. (2021). Nudging for the increased adoption of solar energy? Evidence from a survey in Italy. *Energy Research and Social Science, 74*(1), 101978.
28. Safari, A., et al. (2019). Natural gas: A transition fuel for sustainable energy system transformation? *Energy Science and Engineering, 7*(4), 1075–1094.
29. Wang, H., et al. (2018). Renewable and sustainable energy transitions for countries with different climates and renewable energy sources potentials. *Energies, 11*(12), 3523.
30. Solarin, S. A., Bello, M. O., & Bekun, F. V. (2021). Sustainable electricity generation: the possibility of substituting fossil fuels for hydropower and solar energy in Italy. *International Journal of Sustainable Development and World Ecology, 28*(5), 429–439.
31. Cergibozan, R. (2022). Renewable energy sources as a solution for energy security risk: Empirical evidence from OECD countries. *Renewable Energy, 183*(1), 617–626.
32. Gökgöz, F., & Güvercin, M. T. (2018). Energy security and renewable energy efficiency in EU. *Renewable and Sustainable Energy Reviews, 96*(1), 226–239.
33. Gastaldi, F. C. M., & Trosini, M. (2017). Investments and cleaner energy production: A portfolio analysis in the Italian electricity market. *Journal of Cleaner Production, 142*(1), 121–132.
34. Wang, Y., Xu, L., & Solangi, Y. A. (2020). Strategic renewable energy resources selection for Pakistan: Based on SWOT-Fuzzy AHP approach. *Sustainable Cities and Society, 52*(1), 101861.
35. Shadman, S., et al. (2021). The role of current and future renewable energy policies in fortifying Malaysia's energy security: PESTLE and SWOT analysis through stakeholder engagement. *Progress in Energy and Environment, 16*(1), 1–17.

36. Pramanik, D., Mondal, S. C., & Haldar, A. (2020). A framework for managing uncertainty in information system project selection: An intelligent fuzzy approach. *International Journal of Management Science and Engineering Management, 15*(1), 70–78.
37. Safder, U., Hai, T. N., Loy-Benitez, J., & Yoo, C. K. (2022). Nationwide policymaking strategies to prevent future electricity crises in developing countries using data-driven forecasting and fuzzy-SWOT analyses. *Energy, 259*(1), 124962.
38. Vyas, V., Singh, A. P., & Srivastava, A. (2021). Entropy-based fuzzy SWOT decision-making for condition assessment of airfield pavements. *International Journal of Pavement Engineering, 22*(10), 1226–1237.
39. Srinivas, R., et al. (2018). Sustainable management of a river basin by integrating an improved fuzzy based hybridized SWOT model and geo-statistical weighted thematic overlay analysis. *Journal of Hydrology, 563*(1), 92–105.
40. Karimi, M., Niknamfar, A. H., & Niaki, S. T. A. (2019). An application of fuzzy-logic and grey-relational ANP-based SWOT in the ceramic and tile industry. *Knowledge-Based Systems, 163*(1), 581–594.
41. Karatop, B., & Taşkan, B. (2021). A new integrated approach for determination of Turkey's solar energy production strategies: The fuzzy expanded SWOT. *Gazi Üniversitesi Fen Bilimleri Dergisi Part: C Tasarım ve Teknoloji, 9*(4), 621–644.
42. Amin, S. H. (2011). Supplier selection and order allocation based on fuzzy SWOT analysis and fuzzy linear programming. *Expert Systems with Applications, 38*(1), 334–342.
43. Babar, A. H. K., Ali, Y., & Khan, A. U. (2020). Moving toward green mobility: Overview and analysis of electric vehicle selection, Pakistan a case in point. *Environment, Development and Sustainability*.
44. Khan, F., & Ali, Y. (2022). Moving towards a sustainable circular bio-economy in the agriculture sector of a developing country. *Ecological Economics, 196*(1), 107402.
45. Hassan, Q. (2021). Evaluation and optimization of off-grid and on grid photovoltaic power system for typical household electrification. *Renewable Energy, 164*(1), 375–390.
46. Trotter, P. A., Cooper, N. J., & Wilson, P. R. (2019). A multi-criteria, long-term energy planning optimisation model with integrated on-grid and off-grid electrification – The case of Uganda. *Applied Energy, 243*(1), 288–312.
47. Carlini, E. M., Schroeder, R., Birkebæk, J. M., & Massaro, F. (2019). EU transition in power sector: How RES affects the design and operations of transmission power systems. *Electric Power Systems Research, 169*(1), 74–91.
48. Sun, Y., et al. (2020). Overview of energy storage in renewable energy power fluctuation mitigation. *CSEE Journal of Power and Energy Systems, 6*(1), 160–173.
49. Zsiborács, H., et al. (2019). Intermittent renewable energy sources: The role of energy storage in the european power system of 2040. *Electronics, 8*(7), 729.
50. Nadeem, F., et al. (2018). Comparative review of energy storage systems, their roles, and impacts on future power systems. *IEEE, 7*(1), 4555–4585.
51. Lehtveer, M., & Fridahl, M. (2020). Managing variable renewables with biomass in the European electricity system: Emission targets and investment preferences. *Energy, 213*(1), 118786.
52. Child, M., Kemfert, C., Bogdanov, D., & Breyer, C. (2019). Flexible electricity generation, grid exchange and storage for the transition to a 100% renewable energy system in Europe. *Renewable Energy, 139*(1), 80–101.
53. Child, M., Bogdanov, D., & Breyer, C. (2018). The role of storage technologies for the transition to a 100% renewable energy system in Europe. *Energy Procedia, 155*(1), 44–60.
54. Lowitzsch, J., Hoicka, C., Tulder, F., & v. (2020). Renewable energy communities under the 2019 European Clean Energy Package – Governance model for the energy clusters of the future? *Renewable and Sustainable Energy Reviews, 122*(1), 109489.
55. Baloch, Z. A., et al. (2022). A multi-perspective assessment approach of renewable energy production: policy perspective analysis. *Environment, Development and Sustainability, 24*(1), 2164–2192.

56. Qazi, A., et al. (2019). Towards sustainable energy: A systematic review of renewable energy sources, technologies, and public opinions. *IEEE, 7*(1), 63837–63851.
57. Benedek, J., Sebestyén, T.-T., & Bartók, B. (2018). Evaluation of renewable energy sources in peripheral areas and renewable energy-based rural development. *Renewable and Sustainable Energy Reviews, 90*(1), 516–535.
58. Wu, Y., Xu, C., & Zhang, T. (2018). Evaluation of renewable power sources using a fuzzy MCDM based on cumulative prospect theory: A case in China. *Energy, 147*(1), 1227–1239.
59. Garrett-Peltier, H. (2017). Green versus brown: Comparing the employment impacts of energy efficiency, renewable energy, and fossil fuels using an input-output model. *Economic Modelling, 61*(1), 439–447.
60. Shahsavari, A., & Akbari, M. (2018). Potential of solar energy in developing countries for reducing energy-related emissions. *Renewable and Sustainable Energy Reviews, 90*(1), 275–291.
61. Dhar, A., Naeth, M. A., Jennings, P. D., & El-Din, M. G. (2020). Perspectives on environmental impacts and a land reclamation strategy for solar and wind energy systems. *Science of the Total Environment, 718*, 134602.
62. Howard, D. C., et al. (2009). The impact of sustainable energy production on land use in Britain through to 2050. *Land Use Policy, 26*(1), S284–S292.
63. Wang, S., et al. (2019). Prioritizing among the end uses of excess renewable energy for cost-effective greenhouse gas emission reductions. *Applied Energy, 235*(1), 284–298.
64. Raybould, B., Cheung, W. M., Connor, C., & Butcher, R. (2020). An investigation into UK government policy and legislation to renewable energy and greenhouse gas reduction commitments. *Clean Technologies and Environmental Policy, 22*(1), 371–387.
65. Pfeifer, A., Krajačić, G., Ljubas, D., & Duić, N. (2019). Increasing the integration of solar photovoltaics in energy mix on the road to low emissions energy system – Economic and environmental implications. *Renewable Energy, 143*(1), 1310–1317.
66. Zsiborács, H., et al. (2018). Economic and technical aspects of flexible storage photovoltaic systems in Europe. *Energies, 11*(6), 1445.
67. Aghahosseini, A., Bogdanov, D., & Breyer, C. (2020). Towards sustainable development in the MENA region: Analysing the feasibility of a 100% renewable electricity system in 2030. *Energy Strategy Reviews, 28*(1), 100466.
68. Liu, G., et al. (2018). General indicator for techno-economic assessment of renewable energy resources. *Energy Conversion and Management, 156*(1), 416–426.
69. Deng, X., & Lv, T. (2020). Power system planning with increasing variable renewable energy: A review of optimization models. *Journal of Cleaner Production, 246*(1), 118962.
70. Yang, Y., Bremner, S., Menictas, C., & Kay, M. (2018). Battery energy storage system size determination in renewable energy systems: A review. *Renewable and Sustainable Energy Reviews, 91*(1), 109–125.
71. Diesendorf, M., & Elliston, B. (2018). The feasibility of 100% renewable electricity systems: A response to critics. *Renewable and Sustainable Energy Reviews, 93*(1), 318–330.
72. Ram, M., Aghahosseini, A., & Breyer, C. (2020). Job creation during the global energy transition towards 100% renewable power system by 2050. *Technological Forecasting and Social Change, 151*(1), 119682.
73. Lee, H.-C., & Chang, C.-T. (2018). Comparative analysis of MCDM methods for ranking renewable energy sources in Taiwan. *Renewable and Sustainable Energy Reviews, 92*(1), 883–896.
74. Nock, D., & Baker, E. (2019). Holistic multi-criteria decision analysis evaluation of sustainable electric generation portfolios: New England case study. *Applied Energy, 242*(1), 655–673.
75. Dincer, I., & Acar, C. (2015). A review on clean energy solutions for better sustainability. *International Journal of Energy Research, 39*(5), 585–606.
76. Jurasz, J., et al. (2020). A review on the complementarity of renewable energy sources: Concept, metrics, application and future research directions. *Solar Energy, 195*(1), 703–724.

77. Shen, Y.-C., Lin, G. T., Li, K.-P., & Yuan, B. J. (2010). An assessment of exploiting renewable energy sources with concerns of policy and technology. *Energy Policy, 38*(8), 4604–4616.
78. Suberu, M. Y., Mustafa, M. W., & Bashir, N. (2014). Energy storage systems for renewable energy power sector integration and mitigation of intermittency. *Renewable and Sustainable Energy Reviews, 35*(1), 499–514.
79. González, A., Riba, J.-R., & Rius, A. (2015). Optimal sizing of a hybrid grid-connected photo-voltaic–wind–biomass power system. *Sustainability, 7*(9), 12787–12806.
80. Kamran, M., Fazal, M. R., & Mudassar, M. (2020). Towards empowerment of the renewable energy sector in Pakistan for sustainable energy evolution: SWOT analysis. *Renewable Energy, 146*(1), 543–558.
81. Østergaard, P. A., et al. (2020). Sustainable development using renewable energy technology. *Renewable Energy, 146*(1), 2430–2437.
82. Bódis, K., et al. (2019). A high-resolution geospatial assessment of the rooftop solar pho-tovoltaic potential in the European Union. *Renewable and Sustainable Energy Reviews, 114*(1), 109309.
83. Khan, F., Ali, Y., & Khan, A. U. (2020). Sustainable hybrid electric vehicle selection in the context of a developing country. *Air Quality, Atmosphere and Health, 13*(1), 489–499.
84. Zadeh, L. (1965). Fuzzy sets. *Information and Control, 8*(3), 338–353.
85. Chou, S.-Y., & Chang, Y.-H. (2008). A decision support system for supplier selection based on a strategy-aligned fuzzy SMART approach. *Expert Systems with Applications, 34*(4), 2241–2253.

Digital Platforms, Digital Ecosystems and the Role of Emerging (Digital) Technologies: A Bibliometric Analysis

Martina Mattioli and Antonio D'Andreamatteo

Abstract This research aims to observe the academic discourse developed around digital platforms and digital ecosystems, considering their interconnection with emerging technologies. The study adopts a bibliometric approach to analyze, in a systematic and repeatable manner, 1392 academic contributions published on digital platforms and ecosystems over a time span from 2001 to mid-May 2022. First, we highlighted the key characteristics of the discussion around the topics and the academic community involved in terms of publication and citation trends, the most productive authors and countries, and the most influential authors and articles. Then, we conducted a co-word analysis to observe and analyze the conceptual structure of the dataset. The findings indicate that in the last 10 years has there been a significant growth in academic interest in this research area. The academic discourse on digital platforms is more developed than that on ecosystems, and this could be explained by the various facets and types that result in a broader application of the former topic, which began to be discussed in the early 2000s. The results of the co-word analysis show a strong presence of digital technologies, which was investigated in greater detail to determine the possible influence exerted by technologies on the literature related to the research topics considered. This study provides research insights and suggestions for exploring the knowledge gap identified, namely how emerging technologies interact with digital platforms and ecosystems, as well as analyzing the phenomenon's inevitable further evolution.

Keywords Digital platform · Digital ecosystem · Bibliometric analysis · Emerging technologies

M. Mattioli (✉) · A. D'Andreamatteo
University "G. D'Annunzio" of Chieti-Pescara, Pescara, Italy
e-mail: martina.mattioli@unich.it; antonio.dandreamatteo@unich.it

© The Author(s), under exclusive license to Springer Nature
Switzerland AG 2024
A. Lazazzara et al. (eds.), *Towards Digital and Sustainable Organisations*,
Lecture Notes in Information Systems and Organisation 65,
https://doi.org/10.1007/978-3-031-52880-4_16

1   Introduction

The advent of digitalization, which has drastically changed the way every person lives their daily life, has also led to rapid progress in the business and manufacturing sectors. Some, as noted by Subramaniam et al. [1], have long since begun the process of change, adopting innovative digital strategies both internally and in their supply and distribution networks [2]. Others, more rooted in tradition, must rethink their modus operandi and strive, guided by new technologies, to implement what is called digital transformation [3]. However, this is a complex phenomenon that challenges every area of a company, such as a change of mindset in the holistic approach from decision makers to executive and production power, to the processes of production, supply, and distribution of goods and services in a continuous openness to change with the constant evolution of new technologies adopted universally. It is no coincidence that Karakas [4] states that World 2.0 is a mega-platform, open, flexible, and collaborative, characterized by five changes: creativity, connectivity, collaboration, convergence, and community. Therefore, in order to keep up with progress and stay in the market, companies use the necessary tools for change and organize themselves for innovation.

Over the past two decades, the literature has focused on digital platforms, ecosystems, and emerging technologies. Gawer and Cusumano [5], reviewing the literature on digital platforms, state that the use and meaning of the term often differ. They hypothesize that different types of platforms exist and, therefore, different ways in which platforms can impact the innovation process characterized by the use of new technologies. These are identified by some scholars as Big Data, Internet of Things (IoT), cloud computing, augmented and virtual reality [6], Artificial Intelligence, and cyber-physical systems, in contrast to other authors, such as Fitzgerald et al. [7] who suggest social media, analytics, mobile or embedded devices.

This study aims to explore the literature that has developed around digital platforms and ecosystems, also considering whether and how digital technologies have influenced academic production on these topics over the years. Therefore, the present research seeks to answer the following questions:

RQ1. How has the academic discourse on digital platforms and ecosystems developed, and how is it developing?

RQ2. To what extent have emerging technologies influenced academic production related to digital platforms and ecosystems over the years?

Although reviews of the literature on digital platforms and ecosystems have been carried out before, the present one differs because it adopts a bibliometric approach to observe the academic discourse on these two concepts. Bibliometric analysis was chosen since it allows for systematic and repeatable processing and analysis of a large amount of data. Furthermore, while other reviews analyze these topics separately, this study examines them jointly for a more comprehensive picture of academic interest over time. In addition to conducting a bibliometric analysis, the scope of the research includes the interconnection of digital platforms and ecosystems with emerging technologies. It focuses on determining the possible influence of technologies on the literature related to the research topics. Finally, it seeks to determine which of the emerging technologies considered has the greatest impact on academic production and which has garnered the most attention from the academic community.

The article is organized as follows. After a brief overview of the current literature on digital platforms, ecosystems, and emerging (digital) technologies in Sect. 2, Sect. 3 includes the research methodology divided into three subsections: data collection, data refinement, and data analysis. The latter subsection presents the results of the bibliometric analysis, which contains both descriptive and co-word analysis. Finally, Sect. 4 contains a summary of the paper, conclusions, limitations, and suggestion for future studies.

2 Theoretical Background

2.1 Digital Platform and Digital Ecosystem

Over the years, the academic discourse on digital platforms and ecosystems has become intertwined.

In the 1990s, digital platforms began to attract the interest of academics, giving rise to the distinction between architecture and infrastructure. Architecture, for example, is defined by Ulrich [8] as a logical and conceptual structure of a functional system. Yoo et al. [9], on the other hand, describe a modular layered architecture, where generativity is achieved through loose couplings between layers, meaning that innovations can arise independently in any layer, leading to cascading effects. Moreover, in the wake of Yoo, Kazan et al. [10] theorize a proprietary or open technology architecture consisting of five modular layers—device, system, network, service, and content—each of which has two aspects, i.e., competitive dynamics and implications for market disruption. As infrastructure, a platform, for example, is defined by Hanseth and Lyytinen [11] as "such a complex, evolving and heterogeneous socio-technical system … a shared, evolving, heterogeneous installed base of IT capabilities among a set of user communities based on open and/or standardized interfaces".

In the 2000s, different types of digital platforms also began to be recognized and distinguished. The internal platform or "product platform" originates from a company's need to promote efficiency in terms of economies of scale and scope in design, engineering, and production, to promote innovation of new varieties and types of products, sometimes deriving from existing components and technologies [5]. The supply chain platform, also aimed at improving efficiency and reducing costs, "extends the internal platform concept" to firms that supply products or components, allowing the main firm to "go outside its internal capabilities to find more innovative components or technologies" for the assembly of the final product [5]. The industry platform, similar to internal and supply-chain platforms, is defined by Gawer and Cusumano [5] as "products, services, or technologies that are developed by one or more firms, and which serve as foundations upon which a larger number of firms can build complementary innovations, again, in the form of specific products, related services or component technologies". The last two types form a stable core and act as a mediator between users, sellers, and buyers, shaping the multi-sided platform [12].

Additionally, a platform can be open, closed [13], or "walled garden" [14]. An open platform, by allowing a greater number of outsiders to participate cooperatively, results in a possible increase in opportunities for innovation and value enhancement, as opposed to a closed platform. The "walled garden", by controlling user access to network-based content and services, directs the user's navigation and prevents its accessibility to external content and applications [15]. Every digital platform, according to Hänninen and Paavola [15], has both open and closed elements, because even closed platforms can benefit from opening up to external stakeholders in terms of efficiency and innovation [16].

The adoption of digital technologies has led to the concept of digital organization. As already pointed out, digitalization has brought changes in the way of thinking, operating, attracting and retaining customers, seizing opportunities, and assessing risks in the market. In this context, Godin and Terekhova [17] identify the platform economy and the further development of IT. This has enabled the transition from platform economy, platform as a business model, to ecosystem economy, digital ecosystem as a business model, and more.

Therefore, following this line of reasoning, it is possible to state that "platforms are closely linked to ecosystems" [18]. In the 1990s, Moore [19] conceptualized the notion of a business ecosystem, which implies that an industry can no longer compete alone in one sector but needs to be part of an economic community with its own stable center governed by keystone species, i.e., companies with a leading role, which has as its basis the continuous interaction between organizations and individuals, consumers, producers, competitors, and other stakeholders [20].

In the 2000s, the concept of the ecosystem was introduced to explain the digital ecosystem [21]. In nature, an ecosystem refers to a well-defined portion of the biosphere in which various organisms, animals, and plants, interacting with each other and their surroundings, create, in a unique structural and functional arrangement, a dynamic natural system as they compete to generate and transmit energy and life within the system. In the web, "environments" are characterized by multiple interdependent elements that, despite their differences in origin, structure, purpose, and functioning, act cooperatively and competitively, making the most of their combined capabilities to create innovations, products, and generate the basis for further progress. Like biological ecosystems, business ecosystems – "characterized by a large number of loosely interconnected participants who depend on each other for their mutual effectiveness and survival" [22, 23]—have a life cycle of birth, development, leadership, rebirth, or death [20] in the event that the interaction fails to bring value to the ecosystem by creating knowledge, skills, innovations and, consequently, evolution.

Over the years, further contributions have been made to the already outlined constitution, functionality, and structure of ecosystems. Some authors emphasize their structural characteristics by stating that, in the context of the digital business ecosystem (DBE), the digital ecosystem is either a technology designed to serve specific human purposes, developed to solve dynamic problems in parallel with high efficiency [21], or a technical infrastructure, based on peer-to-peer distributed software technology that finds, transports, and connects services and information over Internet links enabling networked transactions and distribution of digital objects within the infrastructure [24].

Despite the distinction between production and consumption ecosystems and its definition as an alignment structure of the multilateral set of partners that must interact for a value proposition to materialize [25], Subramaniam et al. [1] see the ecosystem as a combination of complex ecosystems managed through a system of interdependencies that facilitate the mutual exchange of information among users.

2.2 Emerging Digital Technologies

Emerging digital technologies characterize Industry 4.0, bring about radical changes, and can be considered "volatile". As they become part of everyday life and of the processes for which they are adopted—i.e., they are normalized—they become commonplace.

For this reason, it can be argued that technologies currently regarded as emerging, as they are already in use but still under development for the first 5–10 years, will eventually cease to be classified as emerging, as in the case of e-mail [26]. Nonetheless, a technology can be considered established in one context and emerging in another, depending on whether it is commercially available and not widely used but could become so in the next few years. Furthermore, emerging technologies can be distinguished by their associated function [27] and digitalization capability: data collection (Internet of Things or IoT), data integration, cloud and blockchain [28], and data analytics, big data, and artificial intelligence [29, 30].

3 Methodology

The aim of this research, in addition to trying to answer the research questions (RQ1 and RQ2), is to monitor the general trend of academic production concerning digital platforms and ecosystems through a bibliometric approach. Moreover, this research aims to assess whether the publication trend has been stable or has seen a sudden but substantial increase, which may have been influenced by the strong wave of digitalization observed during the pandemic period.

Digital platforms and ecosystems, as well as emerging technologies, attract the interest of academia, as evidenced by the rapid multiplication of articles on the subject. The type of analysis selected for this study is bibliometric analysis, as it enables the processing and analysis of a vast amount of information. It involves a set of methods employed in many research fields to study or measure texts and information in large datasets. This approach provides a systematic, transparent, and reproducible data review procedure based on statistical measurement [31]. Its application helps identify the most productive years, journals, and authors and their impact, as well as research themes and trends over time, and focus on the conceptual aspect of the analysis.

Academics agree in attributing two main approaches to bibliometric analysis: performance analysis and scientific mapping [32–34], following a research protocol [35] or, as suggested by Zupic and Čater [36], a standard workflow [31].

In order to answer the research questions, a combination of the techniques described will be observed in the paper. Figure 1 outlines the steps followed in the analysis stages: data collection, data refinement, standardization and homogenization of collected keywords, data analysis and visualization, and interpretation of results.

3.1 Data Collection

To appropriately conduct this analysis, the Scopus database was employed, as it is reputed to be one of the most comprehensive due to the presence of interdisciplinary academic contributions, as well as being one of the most widely used in academic research. In addition, the tools used to perform the analysis are bibliometrix, Excel, and VOSviewer.

Preliminarily, two distinct searches were conducted. The objective was to get an initial idea of the current state of research on digital platforms and ecosystems. In addition, the perceived trend made it essential to identify whether and how the research had experienced a steady and sustained or exponential and abrupt evolution.

In this context, it is possible to anticipate that the academic production on the phenomenon of digital platforms, with respect to the entire time frame considered, is more substantial in the years 2001 to 2022, as compared to the studies on ecosystems, published from 2007 to the present. Thus, the first step resulted in two separate searches on the Scopus database of the keywords "digital platform" and "digital ecosystem," conducted to ascertain the numerical quantity of studies produced on these phenomena. The terms were searched in their singular and plural forms, with the use of an asterisk, in titles, abstracts, and keywords. The individual search results were 6866 for "digital platform" and 1512 for "digital ecosystem," respectively.

Subsequently, the search was narrowed down, limiting the area to "Business, Management, and Accounting" and considering only contributions written in English. This resulted in a decrease in the number of academic contributions in both datasets, 1218 for "digital platform" and 266 for "digital ecosystem." Terms usually

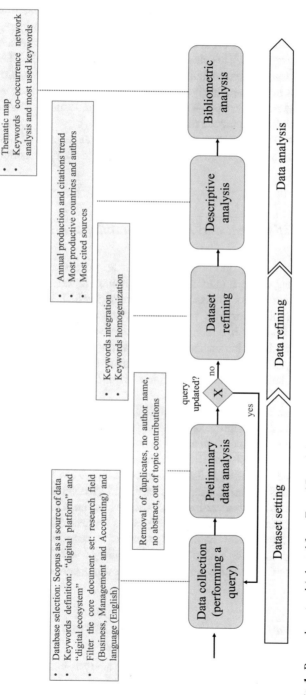

Fig. 1 Research protocol (adapted from Za and Braccini, 2017)

associated with digital platforms and digital ecosystems, such as "platform economy," "multi-sided market," "two-sided market," and "platform ecosystem," were not included in the search queries. The inclusion of the specific terms only—i.e., digital platform and digital ecosystem—gave a general idea of the discourse developed around these topics. This choice made it easier to identify the likely presence of connections to other conceptually similar keywords. In other words, the dataset—though not being completely exhaustive, as it does not include synonyms or extensions of the main concepts—contains a number of documents that can be considered thorough for the purpose of this study.

Finally, the two datasets were merged to form a single dataset of 1484 academic contributions. After the removal of duplicates, the sample comprised 1471 documents.

3.2 Data Refinement and Keyword Standardization

Prior to data processing, the dataset included: 26 articles with missing authors, which, after being checked individually in an attempt to retrieve the missing information, were removed; 31 articles with no abstract, of which 14 were recovered and 17 removed; 2 duplicate articles, which were removed; 1 article that did not contain the selected search terms in either the title, abstract, or keywords, and was therefore deleted; 9 articles that, while including the keywords, where off-topic, and therefore removed; finally, 180 contributions with missing author keywords resulted in individual abstracts being read for the identification and integration of the keywords in question.

A further step, essential for the identification of the conceptual structure, is the homogenization of the authors' keywords. In order to reduce bias, an impartial way of preferring some keywords over others was found by identifying the ones that recurred most in the articles and the ones that had the same meaning. As can be seen in some examples included in Table 1, misspellings were removed, the singular form of terms was preferred over the plural, and vice versa, and keywords were preferred in their American version, standardizing the ones in British English.

After standardization, the number of keywords decreased from 4366 to 4091; the high number of keywords is mainly due to terms that occur only once.

In conclusion, the sample used for the preliminary analysis, which is purely statistical, consists of 1392 academic articles and covers a period from 2001 to 2022.

3.3 Data Analysis and Visualization of Results

Descriptive Analysis The data collected for the analysis make it possible to argue that academic interest in digital platforms and ecosystems, which began about 20 years ago, has observed a steady and growing trend, especially in the last decade.

Table 1 Refined set of keywords

Original authors' keywords	Revised and adopted keywords
AI Artificial Intelligence Artificial Intelligence (AI)	Artificial Intelligence
Blockchain Blockchain Technology	Blockchain
Digital Twin Digital Twin (DT) Digital Twins	Digital Twin
Digitalization Digitalizatio Digitalisation	Digitalization
Digital ecosystem Digital ecosystems	Digital ecosystem
A digital platform Digital platform Digital platforms	Digital platform
"sharing economy" Sharing Economy Sharing Economy (SE)	Sharing Economy

Figure 2 shows the trend in annual academic production.

Although production began in 2001 with one article, the growth of academic discourse was minimal until 2008. This abnormal peak, with 44 scholarly contributions, is mainly due to articles from the "2nd IEEE International Conference on Digital Ecosystems and Technologies," held in 2008. After a steep decline in the following year, a cautious and steady growth can be observed. The number of articles doubled from 2016 to 2017, registering a peak in 2021 with 407 papers.

A crucial element to consider is citations, as they are closely linked to academic production. Figure 3 shows how average citations per article and per year follow different trends compared to production. In 2006, a peak of 246 is observed in the average number of total citations per article, along with a smaller peak of 15.38 in the average number of total citations per year, although only five articles are involved.

Focusing on the most productive and most cited countries and authors is also necessary to get a comprehensive view of academic production and related citations.

Figure 4 shows the 20 most productive countries. The distinction between articles written by authors from the same country (SCP—Single Country Publications) and articles written by authors from different countries (MCP—Multiple Country Publications) makes it possible to affirm that the United States, Italy, and the United Kingdom are the three most productive and collaborative countries. As for production, they register 106, 84, and 69 publications, respectively, while regarding collaboration, there are 32 articles for the UK, 25 for the US, and 24 for Italy. However, it is interesting to note that Denmark, with a total of 17 articles, records more than half of these articles as written by authors from different countries.

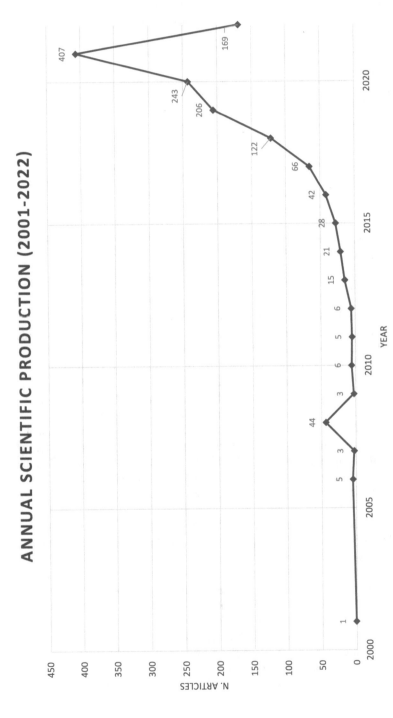

Fig. 2 Annual scientific production since 2001

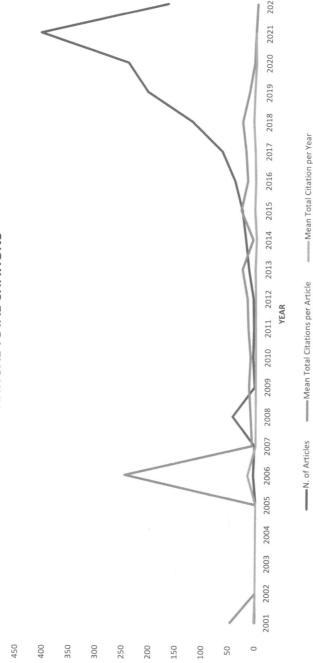

Fig. 3 Total number of citations per year and per article

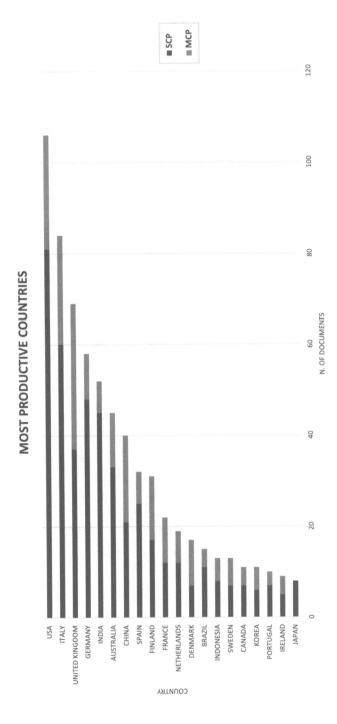

Fig. 4 Most Productive Countries (No.20)

Table 2 Most cited countries (N. 20)

	Country	Total citations	Average article citations		Country	Total citations	Average article citations
1	USA	3239	30,557	11	Denmark	232	13,647
2	United Kingdom	1678	24,319	12	Spain	227	7,094
3	Italy	691	8,226	13	Canada	200	18,182
4	Germany	625	10,776	14	India	194	3,731
5	Australia	505	11,222	15	Norway	123	17,571
6	France	453	20,591	16	Austria	88	17,6
7	China	406	10,15	17	Korea	71	6,455
8	Finland	378	12,194	18	Ghana	63	15,75
9	Sweden	256	19,692	19	Ireland	61	6,778
10	Netherlands	254	13,368	20	Brazil	57	3,8

Table 2 shows the number of citations per country: the US is the most influential and productive country, followed by the UK and Italy. Specifically, there is an average of citations per article of 30.56 for the US, 24.32 for the UK, and 8.23 for Italy, while the total number of citations appears to be 3239, 1678, and 691, respectively. Although the number chosen to identify the most productive and most cited countries is the same, i.e., 20, the sample taken differs. Some countries found among the most productive are absent from the most cited, such as Japan.

Additional parameters to consider, as already mentioned, are the most productive authors and the most cited articles within the analyzed dataset. Figure 5 shows Krcmar H. as the most productive author, with 11 contributions, followed by Trabucchi D., Kumar S., and Buganza T., recording 8, 7, and 7 articles, respectively.

Moreover, Table 3 shows the 10 most cited articles in the dataset. The most cited paper is Rai et al. [37] with 1228 citations and, as highlighted in Fig. 3, it is responsible for the peak in 2006. The second most cited article, which is more recent and noteworthy for its discussion of the literature on digital platforms [18], registers 484 citations, just over one-third of those of the previously mentioned paper. Among the 10 articles, 9 are distributed over a time span from 2015 to 2019, 1 is from 2006, 3 contain the term "ecosystem" and 4 the term "platform" in the title.

Authors' keywords co-occurrences The analyzed dataset produced a thematic map where the clusters are mainly grouped in the second (motor themes) and fourth quadrant (basic themes).

The motor themes, illustrated in Fig. 6, include "digitalization", "digital transformation", and "digital economy", which characterize the "World 2.0" defined by Karakas [4] as a "mega-platform". For example, digitalization has not only transformed everyday reality but has also affected the business world. This reorganization has led to a new way of looking at the organization's relationship with the entire supply chain both from an internal point of view—production processes, warehouse, human capital—and from an external point of view—suppliers, distribution, and customers.

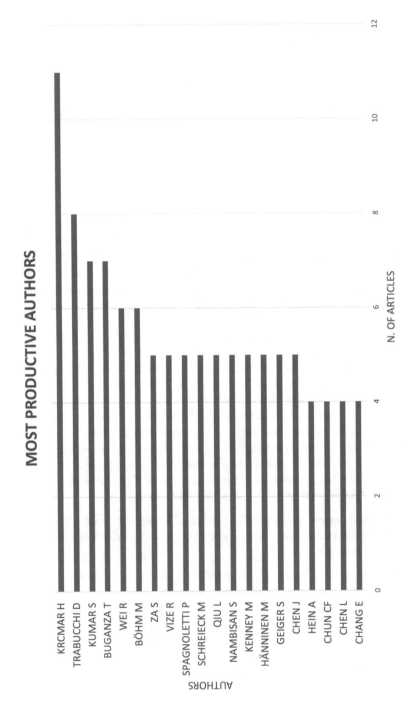

Fig. 5 Most productive authors (No. 20)

Table 3 Most cited articles (N. 10)

Article	N. of citations
Rai A., Patnayakuni R., Seth N., Firm performance impacts of digitally enabled supply chain integration capabilities, 2006, MIS Quarterly: Management Information Systems, 30 (2), pp. 225–246	1228
De Reuver M., Sørensen C., Basole R.C., The digital platform: A research agenda, 2018, Journal of Information Technology, 33 (2), pp. 124–135	484
Nambisan S., Wright M., Feldman M., The digital transformation of innovation and entrepreneurship: Progress, challenges and key themes, 2019, Research Policy, 48 (8)	310
Constantinides P., Henfridsson O., Parker G.G., Platforms and infrastructures in the digital age, 2018, Information Systems Research, 29 (2), pp. 381–400	244
Karimi J., Walter Z., The role of dynamic capabilities in responding to digital disruption: A factor-based study of the newspaper industry, 2015, Journal of Management Information Systems, 32 (1), pp.39–81	244
Helfat C.E., Raubitschek R.S., Dynamic and integrative capabilities for profiting from innovation in digital platform-based ecosystems, 2018, Research Policy, 47 (8), pp.1391–1399	221
Sutherland W., Jarrahi M.H., The sharing economy and digital platforms: A review and research agenda, 2018, International Journal of Information Management, 43, pp. 328–341	218
Sussan F., Acs Z.J., The digital entrepreneurial ecosystem, 2017, Small Business Economics, 49 (1), pp. 55–73	211
Weill P., Woerner S.L., Thriving in an Increasingly Digital Ecosystem, 2015, MIT Sloan Management Review, 56 (4), pp. 27–34	196
Täuscher K., Laudien S.M., Understanding platform business models: A mixed methods study of marketplaces, 2018, European Management Journal, 36 (3), pp. 319–329	195

For this reason, the phenomenon of hyperconnectivity is defined as "the backbone of the digital economy" due to the ever-increasing "interconnectedness of people, organizations, and machines" [38], based on the notion of intensive and extensive applications of ICT [39, 40].

The second quadrant also includes "digital platform", "business model" and "social media". These themes are closely related to the discourse emerging with regard to the first cluster and, in this context, "digital platform"—a distinctive element of the research—becomes essential to the needs and challenges faced by companies [40, 41].

The fourth quadrant comprises two clusters. The first one encompasses general yet relevant themes, such as "entrepreneurship", "ecosystem," and "platform." Among the components of the second cluster, on the other hand, "digital ecosystem" stands out and can be considered to be under development. In light of academic production, this phenomenon has been on the rise in recent years, as shown by the present analysis. In contrast, "digital technologies" and "ICT" are both closely related to digital transformation, digital economy, and digitalization, and can be considered as some of the founding elements of these phenomena. Therefore, they could represent basic themes that "feed" the motor themes.

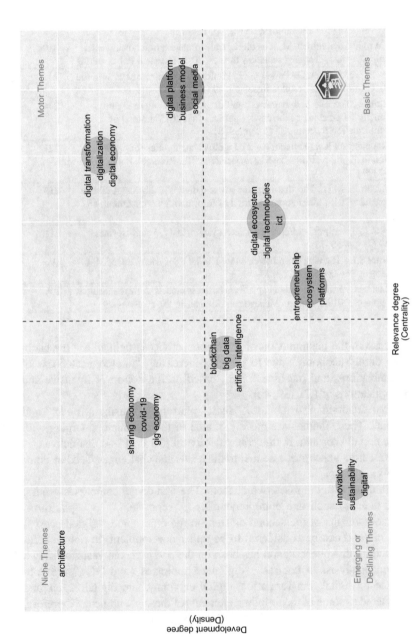

Fig. 6 Thematic map

On the lower left, the third quadrant includes two clusters. The first one contains "blockchain," "big data," and "artificial intelligence," while the second one contains "sustainability," "innovation," and "digital." Unlike the previous themes, these can be considered emerging rather than declining themes. For example, since 2018 there has been growing interest from academia in technologies such as blockchain and artificial intelligence, while since 2015 the focus has been on big data.

Among the niche topics, three main themes are found. The first is "covid-19", which has emphasized the importance and necessity of digitalization in every sector. The second and third terms, often used interchangeably, are "sharing economy" and "gig economy" [42–45]. They share some features, such as the use of digital platforms, intermediaries that enable the matching of supply and demand by allowing peer-to-peer connections for different purposes, respectively the selling or renting and offering resources – on-call, casual, and temporary work, as is the case with Uber and Airbnb.

Figure 7 shows the keywords with the highest number of co-occurrences. The themes that have interested academic research on digital platforms and ecosystems become evident through the analysis of the keywords, which reflect the focus of each article. The 31 most popular keywords, identified from the dataset of 1392 contributions, are divided into five clusters, the largest of which are "digital platform" with 473 occurrences and "digital ecosystem" with 142 occurrences.

The connections between the most recurrent keywords allow five clusters to be distinguished. The blue cluster has "digital platform" as its core, which is connected (see Fig. 7) with the nodes sharing economy, gig economy, multi-sided platforms,

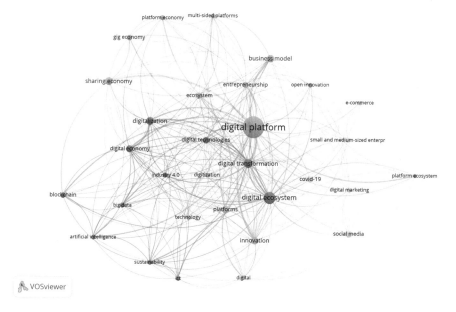

Fig. 7 Keywords co-occurrence graph

and platform economy. The red cluster, which might be referred to as "digital eco-system" due to the large presence of this keyword, includes, in addition to digital transformation and digitalization, closely related topics such as Industry 4.0 and digital technologies, while also distinguishing some individual emerging technologies such as Artificial Intelligence and blockchain. The green cluster seems to have no specific focus, as it includes basic and general keywords such as innovation, entrepreneurship, digital, technologies, ecosystems, and platforms. The yellow cluster includes topics that are mostly related to the Pandemic period, namely Covid-19, e-commerce, social media, digital marketing, and Small and Medium-sized Enterprises. Finally, the purple cluster is the smallest cluster represented in Fig. 7 and includes platform ecosystems (20 occurrences) and open innovation (21 occurrences).

4   Conclusions

This study provided a bibliometric analysis of a dataset consisting of 1392 contributions on digital platforms and ecosystems over a time span from 2001 to mid-May 2022. The analysis involved two phases: descriptive analysis and co-word analysis.

Although academic interest in digital platforms and ecosystems began in 2001, the descriptive study showed that considerable growth has been observed only in the last 10 years, with the highest peak reached in 2021. This could be the result of the significant push toward digitalization that occurred during the pandemic period and saw an exponential increase in the use of digital technology. As a result, the academic literature has observed and analyzed the effects of this situation. It can be argued that the academic discourse on digital platforms is more in-depth than the discourse on ecosystems. This is probably due to the fact that the former topic, which was first discussed in the early 2000s, has a broader application, given its various facets and types, which have already been mentioned.

Furthermore, scientific mapping allowed for a deeper exploration of the themes revealed by the dataset. Some themes are strictly related to digital platforms and ecosystems, such as different types of economies: from general ones, e.g., digital economy and platform economy, to more specific ones, e.g., sharing and gig economy. It is also possible to highlight the presence of "enablers" of platforms and ecosystems, from digital transformation and digitalization to digital technologies, from ICT to artificial intelligence, big data, and blockchain.

Accordingly, throughout the analysis, the strong presence of digital technologies, also referred to as emerging, was noted in the data collected. Therefore, it was deemed appropriate to investigate this aspect further. Hence, a gap can be identified. To the best of our knowledge, there is a limited understanding of how emerging technologies, such as artificial intelligence and blockchain, interact with digital platforms and ecosystems. As a result, the possible interconnection between technologies, platforms, and digital ecosystems is also scarcely explored.

Therefore, following the classification of digital technologies mentioned in the theoretical background—data collection, integration, and analytics—and expanding it with the other classifications mentioned in the paper, the emerging technologies considered for this in-depth study are blockchain, artificial intelligence, social media, big data, and digital technologies in general. The latter is considered because most authors use the generic term, without referring to a specific technology. Thus, the trend of the curve is predominant over that of specific technologies.

Following a preliminary search, it became evident that not all types of technologies were present in the dataset. The results represented in Fig. 8 include emerging technologies found in the papers' titles, abstracts, and/or authors' keywords. For this reason, some technologies such as, for example, machine learning, mentioned only once in an abstract, were not included. Other technologies, on the other hand, were excluded using a predetermined parameter. If a technology did not reach, from the internal search, a total of results greater than 15, it was not included. These technologies encompassed cloud computing, augmented or virtual reality, cyber-physical systems, and mobile or embedded devices. Also, after a careful reading of abstracts, some technologies were grouped under a single term. One example is smart contracts, which were considered part of "blockchain."

Figure 8 comprises 481 articles from the search of individual terms in the dataset out of a total of 1392 academic contributions, and the time frame is from 2015 to 2022.

In addition to the clear predominance of generic references to digital technologies, a steady and growing trend can be observed for the searched terms. Each term had its respective peak in 2021, however differing in the development of the discourse, as Big Data, social media, and "digital technologies in general" have been present since 2015, the Internet of Things (IoT) since 2016, and Artificial Intelligence and blockchain since 2018.

One factor that may have influenced the higher numbers reported in 2021 is the accelerated and forced digitalization that occurred during the pandemic. Emerging

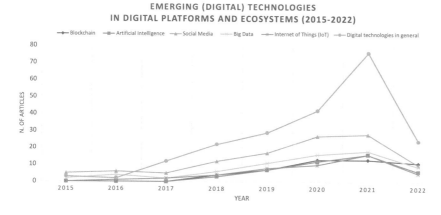

Fig. 8 Number of articles published since 2015 on emerging digital technologies found in the analyzed dataset

digital technologies are enablers of entrepreneurial activity [46, 47] and facilitate digital transformation and Industry 4.0 [47–49]. The trend in the graph reflects what is happening and is being observed by academics: many industries, given the pervasiveness and spread of digitalization, have already adopted emerging technologies (IoT, Big Data, cloud computing, etc.), while others are approaching digital transformation slowly due to the very nature of the company and/or industry they belong to [28, 47].

In conclusion, this study has attempted to make a contribution to the already vast academic literature on digital platforms and ecosystems, as well as emerging digital technologies, by providing research insights and suggestions for analyzing the inevitable further evolution of the phenomenon.

However, this study also has limitations. First, the selected database may represent a limitation. Although Scopus is an interdisciplinary portal and includes a significant number of contributions, other databases that contain additional journals and articles, such as Web of Science, could also be considered for an objective and comprehensive overview. Second, the keywords selected for querying the database are generic. This choice was driven by the need to have as general an idea as possible, which means that terms such as "platform ecosystems" or "platform-based ecosystems" were not specifically included. This led to considering the terms "digital platform" and "digital ecosystem" only separately, instead of considering them jointly or also including related terms, such as "multi-sided market" or "two-sided market."

Finally, Fig. 8 showed the existence of a connection that should be better explored. Future studies could examine the implementation of a specific technology, among those that have been less explored, such as machine learning, cloud computing, or cyber-physical systems, dwelling on the interaction thereof with the use and development of digital platforms and/or ecosystems by a company or a particular industry, through case studies using empirical data. As a result, future research could seek to identify the most affected sectors, defining whether and where the greater application of digital platforms and ecosystems occurs.

References

1. Subramaniam, M., Iyer, B., & Venkatraman, V. (2019). Competing in digital ecosystems. *Business Horizons, 62*, 83–94. https://doi.org/10.1016/j.bushor.2018.08.013
2. Porter, M. E. (1998). *Competitive advantage. Creating and sustaining superior performance.* Free Press.
3. Westerman, G., & Bonnet, D. (2015). Revamping your business through digital transformation. *MIT Sloan Management Review, 56*, 2–5.
4. Karakas, F. (2009). Welcome to World 2.0: The new digital ecosystem. *Journal of Business Strategy, 30*, 23–30. https://doi.org/10.1108/02756660910972622
5. Gawer, A., & Cusumano, M. A. (2014). *Oxford handbooks online platforms and innovation major themes and research findings* (pp. 1–23). doi:https://doi.org/10.1093/oxfordhb/9780199694945.013.014.

6. Urbinati, A., Chiaroni, D., Chiesa, V., & Frattini, F. (2020). The role of digital technologies in open innovation processes: an exploratory multiple case study analysis. *R and D Management, 50*, 136–160. https://doi.org/10.1111/radm.12313

7. Fitzgerald, M., Kruschwitz, N., Bonnet, D., & Welch, M. (2013). Embracing digital technology: A new strategic imperative | Capgemini Consulting Worldwide. *MIT Sloan Management Review, 55*, 1–13.

8. Ulrich, K. (1995). The role of product architecture in the manufacturing firm. *Research Policy, 24*, 419–440. https://doi.org/10.1016/0048-7333(94)00775-3

9. Yoo, Y., Henfridsson, O., & Lyytinen, K. (2010). The new organizing logic of digital innovation: An agenda for information systems research. *Information Systems Research, 21*, 724–735. https://doi.org/10.1287/isre.1100.0322

10. Kazan, E., Tan, C. W., & Lim, E. T. K. (2014). Towards a framework of digital platform disruption: A comparative study of centralized & decentralized digital payment providers. In *Proceedings of the 25th Australasian Conference on Information Systems*. ACIS 2014.

11. Hanseth, O., & Lyytinen, K. (2004). Theorizing about the Design of Information Infrastructures: Design Kernel Theories and Principles. *Sprouts Working Papers on Information Systems, 4*, 207–241.

12. Boudreau, K.J., & Hagiu, A. (2009). Platform rules: Multi-sided platforms as regulators. *Platforms, Markets and Innovation* (pp. 163–191). doi:https://doi.org/10.4337/9781849803311.00014.

13. Tiwana, A. (2014). *Platform ecosystems: Aligning architecture, governance, and strategy*, Waltham, MA.

14. Hazlett, T., Teece, D., & Waverman, L. (2011). Walled Garden Rivalry: The creation of mobile network ecosystems. *George Mason University, Law & Economics* Research *Paper Series, 11*.

15. Hänninen, M., & Paavola, L. (2020). Digital platforms and industry change. In: *Society as an interaction space, a systemic approach* (pp. 213–226). doi:https://doi.org/10.1007/978-981-15-0069-5_10.

16. Boudreau, K. (2010). Open platform strategies and innovation: Granting access vs. devolving control. *Management Science, 56*, 1849–1872. https://doi.org/10.1287/mnsc.1100.1215

17. Godin, V. V., & Terekhova, A. E. (2020). Digital ecosystems as a form of modern business transformation. *CEUR Workshop Proceedings, 2570*, 1–7.

18. de Reuver, M., Sørensen, C., & Basole, R. C. (2018). The digital platform: A research agenda. *Journal of Information Technology, 33*, 124–135. https://doi.org/10.1057/s41265-016-0033-3

19. Moore, J. F. (1993). A new ecology of competition. *Harvard Business Review, 71*, 75–86.

20. Moore, J. F. (1996). *The death of competition: Leadership and strategy in the age of business ecosystems*. Wiley Harper Business.

21. Briscoe, G., Sadedin, S., & De Wilde, P. (2011). Digital ecosystems: Ecosystem-oriented architectures. *Natural Computing, 10*, 1143–1194. https://doi.org/10.1007/s11047-011-9254-0

22. Iansiti, M., & Levien, R. (2004). Strategy as ecology. *Harvard Business Review, 82*(68—78), 126.

23. Iansiti, M., & Levien, R. (2004). *The keystone advantage: What the new dynamics of business ecosystems mean for strategy, innovation, and sustainability*. Presented at the.

24. Nachira, F., Dini, P., & Nicolai, A. (2007). A network of digital business ecosystems for Europe: Roots, processes and perspectives. *European Commission Information Society and Media* (pp. 5–24).

25. Adner, R. (2017). Ecosystem as structure: An actionable construct for strategy. *Journal of Management, 43*, 39–58. https://doi.org/10.1177/0149206316678451

26. Halaweh, M. (2013). Emerging technology: What is it? *Journal of Technology Management & Innovation, 8*, 108–115. https://doi.org/10.4067/s0718-27242013000400010

27. Pagoropoulos, A., Pigosso, D. C. A., & McAloone, T. C. (2017). The emergent role of digital technologies in the circular economy: A review. *Procedia CIRP, 64*, 19–24. https://doi.org/10.1016/j.procir.2017.02.047

28. Ardolino, M., Rapaccini, M., Saccani, N., Gaiardelli, P., & Ruggeri, C. (2017). The role of digital technologies for the service transformation of industrial companies. *International Journal of Production Research, 7543*. https://doi.org/10.1080/00207543.2017.1324224

29. Han, L., Haleem, M. S., Sobeih, T., Liu, Y., Soroka, A., & Han, L. (2018). An automated cloud-based big data analytics platform for customer insights. In *Proceedings of 2017 IEEE International Conference Internet Things. IEEE Green Computing and Communications. IEEE Cyber, Physical and Social Computing. IEEE Smart Data, iThings-GreenCom-CPSCom-SmartData 2017*. 2018-January, 287–292 doi:https://doi.org/10.1109/iThings-GreenCom-CPSCom-SmartData.2017.48.

30. Soroka, A., Liu, Y., Han, L., & Salman, M. (2017). Big data driven customer insights for SMEs in redistributed manufacturing. *Procedia CIRP, 63*, 692–697. https://doi.org/10.1016/j.procir.2017.03.319

31. Aria, M., & Cuccurullo, C. (2017). bibliometrix: An R-tool for comprehensive science mapping analysis. *Journal of Informetrics, 11*, 959–975. https://doi.org/10.1016/j.joi.2017.08.007

32. Noyons, E. C. M., Moed, H. F., & Luwel, M. (1999). Combining mapping and citation analysis for evaluative bibliometric purposes: A bibliometric study. *Journal of the American Society for Information Science, 50*, 115–131. https://doi.org/10.1002/(sici)1097-4571(1999)50:2<115::aid-asi3>3.3.co;2-a

33. Raan, T. (2005). Van: Measuring science. In: *Handbook of quantitative science and technology research*. doi:https://doi.org/10.1007/1-4020-2755-9.

34. Cobo, M. J., López-Herrera, A. G., Herrera-Viedma, E., & Herrera, F. (2011). An approach for detecting, quantifying, and visualizing the evolution of a research field: A practical application to the Fuzzy Sets Theory field. *Journal of Informetrics, 5*, 146–166. https://doi.org/10.1016/j.joi.2010.10.002

35. Za, S., & Braccini, A. M. (2017). Tracing the roots of the organizational benefits of IT services. *Lecture Notes in Business Information Processing, 279*, 3–11. https://doi.org/10.1007/978-3-319-56925-3_1

36. Zupic, I., & Čater, T. (2015). Bibliometric methods in management and organization. *Organizational Research Methods, 18*, 429–472. https://doi.org/10.1177/1094428114562629

37. Rai, A., Patnayakuni, R., & Seth, N. (2006). Firm performance impacts of digitally enabled supply chain integration capabilities. *MIS Quarterly: Management Information Systems, 30*, 225–246. https://doi.org/10.2307/25148729

38. Deloitte: *What is digital economy? Unicorns, transformation and the internet of things*. https://www2.deloitte.com/mt/en/pages/technology/articles/mt-what-is-digital-economy.html.

39. Narasimhan, R. (1983). The socioeconomic significance of information technology to developing countries. *The Information Society, 2*, 65–79.

40. Bukht, R., & Heeks, R. (2018). Defining, conceptualising and measuring the digital economy. *International Organisations Research Journal, 13*, 143–172. https://doi.org/10.17323/1996-7845-2018-02-07

41. Elmasry, T., Barnickel, N., Dib, H., & Bansal, A. (2016). Digital Middle East: Transforming the region into a leading digital economy. *Digital McKinsey, 10*, 1–66.

42. Burtch, G., Carnahan, S., & Greenwood, B. N. (2018). Can you gig it? An empirical examination of the gig economy and entrepreneurial activity. *Management Science, 5497–5520*. https://doi.org/10.1287/mnsc.2017.2916

43. Gorog, G. (2016). The definitions of sharing economy. *Management, 13*, 175–189.

44. Sutherland, W., & Jarrahi, M. H. (2018). The sharing economy and digital platforms: A review and research agenda. *International Journal of Information Management, 43*, 328–341. https://doi.org/10.1016/j.ijinfomgt.2018.07.004

45. Tan, Z. M., Aggarwal, N., Cowls, J., Morley, J., Taddeo, M., & Floridi, L. (2021). The ethical debate about the gig economy: A review and critical analysis. *Technology in Society, 65*, 101594. https://doi.org/10.1016/j.techsoc.2021.101594

46. von Briel, F., Davidsson, P., & Recker, J. (2018). Digital technologies as external enablers of new venture creation in the it hardware sector. *Entrepreneurship Theory and Practice, 42*, 47–69. https://doi.org/10.1177/1042258717732779
47. Elia, G., Margherita, A., & Passiante, G. (2020). Digital entrepreneurship ecosystem: How digital technologies and collective intelligence are reshaping the entrepreneurial process. *Technological Forecasting and Social Change, 150*, 119791. https://doi.org/10.1016/j.techfore.2019.119791
48. WEF - World Economic Forum. (2016). *The Fourth Industrial Revolution: What it means, how to respond.* www.weforum.org.
49. European Commission. (2017). *Digital Transformation Scoreboard 2017.* https://ec.europa.eu/growth/tools-databases/dem/monitor/scoreboard

Entrepreneurial Narcissism in Smart Cities: The Moderating Role of Bonding and Bridging Social Capital

Rebecca Trivelli ⓘ, Francesca Masciarelli ⓘ, and Simona Leonelli ⓘ

Abstract The process of digitization over the years has increasingly taken hold in various areas of our daily lives. When talking about digitization, it is impossible not to talk about smart cities as the two phenomena are linked. Smart cities are supported by digitalization and technological innovations leading to future environmental, social, and financial benefits. The result of digitization in smart cities can be measured by the increase in the quality of life of citizens thus providing a return on the investments made. Digital transformation has enabled smart cities to gain knowledge and understanding of critical issues thus obtaining a competitive advantage over non-digitalized cities. In this paper, we consider the impact of people at the city level focusing on the importance of entrepreneurs' personality traits. Entrepreneurs, through their activity and thanks to their charisma, can bring innovations to the territory. Among the personality traits studied in the literature, we focus on narcissism, considering the positive and negative aspects of this personality trait. Moreover, we also focus on social capital positively influences innovative acquisitions, the geographical location of the entrepreneur is a key factor, that characterizes the performance of the innovative entrepreneurial activity.

Keywords Digitalization · Smart cities · Narcissism · Bonding and bridging social capital · Ethics

R. Trivelli (✉) · F. Masciarelli
University "G. D'Annunzio" of Chieti-Pescara, Pescara, Italy
e-mail: rebecca.trivelli@unich.it; francesca.masciarelli@unich.it

S. Leonelli
Università degli Studi di Modena e Reggio Emilia, Modena, Italy
e-mail: simona.leonelli@unimore.it

A. Lazazzara et al. (eds.), *Towards Digital and Sustainable Organisations*, Lecture Notes in Information Systems and Organisation 65, https://doi.org/10.1007/978-3-031-52880-4_17

1   Introduction

In recent years, many municipalities are focusing on developing smart cities [1]. Smart cities are considered those cities that employ various digital and electronic technologies to transform living environments with information and communication technologies (ICTs) to meet the needs of markets or citizens [2, 3]. Some scholars claim that a city is smart when investments are made in human and social capital and traditional (transport) and modern infrastructure [4] through digital technologies (ICT) [5, 6] fuel sustainable economic growth and high quality of life [4, 7]. Smart cities aim to improve cities' socio-economic, ecological, logistical, and competitive performance. These smart cities are based on a mix of human capital, social capital, and entrepreneurial capital, infrastructures, and are the result of knowledge-intensive strategies [8]. Thus, the process of digitization has increasingly taken hold over the years in various areas of our daily lives [9, 10]. Another important phenomenon that arises with the advent of smart cities is ethics. It is crucial to consider the ethical aspects linked to the analysis and use of data and if and how these data are protected by privacy legislation.

The aim of this article is to propose a new theoretical framework that describes how entrepreneurs' personality traits (i.e., narcissism) affect digitalization levels and ethics in smart cities, considering even the moderator role of social capital.

Smart cities could be considered entrepreneurial cities [11], entrepreneurs initiate technological interventions in their firms that help cities undergo socio-technical transitions and become smart cities. Moreover, technologies adopted in cities generate data which then helps firms to explore new opportunities [11]. According to the Upper Echelon theory [12], the personality of entrepreneurs strongly affects their behavior and strategic choices. For these reasons is crucial to study their impact. According to some authors, narcissists thanks to their art of rhetoric can persuade and influence others, and this allows them to improve their levels of creativity and innovation [13].

We also investigate the role of social capital in cities. Social capital is "the sum of the resources, real or virtual, to which an individual or a group is entitled by possessing a durable network of more or less institutionalized relations of knowledge and mutual recognition" [14]. The concept of social capital refers to the relationships between people in a community [15]. In this paper, the focus will be on the bonding e bridging features of social capital. Previous studies state that social capital is present geographically from cities [16] to regions [17, 18], and finally to nations [19, 20]. Social capital has become an important consideration in smart city planning policy [21]. It enhances the spillover effect of advanced technology by generating a positive effect on urban innovation output from smart cities [22].

Through the analysis of existing literature, it was possible to identify the gap, as there are no studies at the level of smart cities regarding the narcissism of entrepreneurs operating in smart cities, considering digitization and ethics and the moderating role of social capital. This study contributes to the literature underling the importance of the implementation of the territory's wealth, through policies suitable to encourage entrepreneurship and innovation while limiting unethical and unfair attitudes [23].

In the following paragraphs, we review the literature and, based on it, we outline our propositions for future research.

2 Methodology

In our work, a thorough literature review was conducted, which allows for the collection and synthesis of previous research [24, 25], thus allowing for the identification of a possible gap within the literature or the justification for its expansion and deepening [26].

Analysis of the literature related to smart cities, focusing on digitization and ethics, narcissism, and social capital, with a particular focus on linking and bridging aspects.

The literature review was conducted using Google Scholar, as it possesses a huge number of papers surpassing the scientific literature databases of other search engines such as Web of Sciences or Scopus, despite the possible loss of quality due to the high numbers of papers present [27]. The search strategy we followed consisted of two steps.

Firstly, we identified appropriate keywords to search the online database (e.g., smart cities, digitization, ethics, narcissism, social capital, bonding social capital) thus extracting a large set of documents, including journals, books, and conferences, without placing any limits on the database for searching.

Second, based on the study of Meier [28], we have identified three criteria to select the papers to be inserted in our literature review: (1) we included only papers using the English language[1]; (2) we included all documents published in the last 60 years; (3) al articles must be published in peer-reviewed journals with the highest impact factor in the field.

After carefully examining the papers (reading abstracts, methodology, conclusions, and practical implications), we selected 127 papers from books and articles.

Based on the literature review, we put forward some propositions that will be discussed in the article. First, we will analyze the relationship between entrepreneurial narcissism and smart cities (distinguish between digitalization and ethical aspects). Second, we will propose a moderator role of social capital in the above relationships distinguishing between bonding and bridging social capital.

---

[1] We made only one exception including the Meijer and Rodríguez Bolívar (2016) paper that is in French. This is because it has a huge number of citations (1307 quotations) and represents a focal paper in our literature analysis.

3   Literature Review and Propositions

3.1   Smart Cities: A New Way to Conceive Cities

Recent years have witnessed the phenomenon of population migration from rural to urban areas, thus leading to the need for new innovative methods to manage the new urban development. The transformation of metropolises into smart cities to bring improvements to their citizens has become essential [29]. Many municipalities are focusing on developing smart cities through investments and innovations, the implementation of technology, and the use of data for a greater focus on citizens and related social issues and urban development [1, 30].

The concept of smart cities first appeared in the early 1990s. It was born out of the advent of urbanization and the resulting problems of modern cities due to the development of new technologies [31]. However, there is still no single definition of a smart city [32] as there are numerous entities involved for there to be a smart city. In this paper, smart cities are considered cities employing various digital and electronic technologies to transform living environments with information and communication technologies (ICTs) to meet the needs of markets [33] or citizens [2, 3]. According to Washburn [34], smart cities apply intelligent information technologies to infrastructural components, in which hardware, software, and network technologies are integrated. Sensors, electronics, and networks should interface with computer systems, including databases and algorithms for tracking, helping real-time decision-making, and bringing innovative solutions and opportunities [3, 35, 36].

Smart cities' goals are twofold: first, to make better use of public resources such as reducing emissions, smarter the urban transport networks, improving water supply and waste disposal facilities, and making efficient lighting and heating of buildings; second, to improve the quality of life and services offered such as safer public spaces and meeting the needs of an aging population [3, 29]. These goals will reduce the operating costs of public administration and accelerate economic growth and urban competitiveness [37].

Cities are faced with the need to continuously develop in an integrated world with speed [38], having to adapt to the ever-changing environment [39], a city model where technology is at the service of the individual [40]. According to the literature, in the context of smart cities, there is an overemphasis on technology, which plays a central role in smart cities but is not capable on its own of creating value for citizens. That is why human beings are indispensable for implementing smart actions in everyday life, we talk about smart people in smart cities. People, technology, and strategic vision are necessary components for a successful smart program [41–43].

It will require the commitment of public organizations, the state, citizens, and private businesses to achieve sustainability, disaster prevention, business, public safety, and improved quality of life [44].

"No one can oppose the evolution of smart cities if this evolution provides more effective solutions to a whole range of social problems. Smart technologies and smart partnerships are needed to have an educated population and effective institutions to meet the challenges of modern cities" [45].

This paper will focus on two smart cities' characteristics: digitalization and ethics that we will explore in detail in the following two paragraphs.

Digitalization and Smart Cities A smart city must foremost be digital [46]. Smart cities are supported by digitization and technological innovations leading to future environmental, social, and financial benefits [47]. Digitization consists of techniques to improve social and institutional contexts through the adoption or increased use of digital or information technology [47, 48].

Digitalization in smart cities should follow three precise paths in order to be efficient: the first includes the correct use of all the tools that allow data creation. This implies equipping infrastructures (i.e., buildings, transport, and green zones) with sensors (i.e., cameras) for data collection. The second is related to how collected data are communicated thanks to the use of the Internet. Finally, the third path is associated with the ability to manage and interpret collected data to be helpful in smart cities [46].

Information technology changes current urban processes such as transport, health, education, governance, energy, and waste management and is considered a critical factor in the digitization process. Urban services through digitization and their technologies are optimized, creating added value for citizens through the services provided with coordination between different smart services [47, 49].

Digitization allows a large degree of interactivity between users and information. In addition, the control of information obtained through digitization is facilitated as data can be transferred easily [50]. The outcome of digitization in smart cities can be measured through the increase in the quality of life of citizens, thus providing a return on investment [6]. In addition, digital transformation has enabled smart cities to gain knowledge and understanding of critical issues, thus achieving a competitive advantage over non-digitalized cities.

Ethics and Smart Cities Smart cities are based on collecting and using data through intelligent information system technologies [51], making internal operations efficient [52, 53]. However, this massive presence of digitization leaves some doubts about protecting the privacy and security of the population's data and the possible inequalities.

Ethical aspects linked to the analysis and use of data should be considered. Ethics is defined as "an analysis of conduct that may cause benefit or harm to others" [52, 54]. Ethics leads to a breakdown of what is right and what is wrong. Ethical theories or frameworks can enable individuals and organizations to make logical, reasoned, and persuasive decisions [52]. However, embedding ethics in the context of data proves complex, as the legal framework surrounding data analytics operations is often not mature and sometimes not in line with clients' ethical values [52, 55].

With urban big data, companies and governments are constantly working on the data of our daily lives, which can be converted into insights and understandings of individuals and organizations through data analysis [43]. Therefore, ethical issues arise regarding privacy, datafication, dataveillance, and geo-surveillance. Anonymity is a fundamental and necessary approach to protecting personal privacy [52]. Datafication indicates that people are subjected to higher levels of data analysis, even in simple everyday gestures. Dataveillance refers to a mode of surveillance implemented through the generation and sorting of datasets to identify, monitor, track, regulate, predict, and prescribe the behavior of people [56, 57]. Finally, geo-surveillance monitors the location and movement of people, vehicles, goods, and services and the tracking of interactions in space [57, 58]. Other aspects to consider are the use of technology for the transfer of personal information. The exchange of personal information reduces informational inequality, but at the same time produces ethical problems in information disclosure. Invasion of the personal sphere can also occur when information is used to interfere with personal life, influencing decision-making [52, 59]. In fact, ethical issues arise when we consider the data protection consent of many people, such as in the case of urban data in smart cities. Requesting consent from all citizens is quite impossible during data collection and processing. Therefore, the number of privacy agreements is too large to be controlled by individuals in big data circumstances [52, 60].

For these reasons, smart cities should include morals sense through a code of ethics and conduct, an ethics committee, an ethics audit, and an accountability report [61], which could benefit the development of smart cities by giving more trust to citizens.

3.2 Personality Traits and Smart Cities: The Impact of Entrepreneurs' Narcissism

In this paper, we consider the impact of people at the city level focusing on the importance of entrepreneurs' personality traits. According to Penco et colleagues (2020) [62], entrepreneurs have a strong impact on smart cities, particularly on the way people work and live in cities. In fact, entrepreneurs create job opportunities, healthy competition, an inclusive society, and economic growth [62]. Entrepreneurs bring innovations to the territory [63]. However, entrepreneurs' personality traits strongly affect their choices. Personality traits explain why people behave in different ways in front of the same situation [64]. Previous studies show that personality traits affect the entrepreneurial process [65, 66], such as opportunity recognition [13, 67, 68] or career intention [66, 69]. Predominantly, studies have focused on the positive aspects of personality, but in recent years, the dark side of individuals' personalities (e.g., narcissism, Machiavellianism, and psychopathy) has also been addressed [70]. Among the personality traits studied in the literature, we focus on narcissism. Narcissists have a positive view of themselves, admiration, and self-love [13]. Only in extreme cases, narcissism is considered a pathology however, in this paper, we will consider narcissism as a personality trait of the entrepreneur.

According to some authors, narcissists thanks to their art of rhetoric can persuade and influence others, and this allows them to improve their levels of creativity and innovation [64] Moreover, narcissists through social relationships and their status try to gain power [71], narcissists according to studies are considered charismatic subjects and this characteristic allows them to acquire resources from their environment, to have critical skills for the process of creating new ventures [72–74]. Narcissists can bring benefits to organizations due to their visionary and innovative qualities [64, 75–77]. Given the characteristics of the narcissist, it is possible to state that they are attracted to and seek fame and power thinking they are special and unique [78–82], seeking attention and admiration from others [64, 83]. Further studies show a dual correlation with performance, one positive [84] and another negative [85] as narcissists can make a good first impression [86], and over time they exhibit unpleasant behaviors leading to difficulties in maintaining a favorable reputation [74, 87, 88].

Entrepreneurs' narcissism can be studied considering two sides: the visionary and the manipulative sides. The visionary side enables narcissistic entrepreneurs to identify and exploit opportunities, generating important results for the company [76]. In addition, curiosity and perseverance drive entrepreneurs to be more innovative than non-narcissistic entrepreneurs [64, 75] developing new products, new operational initiatives, and new projects [64]. On the contrary, the manipulative side of narcissistic entrepreneurs refers to their ability to control events and people [13]. In order to not lose the admiration of others, they prefer to not undertake high-risk activities and pursue activities only with potential gains [13, 89]. Unlike the exhibitionist side of narcissism, the manipulative side of narcissism constrains the innovativeness of the company and its growth as it will not consider other people's opinions [76] and will try to influence other individuals with its ideas and opinions, generating a single groupthink within the company [90] generating a negative effect on the company [13].

However, to the best of our knowledge, no studies investigated the relationship between entrepreneurs' narcissism and the development of smart cities considering digitalization and ethical features. Therefore, we propose a positive relationship between the visionary side of narcissistic entrepreneurs and digitalization. In particular, the visionary side can push them to consider and implement innovative ideas, be always first, and contribute more prominently to the development of the smart city from a digitalization point of view. On the contrary, the manipulative side of entrepreneurs' narcissism can negatively affect their ethical decisions. In detail, the narcissists' manipulative side can push them to consider an easier way to reach goals than the more ethical ones

Accordingly, we expect that:

P_1: Entrepreneurs' narcissism has a positive relation with digitalization.
P_2: Entrepreneurs' narcissism has a negative relation with ethics.

3.3   *Social Capital Resource*

According to the literature, it is stated that social capital positively influences innovative acquisitions [91] and is defined as "the sum of the resources, real or virtual, to which an individual or a group is entitled by possessing a durable network of more or less institutionalized relations of knowledge and mutual recognition" [14]. Social capital refers to relationships and the intrinsic goods of these relationships such as trust, reliability, and solidarity [92, 93]. Social relations are considered key factors in gaining a competitive advantage [94] such as innovative acquisitions. Social capital is also defined as those network advantages available to an actor within a social context [18, 95].

Social capital is defined by the philosopher Albert O Hirschman as a "moral resource", which is a resource whose supply increases rather than decreases through use and which is exhausted if not used. Social capital can be the basis of progress, where relationships are based on reciprocity, the network that is created facilitates coordination and communication and helps in the transfer of information on the reliability of individuals. Successful collaboration is an effort that nurtures connection and trust [18].

The literature highlights various dimensions of social capital [91]. However, social capital implies advantages and disadvantages and can be defined as a two-sided currency [96]. There is a distinction between bonding and bridging social capital [15]. There is also a need for a balance between bridging and bonding ties [97].

Authors such as Burt [98] and Coleman [95] have opposite visions of social capital, considering a closed network and a network with structural (open) holes. A closed network generates benefits for the community, while an open network with structural holes allows greater competitiveness through the exchange of information from outside.

Bridging social capital is defined as the bond that is established in an open, outward-looking context [15]. Generating a positive effect for innovative acquisitions due to the link and interdependence with other firms but with the possibility of generating non-redundant information (negative effect) [91]. It also generates additional positive aspects such as the existence of technology brokers who facilitate entrepreneurship and innovation [98] who act as mediators of relevant information [99], generating open-mindedness and integration of marginalized groups [100]. At the same time, it also generates other negative effects such as the emergence of subgroups of dissatisfied actors that erode existing organizational structures [94] and the low relevance of shared information for the broad aggregate [101].

Bonding social capital is the bond that is established within a group, strengthening it (positive effect) [92] but limiting (negative effect) innovative transfer and acquisition. In addition, bonding social capital generates many positive effects as the coalescence of goals [102], the respect of common norms [103], greater ease in sharing information [104], and finally the high relevance of shared information for the large aggregate [105]. Negative effects will include the closure of the network to new information [106] and resources controlled by common norms, not by economic rationality [104].

The literature affirms that these two types of social capital, bridging, and bonding, can influence the performance of innovative acquisitions [107]. According to the literature, bridging social capital helps the recognition of the market opportunity, and bonding social capital is used for the implementation and commercialization phase of an innovative idea [107]. Moreover, social capital can benefit both the community (a vision of the collective good) [108] and individuals (a private point of view) [98, 109]. Authors such as Coleman (1990) [110], Putnam et al. 1993 [18], and Fukuyama 1995 [111] affirm that social capital is considered a public good and everyone in each social community can benefit from social capital. Collective social capital creates the relationships between people [95] and is lost when these relationships between people dissolve [98]. The creation of these relationships is called hole bridges [98, 112]. Generate resource exchanges by increasing the efficiency and effectiveness of communication flow and information exchange [112]. The literature considers social capital as a geographically bound phenomenon that is a community rather than an asset of a single actor [18].

The entrepreneur's investment in social relations is also considered in the entrepreneurship literature. Entrepreneurs generally consult within their relationship networks to obtain resources and knowledge [113, 114], so an entrepreneur's social capital has consequences for businesses [115].

Social Capital: Local and Smart Cities Social capital positively affects innovative entrepreneurial activity [23]. Social capital is deeply rooted in local, institutional, historical, and cultural foundations [116], nevertheless, it is possible to have a greater or lesser presence of social capital depending on the areas taken into consideration [23]. Therefore, the geographical location according to literature determines the performance of an entrepreneur [117–119], and how territory and social capital are vital to maintain competitiveness and promote local growth [18, 120]. The presence of social capital will provide connectivity and communication. Successful innovations are enabled by social capital, which will act as a bridge between the various stakeholders [121, 122], creating trust and reliability, thus enabling the entrepreneur to maintain the relationship [123, 124]. A geographical area rich in social capital will have a shared language and communication codes that facilitate the creation and dissemination of knowledge. Mutual understanding between individuals is facilitated by sharing the same localized communication codes and a common language facilitates [23] being able to more easily transfer ideas, share information, and discuss possible problems [93], as to bring solutions.

Previous studies state that social capital is present geographically from cities [16] to regions [17, 18] and finally to nations [19, 20]. Product innovation will be the result of geographically localized social capital. The ability of firms to innovate according to the literature is determined by geographically bound social capital, as it is considered a transmitter of knowledge within geographically bound areas [125]. Open Innovation [126] stems from the need for information and knowledge. Innovation requires heterogeneous, new, and existing knowledge located inside and outside the company. Research shows that companies' innovation processes depend on external actors, such as users, suppliers, universities, and competitors [127–129]. High levels of social interaction fostered by social capital provide informational benefits, and the opportunity to obtain valuable information [98]. Thus, gaining an advantage in the innovative acquisition, implementation, and commercialization in the market. As mentioned above, the role of social capital geographically has different levels of aggregation, and in this paper, we are going to focus on the cities [16], in particular on smart cities.

Smart cities rely on having a variety of creative talents and can offer new and sustainable solutions [8]. According to recent studies, in Japan, there is low social inequality, indicators of bonding and bridging have been examined and it has been defined that each category of social capital is a characteristic of social organizations shown by the combination of three dimensions: 'trust', 'network' and 'norms', which can improve social efficiency by encouraging coordinated actions between individuals. these studies argue that strengthening social capital would revitalize the region with civic activities [21].

The Global Happiness Council in its 2018 report, identified national happiness according to various conditions including social capital. The Cabinet Office of Japan proposed the happiness index in the formulation of a "new growth strategy", which is partially linked to social capital [130]. The concept of social capital refers to the relationships between people in a community [15]. Thus, in this case, social capital has been used as a policy tool for good community management, but also as a performance indicator to check the effects of management policy [21]. Regional efforts toward smart cities can increase residents' happiness [130]. Social capital is used as an indicator to estimate happiness [131] and networking activities [23]. In this case, social capital represents a tool to facilitate community management [132], and smart city efforts are set to continue to accelerate.

Social capital has become an important consideration in smart city planning policy [21]. It enhances the spillover effect of advanced technology by generating a positive effect on urban innovation output from smart cities [22].

Accordingly, we expect that:

P_3: The bonding feature of social capital negatively moderates the relationship between entrepreneurs' narcissism and digitalization.

P_4: The bonding feature of social capital positively moderates the relationship between entrepreneurs' narcissism and ethics.

P_5: The bridging feature of social capital positively moderates the relationship between entrepreneurs' narcissism and digitalization.

P_6: The bridging feature of social capital positively moderates the relationship between entrepreneurs' narcissism and ethics.

In conclusion, all the previously identified relationships enable us to draft the analytical model (Fig. 1).

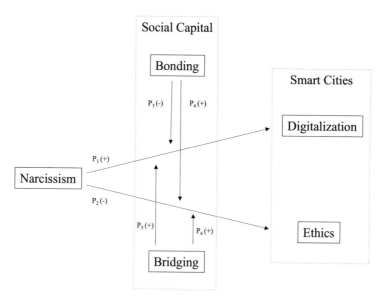

Fig. 1 Analytical model

4 Discussion and Implications

The present study contributes to the existing literature on entrepreneurs' personalities (i.e., narcissism) focusing on the smart city context.

Through the study of the existing literature, we create an ambitious analytical model (Fig. 1) and derive prepositions for future research. Starting from the assumption that entrepreneurs bring innovations to the territory [133], and the choices of each entrepreneur derived from their personality traits, we state that entrepreneurs' narcissism affects innovation positively (acquiring the right resources from the environment and creating new companies and propensity to digitalization) and negatively (manipulation, unethical actions) in some aspects.

Additionally, a pivotal element of our work is social capital, which generates positive effects on entrepreneurship and innovation [13]. Through the presence of bridging and bonding social capital, it is possible to moderate the negative effects of the manipulative narcissist with unethical behavior within smart cities and moderator the aspect of ethics and digitization.

A primary theoretical contribution of this paper is to consider the narcissistic entrepreneur in a smart city context, highlighting how this personality trait can incentivize innovation, a key factor for a city to be smart.

Secondly, we contribute to the literature on narcissism by considering the positive (innovation and digitization) and negative (manipulative aspect) effects in relation to social capital that will help to limit the unethical and incorrect aspects of manipulative entrepreneurship and incentivize innovativeness.

Thirdly, we contribute to the literature on social capital with its moderating role within smart cities in relation to the narcissistic entrepreneur, limiting unethical effects and stimulating innovation and digitization. We highlight how social capital can play a key role within smart cities, as it is used as a city-level indicator to assess citizens' happiness.

Finally, the aim is to create a bridge between the three literatures: smart city, narcissism, and social capital.

Moreover, our study has also practical implications for policymakers and educators.

Policymakers need to recognize the importance of the entrepreneur's personality traits and skills, which can influence the course of innovation at the local level (cities).

In addition, policymakers must give more importance to social capital through which the innovative aspect can be amplified, and the unethical aspect limited.

Universities educators should also develop courses in which they study the personality traits of entrepreneurs.

5 Conclusion

With this theoretical work, we want to analyze the relationship between narcissistic entrepreneurs in smart cities and what role social capital plays, also comparing bridging and bonding social capital with narcissistic entrepreneurs, ethics, and digitalization.

The trait of narcissism in the entrepreneur in relation to smart cities, digitization, social capital, and ethics can generate a positive or negative influence.

A primary theoretical contribution of this work was a positive view of the capabilities of narcissistic entrepreneurs, i.e., the positive influence on innovativeness and digitization and a negative relationship about ethics due to the manipulative behavior that reflects being narcissistic.

Also considered in the paper is the role played by both bridging and bonding social capital, as moderate, about narcissism, ethics, and digitization, thus providing input to policymakers and other authors for future research and input on possible investors.

The limitation of this paper is that it is a theoretical paper and there are no empirical data, it is hoped that it will be used for future research.

References

1. Bosdriesz, Y., Van Sinderen, M., Iacob, M., & Verkroost, P. (2018). A building information model-centered big data platform to support digital transformation in the construction industry. In *Enterprise interoperability: Smart services and business impact of enterprise interoperability*. (pp. 209–215). doi:https://doi.org/10.1002/9781119564034.ch26.
2. Chamran, M. K., Yau, K. L. A., Noor, R. M. D., & Wong, R. (2020). A distributed testbed for 5G scenarios: An experimental study. *Sensors (Switzerland), 20*, 18. https://doi.org/10.3390/s20010018
3. Lai, C. S., Jia, Y., Dong, Z., Wang, D., Tao, Y., Lai, Q. H., Wong, R. T. K., Zobaa, A. F., Wu, R., & Lai, L. L. (2020). A review of technical standards for smart cities. *Clean Technologies, 2*. https://doi.org/10.3390/cleantechnol2030019
4. Caragliu, A., del Bo, C., & Nijkamp, P. (2011). Smart cities in Europe. *Journal of Urban Technology, 18*. https://doi.org/10.1080/10630732.2011.601117
5. Batty, M., Axhausen, K. W., Giannotti, F., Pozdnoukhov, A., Bazzani, A., Wachowicz, M., Ouzounis, G., & Portugali, Y. (2012). Smart cities of the future. *European Physical Journal Special Topics, 214*. https://doi.org/10.1140/epjst/e2012-01703-3
6. Serrano, W. (2018). Digital systems in smart city and infrastructure: Digital as a service. *Smart Cities, 1*, 134–154. https://doi.org/10.3390/smartcities1010008
7. Ylipulli, J., & Luusua, A. (2020). Smart cities with a Nordic twist? Public sector digitalization in Finnish data-rich cities. *Telematics and Informatics, 55*, 101457. https://doi.org/10.1016/j.tele.2020.101457
8. Kourtit, K., & Nijkamp, P. (2012). Smart cities in the innovation age. *Innovation: The European Journal of Social Science Research, 25*, 93–95. https://doi.org/10.1080/13511610.2012.660331
9. Gray, J., & Rumpe, B. (2015). Models for digitalization. *Software and Systems Modeling, 14*, 1319–1320. https://doi.org/10.1007/s10270-015-0494-9
10. Hellsten, P., & Paunu, A. (2020). Digitalization: A concept easier to talk about than to understand. In: *IC3K 2020- Proceedings of the 12th international joint conference on knowledge discovery, knowledge engineering and knowledge management*. doi:https://doi.org/10.5220/0010145302260233.
11. Kummitha, R. K. R. (2019). Smart cities and entrepreneurship: An agenda for future research. *Technological Forecasting and Social Change, 149*, 119763. https://doi.org/10.1016/j.techfore.2019.119763
12. Hambrick, D. C., & Mason, P. A. (1984). Hambrick 1984--UpperEchelons__TheOrganizationasaReflectionofItsTopManagers.pdf.
13. Leonelli, S., Masciarelli, F., & Fontana, F. (2019). The impact of personality traits and abilities on entrepreneurial orientation in SMEs. *Journal of Small Business and Entrepreneurship, 6331*. https://doi.org/10.1080/08276331.2019.1666339
14. Bourdieu, P., & Wacquant, L. J. (1992). *The purpose of reflexive sociology*. The Chicago Workshop.
15. Alone, B. (2001). *Bowling alone: The collapse and revival of American Community*, by Robert Putnam. Simon & Schuster, 2000. Policy (pp. 124–129).
16. Jacobs, J. (1961). *The death and Life of Great American cities*. Randoms House, New York. B. Unpubl. Resour.
17. Beugelsdijk, S., & Van Schaik, T. (2005). Differences in social capital between 54 Western European regions. *Regional Studies, 39*. https://doi.org/10.1080/00343400500328040
18. Putnam, R. (1993). The prosperous community: Social capital and public life. *The American Prospect, 4*.
19. Knack, S., & Keefer, P. (1997). Does social capital have an economic payoff? A cross-country investigation. *The Quarterly Journal of Economics, 112*. https://doi.org/10.1162/003355300555475

20. Zak, P. J., & Knack, S. (2001). Trust and growth. *The Econometrics Journal, 111*. https://doi. org/10.1111/1468-0297.00609
21. Nakano, S., & Washizu, A. (2021). Will smart cities enhance the social capital of residents? The importance of smart neighborhood management. *Cities, 115*, 103244. https://doi. org/10.1016/j.cities.2021.103244
22. Caragliu, A., & Del, C. F. (2018). Technological forecasting & social change smart innovative cities: The impact of Smart City policies on urban innovation. *Technological Forecasting and Social Change, 142*.
23. Masciarelli, F. (2011). *The strategic value of social capital: How firms capitalize on social assets.*
24. Baumeister, R. F., & Leary, M. R. (1997). Writing narrative literature reviews. *Review of General Psychology, 1*, 311–320. https://doi.org/10.1037/1089-2680.1.3.311
25. Tranfield, D., Denyer, D., & Smart, P. (2003). Towards a methodology for developing evidence-informed management knowledge by means of systematic review. *British Journal of Management, 14*, 207–222. https://doi.org/10.1111/1467-8551.00375
26. Snyder, H. (2019). Literature review as a research methodology: An overview and guidelines. *Journal of Business Research, 104*, 333–339. https://doi.org/10.1016/j.jbusres.2019.07.039
27. Halevi, G., Moed, H., & Bar-Ilan, J. (2017). Suitability of Google Scholar as a source of scientific information and as a source of data for scientific evaluation—Review of the Literature. *Journal of Informetrics, 11*, 823–834. https://doi.org/10.1016/j.joi.2017.06.005
28. Meier, M. (2011). Knowledge management in strategic alliances: A review of empirical evidence. *International Journal of Management Reviews, 13*, 1–23. https://doi. org/10.1111/j.1468-2370.2010.00287.x
29. Winkowska, J., Szpilko, D., & Pejić, S. (2019). Smart city concept in the light of the literature review. *Engineering Management in Production and Services, 11*(2), 70–86. https://doi. org/10.2478/emj-2019-0012
30. Anthony Jnr, B., Abbas Petersen, S., Ahlers, D., & Krogstie, J. (2020). API deployment for big data management towards sustainable energy prosumption in smart cities-a layered architecture perspective. *International Journal of Sustainable Energy, 39*, 263–289. https://doi. org/10.1080/14786451.2019.1684287
31. Yin, C. T., Xiong, Z., Chen, H., Wang, J. Y., Cooper, D., & David, B. (2015). A literature survey on smart cities. *Science China Information Sciences, 58*, 1–18. https://doi.org/10.1007/ s11432-015-5397-4
32. Vanolo, A. (2014). Smartmentality: The smart city as disciplinary strategy. *Urban Studies, 51*, 883–898. https://doi.org/10.1177/0042098013494427
33. Christofi, M., Iaia, L., Marchesani, F., & Masciarelli, F. (2021). Marketing innovation and internationalization in smart city development: A systematic review, framework and research agenda. *International Marketing Review, 38*, 948–984. https://doi.org/10.1108/ IMR-01-2021-0027
34. Washburn, D., & Sindhu, U. (2009). Helping CIOs understand "Smart City" initiatives. *Growth, 17*.
35. Hall, R. E., Bowerman, B., Braverman, J., Taylor, J., & Todosow, H. (2000). The vision of a smart city. *2nd Interntionl Life … . 28.*
36. Javidroozi, V., Shah, H., Amini, A., & Cole, A. (2014). Smart city as an integrated enterprise: A business process centric framework addressing challenges in systems integration. In: *3rd International conference on smart systems, devices and technologies.* https://doi. org/10.13140/RG.2.1.2561.1921.
37. Abella, A., Ortiz-de-Urbina-Criado, M., & De-Pablos-Heredero, C. (2017). A model for the analysis of data-driven innovation and value generation in smart cities' ecosystems. *Cities, 64*. https://doi.org/10.1016/j.cities.2017.01.011
38. Hämäläinen, M. (2020). A framework for a smart city design: Digital transformation in the Helsinki Smart City. In: *Contributions to management science.* doi:https://doi. org/10.1007/978-3-030-23604-5_5.

39. Babar, Z., & Yu, E. (2015). Enterprise architecture in the age of digital transformation. In: *Lecture Notes in Business Information Processing*. doi:https://doi.org/10.1007/978-3-319-19243-7_40.

40. Lazaroiu, G. C., & Roscia, M. (2012). Definition methodology for the smart cities model. *Energy, 47*. https://doi.org/10.1016/j.energy.2012.09.028

41. Suppa, A., & Zardini, A. (2011). The implementation of a performance management system in the Italian army. In *Communications in Computer and Information Science 210 CCIS* (pp. 139–146). doi:https://doi.org/10.1007/978-3-642-23065-3_22.

42. Vakali, A., Angelis, L., & Giatsoglou, M. (2013). Sensors talk and humans sense towards a reciprocal collective awareness smart city framework. In *2013 IEEE international conference on communications work. ICC 2013* (pp. 189–193). doi:https://doi.org/10.1109/ICCW.2013.6649226.

43. Paola, D. R., & Rosenthal-Sabroux, C. (2014). *Smart city how to create public and economic value with high technology in urban space.*

44. Lai, C. S., Jia, Y., Dong, Z., Wang, D., Tao, Y., Lai, Q. H., Wong, R. T. K., Zobaa, A. F., Wu, R., & Lai, L. L. (2020). A review of technical standards for smart cities. *Clean Technologies, 2*, 290–310. https://doi.org/10.3390/cleantechnol2030019

45. Meijer, A., & Rodríguez Bolívar, M. P. (2016). La gouvernance des villes intelligentes. Analyse de la littérature sur la gouvernance urbaine intelligente. *Revue Internationale des Sciences Administratives, 82*, 417–435. https://doi.org/10.3917/risa.822.0417

46. Finger, M., & Razaghi, M. (2017). Conceptualizing "smart cities". *Informatik-Spektrum, 40*, 6–13. https://doi.org/10.1007/s00287-016-1002-5

47. Anthony Jnr, B. (2021). Managing digital transformation of smart cities through enterprise architecture–a review and research agenda. *Enterprise Information Systems, 15*, 299–331. https://doi.org/10.1080/17517575.2020.1812006

48. Seth, H., Talwar, S., Bhatia, A., Saxena, A., & Dhir, A. (2020). Consumer resistance and inertia of retail investors: Development of the resistance adoption inertia continuance (RAIC) framework. *Journal of Retailing and Consumer Services, 55*. https://doi.org/10.1016/j.jretconser.2020.102071

49. Talwar, S., Talwar, M., Kaur, P., & Dhir, A. (2020). Consumers' resistance to digital innovations: A systematic review and framework development. *Australasian Marketing Journal, 28*. https://doi.org/10.1016/j.ausmj.2020.06.014

50. Brennen, J. S., & Kreiss, D. (2015). Digitalization. In *The Routledge reader on the sociology of music* (pp. 329–338). doi:https://doi.org/10.4324/9780203736319-36.

51. Mark, R., & Anya, G. (2019). Ethics of using smart city AI and big data: The case of four large European cities. *Orbit Journal, 2*, 1–36. https://doi.org/10.29297/orbit.v2i2.110

52. Chang, V. (2021). An ethical framework for big data and smart cities. *Technological Forecasting and Social Change, 165*, 120559. https://doi.org/10.1016/j.techfore.2020.120559

53. Stelzer, A., Englert, F., Hörold, S., & Mayas, C. (2016). Improving service quality in public transportation systems using automated customer feedback. *Transportation Research Part E Logistics and Transportation Review, 89*. https://doi.org/10.1016/j.tre.2015.05.010

54. Herschel, R., & Miori, V. M. (2017). Ethics and big data. *Technology in Society, 49*, 31–36. https://doi.org/10.1016/j.techsoc.2017.03.003

55. Vidgen, R., Shaw, S., & Grant, D. B. (2017). Management challenges in creating value from business analytics. *European Journal of Operational Research, 261*. https://doi.org/10.1016/j.ejor.2017.02.023

56. Raley, R. (2013). *Dataveillance and Countervailance.* https://escholarship.org/uc/item/2b12683k

57. Kitchin, R. (2016). The ethics of smart cities and urban science. *Philosophical Transactions of the Royal Society A - Mathematical Physical and Engineering Sciences, 374*. https://doi.org/10.1098/rsta.2016.0115

58. Crampton, J. W. (2003). Cartographic rationality and the politics of geosurveillance and security. *Cartography and Geographic Information Science, 30.* https://doi.org/10.1559/152304003100011108

59. Solove, D. J. (2006). *A taxonomy of privacy.* doi:https://doi.org/10.2307/40041279.

60. Solove, D. J. (2013). Introduction: Privacy self-management and the consent dilemma. *Harvard Law Review, 126,* 1880–1903.

61. Calvo, P. (2020). The ethics of Smart City (EoSC): Moral implications of hyperconnectivity, algorithmization and the datafication of urban digital society. *Ethics and Information Technology, 22,* 141–149. https://doi.org/10.1007/s10676-019-09523-0

62. Penco, L., Ivaldi, E., Bruzzi, C., & Musso, E. (2020). Knowledge-based urban environments and entrepreneurship: Inside EU cities. *Cities, 96,* 102443. https://doi.org/10.1016/j.cities.2019.102443

63. Gardner, W. L., & Avolio, B. J. (1998). *The charismatic relationship: A dramaturgical perspective.* doi:https://doi.org/10.5465/AMR.1998.192958.

64. Leonelli, S., Ceci, F., & Masciarelli, F. (2018). The importance of entrepreneurs' traits in explaining start-ups' innovativeness. *Sinergie Italian Journal of Management, 71–85.* https://doi.org/10.7433/s101.2016.05

65. Crant, J. M. (1996). *The proactive personality scale as a predictor of entrepreneurial intentions.*

66. Zhao, H., Hills, G. E., & Seibert, S. E. (2005). The mediating role of self-efficacy in the development of entrepreneurial intentions. *The Journal of Applied Psychology, 90.* https://doi.org/10.1037/0021-9010.90.6.1265

67. Ardichvili, A., Cardozo, R., & Ray, S. (2003). A theory of entrepreneurial opportunity identification and development. *Journal of Business Venturing, 18.* https://doi.org/10.1016/S0883-9026(01)00068-4

68. Leonelli, S., Iaia, L., Masciarelli, F., & Vrontis, D. (2022). Keep dreaming: How personality traits affects the recognition and exploitation of entrepreneurial opportunities in the agritourism industry. *British Food Journal, 124,* 2299–2320. https://doi.org/10.1108/BFJ-10-2021-1150

69. Leonelli, S., Jalal, R. N. U. D., & Fayyaz, U. E. R. (2022). The impact of personal factors and firm dynamics on knowledge workers' counterproductive work behaviour. *The International Journal of Management Education, 16.* https://doi.org/10.1504/IJMIE.2022.121167

70. Do, B. R., & Dadvari, A. (2017). The influence of the dark triad on the relationship between entrepreneurial attitude orientation and entrepreneurial intention: A study among students in Taiwan University. *Asia Pacific Management Review, 22,* 185–191. https://doi.org/10.1016/j.apmrv.2017.07.011

71. Brunell, A. B., Gentry, W. A., Campbell, W. K., Hoffman, B. J., Kuhnert, K. W., & Demarree, K. G. (2008). Leader emergence: The case of the narcissistic leader. *Personality and Social Psychology Bulletin, 34.* https://doi.org/10.1177/0146167208324101

72. Jones, D. N., & Figueredo, A. J. (2013). The core of darkness: Uncovering the heart of the dark triad. *European Journal of Personality, 27.* https://doi.org/10.1002/per.1893

73. O'Reilly, C. A., Doerr, B., Caldwell, D. F., & Chatman, J. A. (2014). Narcissistic CEOs and executive compensation. *The Leadership Quarterly, 25.* https://doi.org/10.1016/j.leaqua.2013.08.002

74. Brownell, K. M., McMullen, J. S., & O'Boyle, E. H. (2021). Fatal attraction: A systematic review and research agenda of the dark triad in entrepreneurship. *Journal of Business Venturing, 36,* 106106. https://doi.org/10.1016/j.jbusvent.2021.106106

75. Goncalo, J. A., Flynn, F. J., & Kim, S. H. (2010). From a mirage to an oasis: Narcissism, perceived creativity and creative performance. In: *Academy of Management 2010 Annual Meeting - Dare to Care: Passion and Compassion in Management Practice and Research, AOM 2010.* doi:https://doi.org/10.5465/ambpp.2010.54496125.

76. Maccoby, M. (2004). *Narcissistic leaders the incredible pros, the inevitable cons.*

77. Maccoby, M. (2003). The productive narcissist: The promise & peril of visionary leadership (Book). *Research-Technology Management, 46.*
78. Campbell, W. K., Goodie, A. S., & Foster, J. D. (2004). Narcissism, confidence, and risk attitude. *Journal of Behavioral Decision Making, 17.* https://doi.org/10.1002/bdm.475
79. Mathieu, C., & St-Jean, É. (2013). Entrepreneurial personality: The role of narcissism. *Personality and Individual Differences, 55.* https://doi.org/10.1016/j.paid.2013.04.026
80. Raskin, R., Novacek, J., & Hogan, R. (1991). Narcissistic self-esteem management. *Journal of Personality and Social Psychology, 60.* https://doi.org/10.1037/0022-3514.60.6.911
81. Humphreys, J. H., Haden, S. P., Novicevic, M. M., Clayton, R. W., & Gibson, J. W. (2011). Lillian McMurry of trumpet records: Integrity and authenticity in the charismatic, constructive narcissist leader. *Journal of Leadership and Organizational Studies, 18.* https://doi.org/10.1177/1548051810383862
82. Rosenthal, S. A., & Pittinsky, T. L. (2006). Narcissistic leadership. *The Leadership Quarterly, 17.* https://doi.org/10.1016/j.leaqua.2006.10.005
83. Gabriel, M. T., Critelli, J. W., & Ee, J. S. (1994). Narcissistic illusions in self-evaluations of intelligence and attractiveness. *Journal of Personality, 62.* https://doi.org/10.1111/j.1467-6494.1994.tb00798.x
84. Wales, W. J., Patel, P. C., & Lumpkin, G. T. (2013). In pursuit of greatness: CEO narcissism, entrepreneurial orientation, and firm performance variance. *Journal of Management Studies, 50.* https://doi.org/10.1111/joms.12034
85. Liu, Y., Li, Y., Hao, X., & Zhang, Y. (2019). Narcissism and learning from entrepreneurial failure. *Journal of Business Venturing, 34.* https://doi.org/10.1016/j.jbusvent.2019.01.003
86. Carlson, E. N., Vazire, S., & Oltmanns, T. F. (2011). You probably think this paper's about you: Narcissists' perceptions of their personality and reputation. *Journal of Personality and Social Psychology, 101,* 185–201. https://doi.org/10.1037/a0023781
87. Keith Campbell, W., & Foster, J. D. (2011). The narcissistic self: Background, an extended agency model, and ongoing controversies. *Self, 9780203818,* 115–138. https://doi.org/10.4324/9780203818572
88. Paulhus, D. L. (1998). Interpersonal and intrapsychic adaptiveness of trait self-enhancement: A mixed blessing? *Journal of Personality and Social Psychology, 74.* https://doi.org/10.1037/0022-3514.74.5.1197
89. Blair, C. A., Helland, K., & Walton, B. (2017). Leaders behaving badly: the relationship between narcissism and unethical leadership. *Leadership and Organization Development Journal, 38.* https://doi.org/10.1108/LODJ-09-2015-0209
90. Glebovskiy, A. (2019). Criminogenic isomorphism and groupthink in the business context. *International Journal of Organization Theory and Behavior, 22*(2). https://doi.org/10.1108/IJOTB-03-2018-0024
91. Eklinder-Frick, J., Eriksson, L. T., & Hallén, L. (2012). Effects of social capital on processes in a regional strategic network. *Industrial Marketing Management, 41,* 800–806. https://doi.org/10.1016/j.indmarman.2012.06.007
92. Adler, P. S., & Kwon, S. W. (2002). *Social capital: Prospects for a new concept.* https://doi.org/10.5465/AMR.2002.5922314
93. Nahapiet, J., & Ghoshal, S. (1998). Social capital, intellectual capital, and the organizational advantage. *The Academy of Management Review, 23,* 242–266. https://doi.org/10.5465/AMR.1998.533225
94. Portes, A. (2009). Social capital: Its origins and applications in modern sociology. *Knowledge and Social Capital, 43–68.* https://doi.org/10.1016/b978-0-7506-7222-1.50006-4
95. Coleman, J. S. (1988). Social capital in the creation of human capital. *The American Journal of Sociology, 94,* S95–S120.
96. Eklinder-Frick, J., Eriksson L. T., & Hallén, L. (2011). The impact of social capital on renewal through cluster initiatives. In: *Studies in industrial renewal: Coping with changing contexts* (pp. 129–146).

97. Parmigiani, A., & Rivera-Santos, M. (2011). Clearing a path through the forest: A meta-review of interorganizational relationships. *Journal of Management, 37*(4), 1108–1136. https://doi.org/10.1177/0149206311407507

98. Burt, R. S. (1992). *Structural holes: The social structure of competition.*

99. Hansen, M. T. (1999). The search-transfer problem: The role of weak ties in sharing knowledge across organization subunits. *Administrative Science Quarterly, 44.* https://doi.org/10.2307/2667032

100. Naylor, T. D., & Florida, R. (2003). The rise of the creative class: And how it's transforming work, leisure, community and everyday life. *Canadian Public Policy/Analyse De Politiques, 29,* 378. https://doi.org/10.2307/3552294

101. Gabbay, S. M., & Zuckerman, E. W. (1998). Social capital and opportunity in corporate R&D: The contingent effect of contact density on mobility expectations. *Social Science Research, 27.* https://doi.org/10.1006/ssre.1998.0620

102. Dhanaraj, C., & Parkhe, A. (2006). Orchestrating innovation networks. *Academy of management review, 31*(3), 659–669. https://doi.org/10.5465/amr.2006.21318923

103. Ouchi, W. G. (1980). Markets, bureaucracy, and clans. *Administrative Science Quarterly, 25.*

104. Uzzi, B. (1997). Social structure and competition in interfirm networks: The paradox of embeddedness. *Administrative Science Quarterly, 42.* https://doi.org/10.2307/2393808

105. Krackhardt, D., & Hanson, J. R. (1993). Informal networks: The company behind the chart. *Harvard Business Review, 71.* https://doi.org/10.1093/oso/9780195159509.003.0016

106. Parra-Requena, G., Molina-Morales, F. X., & García-Villaverde, P. M. (2010). The mediating effect of cognitive social capital on knowledge acquisition in clustered firms. *Growth and Change, 41.* https://doi.org/10.1111/j.1468-2257.2009.00516.x

107. Ceci, F., Masciarelli, F., & Poledrini, S. (2020). How social capital affects innovation in a cultural network: Exploring the role of bonding and bridging social capital. *European Journal of Innovation Management, 23,* 895–918. https://doi.org/10.1108/EJIM-06-2018-0114

108. Leana, C. R., & Van Buren, H. J. (1999). Organizational social capital and employment practices. *The Academy of Management Review, 24.* https://doi.org/10.5465/AMR.1999.2202136

109. Seibert, S. E., Kraimer, M. L., & Liden, R. C. (2001). A social capital theory of career success. *The Academy of Management Journal, 44.* https://doi.org/10.2307/3069452

110. Coleman, J. S. (1990). Social capital. In *Foundations of Social Theory, 69.*

111. Fukuyama, F. (1995). *Trust: Social virtues and the creation of prosperity.* Francis Fukuyama.

112. Burt, R. S. (2000). The network structure of social capital. *Research in Organizational Behavior, 22.* https://doi.org/10.1016/s0191-3085(00)22009-1

113. Larson, A., & Starr, J. A. (1993). A network model of organization formation. *Entrepreneurship Theory and Practice, 17.* https://doi.org/10.1177/104225879301700201

114. Stuart, T., & Sorenson, O. (2003). The geography of opportunity: Spatial heterogeneity in founding rates and the performance of biotechnology firms. *Research Policy, 32.* https://doi.org/10.1016/S0048-7333(02)00098-7

115. Shane, S. (2002). Selling university technology: Patterns from MIT. *Management Science.* https://doi.org/10.1287/mnsc.48.1.122.14281

116. Putnam, R. D. (1995). Bowling alone: America's declining social capital. *Journal of Democracy, 6.* https://doi.org/10.1353/jod.1995.0002

117. Boschma, R. A. (2005). Proximity and innovation: A critical assessment. *Regional Studies, 39.* https://doi.org/10.1080/0034340052000320887

118. Fritsch, M., & Franke, G. (2004). Innovation, regional knowledge spillovers and R&D cooperation. *Research Policy, 33.* https://doi.org/10.1016/S0048-7333(03)00123-9

119. Morgan, K. (1997). The learning region: Institutions, innovation and regional renewal. *Regional Studies, 31.* https://doi.org/10.1080/00343409750132289

120. Florida, R. (2002). *The economic geography of talent.* doi:https://doi.org/10.1111/1467-8306.00314.

121. Fleming, L., & Sorenson, O. (2004). Science as a map in technological search. *Strategic Management Journal, 25.* https://doi.org/10.1002/smj.384

122. Rosenkopf, L., & Nerkar, A. (2001). Beyond local search: Boundary-spanning, exploration, and impact in the optical disk industry. *Strategic Management Journal, 22*, 287–306. https://doi.org/10.1002/smj.160

123. Larson, A. (1992). Network dyads in entrepreneurial settings: A study of the governance of exchange relationships. *Administrative Science Quarterly, 37*. https://doi.org/10.2307/2393534

124. Ring, P. S., & van de Ven, A. H. (1994). Developmental processes of cooperative interorganizational relationships. *The Academy of Management Review, 19*. https://doi.org/10.2307/258836

125. Laursen, K., Masciarelli, F., & Prencipe, A. (2012). Regions matter: How localized social capital affects innovation and external knowledge acquisition. *Organization Science, 23*, 177–193. https://doi.org/10.1287/orsc.1110.0650

126. Chesbrough, H. (2003). *Open innovation: The new imperative for creating and profiting.*

127. Arora, A., Fosfuri, A., & Gambardella, A. (2002). *Book review markets for technology: The economics of innovation and corporate strategy.* The MIT Press. Managerial and Decision Economics, 23.

128. Shan, W., Walker, G., & Kogut, B. (1994). Interfirm cooperation and startup innovation in the biotechnology industry. *Strategic Management Journal, 15*. https://doi.org/10.1002/smj.4250150505

129. Israel, P., & von Hippel, E. (1990). The sources of innovation. *Technology and Culture, 31*, 333. https://doi.org/10.2307/3105687

130. Commission, T., on Measuring Well being, J. (2011). *Measuring national well-being - proposed well-being indicators - 5th December, 2011.* The Commission on Measuring Well-being, Japan.

131. aniaostudio. (2018). *Global Happiness Policy Report 2018 Global Happiness Council.*

132. Shiga University and Economic and Social Research Institute of Cabinet Office. (2006). *Revitalization of neighborhoods by utilizing the richness of social capital.* www.esri.go.jp/jp/prj/hou/hou075/hou075.ht%0Aml (in Japanese).

133. Solove, D. J. (2013). Introduction: Privacy self-management and the consent dilemma. *Harvard Law Review, 126.*

Characterizing Smartness in the Manufacturing Domain: Literature Review and Development of a Classification Framework

Philipp Scharfe

Abstract Smartness represents a key phenomenon in the digital era. This also applies to the manufacturing domain, where researchers and practitioners discuss concepts such as smart machines, smart manufacturing systems, or smart maintenance services. While all those concepts are called smart, it remains vague what this smartness means. Considering this background, we want to understand what similar characteristics are implemented in those smart devices, systems, and services of the manufacturing domain that make them smart. Therefore, we conducted a systematic review of literature focusing on multiple characteristics associated with the smartness of devices, systems, and services in this domain. We synthesize our results in a classification framework—consisting of 9 dimensions and 37 characteristics. Our classification framework contributes to the existing body of knowledge by providing a more nuanced understanding of the implementation of smartness in the manufacturing domain and offering manufacturing practitioners a 'guidance tool' for exploring and designing smart devices, systems, and services. We conclude by discussing some gaps in the identified literature and corresponding future research opportunities.

Keywords Smart devices · systems and services · Manufacturing · Literature review · Classification framework

1 Introduction

In practice and research exist a wide range of things called "smart". This also applies to the manufacturing domain, where we talk about concepts such as smart quality management, smart planning, smart manufacturing machines, or smart factories. These concepts are also associated with new benefits and opportunities. For example, in a smart

P. Scharfe (✉)
Business Information Systems, esp. Business Engineering, TU Dresden, Dresden, Germany
e-mail: philipp.scharfe@tu-dresden.de

© The Author(s), under exclusive license to Springer Nature Switzerland AG 2024
A. Lazazzara et al. (eds.), *Towards Digital and Sustainable Organisations*,
Lecture Notes in Information Systems and Organisation 65,
https://doi.org/10.1007/978-3-031-52880-4_18

manufacturing environment, energy consumption is expected to be reduced by up to 40% and maintenance costs by 10–40% compared to a traditional one [1]. Moreover, smart manufacturing equipment facilitates new beneficial services, such as predictive maintenance, or new business models, such as pay-per-use ones [2]. While we are using the term "smart" for all those beneficial concepts, it is unclear what this smartness really means. We associate smartness either with the vague description of using large and impressive IT capabilities or with properties similar to humans' intelligence [3]. A few publications have already addressed this issue and started to define and characterize the meaning of smartness in the context of smart devices, systems, and services (e.g., [3, 4]). However, these characterizations miss important smart capabilities, such as knowledge acquisition in the case of [3]. Moreover, these descriptions have a very general focus. Since the manufacturing domain has some unique characteristics (e.g., unique information sources such as manufacturing design solutions or specific outcomes such as manufacturing quality management [5]), it remains questionable if these characterizations can be applied to this domain without further ado. Moreover, the manufacturing domain is highly relevant as it contributes high value-added in many developed countries [6]. Considering this background, we conclude that it is necessary to investigate the concept of smartness in the manufacturing domain with its particularities. More specifically, we want to understand what similar characteristics are implemented in smart devices, systems, and services of the manufacturing domain that make them smart.

This need for understanding also seems relevant from a practical perspective. Companies in the manufacturing domain are undergoing a smartification process, where they transform their traditional devices, systems, and services into smart ones. However, this remains a challenging endeavor, and many companies are still at the beginning of this transformation, particularly the manufacturing domain dominating small and medium-sized firms [7]. Studies found that this transformation remains challenging because these firms lack knowledge about new characteristics, requirements, and technologies associated with the smartness of devices, systems, and services [7, 8]. Considering this background, we want to investigate the following research question: *What are key characteristics for describing the implementation of smartness in smart devices, systems, and services of the manufacturing domain?* Research has already started to answer this question by investigating multiple individual characteristics associated with the smartness of devices, systems, and services in the manufacturing domain. For example, they outlined various approaches how smart devices, systems, and services in this domain can learn (e.g., [9, 10]) or how they collect and process information (e.g., [11, 12]). We conducted a literature review following established guidelines [13–15], collecting this literature and synthesizing it into a classification framework that characterizes the implementation of smartness in devices, systems, and services of the manufacturing domain. In this way, our study aims to contribute to the existing body of knowledge by elaborating on the concept of smartness in this specific domain, thereby also providing insights that are transferrable to a more general level. Moreover, with its dimensions and characteristics, our classification framework offers design options that can guide manufacturing practitioners in developing or enhancing smart devices, systems, and services. Since we consider some of the identified characteristics as very innovative and we identified some research gaps, we discuss opportunities for future smartness research in manufacturing.

The remainder of this paper is structured as follows. In the second section, we describe relevant foundations. Section 3 introduces our research approach. We present and describe our classification framework in Sect. 4. Section 5 illustrates our classification framework based on three examples from practice. Section 6 discusses the results, research opportunities, and limitations. Finally, Sect. 7 concludes our study.

2 Research Background

2.1 Smartness and Manufacturing

The term "smart" is widely used in practice and research. However, it remains unclear or vague what the smartness of devices, systems, or services means. Only a few academic studies offer more detailed explanations (see Table 1).

While the definitions shown in Table 1 differ in their wordings, they refer to similar characteristics to describe smartness. On this basis, we define smartness as a set of capabilities that enable smart devices, systems, and services to collect, transmit and process information, as well as, to make decisions autonomously, to learn, and/ or to communicate and coordinate with their environment.

Manufacturing refers to processes that convert "raw materials into useful products" [18 , p. 69]. These processes can be summarized within six main steps: (1) product design, (2) manufacturing process planning, scheduling, and improvement, (3) material distribution, (4) actual manufacturing (i.e., physical material transformation), (5) quality control, and (6) delivery. In addition, another permanent seventh step is the maintenance of the equipment needed for manufacturing [19].

2.2 Analytical Framework of Smartness

For structuring the identified literature and as basis for developing our classification framework, we decided to rely on a framework. Such a framework adds value since it provides a comprehensive theoretical grounding. We identified two suitable smartness frameworks in the literature. The framework of Alter [3] characterizes smartness along four categories: information processing, knowledge acquisition, internal regulation, and action in the world. The framework of Boukhris and

Table 1 Definitions of smartness in academic literature

Refs.	Definition
[16, p. 21]	"... being connected and able to act with partial autonomy based on own decision making while cooperating and coordinating with others."
[17, p. iii]	"... capable of learning, dynamic adaptation, and decision making based upon data received, transmitted, and/or processed to improve its response to a future situation."
[3 , p. 384]	"... apply automated capabilities and other [...] resources for processing information, interpreting information, and/or learning from information ..."

Fritzsche [4] describes smartness along five dimensions: data richness, design support engine, outcome, the architecture of stakeholders, and automation of service processes. We choose the framework of Alter [3] since this framework aggregates the five categories of Boukhris and Fritzsche [4] into three ones and has additionally the relevant category knowledge acquisition that is missing in the other framework [4].

In the following, we describe the four categories of smartness in Alter's [3] framework: *(1) Information processing* refers to the ability to collect information from multiple sources and transmit, store, retrieve, and manipulate this information. *(2) Internal regulation* refers to the ability to make decisions autonomously. *(3) Knowledge acquisition* refers to the ability to accumulate knowledge (i.e., to learn). *(4) Action in the world* refers to the ability to communicate and interact with and perform actions in the environment beyond the nominally smart device, system, or service. According to Alter [3], the second, third, and fourth categories rely on the capabilities of the first. Moreover, Alter [3] argues that it is possible that smart devices, systems, or services do not have capabilities in all four categories (e.g., a smart machine may be able to process information for learning purposes and communicate the learning results but do not make decisions based on them). We follow this direction and define that a device, system, or service is already smart if it has at least information processing capabilities and some action in the world capabilities to act as the outcome of the processed information. For example, we consider a monitoring service that collects information from sensors, aggregates, and presents this information without decision making and knowledge acquisition in a dashboard as already smart. This is also in line with Porter and Heppelmann [20], who also defines such a monitoring service as already smart.

Since Alter's [3] categories refer to the smartness of devices, systems, and services, we describe these three conceptual levels in the following in a manufacturing context. *(1) Smart devices* are individual physical objects (e.g., machines) equipped with hardware and software components that enable the capabilities outlined in the four categories of Alter [3, 4, 21]. *(2) Smart systems* describe networks with multiple smart devices and other physical and computational elements that interact with each other and their surrounding world (e.g., a smart factory) [22]. *(3) Smart services* are new forms of value creation that exist in addition to the basic manufacturing functionalities of smart devices and systems (e.g., predictive maintenance services) [23, 24].

3   Methodology

To develop our classification framework that characterizes the implementation of smartness in smart devices, systems, and services of the manufacturing domain, we conducted an explorative investigation of the topic based on a systematic literature review. We followed established methodological approaches for literature reviews in our literature search, selection, and analysis [13–15].

3.1   Literature Search

To identify relevant publications, we employed a five-step process. In the first step, we used the literature mentioned in the theoretical background section to formulate a search string: (smart* OR intellig* OR digit*) AND (manufact* OR engineer* OR industr*). In the second step, we used this string to search the title, abstract, and keywords of nine leading IS journals and the proceedings of two leading conferences (Basket of Eight Journals, Business & Information Systems Engineering Journal, ICIS, and ECIS). We reviewed the title and abstract of the resulting 378 publications and applied four initially defined exclusion criteria for the paper selection. Two of them are formal exclusion criteria: (1) We dismissed: research-in-progress publications since it remained unclear if their research would lead to valuable results, and (2) not peer-reviewed publications to ensure a certain quality level. Two more criteria were content-related: (3) We dismissed publications that did not focus on the manufacturing domain as outlined in the six processes of the manufacturing domain, and (4) that did not focus from a design-oriented perspective on the implementation of smartness. For example, we excluded publications that discuss the (organizational and business model) implications resulting from the smartness and the smartification process. After applying these four exclusion criteria, 14 of the 378 publications were left. We conducted a backward search within the third step and identified 13 more relevant publications. The fourth step included a forward search using Google Scholar, leading to another 16 relevant publications. In the fourth step, we used our search string for a database search in the AIS eLibary (1117 results). We searched in title and abstract. After merging duplicates and reading the title and abstract, we identified another 19 relevant publications. In the fifth and final step, we read the full text of the remaining 62 publications, which led to the exclusion of another 24 publications. As a result, our review sample includes 38 relevant publications (see Appendix).

3.2   Literature Analysis and Classification Framework Development

After identifying the relevant literature, we proceeded with their analysis and the classification framework development. A classification framework seems suitable since such an artifact structures knowledge in a certain field of interest [25]. We developed the classification framework in a three-step process. In the first step, we started by determining the following information from each publication: title, author, outlet, outlet type (i.e., journal or conference), year of publication, and the main content. Most identified publications were published within the last 4 years (25 publications, 66%). Moreover, almost all of the publications (36 publications, 95%) were published at conferences, most at HICSS, ECIS, and Wirtschaftsinformatik. In the second step, we added in these summaries which of the four categories the publications mainly focus on (we allowed publications to focus on more than one category). In the third step, we focused on the publications within each of the four smart categories and identified codes representing the publications' main topic. Based on these codes, we developed a concept matrix with the dimensions and more concrete characteristics (see Appendix). Generally, the identified characteristics were identified in two ways or a combination of both. Either, we further summarized/ synthesized existing reviews/systematizations (marked as 'R' in the Appendix). For example, multiple studies [26–28] systemize action outcomes. We further summarized them to our classification framework's corresponding four main characteristics. Otherwise, we discovered characteristic patterns within studies describing or designing individual smart devices, systems, or services (marked as 'I' in the Appendix). For example, we discovered multiple knowledge acquisition approaches in the identified studies. Based on additional literature [29], we synthesized these approaches within the three mentioned characteristics.

4   Classification Framework

In the following, we present our classification framework for characterizing the implementation of smartness in smart devices, systems, and services of the manufacturing domain (see Table 2). Our classification framework is structured along the categories outlined in the framework of Alter [3]. We identified for each category one or multiple dimensions with concrete associated characteristics. As argued in the research background section, smart devices, systems, or services must have capabilities in the information processing and action in the world category but not in all four ones. Moreover, the dimension of human interaction is a specification of the characteristic human information presentation. All dimensions of our classification framework are not exclusive (i.e., multiple characteristics can be applied to a single classified object). Since in our classification framework not every classified object needs to be described by every dimension and not all dimensions are exclusive, we do not follow some important taxonomy characteristics as defined by Nickerson et al. [30]. Therefore, we avoid this term and call our artifact "classification framework."

4.1   Information Processing

Information processing refers to the capability of smart devices, systems, and services to collect, transmit, store, and analyze information. The other three categories rely to some extent on this first category. We characterize information processing along with the dimension's information sources, deployment scenarios, and implementation partners. The identified literature points to multiple *sources information* is collected from: sensors, equipment operation systems, manufacturing IS, development systems, human user input, public databases, and social media. Sensors, as the first-mentioned source, provide original values (e.g., the pressure at a tool) [5, 11, 31]. As another important source, equipment operation systems provide

Table 2 Classification framework for characterizing smartness in manufacturing

Category	Dimensions	Characteristics						
Information processing	Inform. sources	Sensors	Operat. systems	Manuf. IS	Develop. systems	Human user	Public DB	Social media
	Deploym. scenarios	Edge-based		Central platform-based				
	Implem. partners	Equipment providers	Software providers	Retrofit companies		Platform providers	End users	
Knowledge acquisition	Approaches	Explicit human programming		Self-learning (shallow machine learning)		Self-learning (deep learning)		
Internal regulation	Decision types	Process deviation identification		Process control		Process optimization		
	Decision auto.	Semi-automated (human-based)		Semi-automated (data-driven)		Fully automated		
Action in the world	Action outcomes	Maintenance and service		Design support	Man. planning and control	Performance-based contracting		
	Acting appr.	Automated instructing		Automatedphysical acting		Human information presentation		
	Human interact.	Dashboards	Tactile	Virtual Reality	Lights	Speech	Gestures	Augm. Reality

operational information (e.g., machine operation times) [5, 31]. Manufacturing IS (e.g., ERP) provide administrative and management information (e.g., about component inventory) [5, 31, 32]. On the other side, deliver development systems rather technical information resulting from design and development processes (e.g., CAD information). Literature also considers human users with their knowledge, experience, and unique sensing capabilities as another important source of information. Furthermore, information can be collected from public databases (DB) (e.g., manufacturing norms) [5, 31]. From our perspective is social media another interesting source of information. For example, Petrik et al. [33] describe social media as a source for identifying user trends and feedback by analyzing posts on Twitter.

After the collection, the information is transmitted for storage and analysis. There are two *deployment scenarios* for this: edge-based and central platform-based. The first option means that information is stored and analyzed on the edge in the manufacturing environment (e.g., locally on the smart machine). This scenario is suitable in case of low transmission bandwidth. The second option—on a central platform—is more suitable if larger quantities of information need to be stored and analyzed since the required advanced capabilities are available on the central platform (e.g., in the cloud) [11, 12].

We identified in the literature multiple *partners* that are necessary for *implementing* the information processing capabilities of smart devices, systems, and services (for the initial setup and following usage). We classified these partners into five main types: equipment providers, software providers, retrofit companies, platform providers, and end-users. Equipment providers offer the final user equipment (e.g., machine tools) or components that are part of it (e.g., sensors, robot arms, or communication technology). Moreover, they often still have access to the equipment during usage for remote maintenance, troubleshooting, and update installation [34–36]. Often larger equipment providers also develop the software for the equipment themselves. However, they also cooperate with companies developing the required software and programs. To this partner type also belong data analytics providers that offer advanced data analytics capabilities [35, 36]. Retrofit companies, as the third type, focus on the smartification of older equipment by providing the necessary knowledge, hardware, and software capabilities [36]. We identified platform providers as another partner since many smartification projects rely on Industrial Internet of Things (IIoT) platforms. These platforms provide the technical infrastructure to transmit and process information and an integrating ecosystem (e.g., to integrate third-party software applications) [35–37]. The end users also play a crucial role as they provide the required infrastructure (e.g., in their plant for information transmission) and handle the implementation and usage [35, 36].

4.2 Knowledge Acquisition

Knowledge acquisition refers to the capability of smart devices, systems, and services to accumulate their knowledge base. For this category exist the dimension learning *approaches* with their characteristics explicit human programming, self-learning (shallow machine learning (ML)), and self-learning (deep learning). Explicit human programming refers to the paradigm of handcrafted model building. Many smart devices, systems, and services rely on this form of knowledge acquisition (e.g., rule-based decision and expert systems) [29]. In contrast to human programming, the other two characteristics rely on the self-learning capabilities of smart devices, systems, and services. To do so, they apply ML, which describes the capability "to learn from problem-specific training data to automate the process of analytical model building" [29 , p. 685]. Based on the literature, we distinguish between the two ML concepts: shallow ML (e.g., [38–40]) and deep learning (e.g., [41, 42]). The latter can be considered more advanced as it does not require handcrafted feature engineering anymore since the required feature representation can be automatically learned by a deep neural network with many hidden layers [29]. We found examples for both concepts in the literature. For example, Singh et al. [40] describe a quality control service that applies a simple decision tree belonging to shallow ML. On the other hand, Elnagar and Thomas [41] describe the implementation and usage of a deep learning model in a smart manufacturing system.

4.3   Internal Regulation

Internal regulation refers to the ability of smart devices, systems, and services to analyze the collected information to make decisions based on the knowledge base. We characterize this category based on the dimensions: decision types and decision automations. Within the first dimension—*decision types*—we distinguish based on the identified literature with an increasing level of advancement between process deviation identification (e.g., [9, 43]), control (e.g., [40, 44]), and optimization (e.g., [45, 46]). Suschnigg et al. [43] provide an example for the first one. They describe a service that identifies quality deviations within manufacturing processes. An example of the following type of process control provide Koppe and Schatz [44]. They present a visual inspection service that conducts control decisions, meaning there is not only a deviation identified but also a decision made on the appropriate action resulting from the deviation. On the most advanced level are manufacturing process optimization decisions. This type tries to make the best possible control decision(s) for the manufacturing processes. Kauke et al. [45] describe an example of this type and present a service that optimizes picking in a warehouse.

The second dimension, *decision automations*, refers to human decision-making. Based on multiple identified smart devices, systems, and services described in the literature, we distinguish between semi-automated (human-based), semi-automated (data-driven), and fully automated decision making. In the case of semi-automated human-based decision making (e.g., [9, 43]) is the decision primary made by humans with some limited IT support. For example, Jecik et al. [9] describe the case where a monitoring service identifies atypical distributions but the human need to decide if this atypical distribution is relevant and what the reason is. In the case of more advanced semi-automated data-driven decision making (e.g., [40, 47]), pre-analyzes the smart device, system, or service relevant data and subsequently collaborate with the human for the final decision making (i.e., IT and human make the decision together). For example, in the mentioned case of Singh et al. [40], the smart service automatically predicts quality failures in manufacturing processes and points to possible failure explanations. The human user needs to decide on the correct failure explanation finally. Fully automated (e.g., [44–46]) means that there is (almost) no human involvement in decision-making. For example, the already mentioned warehouse order picking service makes essential planning decisions such as the size of picking tours or the employee scheduling entirely on its own [45]. Literature also highlights the need to explain the automated decision-making by smart devices, systems, or services. Otherwise, the human users lose trust in the automatically made decisions, even if they are more superior than human decisions made by their intuition [10, 48].

4.4   Action in the World

Action in the world describes the ability of smart devices, systems, and services to perform actions in and interact with the environment. We identified three dimensions belonging to this category: action outcomes, acting approaches, and human interaction approaches. The third dimension specifies the human interaction approaches (third characteristic in the second dimension). The first dimension systemizes the *outcomes of actions* of smart products, systems, and services for their users. Based on the literature, these outcomes can be summarized within four main categories: maintenance and service, design support, manufacturing process planning, and control, as well as performance based contracting [26–28]. The first outcome maintenance and service support compromise regular maintenance in the case of errors and predictive maintenance to optimize manufacturing equipment operations. The second outcome, design support, means that users can design and manufacture their products in an interruption-free process due to the integration and compatibility of the tools used in this process (i.e., design and simulation software, manufacturing equipment) [5]. The third outcome manufacturing process planning and control comprise the production planning, production preparation (e.g., tool supply), the conduction of the actual manufacturing (i.e., the physical transformation of the material), and quality management [26–28]. The last outcome, performance-based contracting, marks a fundamental shift in the business model of smart equipment manufacturers. Instead of selling equipment, the user pays based on monitored values a usage-based fee. For example, instead of buying a smart printing machine, the user pays in addition to a basic usage fee only for each printed page [28].

While the first dimension of this category describes the outcomes of action, focus this category on the *acting approaches* (i.e., approaches on how the outcome is generated). We differentiate between the following approaches: automated instructing (e.g., [48, 49]), automated physical acting (e.g., [46, 47]), and human information presentation for learning and instructing (e.g., [49, 50]). Automated instructing means that smart devices, systems, and services provide information to instruct other smart devices, systems, and services. For example, Hakanen et al. [49] describe the case where information (e.g., process parameters) about manufactured steel workpieces is shared along the production value chain. This allows the other smart machines along this chain to adapt their behavior to the individual workpieces. Automated physical acting means that smart devices, systems, or services conduct some physical actions themselves. For example, Scharfe and Wiener [5] present types of automated physical actions of smart machines. Moreover, literature provides multiple examples of smart devices, systems, and services presenting information to humans for learning and instruction. Based on this information, humans then conduct actions. Mättig and Kretzschmar [50] describe an example for the instruction purpose. They present a smart service that decides how to pack products and then communicate this decision to human workers who conduct the actual packing task. For the learning purpose, the dashboard service of Jekic et al. [9] enables shop floor workers to gain new knowledge about manufacturing processes.

Literature points to multiple specific approaches for the *human interaction*: dashboards (e.g., [9, 46, 51]), tactile functions [52], virtual reality (VR) [53], LED lights [50], speech [54], gestures [54], and augmented reality (AR) (e.g., [55–57]). Interesting is the ambiguity in how users evaluate the usability of AR technology. In the publications of Aaroma et al. [55] and Saggiomo et al. [58] got the AR approach a very positive usability rating. In contrast, in the study of Mättig and Kretschmer [50] preferred the users an alternative approach since the AR one caused increasing temporal stress.

5 Empirical Illustration of the Classification Framework

To illustrate the usefulness of our classification framework, we applied it to three real-world examples: a smart transport robot (smart device), an injection molding work cell (smart system), and a smart AR maintenance instruction service (see Table 3). In selecting the three examples, we first searched the identified literature for one type of smart device, system, and service that is frequently mentioned (e.g., smart AR maintenance instruction services are frequently mentioned). Second, we searched the web for a well-described real-world example of each of the three identified types (e.g., Bitnamic provides a smart AR maintenance instruction service).

The **smart AR maintenance instruction service** of the startup Bitnamic connects a human worker wearing AR glasses with a technician, who gives the worker maintenance instructions via the glasses (*action outcome; acting approach*). These AR glasses also have a camera and a headset to transmit the workers' view and speech to the technician (who sees this view on a dashboard screen and hears the voice). Then the technician can give instructions back to the worker via the headset or AR functionalities (*information sources; human interaction*). The implementation of this service relies on the software provider Bitnamic, the smart glass

Table 3 Classification of examples along the classification framework dimensions

Dimensions	Smart AR maintenance instruction service	Smart injection molding work cell (smart system)	Smart transport robot (smart device)
Inform. sources	Sensors, Human users	Sensors	Sensors, Human users
Deployment scenarios	Central-platform based	Edge-based	Edge-based
Implementation partners	Equipment, software, and platform providers, end users	Equipment and software provider, end user	Equipment provider, end user
Knowledge acquisition	*No knowledge acquisition capability*	Explicit human programming	Explicit human programming, Self-learning
Decision types	*No internal regulation capability*	Process optimization	Process optimization
Decision automations	*No internal regulation capability*	Fully automated	Fully automated
Action outcomes	Maintenance and service	Manufacturing planning and control	Manuf. planning and control
Acting approaches	Human information presentation	Automated physical acting; human information presentation	Automated physical acting; human inf. presentation
Human inter. approaches	AR, speech, dashboard	Dashboard	Dashboard

equipment provider Microsoft, an IIoT platform provider, who hosts the application in the cloud, and the end-users (AR using worker and the instructing technician) (*deployment scenario; implementation partners*). This instruction service has no capabilities belonging to the knowledge acquisition and internal regulation categories.

The **smart injection molding work cell** of the company Wittmann Battenfeld consists of multiple connected smart devices: an injection molding machine, a dryer, a dosing device, and a pump. This work cell collects information from sensors and the device's operating systems (*information sources*). This information is processed on the edge (directly on the cell; *deployment scenario*). Based on the collected information, the cell optimizes the molding process fully automated and conducts the molding with its physical actuators (*decision type; decision automation; acting approach; action outcome*). For process optimization, the cell relies on rules programmed by humans (*knowledge acquisition approach*). Moreover, the cell informs a user about its condition on a dashboard (*acting approach; human interaction*). For the *implementation*, the equipment provider Wittmann Battenfeld corporates with the software provider MPDV. The user is also an important *partner* (e.g., for set up and control).

The **smart transport robot** of the company Omron transports products autonomously in plants (*action outcome, acting approach*). The robot relies primarily on laser sensor information for navigation and control and human user input to tell the robot the transport destinations (*information sources*). The collected information is processed within the robot (on the edge; *deployment scenario*). Moreover, the robot is able to optimize its way in the plant fully automated (*decision type; decision autonomy*). According to Omron, they use ML for training their robots to react to unforeseen situations. We could not identify the concrete *knowledge acquisition approach* for that learning task. Moreover, the robot has a little screen showing operation parameters to humans on a dashboard (*human interaction*). In addition to Omron as an equipment provider, the end users play an important role as *implementation partner* for installation and usage. For example, the end user must set up the robot and program ways within the plant. There was no other information about further implementation partners for this robot available.

6 Discussion

The objective of this paper was to investigate characteristics for describing the implementation of smartness in smart devices, systems, and services of the manufacturing domain. To do so, we conducted a systematic literature review and synthesized the results into a classification framework of 9 dimensions with 37 characteristics.

6.1 Contributions and Implications

Our study contributes to the literature by clarifying the concept of smartness in the manufacturing domain. Therefore, we describe and synthesize key characteristics along the four smart capability categories information processing, knowledge acquisition, internal regulation, and action in the world. Some of our identified characteristics are manufacturing-specific, such as the ones in the dimensions' information sources and action outcomes. On the other hand, some dimension's point to characteristics that are relevant to characterize smartness on a more general level and have not been discussed in corresponding available frameworks on smartness (e.g., knowledge acquisition approaches, human interaction approaches) [3, 4]. In this way, our classification framework is not only clarifying the concept of smartness in the manufacturing domain but although on a more general level. Moreover, we show that the concept of smartness is reflected by different capabilities with different levels of advancement. Of the described examples has the smart AR maintenance instruction service only capabilities in the information processing and action in the world capability category. In contrast, the smart transport robot is more advanced as it additionally can make decisions and has self-learning capabilities. Since our research contributes to clarifying the concept of smartness, we respond to recent calls for research (e.g., [3, 59]).

Our study results are also relevant for manufacturing practitioners (e.g., engineers, managers, designers). Since the smartification of devices, systems, and services is a challenging endeavor, practitioners can use our classification framework to assess and identify additional capability and design options [7, 8]. On the one hand, points our classification framework to rather 'traditional' options (such as dashboards for user interaction). These are more relevant for firms at the beginning of their smartification trajectory. In contrast, since we conducted a literature review and research often points to new innovative topics that are later implemented in practice, we were also able to identify characteristics (such as performance-based contracts as action outcome or social media as an information source) that are more advanced and therefore interesting for companies that are already further in their smartification process.

6.2   Future Research Directions

Since we conducted a literature review for our classification framework development, we identified gaps and interesting topics for future smartness research in manufacturing. First, we consider social media an interesting source of information that was not yet the focus of research. Further studies could investigate what kind of manufacturing relevant information can be selected from this source (e.g., maintenance instructions, manufactured product user reviews). Moreover, it would also be interesting to study what type of social media to use as an information source (e.g., general social networking sites such as Twitter or domain-specific discussion forums such as woodworker) and for what purpose. Second, the literature review shows a growing number of devices, systems, and services with semi- or fully automated decision-making. In addition to encouraging researchers to design and describe more of such ones, we see the coordination of decision making tasks between humans and the devices, systems, and services underlying algorithms as another promising avenue for future research. For example, researchers could study the complementary expertise of human users and algorithms in manufacturing and the resulting division of decision making tasks between them [60]. Moreover, suppose humans collaborate for decision-making with smart devices, systems, or services. In that case, it is also interesting to study how humans perceive these devices, systems, or services (as a teammate or tools) and how this influences their collaboration. For such investigations, researchers could apply human-agent theories [61]. Third, the literature describes different approaches to human interaction but focuses on AR technology. Some studies positively review AR technology (e.g., [57]). In contrast, the study of Mättig and Kretschmer [50] describes barriers that still hinder the use of AR in practice (e.g., AR causes temporal stress). Therefore, we suggest investigating the reasons for these different evaluations of AR solutions. Moreover, there are other promising and less studied human interaction approaches in manufacturing, such as interaction via speech. This approach avoids distraction since users have their hands free, and no visual attention to a display is necessary [62].

6.3   *Limitations*

As with any research, our study is not free of limitations. First, selecting relevant publications and collating and synthesizing them within dimensions and character-istics depends on individual judgment. We wanted to mitigate that limitation by formulating clear exclusion criteria and dimension/characteristics definitions. Second, even though our classification framework was already developed based on practical-oriented literature, the analysis of additional practical examples may pro-vide further insights that could result in an extension or adaption of the classifica-tion framework. Finally, we relied in our review primarily on literature published in IS outlets since smartness is a key topic in this field, with a focus on certain applica-tion domains, such as manufacturing [59]. However, there may be other relevant literature outside the IS domain (e.g., in manufacturing) that could further enhance our conceptual framework.

7   Conclusion

In conclusion, we hope that our study will contribute to the understanding of the interesting phenomenon of smartness in manufacturing, stimulate future research in this area, and assist companies in their smartification efforts.

Appendix

Column groups — **Information processing** > Information sources: DS (Deployment scenarios), IP (Implementation partners); **KA** (Knowledge acquisition); **IR** (Internal regulation): DT (Decision types), DA (Decision automations); **Action in the world**: AO (Action outcomes), AA (Acting approaches), HI (Human interaction).

Reference	Sensors	Operation systems	Manufacturing IS	Development systems	Human users	Public DB	Social media	Edge-based	Central platform-based	Equipment providers	Software providers	Retrofit companies	Platform providers	End users	Explicit human programming	Self-learning (shallow ML)	Self-learning (deep learning)	Process monitoring	Process control	Process optimization	Semi-automated (human-based)	Semi-automated (data-driven)	Fully automated	Maintenance and service	Design support	Manufacturing planning and	Performance-based contracts	Automated instructing	Automated physical acting	Human information presenta-	Dashboards	Tactile	Virtual Reality	Lights	Speech	Gestures	Augmented Reality	Type
5	•	•	•	•	•	•		•	•															•	•	•				•								R
9																•						•						•	•									I
10																•			•			•	•															I
11	•	•	•	•				•	•																													I
12								•	•																													I
26																								•	•	•												R
27																								•	•	•	•											R
28																								•	•	•	•											R
31	•	•	•	•	•	•		•	•															•	•	•			•									R
32		•																																				R
33								•		•	•		•	•																•								I
34										•																												R
35										•	•	•	•	•																								R
36										•	•	•	•	•																								R
38														•												•												I
39														•						•					•			•									I
40														•							•				•			•									I
41																	•																					I
42																	•																					I
43															•					•									•	•								I
44													•	•	•				•						•				•									I
45													•			•			•						•			•									I
46													•			•			•						•			•	•								I
47													•				•								•				•	•							I
48													•				•								•			•	•								I
49													•												•		•										I
50													•												•		•		•						•	•	I
51													•	•												•	•	•									I
52													•										•			•	•					•					I
53													•												•		•						•		•	I
54													•												•		•						•	•	•	I
55													•											•		•									•	I
56										•	•												•			•									•	I
57													•										•		•									•	I
58													•										•		•										I
63													•	•	•									•												R
64													•		•					•					•											I
65													•	•	•																					R

Focus marked with a point "•"; **Description type:** Review/ overview of multiple smart devices, systems, or services (R); Description of individual smart devices, systems, or services (I); **Abbreviations**: acting approaches (AA); action outcomes (AO); decision automations (DA); decision types (DT); deployment scenarios (DS); human interaction approaches (HI); implementation partners (IP); internal regulation (IR); knowledge acquisition approaches (KA)

Focus marked with a point "●"; **Description type:** Review/ overview of multiple smart devices, systems, or services (R); Description of individual smart devices, systems, or services (I). *AA* acting approaches, *AO* action outcomes, *DA* decision automations, *DT* decision types, *DS* deployment scenarios, *HI* human interaction approaches, *IP* implementation partners, *IR* internal regulation, *KA* knowledge acquisition approaches

References

1. McKinsey. Last accessed 2022/04/04, from http://globaltrends.thedialogue.org/publication/the-internet-of-things-mapping-the-value-beyond-the-hype/
2. Bock, M., Wiener, M., Gronau, R., & Martin, A. (2018). Industry 4.0 enabling smart air: Digital transformation at KAESER COMPRESSORS. In N. Urbach & M. Röglinger (Eds.), *Digitalization cases: How organizations rethink their business for the digital age* (pp. 101–117). Springer.
3. Alter, S. (2019). Making sense of smartness in the context of smart devices and smart systems. *Information Systems Frontiers, 22*(2), 381–393.
4. Boukhris, A., & Fritzsche, A. (2019). What is smart about services? Breaking the bond between the smart product and the service. In: *Proceedings of the 27th European conference on information systems* (pp. 1–16). Association for Information Systems, Stockholm-Uppsala
5. Scharfe, P., & Wiener, M. (2020). A taxonomy of smart machines in the mechanical engineering industry: Toward structuring the design solution space. In: *Proceedings of the 41st international conference on information systems* (pp. 1–17). Association for Information Systems, Hyderabad
6. OECD. Last accessed 2022/04/04, from https://stats.oecd.org/Index.aspx?DataSetCode=SNA_TABLE6A
7. VDMA. Last accessed 2022/02/03, from https://industrie40.vdma.org/documents/4214230/26342484/Industrie_40_Readiness_Study_1529498007918.pdf/0b5fd521-9ee2-2de0-f377-93bdd01ed1c8
8. Rijsdijk, S. A., & Hultink, E. J. (2009). How today's consumers perceive tomorrow's smart products. *Journal of Product Innovation Management, 26*(1), 24–42.
9. Jekic, N., Schreyer, M., Neubert, S., Belgin, M., & Schreck, T. (2021). Visual data analysis of production quality data for aluminum casting. In: *Proceedings of the 54th Hawaii international conference on system sciences* (pp. 1487–1498). IEEE.
10. Mehdiyev, N., & Fettke, P. (2021). Local post-hoc explanations for predictive process monitoring in manufacturing. In: *Proceedings of the 29th European conference on information systems* (pp. 1–17). Association for Information Systems. Marrakesh, Morocco/A Virtual AIS Conference.
11. Dreyer, S., Olivotti, D., Lebek, B., & Breitner, M. H. (2017). Towards a smart services enabling information architecture for installed base management in manufacturing. In: *Proceedings of the 13th international conference on Wirtschaftsinformatik* (pp. 31–45). St. Gallen
12. Herterich, M. (2017). On the design of digitized industrial products as key resources of service platforms for industrial service innovation. In A. Maechde, J. vom Brocke, & A. Hevner (Eds.), *DESRIST2017, LNCS* (Vol. 10243, pp. 364–380). Springer.
13. Arksey, H., & O'Malley, L. (2005). Scoping studies: Towards a methodological framework. *International Journal of Social Research Methodology, 8*(1), 19–32.
14. vom Brocke, J., Simons, A., Riemer, K., Niehaves, B., Plattfaut, R., & Cleven, A. (2015). Standing on the shoulders of giants: Challenges and recommendations of literature search in

information systems research. *Communications of the Association for Information Systems, 37*(1), 205–224.

15. Webster, J., & Watson, R. T. (2002). Analyzing the past to prepare for the future: Writing a literature review. *MIS Quarterly, 26*(2), xiii–xxiii.
16. Bures, T., Weynes, D., Schmerl, B., & Tovar, E. (2017). Software engineering for smart cyber-physical systems: Challenges and promising solutions. *ACM SIGSOFT Software Engineering Notes, 42*(2), 19–24.
17. Medina-Borja, A. (2015). Editorial column—Smart things as service providers: A call for convergence of disciplines to build a research agenda for the service systems of the future. *Service Science, 7*(1), ii–iv.
18. Dahotre, N. B., & Harimkar, S. P. (2008). *Laser fabrication and machining of materials* (1st ed.). Springer.
19. Eversheim, W. (1996). *Organisation in der Produktionstechnik Band 1 Grundlagen* (3rd ed.). Springer.
20. Porter, M. E., & Heppelmann, J. E. (2014). How smart, connected products are transforming competition. *Harvard Business Review, 92*(11), 64–88.
21. Hicking, J., Zeller, V., & Schuh, G. (2018). Goal-oriented approach to enable new business models for SME using smart products. In P. Chiabert, A. Bouras, F. Noël, & J. Ríos (Eds.), *Product lifecycle management to support industry 4.0. PLM 2018. IFIP advances in information and communication technology* (Vol. 540, pp. 147–158). Springer.
22. Romero, M., Guédria, W., Panetto, H., & Barafort, B. (2020). Towards a characterisation of smart systems: A systematic literature review. *Computers in Industry, 120*, 1–23.
23. Allmendinger, G., & Lombreglia, R. (2005). Four strategies for the age of smart services. *Harvard Business Review, 83*(10), 131–145.
24. Beverungen, D., Müller, O., Matzner, M., Mendling, J., & vom Brocke, J. (2019). Conceptualizing smart service systems. *Electronic Markets, 29*(1), 7–18.
25. Glass, R. L., & Vessey, I. (1995). Contemporary application-domain taxonomies. *IEEE Software, 12*(4), 63–76.
26. Azkan, C., Iggena, L., Gür, I., Möller, F., & Otto, B. (2020). A taxonomy for data-driven services in manufacturing industries. In: *Proceedings of the 24th Pacific Asia conference on information systems* (pp. 1–14). Association for Information Systems, Dubai, UA
27. Herterich, M., Eck, A., & Uebernickel, F. (2016). Exploring how digitized products enable industrial service innovation – An affordance perspective. In: *Proceedings of the 24th European conference on information systems* (pp. 1–17). Association for Information Systems, İstanbul
28. Heuchert, M., Verhoeven, Y., & Cordes, A.-C. (2020). Becker: Smart service systems in manufacturing: An investigation of theory and practice. In: *Proceedings of the 53th Hawaii international conference on system sciences* (pp. 1686–1695). IEEE, Maui, Hawaii
29. Janiesch, C., Zschech, P., & Heinrich, K. (2021). Machine learning and deep learning. *Electronic Markets, 31*, 685–695.
30. Nickerson, R. C., Varshney, U., & Muntermann, J. (2013). A method for taxonomy development and its application in information systems. *European Journal of Information Systems, 22*, 336–359.
31. Scharfe, P., & Wiener, M. (2021). Smartification in the mechanical engineering industry: A typology of smart machines. In: *Proceedings of the 27th Americas conference on information systems* (pp. 1–10). Association for Information Systems.
32. Hänel, T., & Felden, C. (2013). Operational business intelligence meets manufacturing. In: *Proceedings of the nineteenth Americas conference on information systems* (pp. 1–10). Association for Information Systems, Chicago, IL.
33. Petrik, D., Pantow, K., Zschech, P., & Herzwurm, G. (2019). Tweeting in IIoT ecosystems – Empirical insights from social media analytics about IIoT platforms. In: *Proceedings of the 16th international conference on Wirtschaftsinformatik* (pp. 455–472). Siegen.
34. Werner, P., & Petrik, D. (2019). Criteria catalog for industrial IoT platforms from the perspective of the machine tool industry. In: *Proceedings of the 14th international conference on Wirtschaftsinformatik* (pp. 1940–1951). Siegen

35. Guggenberger, T. M., Hunke, F., Möller, F., Eimer, A.-C., Satzger, G., & Otto, B. (2021). How to design IIoT-platforms your partners are eager to join: Learnings from an emerging ecosystem. In F. Ahlemann, R. Schütte, & S. Stieglitz (Eds.), *Innovation through information systems. WI 2021. LNISO* (Vol. 48, pp. 489–504). Springer.
36. Petrik, D., & Herzwurm, G. (2020). Towards the IIoT ecosystem development - understanding the stakeholder perspective. In: *Proceedings of the 28th European conference on information systems* (pp. 1–15). Association for Information Systems, A Virtual AIS Conference.
37. Pauli, T., Fielt, E., & Matzner, M. (2021). Digital industrial platforms. *Business and Information Systems Engineering, 63*(2), 181–190.
38. Rudolph, L., Schoch, J., & Fromm, H. (2020). Towards predictive part quality and predictive maintenance in industrial machining - a data-driven approach. In: *Proceedings of the 53th Hawaii international conference on system sciences* (pp. 1580–1588). IEEE, Maui, HI
39. Stein, F., & Flath, C. (2017). Applying data science for shopfloor performance prediction. In: *Proceedings of the 25th European conference on information systems* (pp. 1–14). Association for Information Systems, Guimarães.
40. Singh, R., Redmond, R., & Yoon, V. (2006). Design artifact to support knowledge-driven predictive and explanatory decision analytics. In: *Proceedings of the 27th international conference on information systems* (pp. 1–16). Association for Information Systems, Milwaukee, WI.
41. Elnagar, S., & Thomas, M. A. (2020). Federated deep learning: A conceptual model and applied framework for industry 4.0. In: *Proceedings of the 26th Americas conference on information systems* (pp. 1–10). Association for Information Systems.
42. Hodapp, J., Schiemann, M., Arcidiacono, C., Reichenbach, M., & Bilous, V. (2020). Advances in automated generation of convolutional neural networks from synthetic data in industrial environments. In: *Proceedings of the 53th Hawaii international conference on system sciences* (pp. 4620–4626). IEEE, Maui, HI.
43. Suschnigg, J., Ziessler, F., Brillinger, M., Vukovic, M., Mangler, J., Schreck, T., & Thalmann, S. (2020). Industrial production process improvement by a process engine visual analytics dashboard. In: *Proceedings of the 53rd Hawaii international conference on system sciences* (pp. 1320–1329). IEEE, Maui, HI.
44. Koppe, T., & Schatz, J. (2021). Cloud-based ML technologies for visual inspection: A case study in manufacturing. In: *Proceedings of the 54th Hawaii international conference on system sciences* (pp. 1020–1029). IEEE.
45. Kauke, D., Galka, S., & Fottner, J. (2021). Digital twins in order picking systems for operational decision support. In: *Proceedings of the 54th Hawaii international conference on system sciences* (pp. 1655–1664). IEEE.
46. Lee, C. (2018). Development of an Industrial Internet of Things (IIoT) based Smart Robotic Warehouse Management System. In: *Proceedings of the CONF-IRM* (pp. 1–13). Ningbo.
47. Naik, H. S., & Fritzsche, A. (2017). Enabling the democratization of innovation with smart toolkits. In: *Proceedings of the 37th international conference on information systems* (pp. 1–18). Association for Information Systems, pp. 1–13, South Korea.
48. Rehse, J.-R., Mehdiyev, N., & Fettke, P. (2019). Towards explainable process predictions for industry 4.0 in the DFKI-Smart-Lego-Factory. *KI-Künstliche Intelligenz, 33*, 181–187.
49. Hakanen, E., Eloranta, V., Töytäri, P., Rajala, R., & Turunen, T. (2017). Material intelligence: Cross-organizational collaboration driven by detailed material data. In: *Proceedings of the 50th Hawaii international conference on system sciences* (pp. 360–369). IEEE, Big Island, HI.
50. Mättig, B., & Kretschmer, V. (2019). Smart packaging in intralogistics: An evaluation study of human-technology interaction in applying new collaboration technologies. In: *Proceedings of the 52th Hawaii international conference on system sciences* (pp. 739–748). IEEE, Maui, HI.
51. Wache, H., & Dinter, B. (2021). Digital twins at the heart of smart service systems- an action design research study. In: *Proceedings of the 29th European conference on information systems* (pp. 1–17). Association for Information Systems, Marrakesh, Morocco/A Virtual AIS Conference.
52. Zenker, S., & Hobert, S. (2019). Design and implementation of a collaborative smartwatch application supporting employees in industrial workflows. In: *Proceedings of the 27th*

European conference on information systems (pp. 1–16). Association for Information Systems, Stockholm-Uppsala.

53. Metzger, D., Niemöller, C., Wingert, B., Schultze, T., Bues, M., & Thomas, O. (2017). How machines are serviced – design of a virtual reality-based training system for technical customer services. In: *Proceedings of the 13th international conference on Wirtschaftsinformatik*, St. Gallen

54. Berkemeier, L., Zobel, B., Werning, S., Ickerott, I., & Thomas, O. (2019). Engineering of augmented reality-based information systems - Design and implementation for intralogistics services. *Business and Information Systems Engineering, 61*(1), 67–89.

55. Aromaa, S., Väätänen, A., Hakkarainen, M., & Kaasinen, E. (2017). User experience and user acceptance of an augmented reality based knowledge-sharing solution in industrial maintenance work. In T. Ahram & C. Falcão (Eds.), *Advances in usability and user experience. AHFE 2017. Advances in intelligent systems and computing* (Vol. 607, pp. 145–156). Springer.

56. Kohn, V., & Harborth, D. (2018). Augmented reality – A game changing technology for manufacturing processes? In: *Proceedings of the 26th European conference on information systems* (pp. 1–18). Association for Information Systems, Portsmouth.

57. Niemöller, C., Metzger, D., & Thomas, O. (2017). Design and evaluation of a smart-glasses-based service support system. In *Proceedings of the 13th international conference on Wirtschaftsinformatik* (pp. 106–120). St. Gallen.

58. Saggiomo, M., Loehrer, M., Kerpen, D., Lemm, J., & Gloy, Y. (2016). Human- and task-centered assistance systems in production processes of the textile industry: Determination of operator-critical weaving machine components for AR-prototype development. In: *Proceedings of the 49th Hawaii international conference on system sciences* (pp. 560–568). IEEE, Kaui, HI.

59. Yang, Y.-C., Ying, H., Jin, Y., Cheng, H. K., & Liang, T.-P. (2021). Special issue editorial: Information systems research in the age of smart services. *Journal of the Association for Information Systems, 22*(3), 579–590.

60. Fraunhofer. Last accessed 2022/04/04, from https://www.produktionsarbeit.de/content/dam/produktionsarbeit/de/documents/Fraunhofer-IAO-Studie_Produktionsarbeit_der_Zukunft-Industrie_4_0.pdf

61. Wynne, K. T., & Lyons, J. B. (2018). An integrative model of autonomous agent teammate-likeness. *Theoretical Issues in Ergonomics Science, 19)3*, 353–374.

62. Fischer, J., Pantförder, D., & Vogel-Heuser, B. (2017). Improvement of maintenance through speech interaction in cyber-physical production systems. In: *Proceedings of the 15th international conference on industrial informatics (INDIN)* (pp. 290–295). IEEE, Emden.

63. Horn, R., & Zschech, P.. (2019). Application of process mining techniques to support maintenance-related objectives. In: *Proceedings of the 14th international conference on Wirtschaftsinformatik* (pp. 1856–1867). Siegen.

64. Wang, Y., Hulstijn, J., & Tan, Y.-H. (2018). Analyzing transaction codes in manufacturing for compliance monitoring. In: *Proceedings of the 24th Americas conference on information systems* (pp. 1–10). Association for Information Systems, New Orleans, LA.

65. Zschech, P. (2018). A taxonomy of recurring data analysis problems in maintenance analytics. In: *Proceedings of the 26th European conference on information systems* (pp. 1–16). Association for Information Systems, Portsmouth.

Printed in the United States
by Baker & Taylor Publisher Services